FREEDOM AND GROWTH IN MARRIAGE

FREEDOM AND GROWTH IN MARRIAGE

Second Edition

JAMES LESLIE McCARY

JOHN WILEY AND SONS

New York · Chichester · Brisbane · Toronto

Picture Researcher: Cheryl Moch

Picture Editor: Stella Kupferberg

Library of Congress Cataloging in Publication Data

McCary, James Leslie.
    Freedom and growth in marriage.

    Bibliography: p.
    Includes index.
    1. Marriage. 2. Interpersonal relations. 3. Self-
actualization (Psychology) I. Title.
HQ734.M16 1980   301.42   79-17199
ISBN 0-471-05341-4

Printed in the United States of America

10 9 8 7 6 5 4 3 2

PREFACE

Marriage . . . is a damnably serious business, particularly around
Boston.
JOHN PHILLIPS MARQUAND

When anyone raises questions about the meaningfulness or workability of traditional marriage in present-day society, he is liable to be peremptorily judged as a foe of home, children, or even the American way of life! Such judgment is not only unfair, but is utter nonsense because the question of whether an old system fits into a rapidly changing new world is a logical and necessary one.

It should be apparent that traditional marriage and family life no longer serve the needs of the people as successfully as they once did. It seems equally clear that serious new thought must be given to the purposes and structure of both institutions. But what are those professionals who are best equipped to generate fresh new thought doing to re-form public thinking about the realities of marriage? With few exceptions, those considered experts in the field of marriage and the family are shirking their responsibility. For either they neglect to define the often monumental problems inherent in marital and family relationships, or they do not offer appropriate solutions to them. In teaching and writing they fail to "tell it like it is," meaning that endless lectures and rows of books contain the same obsolete, irrelevant trivia—the kinship system, the Nayars of India, a propinquity model for dating and courtship—that has bored students and lay persons for generations.

One fact has emerged clearly from my contacts with students, at my own and the other universities at which I lecture, and in my clinical practice, where I do much marriage counseling. I find consistently that they want information that is relevant to their lives *today*. Why, they ask, does the concept of monogamous marriage appear to be in a state of erosion? Why is so little being done, so little being accomplished, either theoretically or practically, to preserve monogamy? Implied in this question, of course, is a bigger one: is the traditional monogamous marriage workable in the 1980s; is it worth saving? Certainly the country's high divorce rate and the ever-increasing experimentation of young people with new and different kinds of relationships suggest that traditional marriage is in serious trouble.

V

Many parameters must be examined in any evaluation of marriage. What is the impact on human relationships in this rapidly changing world, in which roles of men and women shift constantly and often merge? What is the impact on society when its individual members place greater importance on satisfying their personal needs than on the preservation of any particular life style or social system? What happens to young people when the style of family life observed in their childhood does not provide, as it would have in a more static society, the training necessary for satisfactory permanent relationships?

The problem of marriage in the 1980s does not end with those not yet married. Why are those already married afraid to look honestly at their own conjugal relationship and judge it for what it really is? Are the needs of both spouses being met? Is the relationship healthy, in that it permits the growth of each partner? Is either spouse trapped, a mere possession of the other, unable to achieve any sort of self-realization, despite occasional clawing attempts to achieve at least partial freedom? Concerned married people today also want to know how to achieve a balance within themselves and within their marriage, given the cultural and societal upheaval in which they live.

This book would deserve neither the printing nor the reading were I to presume to supply solutions to all the perplexities of marital and parental relationships. Rather, I have attempted to put the subject in the ball park where the game is being played. And the name of the game is *human relationships*. I believe that the topics dealt with herein are pertinent to anyone who wants something other than superficial associations with others, whether within marriage or outside it. This approach alone is, in my opinion, a distinct departure from the way the subject is typically presented from the lecture podium or on the printed page.

As will be easily detected by any reader of this book, I have a burning belief in the rights of the individual—especially the right to individuality. It does not seem unreasonable that all people should experience the fullest and most satisfying lives possible without, of course, those experiences adversely affecting the lives of others. Such experiences when one is living alone cannot be nearly as satisfying and fulfilling as they are when shared in a loving relationship. The Book of Genesis contains a profoundly prophetic statement to this effect by its declaration that it is not good for a person to live alone, and that each person should have a helpmate. Marriage is the best solution developed to this date to the dilemma of aloneness. Because most people do marry, and spend most of their lives in the married state, the hope for satisfying the goals of personal maturity and emotional fulfillment would seem to lie within marriage. When that hope is not reached within a particular marriage, that marriage has failed, whether there is divorce or not. Conversely, when full and satisfying lives are lived within the marital framework, one will usually find that the relationship has allowed maximum freedom and growth for both partners.

As should be expected in any book such as this one, the author's own background and personal experiences produce and set a bias of the presentation. I certainly recognize that my bias is present in this volume, in spite of the fact that the vast amount of the material presented is based on experimental research data and basically objective observations of social scientists.

In my opinion I have been exceedingly fortunate in both my personal life and professional life. In my family of origin I was exposed to the role separation of men and women common of that time; however, there was much more sharing, equality, and overlapping of roles in my family than in the families of many of my friends. More important, there was never any doubt in my mind or in the minds of my parents, brother, or sister that love, understanding, and acceptance flowed freely among all of us.

In my family of procreation we have shared the same type of love, understanding and acceptance, beginning with my marriage, celebrating its fortieth year, through the birth of our daughter and our son. Furthermore there has been an inordinate amount of encouragement and cooperation among members of both of my families to seek their own goals and fulfillment by doing their own thing. I have always felt a little sorry for those families that did not have the freedom to grow that we have had.

My professional life has been affected by the teaching and compassion of such people as D. B. Klein, Roy Crouch, James A. Brown, Mary Calderone, Carl Rogers, A. H. Maslow, and many others too numerous to mention. Many of my long-time associates have aided significantly in bringing the present work to fruition. Those contributing the most are Elizabeth Smith, Carmen Perez, Mary Sieber, Joan Black, Vicki Hammett and Betty Stewart. This second edition has come about largely through the efforts of Johnnie Newlin, who researched and updated much of the material, and Glenn F. Sternes, who edited and proofread the final copy. My thanks go to all these people and to John Crosby, University of Kentucky; David Barker, San Diego Mesa College and Charles F. Petranek, Indiana State University, who reviewed the manuscript.

JAMES LESLIE MCCARY

ABOUT THE AUTHOR

JAMES LESLIE McCARY received his Ph.D. degree from the University of Texas in 1948, at which time he joined the faculty of the University of Houston, where he established and for fourteen years directed the clinical psychology training program. At the time of his death, in August, 1978, he was professor of psychology at the University of Houston, where he taught marriage and family life and sex education courses. He was also a lecturer at the University of Texas Medical School, Galveston, and the director of psychological services of Almeda Clinic, Houston. Dr. McCary was past-president of the Houston Psychological Association, the Texas Psychological Association, and the Southwestern Psychological Association; was a director of the American Association of Marriage and Family Counselors; a member of the certification board of sex therapists for the American Association of Sex Educators, Counselors and Therapists (AASECT), and was certified as a sex educator and sex therapist by the same organization. He was a member of the APA Council of Representatives, was on the Board of Governors of the Council for the Advancement of the Psychological Professions and Sciences (CAPPS), was on the advisory board of the Institute for Rational Living, and was a past-director of Sex Education and Information Council of the United States (SIECUS).

The author had been the recipient of several teaching awards, including his university's 1970 President's Teaching Excellence Award, the Minnie Stevens Piper Foundation's 1971 Award for Outstanding Scholarly and Academic Achievement among Texas College Teachers, the American Psychological Foundation's 1972 Award for Outstanding Contributions to Education in Psychology, AASECT's 1977 National Award for Outstanding Sex Educator and Sex Therapist, and he was nominated by his university to appear in the 1975 edition of *Outstanding Educators of America*.

He published more than 70 articles in professional journals and wrote several books, including his award-winning *Human Sexuality, Sexual Myths and Fallacies, The Abbreviated Bible* (with Mark McElhaney), and *A Complete Sex Education for Parents, Teenagers and Young Adults*.

Dr. McCary was assisted in the updating of the second edition of this book by Johnnie Newlin, M.A., M.S.W. Final editing was done by Glenn F. Sternes, Ph.D., clinical psychologist and staff member of the Almeda Clinic, Houston.

viii

CONTENTS

A good relationship has a pattern like a dance and is built on some of the same rules. The partners do not need to hold on tightly, because they move confidently in the same pattern, intricate but gay and swift and free, like a country dance of Mozart's. There is no place here for the possessive clutch, the clinging arm, the heavy hand; only the barest touch in passing. Now arm in arm, now face to face, now back to back— it does not matter which. Because they know they are partners moving to the same rhythm, creating a pattern together, and being invisibly nourished by it. ANNE MORROW LINDBERGH

THE FAMILY VS. THE INDIVIDUAL

Marriage, as it exists in our Western culture and in most advanced societies of the world, is coming under increasing scrutiny, and is being criticized as an anachronism. Critics decry its hypocrisy, its frequent disappointments, and assert that it has become a consumer unit exploited by society and business which degrades both women and men and hampers their freedom to develop their potential.

The greatest source of concern is the disparity between the goals and values of our traditional form of marriage and the goals and values that human beings nowadays have for themselves as individuals. Humanity has made a collective effort to explore and conquer the world, even extending this exploration into extraterrestrial territory. Many individuals, however, find themselves small, isolated beings in an increasingly complex society. Automation and technology have reduced the need for physical conquests, and people are now turning to a most exciting and mysterious challenge—themselves. To become acquainted with oneself, to know and be oneself, fully and completely, to experience life in all its joy and pain and conflict, to utilize all of one's senses as well as one's intellect—these are the goals of modern men and women.

To realize these goals, or even to strive toward these goals, requires freedom of thought and action unhampered by too strict a religious, societal, or marital conformity. To develop one's full potential as a human being means to expose oneself to the uncertainties and the perils that exist in any exploration into the unknown. To become one's own person requires faith in oneself and the courage to experience failure as well as success.

The very nature of our traditional form of marriage does much to preclude the possibility of such risks and therefore of human development. The **yoked** *nature of most marital relationships provides a buffer against the terror of loneliness, but at the same*

1

time it forces two people into a compromise. If one partner feels inclined to go in one direction to add a new dimension to awareness and selfhood, and the other is inclined in another direction, the choice is to compromise and take some middle path—or move in one direction at the expense of the other partner. If they plod forward, yoked together in a rigid marital harness that allows no personal deviation, each may very well feel a gnawing sense of dissatisfaction and a secret regret that the adventure and experience of becoming the person each knows he or she could be is forever denied by the need to conform to the marital expectations of society.

An example of compromise conformity is the couple who never go anywhere together because he likes opera and she hates it; she likes movies and he hates them; he likes the symphony and she likes rock concerts. They compromise by staying home and watching TV reruns and feeling resentful and disappointed. Yet their yoked ties are so inflexible that neither could countenance the other's going alone—or worse, with a same-sex friend, and intolerable, with a friend of the opposite sex—to the kind of entertainment that is preferred. To the yoked pair, doing anything without the other, except for reasons of employment, is tantamount to disloyalty and is threatening to the marriage.

The basis for the fear of independent or autonomous activity is most often the fear of loss of the other. "He might meet somebody else who enjoys the same things he enjoys, and decide he doesn't love me anymore!" Better that the other partner be doomed to a life of doing none of the things he enjoys than the possibility that he will meet and enjoy the company of somebody else, or that he will meet and be attracted to somebody else.

A particular threat to the couple who have a togetherness compulsion is the possibility of extramarital sexual interest or activity. Our culture is so steeped in the romantic notion that sexual attraction is the equivalent to "falling in love" that the yoked couple will frequently subject themselves to a marriage deadened by suspicion, accusation, and fear of abandonment because of sexual jealousy. The sexual act has been so romanticized and idealized that yoked couples are willing to terminate their marriages if the act is performed by one partner with someone other than the spouse. And if one partner does have a sexual relationship outside the marriage and is discovered or feels obliged to "confess" to the other and is subsequently "forgiven," the marriage henceforth may be based on the guilt of the one and the generosity of the other.

Wives and husbands are frequently exhorted by newspaper ad-

vice columnists and by ministers and marriage counselors to **forgive** a sexually errant spouse and to give him or her a second chance. All parties involved overlook the fact that forgiveness is an emotion that exists solely in connection with judgment and condemnation. To say "I forgive you" means "I have judged you and found you lacking in qualities that are worthy of respect. I have these qualities, but you do not. I recognize my superior moral strength and your weakness. We will henceforth have a relationship based on that recognition." The forgiven is unconsciously aware of a morally subordinate position, but to express resentment or anger would make this partner look even more unworthy of the other's magnanimous "love."

Each member of a yoked union is therefore in the position of being both a potential sinner and a judge. The fear of being judged by the other while simultaneously judging the other creates a relationship that is not likely to foster trust, self-confidence, or total acceptance between the partners. And it is definitely not one that will foster the independent growth of human beings who have the urge to become completely self-actualized individuals. The traditional marriage, then, seems counter to the emotional growth needs of individuals.

The paradox is that individuals reach their greatest potential and experience their fullest humanity when they are involved in a close relationship with another person with whom they can share their triumphs and failures, to whom they can open themselves and be unconditionally accepted, with whom they can experience honest conflict that is either resolved satisfactorily or accepted as unresolvable, and toward whom they can fearlessly express the tenderness, eroticism, dependency, nurturance, admiration, and anger that all who live intimately together feel toward one another.

Without such relationships, human beings would be closed in upon themselves, living solitary emotional lives, always peripherally involved with others, and never deeply involved. We would become a society that relied on sensory experiences alone to define ourselves. Our emotional responses of compassion, love, desire, and empathy would be denied full expression. Rather than becoming more fully human, we would become less human and less aware of ourselves and of others. For most human beings, the closeness of a rewarding relationship is best realized in a union of a man and a woman who live together with the sanction of society, and this is a **marriage**.

It is likely that some form of marriage must form the basis of a large social structure. For civilization to continue, new genera-

"I'd like to go where the wild goose goes."

tions must be born and nurtured, educated and socialized. The ability to love, to relate to others, and to have the desire and the courage to strive for self-actualization comes about through interaction with other human beings. Infants, helpless and dependent, require an atmosphere that provides not only for physical needs, but for affectional needs as well. They must, if they are to grow into adulthood as complete individuals, experience acceptance and the freedom to be themselves. These needs can best be met within the framework of an ongoing family. The elimination of the institutions of marriage and family would therefore not only be chaotic for society, but could also be a pathogenic factor in the lives of many individuals.

The forms that family patterns take are multivariate, and are only partially constructed by the individual members. Society and culture place powerful constraints on certain features of any design; for instance, on the roles of men and women within the family, on the presence or absence of children, on sexual conduct,

4   The Family vs. the Individual

etc. Some of the means by which these constraints operate are laws about marriage, divorce, inheritance, and sex, family pressures to conform, one's own previous enculturation, and a multitude of other overt and covert measures. To go very far against the constraints requires a degree of effort and determination that most people are unwilling to exert. Nevertheless, some do attempt it and are sometimes successful, sometimes not so successful. "Success" is often difficult to judge. For example, a couple may be pleased about some particular variation or divergence from convention that they have accomplished, while their children may despise their "difference" and wish they were like everyone else.

The family will probably endure, in one form or another, as long as humanity exists. However, our present form of marriage must be reevaluated in light of the individual partners' needs for human growth. That our present form is not satisfactory to society or to individuals requires no elucidation. Its deficiencies are all too apparent to even the most disinterested observer. That changes must come about in our marriage form is also apparent.

We must, for the sake of the individual and society, develop a form of marriage that allows the partners to freely realize their own human potential, to experience the close sharing of each other's adventure in human growth, and to foster the development of emotionally secure children who can also form close personal involvements as adults. This, then, is the challenge that faces us today: to retain the function of the family while restructuring the institution of marriage.

CHAPTER 1

THE SELF
IN MARRIAGE

Once the realization is accepted that even between the closest human beings infinite distances continue to exist, a wonderful living side by side can grow up, if they succeed in loving the distance between them which makes it possible for each to see the other whole against the sky.
RAINER MARIA RILKE

Ask almost any young person today what he or she wants out of life, and the answer is almost always something like, "I want to be myself." "Doing your own thing" has become almost a mandate for the young, and the idea of following one's own inclinations and interests in spite of society's expectations has filtered to the older generation as well. The *desire* to be one's real self and to do one's own thing, however, is sometimes a far cry from the knowledge of what one's real self *is,* or what one really *wants* to do.

"I made myself up"

Phyllis had been in group psychotherapy for several weeks before she allowed her facade of bubbly cheerfulness to be penetrated. "It seems to me," she said, "that people have an inner core to them—their *self*—and their personalities sort of reflect that core. I'm different. I made myself up. I don't think I *have* a self. If you stripped off all the fake layers and got down to my inner core, you'd find it empty—just a hollow thing. I can't *be* myself because I don't *have* a self!"

Phyllis' feeling of having "made herself up" came from her efforts to conform to the expectations of her parents, her church, her husband, her friends, and the nebulous "they" of society. Outwardly, she was the epitome of a mentally healthy and emotionally adjusted young woman, but inwardly she was desperate and empty. As a result, she found no joy in her marriage and no sense of fulfillment within herself.

THE DESIRE TO BE "NORMAL"

The desire to be considered "mentally healthy" or "emotionally adjusted" has led many in our society to be overly concerned with **normality**—a concern that causes everybody to watch everybody else to get cues as to what behavior or emotions are "normal" or "right." Nobody wants to appear mentally *un*healthy or emotionally *mal*adjusted, so countless people paste on artificial airs of warmth and self-confidence, thereby gaining society's stamp of approval, **mentally healthy**—meaning that they behave differently from individuals who have been diagnosed as maladjusted, neurotic, or psychotic.

The difficulty is that people hiding behind a facade become increasingly aware of the difference between their feelings and their actions. They come to believe that their feelings are abnormal and unhealthy—different from the feelings of others. As others respond to their actions rather than to their feelings, they become more alienated, more afraid to act on their true feelings, and less sure of what their true feelings really are. For these persons, the admonition to "just be yourself" only adds to their sense of confusion.

Similarly, the concept of **adjustment** is often cited as a criterion of emotional health (White, 1966), on the assumption that the strong, healthy personality can and should adjust to each and every de-

mand that the surrounding society imposes. By implication, then, only the weak and neurotic attempt to change the traditional institutions of their society, or criticize or rebel against them in any way, no matter how detrimental to human dignity those institutions may be.

Obviously, struggling to adjust to a restricting situation, rather than attempting to alter it, will inevitably narrow one's range of interests and activities. The result is a blockage of emotional growth, a loss of capacity to enjoy life and living, and an inability to live creatively (White, 1966).

When one's main goal in life is to conform to society's expectations, individuality is necessarily repressed. One's sense of worth and one's feeling of competence then come from the value judgments of others, and not from an inner sense of achievement. Whether the judgment be in matters of sexual desirability, occupational competence, marital happiness, or personal worth, it is the opinion of the rest of the world that is important, and not one's own feelings.

Popular magazines capitalize on this mass insecurity by publishing inane quizzes designed to inform people if they have sex appeal or happy marriages. And countless people who were reasonably content before taking such a quiz may find that they "fail" the test and dismally conclude—at least for the moment—that they are not all that they "should" be.

GROWTH OF THE SELF

What is the **self**? Is it the personality that you project to others? Is it your own private thoughts and fears that others never know about? Is it a combination of the two? Or is it, as Phyllis said, an inner core that is reflected by your personality and your inner emotional life?

How does one know oneself? And if one doesn't, how does one discover the true self? There are some who advocate the "drop out, turn on, tune in" approach to self-discovery, but all too often this is an escape from self-discovery rather than an avenue to it. One's self is not discovered, nor does it become actualized, through drugs or mysticism but, rather, through open and honest interaction with the world and with other people.

The growth of one's sense of self and the ability to express that self is a process that begins in infancy and continues to young adulthood and beyond. It begins when the infant begins to differentiate between self and the environment, to experience the difference between what is "me" and what is "not me." It continues as the child develops and acquires a sense of competence and an awareness of others' judgments. In infantile relationships, basic security is of foremost importance.

As children move toward mature relationships, they proceed through several stages of emotional growth. When they have their early experiences with the world (outside their families), they may become frustrated, since they operate with a set of expectations acquired in interacting with their own families, which may be dissimilar to others' in some respects. Children respond to their teachers much as if they were their parents, and to their schoolmates as their brothers and sisters. Self-concept undergoes some alterations during this time, since they must adapt to different ways of being. During adolescence, the sense of self-identity is particularly dependent on the judgments of peers. A certain amount of role diffusion occurs at that time, with the individual trying out a variety of personalities by copying the personalities of others (White, 1966).

It is possible to become fixed in (i.e., stuck at) these early stages of development. Ideally, however, emotional growth is free and relatively unrestricted, and children move steadily toward relationships in which they are both capable of expressing their own natures and responsive to others'. If there is undue restriction, they are likely to remain in an immature pattern of egocentricity in which they are so intent on making a good impression on others that they fail to clearly perceive those around them. If their anxiety is high, it will be so distracting that they will be incapable of relating to others on any but a superficial level. And unless their defenses are adaptive, their repertoire of safe social behaviors will be frozen, and any attempts to learn new responses will be thwarted (White, 1966).

People whose social learning progresses satisfactorily learn to respond to others in their own right and to experience themselves in their own right. They are neither so uncertain of their own worth that they constantly search for proof of affection in their relationships with others, nor are they closed off from emotional responses to others. They are therefore free to fully perceive both other people and themselves, and they are able to learn new attitudes and new ways of behaving (White, 1966).

As the sense of identity becomes more stable, people are able to become more free and flexible in their personal relationships. They are less anxious, less defensive, and better able to throw off reactions that are inappropriate. Simultaneously, people become warmer

12   The Self in Marriage

CHRISTIANSON

"This is it? This is life?"

and more respectful toward others, as well as more assertive and honest. The capacity to live in good relationships with other people increases.

Furthermore, as the sense of self-identity becomes more stable, people are able to use relativity in moral judgments. From a childish concept of the value of rules in themselves, they come to perceive the rules in the context of their social function (Piaget, 1932; Kohlberg, 1971). To a young child, for example, a red traffic light is an authority in itself, a mysterious force that must be obeyed simply because it exists. As the child matures, the traffic light comes to be seen as a means that has been devised by governing bodies to regulate the flow of traffic and thus protect the lives of drivers or pedestrians. So it is with rules governing human relationships. Blind obedience to a rule formulated by parents, church, school, or government becomes modified by an awareness of the original reason for the rule and an evaluation of the rule in its present social context. This is essentially a process of humanizing personal values (White, 1966), as people's values become increasingly their own according to their own experiences and goals. Mature

Growth of the Self **13**

individuals no longer accept a moral precept blindly, but accept it only if it has personal meaning and value.

The humanization of values comes about as people become more free and open to new experiences and new ideas. Inevitably, existing values will come into conflict with new values, and individuals are faced with value choices. If a new value is rejected in favor of the old, there must be a new perception of the matter involved, and a personal definition of the goals and motives that are retained. If allegiance is given to the new value, there must be a clear realization of what is involved in both the old and the new (White, 1966). In either case, the resolution of the conflict results in personal growth and a heightened sense of self.

Sometimes growth occurs when people obtain unexpectedly unpleasant results from acting on cherished values (White, 1966). Individuals who hold moral righteousness as a strongly motivating value, for example, may discover that they have hurt others by cruel judgment, and that they are prevented from having intimate friends by their sense of self-righteousness.

As people deal with the need to humanize their values, they discover the need to form a unifying philosophy of life into which all their values fit in a congruent, interlocking whole (Allport, 1937). Thus, the sense of **self-identity**—what a person is and believes in—is further strengthened. People who have well-knit systems of inherited values will find that their philosophies will become much less fixed as the values within the philosophical framework are humanized (White, 1966). They may for a time be alarmed by their own inconsistency of views, but if they remain flexible and self-confident in this fluid state, they will progress toward new stable philosophies.

The final state in the process of establishing a strong sense of identity comes about as individuals outgrow the egotistical urge to be superior to others (Adler, 1927). At that time, people are free to extend the sense of self and to care enough about other persons, or valued ideals, for them to become as important to them as their own selves (Allport, 1961). This is not to say that the person with a strong sense of identity loses this identity in a concern for another person or for an ideal. Rather, one with a clear awareness of his or her own identity is able to maintain that awareness and to maintain integrity, keeping one's own definition distinct from those people or ideals for whom deep concern is felt. A recent definition of "individuation" is that of Karpel's (1976, pp. 66-67). He says it

. . . refers to the process by which a person becomes increasingly differentiated from a past or present relational context. It in-

14 The Self in Marriage

volves the subtle but crucial phenomenological shifts by which a person comes to see him/herself as separate and distinct within the relational context in which s/he has been embedded. It is the increasing definition of an "I" within a "We."

Karpel differentiates the concept from that of "fusion," in which a person is embedded in an *un*differentiated manner within the relational context.

An immature relationship is characterized by a low degree of individuation, the partners preferring to hand over to each other the responsibility for self. Mature people, on the other hand, accept responsibility for their selves and their relationships are based on differentiation rather than identification. In a mature relationship there is successful integration of the "I" and "We" components, so that the participants fear neither isolation nor suffocation. In less mature relationships, a variety of unsatisfactory compromises are made between these two polarities of unrelatedness and fusion (Karpel, 1976).

SURVIVAL OF EARLY EXPERIENCES

In striving for a stable self-identity, every individual has periods of growth and periods of plateaus. Furthermore, we never completely leave behind us the preceding levels of awareness. Instead, we expand our repertoire of behaviors by building on each level of growth. The range of behavior available to adults is therefore a mixture of all the experiences that they have had throughout their lives, and they may draw on all of them in their interactions with others. When people feel overwhelmed by responsibility and cares, for example, they may revert to infantile responses of self-indulgence and selfishness. Or, they may draw on the memory of their parent models and adopt judgmental, critical attitudes when they feel that their own importance has been reduced. When people are relatively secure and self-confident, they will freely relate to others according to the particular situation.

Thomas Harris, in *I'm OK, You're OK* (1967), discusses the fact that within every person there are three aspects of the self—Parent, Child, and Adult. The Parent represents the judgmental, critical, evaluative aspects of a person, derived from his memories of his own parents' opinions of what was proper and right. The Child is composed primarily of the feelings that a person had when he was very small and unable to verbalize his reactions to his environment. According to Harris, the Child always has the feeling of "I'm not

Survival of Early Experiences **15**

OK," because children are constantly made aware of their inferior position in relation to their parents. It is the Child within a person who reacts with strong emotions to a situation, whether the emotion be a feeling of abandonment, anger, fear, or overwhelming joy. The Child wants what he wants *now,* and he is not aware of any realistic contingencies that might make his desires impossible to attain or harmful to him or to others if he did attain them. The Adult, unlike either the Parent or the Child, acts according to objective reality. The Adult is able to delay gratification of a desire if the delay will bring greater satisfaction later. He is able to judge his own or another's behavior according to the situation in which the behavior occurs, and not according to some parental rule that says one "should" or one "ought to" *always* behave in a certain way. While the Child says to others, "I'm not OK, you're OK," the Adult says "I'm OK, you're OK," and behaves accordingly, without the critical or restrictive attitude of the Parent.

The idea of being Parent, Child, and Adult becomes particularly significant when one considers that one person may be behaving as Child in a situation, and his spouse may be behaving as Parent or Adult. If Mary dents the fender of their new car, she may react as her Adult and say to John, "I dented the fender of the car. I'll call the garage Monday about getting it fixed." If John's Parent is in charge, he may fume, "You could at least say you're sorry!" On the other hand, if Mary's Child is in charge, she may greet John with tears and rationalizations. If John's Child reacts, he may become furious and yell and curse because his new toy is damaged. Ideally, John will react as his Adult, and respond to Mary's Adult with "I'll see about renting a car while the fender's being repaired."

Frequently, the feelings that people have in response to particular situations may be so intense and so powerful that they overwhelm the person, but the person may be unable to say what the feeling is. According to Harris, these feelings are usually evoked by the memory of something that happened when the person was in the preverbal stage before the age of two. Intense feelings of grief, abandonment, or despair may be triggered by an incident that somehow reminds one of an incident in infancy that evoked the same feelings. It is then that the Child takes over, and the person becomes engulfed by feelings without understanding their true source.

The feeling that we call jealousy may very well have its origins in the preverbal period when a child is swept with feelings of being abandoned if his mother goes away. When she returns, the infant is flooded with joy and feels loved again. Mother's presence then becomes synonymous with Mother's love, and Mother's absence, no

matter how often it occurs, is translated into a loss of Mother's love. In a person's relationship with a mate, then, the attention the mate pays to another person, or the time spent with another person, may stir up infantile feelings of abandonment and loss of love. The Child, who believes that love and the physical presence of the loved one are the same, becomes supreme in the psyche of the individual. If such a person were able to let the Adult view the situation objectively and act accordingly, both behavior and feelings would be entirely different. Every person can therefore better understand his or her own feelings and behaviors, as well as those of others, if there is awareness of the Child, Parent, and Adult in oneself and in others.

Interpersonal relationships are crucial in establishing self-identity. While there are other environmental and situational factors that influence a person's sense of self, people are primarily social beings, and they define themselves best through interacting with others. Blocking in interpersonal relationships prevents persons from fully defining themselves and achieving a strong sense of identity.

BECOMING

Individuals who set out in the groping, uncertain path toward becoming what they would like to be learn quickly that such a quest is not for the timid or the faint-hearted. It is also not for those who are anxious about *closure*—needing to have all the loose ends of life neatly tied up or tucked away out of sight. Instead, becoming what Kierkegaard (1941a) calls "the self which one truly is" is a continuing way of life that is never completed. It involves stretching and changing as one achieves potentialities, and this change is sometimes painful. Sometimes it happens that personal growth conflicts with the growth of a partnership. Thus, from time to time a couple must decide on how much of the partnership they are willing to give up for personal growth. In these cases, several alternatives are open to the couple, including the possibility that they may grow *apart*. Ideally, of course, they grow along together at approximately the same rate and on the same course, but this is not always the case. The issue inevitably comes up in any relationship of long standing, and couples should be prepared to deal with it. The vast majority of those people willing to pay the price for personal growth, however, find the results to be well worth their investment, and growth of the partnership as well is very often the chief by-product of this change.

The quest for self-fulfillment within marriage doubles both the joy of achievement and the pain of disappointment. It requires the maturity to live with some discomfort, to learn new patterns of relating to others, and to dispense with superficial games which people sometimes use to manipulate and dominate one another (Crosby, 1973).

People who look for personal fulfillment together must have the maturity to look at themselves without becoming defensive or compulsive in compensating for faults (Crosby, 1973). People who can accept themselves are more able to accept the foibles and hangups of their mates.

In addition, the dream of perfectionism must fade if a couple is to achieve fulfillment within marriage. Perfectionists expect someday to be completely happy, to reach an ultimate goal. Mature people know that perfectionism is a fallacy and that expecting perfection makes one live continually in the future rather than in the imperfect present (Crosby, 1973).

"OK, then . . ."

Pete and Robin are a delightful couple who have been married nine years. Their relationship is unusual in its complete candor and its open expression of feelings. In a casual conversation with friends, Pete says of a recent trip through snow. "I finally decided to go about 12 o'clock." "You did not," says Robin firmly, "you left the whole goddamned decision up to me. You kept saying, 'Well, whatever you think,' and you had *me* call the highway department and the trucking lines and everybody else to see if we could get through. *I* decided to go."

"I was at work," says Pete heatedly, "and you were at home. You had the time to make those calls, and since you were the one with the information, I relied on your judgment." "OK, then," smiles Robin, "we *both* made the decision to go." "Yeah," nods Pete.

The significant thing about their interchange was that it took place at a social gathering and that it was typical of the way they interact. They *could* have postponed their discussion until they were alone, but the incident in question seemed both too trivial and too important to them to delay settling. *All* of their differences of opinion and their feelings toward each other are aired just as freely and with just as little self-consciousness. They are sometimes like children at play who intersperse their fun with free expression of dissatisfaction and anger at the other.

They both say that they prefer each other's company to anyone else's and that after nine years of intimate life together, they wake up each day excited at being together. They do almost everything as a twosome, because each finds the other exhilarating and exciting, yet they are each fiercely independent and honest with each other. They feel no compulsion to conform to the marital patterns of their friends, in which separate activities are stressed. "We will go off and do anything by ourselves anytime we want to," they declare, "but as long as we prefer doing things together, we will." This is not a yoked couple, then, but a self-actualized couple who prefer togetherness for its personal rewards. By harboring no resentments, by spontaneously expressing irritation or annoyance, rather than piling it into a state of anger, they are free to delight in one another.

There is little doubt that self-actualizing couples pay a price in the form of some pain and discomfort, but those who choose this form of relationship seem to be unanimous in their opinion that the price is well worth it (Crosby, 1973).

THE PERSONAL JOURNEY

In our automated, impersonal world, it is sometimes necessary to gain a base of self-knowledge through psychotherapy before one can begin to know oneself. People whose personal growth has been blocked in the course of development can remove the blocks in psychotherapy and thereby experience the same growth that they would have experienced in the normal process of development if the blocks had not been present (White, 1966).

Psychotherapists have found that individuals develop the capacity for self-actualization in an atmosphere of acceptance and approval, in a relationship between client and therapist in which the therapist experiences genuinely warm approval for the client. In this atmosphere, individuals are free to explore themselves and their own feelings and to gain the trust and self-confidence that they must have in order to be themselves.

Carl Rogers (1961) has outlined the steps that individuals take in their quest for self-actualization in a therapeutic relationship with a psychotherapist. The **therapeutic relationship** is essentially a close, accepting interpersonal relationship between two people and there is no reason that a marriage—also a close interpersonal relationship—cannot provide a similarly accepting, approving atmosphere that is conducive to personal growth. The steps individuals take are these:

1. They move toward autonomy by beginning to choose for themselves goals and directions that have relevance *for them*. In

doing so, they take responsibility for themselves and move toward the freedom of being themselves.

2. They move outside static, rigid states of mind and become fluid, changing beings who are not disturbed by inconsistencies in themselves or in others, who do not demand final conclusions or end states, but recognize that existence means a constant process of becoming (Kierkegaard, 1941b).

3. They establish open, friendly, close relationships with their own experiences. They step outside objectivity and embrace experiences as they occur.

4. They begin to value and appreciate not only their own experiences but those of others for what the experiences *are*. They do not demand that circumstances or people be other than they are, but simply note what *is* and uncritically accept all that exists in themselves and in others.

5. As they become self-actualized, there is greater trust in themselves and in their own feelings. They begin to listen to their own inner voices and to live by the values within themselves and to express themselves in their own ways.

As people take these steps toward becoming themselves, they are moving away from being reflections of what society wants and expects them to be. Their values are no longer based on what some external authority thinks they "ought" to be, or on pleasing others

"Momma! Look at William's erection!"

or meeting society's expectations. Instead, they are becoming fully themselves (Rogers, 1961).

"I don't want to **be** jealous"

Edward and Lois had been married ten years, and they had established a relationship that was richly rewarding to both of them. Each believed that intimate friendships with other people added new dimensions to their personal growth, and each believed that their marriage had benefited from their extramarital relationships. They had learned to be honest with each other, and their relationship seemed to be a dynamic, growth-producing one because of their growth as individuals. Both were therefore shocked and confused when Edward became attached to another woman and was unable to decide between her and Lois. He remained in a state of indecision until Lois demanded that they seek counseling. By that time, Lois was both ashamed of her jealousy and defiant in her resentment.

"I love Edward," she said, "and if this woman is better for him than

I am, then I *should* want him to go to her, but I just feel miserable and jealous. I never believed that I could feel this much jealousy—it consumes me and I simply can't control it. But I don't want to *be* a jealous, possessive woman!"

Edward continued to be confused and undecided, and a meeting was finally arranged so that all three could discuss the problem. Lois wrestled with her feelings when they met, trying in vain to feel giving and loving toward both of them. She only succeeded in feeling self-pity and resentment. Her inner turmoil finally exploded in an attack in which Lois later described herself as being "pure bitch." "I heard myself saying things that were hurting, cutting, destroying things," she told the counselor. "I *became* my jealousy and hatred, I couldn't control them. I *was* them, and there was a kind of wild, exhilarated feeling of freedom in doing it. As bad as I was, I was being *myself*."

"But a funny thing happened," she continued. "Afterwards, I felt strong and sure of myself. My self-pity was gone. My fears of inadequacy were gone. And I suddenly experienced a new feeling of love and tenderness for Edward. I honestly *wanted* him to leave me if it would make him happier. It was no longer a threat to me." Perhaps drawn to her new strength, Edward soon decided that his commitment to Lois was still of foremost importance to him.

"It's such a curious thing," mused Lois later. "It was when I discovered the meanness in myself that I also discovered my strength. And, somehow, I don't dislike my mean self. I can accept it and feel understanding and even affection for it. It's as if," she laughed, "my feelings were relatives and I had gone to a family reunion where there were relatives I'd never met. Some members of my family are admirable and I'm proud of them, and the majority of the others are OK—just nice, friendly, gentle things. But there are a few members of my 'family' that are ugly and mean and spiteful, and these are the feelings that have been locked up in the basement of my psyche, and I didn't know they existed until they came upstairs. It was a shock to meet them, but I'm not ashamed of them, and I think they should be allowed to stay out with the other 'relatives.' I don't intend to try to deny them. They're part of myself, and I'm not afraid of them. Maybe they'll become more mellow in time with association with my more positive feelings, but in the meantime I accept them completely, and I'm grateful to them for introducing me to my strength."

Lois' experience was typical of those persons who open themselves to their feelings and who allow themselves to experience their emotions completely. In experiencing her hatred, she was able to discover greater love, and in allowing herself to be buffeted by jealousy and spite, she freed her feelings of strength and self-confidence. We do not become *better* people by denying our negative feelings—we simply become more inhibited people who never experience positive feelings either.

NEEDS AND SELF-FULFILLMENT

Maslow (1943) proposed a hierarchy of **developmental needs** that must be fulfilled in order for an individual to become capable of self-fulfillment. In their order of development, these needs are:

Physiological needs (e.g., hunger, thirst)
Safety needs (security, order)
Belongingness and love needs (affection, identification)
Esteem needs (prestige, success, self-respect)
Self-actualization needs (the desire for self-fulfillment)

During an individual's development, the first need at the lower end of the hierarchy must be satisfied before the next need can emerge, and so on up the hierarchical ladder. Unless a person's need for esteem has been met, for example, he or she will never have a need for self-actualization. Furthermore, even though a higher-order need has emerged, a deprivation in a lower-order need can make it again compelling. Jewish prisoners in Nazi prison camps during World War II, for example, lost their need for esteem in their compelling need for food and shelter (Frankl, 1963).

With the exception of physiological and safety needs, one's needs may not be consciously acknowledged. Sometimes people try to make up deficiencies at one level by working very hard to gain fulfillment of needs at the next level. Men or women may therefore drive themselves unmercifully in an attempt to gain prestige and professional success (esteem needs), when the psychological deficit is actually in the need for affection (love needs). All the success in the world will not relieve a person's sense of unfulfillment, unless love needs are also met.

"Show me you love me"

Bill and Mary had been married for six years, during which time they became progressively distant. When they came for counseling, neither could explain what had happened to their marriage. In the beginning, they had been happy with each other, but as time went on, Bill became more and more withdrawn and Mary became less and less sexually responsive. In time, she began an affair with another man, with whom she had emotional rapport, and she found her association with him richly rewarding. Although both were unhappy about their marriage, the difference in their behavior was marked. Mary was relaxed, open, and voiced concern over the lack of communication between them. Bill was rigid, closed, and seemingly indifferent. "I just don't give a damn," he said coolly, "about anything."

During subsequent psychotherapy, it became apparent that Bill had been deprived of love and esteem throughout his childhood and adolescence. His father was an alcoholic, and his mother worked long hours to support a large family. Bill suffered the humiliation of profound poverty as well as the loneliness of being a child who was always alone. He managed to work his way through college and to achieve success in his career. He attempted to fulfill his deficiencies in both love and esteem by gaining prestige and wealth. He wore the most expensive clothes, drove the most expensive automobile, owned fine paintings, traveled in the best circles. In spite of these material possessions, he became increasingly withdrawn, and later described his feeling of having a plastic shield between himself and the rest of the world.

Without realizing it, he had looked to Mary to ease the longing he had for love and affection, yet he was not able to offer her love to which she could respond. When she did not fulfill his love deficit, he believed that he had "fallen out of love" with her, but the truth was that his needs were too insatiable for anybody to fulfill. Through psychotherapy, Bill was able to find the self-esteem and feeling of self-worth that he had been denied as a child. Mary's love for him had died, however, when his demands became insatiable, and the marriage could not be revived. All too often, this is the case when couples have entered marriage expecting their spouse to fulfill all the deficiencies they have within themselves.

When people's basic needs have not been sufficiently met, they are likely to look to their marriage partners to meet them. Children whose needs for love are not sufficiently met by their parents, for example, may take their love deficit with them into marriage and place inordinate demands on their spouses to reassure them that they are loved. If the deficit is great, no amount of reassurance on the part of their spouses will allay their anxiety, and they will end up blaming their mates for not loving them and for not giving them the emotional support they need. If two people with love deficits marry, they will each look to the other for fulfillment of their need for love, but neither will have the self-love necessary for the giving of love.

Similarly, people whose parents or teachers used shame and crit-

icism as disciplinary measures will grow up with deficits in esteem needs and will look to their marriage partners to fulfill these needs by constant praise and approval. Any anger or criticism will be interpreted as a withdrawal of love and esteem by these individuals, with resulting neurotic marital patterns that deny normal conflict.

"If she really loved me"

Mark grew up in a family whose religion stressed the importance of the observance of rigid rules of behavior. Any infraction of a rule, however minor, meant strong disapproval from his parents. In spite of high intelligence and capability, he was completely lacking in ambition. After his marriage to Susan, he dropped out of college and took a menial job making very little money. When Susan expressed her disappointment and failure to understand his seeming lack of concern for their financial future, he interpreted this as a lack of love on her part. "If she really loved me, she would love me regardless of what kind of job I had," he said. "Apparently she only married me so that I could be a meal ticket for her."

In psychotherapy, Mark learned that he suffered a deep deprivation in his need for love. Having won his parents' affection and approval only when he kept the rules of their religion, he had never experienced the feeling of being loved just for himself. His deep need for love therefore had not been sufficiently fulfilled for his need for esteem—prestige, success—to become important to him. Furthermore, he was testing Susan's love for him by breaking the rules and not fulfilling the expectations that she and others had for him. Mark did not begin to live up to his intellectual capacities until he learned to feel worthwhile as a person, and not merely as a rule-keeper.

Once physiological, safety, love, and esteem needs of individuals are reasonably satisfied, they are free to realize their potentialities and desires—to become self-actualized. Maslow describes the process of becoming self-actualized as "the desire to become more and more what one is, to become everything that one is capable of becoming" (Maslow, 1943). And it is the freedom of individuals to become self-actualized that our marriage forms must provide. Without such freedom and growth no marital relationship can be truly successful.

NEEDS AND LOVE

Maslow (1962) terms the basic physiological, safety, esteem, and love needs **D-needs** (dependency needs), and the needs for self-actualization **B-needs** (being needs). People who are still motivated by D-needs are not apt to be able to achieve satisfying marriages unless they are able to recognize their own needs as their responsibility and not the responsibility of their mates. Love is described by Maslow as either **D-love**, which seeks happiness by taking love from another, or **B-love**, which achieves inner happiness from loving another person.

Two people who have both progressed from D-needs to B-needs are therefore free to share B-love. Maslow contrasts B-lovers and D-lovers according to their degree of self-esteem and their ability to *give* love rather than always needing to receive love. B-lovers are less possessive or jealous of their loved one. They tend to be more independent, autonomous, and individual than D-lovers are, yet at the same time they are more eager to help the other toward self-actualization. They are more proud of the other's triumphs, and are more generous and giving in their love (Maslow, 1962).

Not understanding one's own particular needs can result in a person's confusing the neurotic need for affection with "being in love." In **love**, the feeling of affection is primary, whereas in the neurotic need for affection, the primary feeling is a need for reassurance (Horney, 1937). People who need the affection of others as buffers against anxiety frequently believe that their responses of gratitude or trust or infatuation are really feelings of spontaneous love. They will constantly be on guard for evidence of any interest the other may take in a third party, and will interpret that interest as neglect of themselves. If any criticism is directed toward them by another, they will interpret it as humiliation (Horney, 1937). Thus, what a person experiences as "being in love" may be a response to another who one hopes can fulfill unmet needs carried over from earlier developmental experiences (Crosby, 1973).

Unmet developmental needs are satisfied in some manner, and the responsibility for this is frequently passed to the marriage partner along with the wedding ring. Overdependency arises from feelings of worthlessness, shame, guilt, and self-doubt, and those with such characteristics cling to their mates and try to possess them. They want their mates to provide them with strength, succor, and self-esteem that should arise from within themselves. Lacking self-acceptance and self-love, they attempt to manipulate others into giving it to them. Often, however, their partners tire of insatiable demands and come to feel disgust and resentment (Crosby, 1973).

All too often, men and women enter marriage with the expectation that their feelings of self-worth will be provided by the other. It is true that individuals who already believe themselves to be worth loving gain additional feelings of self-worth from the love of their mates. But marriage can never change the self-evaluation of people who failed to get enough love as children and therefore believe themselves to be worthless.

The expectation of some that love and marriage will cure all personal ills is so strong that it seems similar to the developmental level of children for whom fairy tales are written, which end, "So they were married and lived happily ever after." Marriage in itself does not lead to happiness, nor is it an antidote for loneliness. Happy marriages are achieved by already happy people, and marital happiness is a by-product of self-fulfillment and self-actualization (Crosby, 1973). The most disillusioned and disappointed people in the world are those unhappy people who marry expecting their mates to make them happy. Two people who are already essentially happy, however, with a reasonable amount of self-worth, self-acceptance, self-trust, and self-esteem can grow together in love and trust and self-expression. Marital happiness therefore lies primarily within oneself and only secondarily in one's mate (Crosby, 1973).

PATTERNS OF MANIPULATION

Individuals whose attractions are based on unconscious needs tend to enter into manipulative relationships, which Shostrom (1972) describes as falling into one of six patterns. The first pattern is the **Mother-Son** pattern, in which a man chooses as a wife someone who will allow him to continue feeling protected, as his mother did. When this happens, the husband repeats the same problems he had when he was growing up. Just as his mother was strong and adequate and he was weak and passive, his wife will be the stronger of the two, and he will remain the weaker.

The women in such marital relationships frequently marry because of the man's "potential" as a husband and as a complete person. Their strength may cause them to stay in the marriage long after they are aware that this "potential" will never be realized. They may resent their position as the stronger of the two, but they fear the total destruction of their families if they abdicate their position of power. Obviously, this pattern is one that creates unhappiness and resentment in a marriage.

The second pattern is the reverse of the mother-son relationship, in that the husband is the strong figure and the wife is the passive, weaker one. Termed the **Daddy-Doll** relationship, it is characterized by a husband who makes all the decisions, and a wife who fails to gain strength or awareness. This pattern is satisfying for a while, but in time the husband may tire of being married to a doll and look for a more mature woman. The doll, of course, remains confused and unhappy and fails to understand why her former manipulative tactics no longer work. She may meet a new man who is temporarily flattered by her doll-like mindlessness, only to have that relationship also end in boredom and disgust.

One of the most common patterns in our society is that termed the **Bitch-Nice Guy** relationship. This pattern may develop when a woman feels a need to become strong and equal. If her husband is threatened by her strivings for equality, he may unconsciously decide to outmaneuver her by becoming passive and weak, thereby manipulating her through passive-aggressive means. He therefore controls, in an unconscious manner, his strong, frustrated wife, and she continues to enjoy his nurturance and passivity.

The **Master-Servant** pattern is one that is often seen when a strong, adequate man marries a weak, servile woman. In some cases, as in Shaw's *Pygmalion* (1967), the husband is from a more educated or refined environment, and he undertakes the remolding of his less educated wife. The pattern may be satisfying to both—at least until the woman has been changed into the image that her husband thinks he wants.

This pattern is very frequently seen in our society when a man marries a woman who achieves her own feelings of identity through him. Such a woman will make herself her husband's slave. She will try to anticipate his every need, and she will arrange her entire life so as to be more accessible to him. This servant-girl wife will make her husband her entire life—and she will tell him so at every opportunity. While a man may believe that it would be a delight to have a wife whose only desire was for his comfort and well-being, he eventually becomes weary of so much attention and wishes that she would find something or someone else on which to focus her energy. As he attempts to extricate himself from her ever-present solicitousness, she will redouble her efforts to make him happy and to take care of him. If he leaves her, she will literally believe that her life is ended. Never having built a life for herself, she is utterly shattered if the man through whom she has lived is no longer able to stand the strain of being another person's sole reason for living. In this type of relationship neither person *lives*, in one sense of the word.

Another marital pattern is the **Hawks** pattern, in which two very strong competitive people marry and attempt to gain control of each other. Until and unless two hawks decide that neither will ever dominate the other, their marriage will be like that of Albee's characters in *Who's Afraid of Virginia Woolf* (1962), who almost systematically destroy each other in their compulsion to be the dominant partner.

The opposite pattern is found in the **Dove** relationship, in which two people, who are each determined to be submissive to the wants of the other, marry. Dove couples are masters at the game of "Where do you want to go? . . . I don't care, where do you want to go? . . . Anywhere you want to go is fine with me . . . ," ad infinitum. Each is angered that the other will not give him or her the satisfaction of being the self-sacrificing one, and each submerges identity and personality in an effort to win in the virtue department.

In contrast to these manipulative relationships is that of the self-actualizing pair who have each discovered and accepted themselves as worthwhile, lovable human beings who do not expect someone else to make up for their own deficiencies. When these two join in marriage, each remains responsible for developing the parts of themselves that remain undeveloped. The marriage therefore becomes a kind of workshop for growth, and the individuals in it continue to work on their own individual growth as well as working on the growth of the marriage (Shostrom & Kavanaugh, 1971).

ORIENTATIONS TOWARD MARRIAGE

Individuals entering marriage usually do so with one of four basic character orientations (Fromm, 1947). These orientations determine the expectations people will have for their marriage partners, since they are based on the nature of the unmet needs that people bring into marriage.

A **receptive** orientation is held by people who are primarily characterized by dependence on others to take care of them and meet their needs. Fear of losing the nurturance of others causes these people to repress feelings of anger, resentment, and hostility, and to go to great lengths to please others and to submit to authority. Their feelings of self-worth come from external sources—what other people think—so they depend on the praise and accolades of others for their self-esteem.

Individuals with strong receptive orientations will continually place demands on their marriage partners, and will manipulate their partners through shows of helplessness. Their mates are likely to tire of the dependency and feel resentment and a loss of the feeling of being in love.

In their relationships with their children, receptive personalities will abrogate their parental duties of discipline and guidance and instead subtly align themselves with the children against the other parent. By forcing their mates to always mete out punishment and make and enforce rules, receptive persons hope to gain the love of their children by being permissive and noncommital. They lose their bid for "the most popular parent," however, as the children grow in awareness and realize that their passive parents were more interested in gaining their allegiance than they were in helping them grow up to be responsible people.

An **exploitative** orientation causes people to constantly need to maintain a feeling of being "over" or "one-up" in all relationships. These persons cannot tolerate equality with others, because of the need to retain the feeling of power and control—to prevent *being* controlled or manipulated. In attempting to maintain control, these people are manipulative and sometimes ruthless.

People with marked tendencies to dominate others threaten the stability of any relationship, and certainly destroy the happiness and love in marital relationships. They *demand* their partners' love as well as their persons. They are supremely confident that their partners will never be interested in another person, because their belief in their own superiority makes them convinced that they are everything that their partners would ever want or need. Their attitude is that their partners would never *dare* have an interest—or a thought—that was not related to them. Such unrealistic efforts to control their partners lead to dehumanization of their mates and to chaos and disillusionment in their marriages.

Exploitative personalities also dominate and control their children. Telling them what to think and how to live, these parents will brook no deviation from their dictates. A child who displays any degree of independence or autonomous thinking is quickly squelched. As the child matures, future education, career, and marital pattern are planned by the parent. Exploitative parents either manipulate the offspring into following the plans, so that the children remain shadows of the parents, or completely alienate them and lose any influence they may have had in their lives.

People with a **hoarding** orientation think of love as a possession, and since their security is based on hoarding and saving, they are not willing to grant any independence or freedom to their mates. Spending is a threat to them, whether it be money or themselves, and they are overpossessive and jealous because they never believe themselves lovable no matter how much reassurance they get from others. People with this orientation tend to hold onto everything—possessions, money, memories—and to be excessively orderly and punctual. Their constant need for reassurance that they are loved, plus their inability to give anything of themselves to the other, quickly lead to an end of marital happiness.

Hoarding individuals are unable to let their children go, as they are also seen as possessions. When a child marries, the hoarding parent insists, either directly or by indirect manipulative methods,

that the married child live nearby. The married offspring's family becomes an extension of the hoarding parent's family, and the grandchildren are viewed as possessions also, with the result that not one but two families may be made miserable by persons who are compelled to hoard those close to them.

Persons with a **marketing** orientation derive their sense of identity from their success in the world of business, politics, industry, sales, or commerce. The value they place on themselves depends on the status they command, rather than on an inner sense of worth. If such people lose their status, as in the case of a man or woman who retires from a successful career, there will be a loss of a sense of identity and a profound sense of loss of self.

People with a marketing orientation are not likely to seek fulfilling marital relationships, since they seek their identity through the world of work. Their lack of inner feelings of self-worth, self-fulfillment, and self-acceptance will cause their marriages to be unfulfilling, and if the hoped-for evaluation from others does not materialize, the marital relationship will be weakened and will ultimately deteriorate.

In our own society, the marketing orientation is particularly prevalent and has almost come to be accepted as the norm. It is for this reason that many women experience the "empty-nest syndrome"

Orientations Toward Marriage **33**

when their last child leaves home, and that men who have been vigorous and active frequently become withdrawn and apathetic when they retire. No longer having a role from which they derive a feeling of self-identity, they are unable to create a new center within themselves.

The children of a person with a marketing orientation are viewed as investments and are expected to yield returns. They are expected to make the best grades, to be popular, to marry the most desirable person, and to have highly successful careers. They are, in effect, expected to adopt the same marketing orientation as the parent and to sublimate any needs for love and emotional closeness by achieving success in the business or professional world. Thus, persons with a marketing orientation either succeed in molding replicas of themselves, or they face a confrontation in which conflicting values lead to a lack of understanding and respect between parents and offspring.

All of us have one of these orientations to some degree, and most of us have elements of all of them in our personality makeup. They become destructive forces only when we deny their existence and adhere to them in an extreme and inflexible manner. Self-actualizing persons are no longer controlled by these approaches to life. Instead, they have freed themselves to the extent that they are able to be flexible in their adoption of different principles and values.

CONCLUSION

It is apparent that the success or failure of a marriage largely depends upon the inner resources and the personality orientation of the marriage partners as individuals. Sometimes people are so afraid of appearing conceited or self-preoccupied that they do not pay enough attention to themselves. "For most people . . . the danger is not too much self-involvement but one of too little self-awareness" (Schulz & Rodgers, 1975). Thus, a person whose single life is rich and satisfying is far more likely to find married life rewarding and worthwhile than is a lonely, miserable single person.

However, one does not simply continue the same pattern of living when the switch is made from a single state to a married one. There are elements inherent in a marital relationship that affect the individuals in it, and these elements must be firmly understood if partners are to grasp the issues that must be faced in marriage. The following chapter will deal with the issues inherent in a modern marriage that can greatly affect both individual and marital happiness.

CHAPTER 2

ISSUES FACING
MODERN
MARRIAGE

Is not marriage an open question, when it is alleged, from the beginning of the world, that such as are in the institution wish to get out, and such as are out wish to get in?   RALPH WALDO EMERSON

When one considers the conditions that are needed for the self-actualization of an individual, it is apparent that our traditional marriage forms tend to be restrictive rather than free, punitive rather than accepting, and conducive to dissatisfaction and stunted growth rather than to emotional freedom and autonomy. Without the freedom to grow and expand, the lives of married individuals become blocked and constricted, thus cutting them off from avenues to self-actualization.

In order to construct a marital environment that allows for human growth and self-actualization, but that still retains the function of the family, we must resolve certain basic issues that confront us with regard to marriage. These issues involve elements of the institution of marriage that have been unquestioned for centuries in Western civilization—the marital relationship itself, the sexual fidelity of the married couple, and the parental responsibility of the couple.

THE RELATIONSHIP ITSELF

For the first time in the history of mankind, men and women are considering the marital *relationship* rather than the marital *function* as the most important aspect of marriage. The traditional reasons for marrying have been both familial and societal, but now people marry for reasons of personal fulfillment and emotional security as well (Mace, 1972).

Woman's changing status. The changing status of women has greatly affected the manner in which both men and women view the marital relationship. In the near past, a woman who did not marry was doomed to life as the family spinster who had to be supported by her family. She suffered not only the humiliation of being unwanted and unloved, but also the degradation of being dependent on others for her survival.

When a woman married, she was protected, physically and economically, by marriage. In return for this protection, she provided sex, children, and housekeeping chores. With relatively few exceptions, women have been economically and physically dependent upon men. Even those women with higher education have been assigned by societal role expectations primarily to homemaking and childrearing. Until the last few decades, when a woman's youngest child was grown, she frequently had grandchildren by her older children and continued her childrearing duties by assisting her married children. The "maternal instinct" was considered universal and axiomatic to femininity.

With the industrialization and automation of our society came labor-saving housekeeping devices that allowed women more time for personal growth and study. As the necessity for producing sons to help with the family farm decreased, women began to limit the size of their families and to end their childbearing years sooner. The nature of work itself has shifted; most jobs now consist of light labor that is clean and safe. Furthermore, people are less ambitious, and more interested in personal involvements than heretofore.

As machines took the place of muscles in the labor force, women became equally capable of working at some occupations outside the home. In World War II they proved their ability to perform well in a man's world, and they returned to their kitchens reluctantly when the soldiers came home and took over their previous jobs. Since that time, women have been entering the labor force in increasing numbers and have renounced their role as solely that of childbearing and childrearing. Nevertheless, societal expectations have continued to channel women into **nurturant** occupations such as nursing and teaching, or into clerical or paraprofessional jobs. Attitudes are changing, however, and the modern woman is beginning to think in broader terms when selecting a career. The sex-role division that has traditionally reserved medicine, law, engineering, and

business management for men and elementary school teaching, nursing, secretarial work, and medical and dental assistantship for women is breaking down. Society is belatedly recognizing the fact that a woman is intellectually capable of the same professional achievements that a man is capable of, and that a man can be as clerically efficient or as tenderly nurturant as a woman can be.

For the younger woman, the changing status of women in our society means that she has more equality with men sexually, economically, and socially. The birth-control pill has allowed women to enjoy sex without the fear of pregnancy, and more liberal attitudes toward abortion have made marriage more a matter of choice than of necessity as it too often was in the past. Furthermore, women are waiting longer to marry, and if they decide on a career instead of or in addition to marriage, they can expect to be paid on a more equal basis with men, although many industries and businesses still base their wages on a sexual dichotomy ("A woman has a husband to support her and shouldn't be paid as much as a man").

What these changes mean is that women are beginning to think of themselves as human beings first and females second, and to voice their opinions and ideas openly. Significantly, more and more men are beginning to understand the full import of the women's liberation movement, and are supporting women in their demands to be freed from the stereotype of mother and housewife, so that they can *choose* these roles if they wish, but are not forced into them by economic necessity or by societal pressure.

Women have not only been assigned to traditionally "feminine" sex roles but have been pushed—by both subtle and overt societal pressure—into adopting traditionally "feminine" personality patterns. A woman who is aggressive in her dealings with others—and especially with men—has been scornfully labeled a "castrating woman," often meaning that she fails to butter up the masculine egos around her. Even professionals in the mental health field subscribe to the idea of so-called "feminine" traits as the hallmark of a mentally healthy woman. When a group of male and female psychologists, psychiatrists, and social workers were asked to list traits they considered to be present in mentally healthy adults (sex unspecified), they were found to consider these traits ideal for men, but not for women. Femininity was seen as going hand in hand with submissiveness, dependency, timidity, and passivity. Women were also believed by these professionals to be more easily influenced, less competitive, more excitable in minor crises, more easily hurt, more emotional, more conceited about their appearance, less objective, and less interested in mathematics and science. All of these "feminine" traits were considered less socially desirable than their opposites and less healthy for a competent adult (Broverman et al., 1970). Clearly, from this standpoint, a woman has a choice of adjusting to the stereotypes of femininity—at whatever cost to her evaluation and self-esteem—and being *considered* mentally healthy, or of striving for competence and self-expression and being considered unfeminine and abnormal.

Nevertheless, evolvement toward equality between the sexes continues. In education, the gap between the ratio of men to women is narrowing, and women comprise about half of those enrolled in higher education (Rapoport & Rapoport, 1976). While there still exists a discrepancy between the number of men and number of women in high-status, well-paying jobs, and while more men have a positive *attitude* for equal responsibility than actually *practice* it, people do tend to be working toward more reciprocal, egalitarian relationships. "Perhaps the most promising possibility for structural rearrangement lies with the tendency toward job restructuring, providing more flexibility and more part-time job options for men as well as women" (Rapoport & Rapoport, 1976, p. 97).

Differences between women and men. Married couples who want and expect such an egalitarian relationship frequently find to their disappointment that they cannot simply enter a relationship as equals and achieve the feeling of partnership and mature love that they hope for. Sometimes, differences between the sexes over and beyond the biological differences lead to conflicting points of view and contrasting behavior. It is the manner in which the individuals in the marriage view these differences and the reasons behind them that can lead to a mutually satisfying relationship or one that is frustrating and confusing to both. How an individual views the reasons for the differences between men and women has a lot to do with his concept of the appropriate role of a man or a woman.

Basically, there are four positions which define the differences between men and women beyond those that are biological (Way, 1973). The traditional position, which has been furthered by the Church and by secular institutions alike, is that the male is the superior being and that his superiority derives from the very nature of creation. This view holds that God created man in His likeness and then created woman as a subordinate being to be a helpmate for man. According to this position, the superordinate position of man is assumed as a *given*, and the philosophy is expressed in the Church, in the business world, in education, and in the home. It is exemplified by the fact that men are ministers and priests and rabbis, while women arrange the floral offerings; men are doctors,

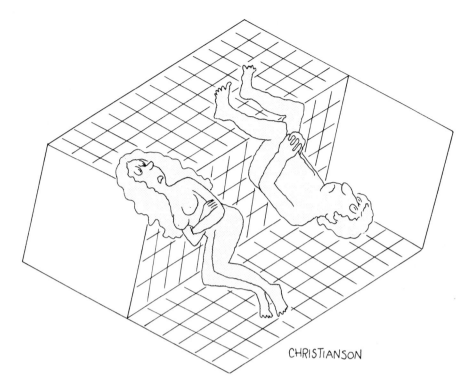

CHRISTIANSON

"You know why we don't get along, Edwin? We live
in two different worlds."

women are nurses; men are executives, women are secretaries; men earn the family's income, women clean the toilets. A husband who believes in the innate superiority of men will be extremely threatened by a wife who demands the right to a career of her own.

The second position, advanced by Erik Erickson (1968), holds that sexual differences are due to differences in the experiences that men and women have because of their biological differences. Because women experience sexuality as inward space and men experience it as outward thrusting, their perception of their world is different. Similarly, the duality of such experiences as menstruation, noctural emissions, lactation, and ejaculation causes other differences in the manner in which the two sexes view and approach the world. According to this view, the duality of experience leads to a complementary relationship between the sexes. What one sex lacks, the other has; what one sex needs, the other needs to give. Neither sex is superordinate or subordinate; they are equal, with differing experiential bases.

The Relationship Itself **41**

The third position, espoused by feminists such as Kate Millett, holds that all sexual differences are culturally imposed. This position can be covered loosely by the term **androgyny**, which means that men and women each possess the potential for both male and female traits, and that culture alone decides which will predominate.

The fourth view, and the newest, is the backlash idea of female superiority. Those who hold this view point to the biological superiority of women and to the fact that, in embryonic development, the female is the primal sex. A female has a greater chance of surviving if she is born prematurely than a male does, and she outlives him by about ten years. To the believer in female superiority, Eve was created for the purpose of overseeing Adam and keeping him from making a complete mess of things rather than for the purpose of helping him carry out his decisions.

While these differences in opinion about the basic nature of the sexes may seem trivial, they actually are the basis of much marital discord. A woman who has been brought up to believe that a husband is lord and master of the home will be confused and miserable with a husband who believes that men and women should share the responsibility of making all decisions. She, believing that all important decisions are for the man to make, will retire gracefully to the background and busy herself with training English ivy to climb, while her husband resentfully wrestles with the major issues in their lives and feels that his wife is shirking her responsibilities as a partner in the marriage.

Similarly, an ardent believer in women's superiority is hardly likely to find emotional satisfaction in a marriage with a man who believes that God just naturally created man as a superior being while He created woman as a slightly inferior being or, as Aristotle believed, that woman was created first in an unsuccessful attempt by the gods to create man.

For a married pair to achieve an egalitarian relationship as partners and as lovers, they must have similar views as to the appropriate roles of a husband and a wife, and they must each be satisfied with their own and their spouse's role performance.

Sex-role learning. In the past, sex-role learning has perpetuated the stereotypic views of masculinity and femininity in terms of dominance and submission. Different behavior has been taught by making a distinction between the sexes and by responding to them in different ways. Boy babies are more likely to be bounced and tumbled than girl babies are, for example, and girl babies are more likely to be stroked and patted gently. This difference in response continues as the child grows, so that the child is taught that there are differences in the way others respond to the different sexes.

Among primates, dominance is based on morphology, with the larger of the monkeys assuming the dominant role (Maslow, 1936a, b, c, d). If a monkey who is dominant in an encounter with a smaller monkey meets a larger monkey on his path, he will instantly become a submissive one, and assume a female "presenting" position as a pseudosexual acknowledgment of the other's dominance. If both monkeys are equal in size, the monkey who behaves in the more aggressive manner becomes the dominant one. Since female monkeys are usually smaller in size than male monkeys, the female is usually submissive.

Unlike subhuman animals, however, dominance among human beings is not dependent on the particular situation, but is more of a consistent personality trait. While a woman can be as dominant as a man, society expects males to be more dominant than females, and women are frequently labeled "unfeminine" if they are aggressively dominant. Women may therefore fall into the unhappy trap of denying intellectual, physical, or emotional strength because they fear being considered "masculine," and men may deny their

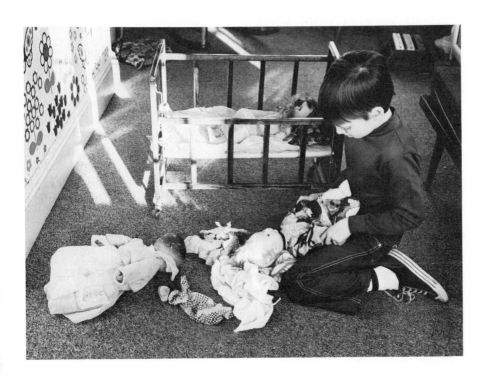

own natural emotional responses lest they be labeled "sissies" or unmanly.

Since girls traditionally have been expected to grow up to be wives and mothers, it has been easier for them to learn the role behaviors that were considered appropriate by society. A girl has her mother and other women as role models, and she is therefore able to learn "feminine" role behavior in a leisurely, natural manner. Boys do not have such accessible and visible role models, however, and it is therefore sometimes difficult for boys to learn "masculine" role behavior in an easy, natural manner. In addition, boys have traditionally not been given clear-cut instructions as to *what* men do and *how* they do it. Instead, they are told what men do *not* do (they do not cry, they do not play with dolls, they do not wear skirts, they do not paint their faces with cosmetics). Since these negative instructions are usually accompanied by punishment for behaving in a "feminine" manner, a boy learns early to dislike feminine activities, and possibly females as well (Lynn, 1964).

Furthermore, a boy is forced to abstract from these injunctions and punishments the appropriate male roles in our society. It is not surprising, therefore, that boys develop a masculine identity at a later age than girls develop feminine identities.

In addition to providing girls with more explicit and visible role training, our culture allows girls a considerable degree of cross-sex behavior, while it insists on a rigid adherence to a monosex role in boys practically from infancy. A girl can dress in jeans and sweatshirt and play baseball with the boys, and the adults around her smile with amused approval, content in their confidence that she will, when the time comes, adopt appropriate feminine attire and behavior. One of the most popular *Saturday Evening Post* covers by artist Norman Rockwell pictured a young girl in sweatshirt, jeans, and sneakers, holding a beautiful, frothy evening gown in front of her as she looked into a full-length mirror. The painting captured both the mirrored reflection of the dainty, feminine frontal view, and the rumpled, tomboy back view of the girl. Millions of Americans chuckled at the cover, reminded of a daughter, niece, or friend. If the cover had depicted an adolescent boy in a dress, holding a formal tuxedo up to the mirror, the reaction would doubtless have been one of disgust and revulsion.

Our society does not have the same confidence that boys will grow up to be masculine simply because they are anatomically male. A little boy who joins his sisters in "dressing up" in his mother's clothes is more likely to be punished or teased than he is to be admired. We seem to believe that any deviation from a rigid masculine role in boys will predispose them to homosexuality or effeminacy as adults.

Perhaps because they internalize the uncertainty of their elders, there is considerable anxiety in adolescent boys as to their masculinity. With the exception of the Jewish Bar Mitzvah, we have no equivalent ritual to the **rites of passage** with which primitive people mark the transition from childhood to adulthood, and males in our society frequently feel that they must somehow prove that they have come of age as men. Often, this "proof" remains a need throughout a man's life, and it may involve rejecting all behavior that does not fit the rigid stereotype of the tough, taciturn "he-man." A man who needs to continually prove to himself that he is indeed a man may do so by trying to seduce as many women as possible, believing that sexual seduction is equivalent to masculinity. Called **Don Juanism**, this behavior seldom results in emotional satisfaction for the man, and he must continually make new conquests in an effort to achieve the feeling of being a "real" man. If he does not resort to Don Juanism to assert his masculinity, a man whose sexual identity is shaky may instead try to affirm it by **John Waynism**—proving his masculinity by aggressive and chauvinistic patriotic fervor.

Roles in marriage. When a man with an unstable sexual identity marries, he needs to abstain from "feminine" behavior and his training to perform strictly "masculine" activities are frequently motivations to turn all chores and responsibilities of a "feminine" nature over to his wife. Those responsibilities have traditionally included the responsibility of the house, the children—the boys as well as the girls—and all duties of a domestic or nurturant quality.

Even if a man helps his wife with the care of the children or with some household chores, in his need to affirm his "masculinity" he may perform the tasks in an incomplete manner, as a reminder to his wife that it is really not *his* job. He may wash and dry the dishes, for example, but fail to put them away; or he may change a baby's diaper and leave the soiled diaper for his wife to rinse and put in the diaper pail (Henry, 1971). To do otherwise would make him feel henpecked and unmasculine.

A woman who holds a job in addition to caring for her home and children, or who is immersed in the endless duties involved in caring for small children, will interpret such "masculine" omissions as direct insults to her, and overt reminders that her position is that of a scullery maid in the home, and she may withhold any expression of appreciation for her husband's help, thus making him feel deprived and unloved (Henry, 1971). From such seemingly trivial

CHRISTIANSON

"I don't know, Shirley. I've never let Harold work.
I've always felt that a man's place is in the home."

incidents arising from the sex-role dichotomy inherent in our culture, a deep-seated distrust and antagonism can arise in a marriage.

There are healthy changes taking place, however, especially among the college-educated. The home and the children are becoming more of an egalitarian responsibility between husband and wife, and the duties at home are more likely to be divided according to ability and convenience rather than sex.

One researcher (Giele, 1976) sees two significant changes taking place in marriage. One has to do with the division of labor and the other with the expression of love and degree of commitment. The future direction of the former is fairly clear; that is, that there is likely to be more and more overlap in the kinds of responsibilities men and women assume. Abernathy (1976) has noted that nowadays the feature of whether or not one bears children is more important in determining the activities of a person than is the male-female distinction. Thus, the life role of a career woman without children may be more similar to a man's than it is to a woman who cares for her children at home.

For the couple who desire equality in responsibility, there is no platitudinous belief that it can exist in a marital framework in which the wife makes the decisions "inside" the home and the husband makes them "outside." As women know, that philosophy resembles a paternalistic pat on the head that says, "Of course the decision of whether to have peas or carrots for dinner is just as important as the decision of whether to buy stock or real estate." A woman may tell the world that this arrangement offers her equal responsibility in the marriage, but it is probable that she is only fooling herself. It is likely that having only these small responsibilities prompts a woman to do volunteer work in the hope of gaining a sense of importance. She may not make decisions of importance as a volunteer, either, but there are people who look up to her and consider her an important person. Younger women today are less likely to need to prove their own importance by such contrived means, since they are more likely to feel a sense of importance from real accomplishments. If they do volunteer work, then, it will be out of a sense of civic responsibility and not out of a search for equal responsibility.

A marriage with symmetry of work roles creates a stronger bond because of the functional interdependence that is intrinsic to it. While divorce still occurs with this type of marriage, it is usually followed by a similar type of pair-bond (Giele, 1976).

In regard to the other change noted by Giele in the area of emotional expression and degree of commitment, a specific trend is less clear. While there have been many attempts to alter and redefine marital boundaries, experiments in this area have not been as successful as those with dual-career marriages, which are more and more common.

SEXUAL EXCLUSIVENESS IN MARRIAGE

The need to form a paired relationship seems to be very basic to the nature of human beings; the *intensity* of that need is variable. The concept of sexual exclusiveness in marriage is so ingrained in our own culture that we tend to believe that it is a universal standard. The truth is, however, that only 5 percent of all societies of the world actually prohibit sexual expression outside of marriage, although almost all disapprove of it (Murdock, 1949). Even in some monogamous societies, other partners in sex are allowed and even specified for the married pair. And societies that have plural marriages as their sanctioned marriage form do not always restrict sex to only those within a marriage (O'Neill & O'Neill, 1972).

Possible origins. In the animal world, sexual exclusiveness is exemplified by **pair-bonding**, whereby the animal chooses a mate and remains exclusively with that mate until death. Animals that practice pair-bonding are found among all species of animals—except Homo sapiens (Morgan, 1972). In spite of most societies' disapproval of marital infidelity, man has never been an animal who remained totally faithful to one partner, although his sexual infidelity has caused him guilt, grief, broken marriages, and broken trust.

The traditionally accepted explanation for the value placed on sexual exclusiveness was that hominid males needed to equally divide all the females among themselves in a one-to-one ratio in order to insure their close cooperation when they were hunting. This theory presumes that sexual jealousy among the males would destroy their camaraderie and cause them to be less effective as hunters. The assumption of this theory is that the female hominids were docile and submissive creatures and that they had no say at all in the matter of being divvied up among the males. The truth is that the female hominid was probably quite independent from the

males, since she was left to fend for herself and her young for long periods of time. She also was the gathering half of the hunting-gathering economy, and she and her young could survive on the grains and other edible vegetation that she provided, without relying on the meat that the male hominid presumably brought back. (The premise that he dragged the carcasses of animals home to share with the females and children may be one that attributes far too much altruism to early man.) Furthermore, it is quite likely that man was often dependent on the grains that the females gathered for his own survival, since animals could not always be depended upon to obligingly allow themselves to be killed. At any rate, it is doubtful that the female hominids would have submissively allowed themselves to be parceled out to the men unless the arrangement offered something they wanted and needed.

A more plausible, if less scientifically accepted, theory is that advanced by Morgan in *The Descent of Woman* (1972). Morgan's theory is that sexual exclusiveness developed as an accepted part of male-female relationships because of the hunting-gathering economy of the hominids in the Pleistocene era and not because of any sexual jealousy. As she points out, sexual jealousy was probably as absent in the hominid as it is in the primate, who will casually watch his mate copulating with another primate with no concern whatsoever.

Among the hominids, the first nuclear families were the females and their young. And it was the female who established the place to which the young returned when they were hungry or when they wanted the close companionship of others. As in primate groups, the bond of mother and children probably lasted for at least ten years among the hominids, and, as Morgan notes, the practice of going to a special place where a female provided food would undoubtedly become ingrained in the male hominid so that he would come to view the distribution of food as one of the functions of a female. When his own mother died, or when the matrifocal bond was weakened, a male would quite naturally turn to another female to continue supplying him with food.

According to Morgan's theory, the supply of sex was far more plentiful than was the supply of food, and primal man was far more likely to fight over the food that a woman dispensed than he was over the sex that she dispensed, since sex was not diminished for one man if it had previously been shared with another man. The rub was that a female hominid was more likely to share her food with a man who provided her with sexual pleasure than she was with one who simply presented himself with his hand out. Thus, a hominid who wanted the exclusive right to a woman's food supply would have to spend a good deal of time satisfying her sexually, and sexual exclusiveness thus became a part of feeding exclusiveness. In time, according to Morgan's theory, the male acquired a sense of ownership and moved in with the female and her children, and the nuclear family thus came to include the father as well as the mother of the young.

The concept of lifelong monogamy apparently evolved over a period of two or three thousand years—from a time when pestilence, famine, maternal and infant death, war, and similar dreaded happenings limited the average life span to about 22 years, to approximately 100 years ago when the average life span reached about 40 years (now the average American male can expect to live to age 69, and the female to 77). During this early period of history when women frequently died in childbirth, a man might bury two or three wives in his own lifetime. A man, therefore, was not bound to a sexually exclusive existence with one particular woman for more than a few years before his wife's death, and his remarriage brought him a new sexual partner. Of course women, who were regarded as chattel in any case, were expected to have only one sexual partner in their lifetime. To a large extent, then, the sexual double standard was present at that time, even in loyal monogamous marriages.

Extramarital sex. Whatever the origins of the importance that so many people attach to sexual exclusiveness in marriage, it has been and remains a central element in the concept of monogamy. In our own society, sexual activity outside marriage is termed **adultery**, and implies breaking a trust by deceitfully and illicitly engaging in sexual intercourse with someone other than the spouse, when each has pledged permanent fidelity to the other. The consequences of breaking the trust on which such a relationship has been built are painful and destructive, and many adulterous married partners have regretfully concluded that the illicit pleasure was not worth the price.

Obviously, if a couple pledge to each other both marital fidelity and complete honesty in their interpersonal relationship, adultery destroys one or both of these commitments. If one commits adultery and is deceitful and secretive about it, there is a resulting loss of closeness and open communication. On the other hand, if one commits adultery and is openly honest about it, he runs the risk of seeing the marriage dissolve. Most adulterous partners have chosen to be unfaithful and deceitful, and the consequences are frequently a marriage that is empty of meaningful communication.

Our culture's ban on adultery stems from the Jewish law that made adultery a sin. The sin, however, involved property rights, and not the sexual relationship between two individuals. To the ancient Hebrews, a woman was a man's possession, as his cattle were possessions, and a man who had sexual intercourse with another man's wife had taken his property.

Furthermore, since a woman's body was thought to be the "soil" in which a man's "seeds" grew to produce new generations, it was very important to have perfect, unspoiled soil. If another man's seed had been deposited in his wife's body, a Hebrew man considered his wife's "soil" to be contaminated and unfit for his own seed. Adultery thus constituted stealing a man's possession and rendering it useless for its function before returning it.

Although women are no longer considered chattel or "soil," the concept of **ownership** persists between both men and women. To be married means to many to own another individual ("my woman," "my man"), and few people want to "share" the person they own with anyone else. The fact is, however, that a large number of married couples are sharing each other with other people, whether or not they agree to do so, and whether or not they believe in the morality of what they do. The rules governing adultery have been undergoing some interesting changes in recent years.

Today, there is a certain amount of tolerance for extramarital involvement. Sometimes these involvements are deep friendships without a sexual relationship, and frequently there are flirtations that are generally considered harmless, such as at parties and other social gatherings. Although the spouse may feel twinges of jealousy at times, ordinarily these friendships and flirtations are not seriously disruptive to marriages.

Sexual freedom in marriage. Many people today believe that imposing permanent sexual fidelity on a married couple constitutes a hypocritical, unrealistic stricture that is likely to be broken, with a resulting sense of guilt and a loss of open communication between the married partners. A revolutionary kind of marriage has therefore been proposed in which sexual exclusiveness is not the foundation of the marriage. Instead, a married couple could place the emphasis on the total quality of the marriage and on the couple's commitment to have a mutually satisfying growth relationship. Advocates of such marital relationships believe that men and women can and should seek vitality and dynamic understanding instead of sexual fidelity. They furthermore believe that the commitment to sexual fidelity reduces love and sex to duty and obligation instead of raising them to experiences to be shared and enjoyed in their own right. Sex in marriage is therefore seen as simply one aspect of the totality of love, and a lifelong commitment to sexual fidelity is seen as a fixation that can destroy both the growth of the individuals and the love between them (O'Neill & O'Neill, 1972).

To those who seek to establish such marital relations, *trust* lies in the couple's faith in each other to be open and honest in the *total* relationship, and not in faith that each will observe a particular societal rule governing marriage. In this type of marriage, the partners can allow each other the freedom to be themselves rather than demanding that some particular societal expectation be met. Fidelity for these couples is an equal commitment to one's own growth and that of one's partner, and the shared self-discovery that comes from such growth. Loyalty and faithfulness are to that shared growth, to integrity of self and respect for the other, and not to sexual bondage to each other (O'Neill & O'Neill, 1972). It should be noted that this type of marital commitment does not demand or expect sexual relationships outside marriage. Instead, such relationships are *allowed*, and they are therefore not signs of a broken trust or violated commitment.

The word "adultery" is not descriptive of the type of extramarital relationships that advocates of sexual freedom in marriage propose. Those who advocate sexual permissiveness within marriage do so while also advocating honesty and fairness among all parties con-

cerned. Thus, sexual permissiveness becomes an aspect of a new philosophy, and is not a matter of breaking a rule. A vast difference exists between someone who violates a rule and someone who does not accept the rule as being valid for himself (Cuber, 1972). If a couple's commitment to one another allows for individual sexual freedom, then sex outside marriage is not adultery, but a part of the total philosophy on which the marriage is based. Those people who truly guide their marriage with this philosophy maintain faith in each other and in their relationship.

Arguments for sexual fidelity and open marriage. The concept of sexual freedom in marriage is disturbing to many people, since it is counter to their ethical values concerning marital fidelity. Many people seriously question the proposition that a marriage can be a vital, loving, interpersonal relationship while at the same time allowing sexual freedom (Crosby, 1973). To these people, sexual fidelity is not a matter of sexual bondage, but a mature ability to give up certain physical pleasures in favor of the greater pleasure they derive from being able to trust the other. While they might occasionally wish for extramarital sex, they consider the risks too great for the rewards. These married couples prefer to find sexual variety by varying their own sexual performance together, and they believe that they can add to the richness and depth of their relationship by making a conscious effort to keep their physical and emotional relationship vital. To them, sexual permissiveness in marriage is a "cop-out" that allows a married couple to seek sexual excitement from outside sources when marital boredom sets in. Rather than make an effort to use ingenuity and creativity to infuse their marriage with excitement, they take the easier way out and seek individual excitement.

Those who believe in the superiority of sexual fidelity feel that seeking sexual excitement outside marriage denies the partners the experience of a lifelong partnership in which each actively seeks to dispel marital boredom. Furthermore, many advocates of marital sexual fidelity believe that sex for the sake of sex is far too insignificant in importance to allow it to tarnish the very special intimacy that a married couple may have together. To have a brief sexual affair, however exciting and fun, seems to those who are particularly close and intimate an immature rejection of lasting, trusting love in favor of a the cheap thrill of a short ego trip. People who believe that it is possible to achieve both excitement and sexual fidelity in marriage can be found among both the older and the younger generation, but there is a slight difference in the philosophies behind the views.

Two studies, one conducted in 1939 and one almost 30 years later in 1968, were compared, and it was found that there was no significant difference in the percentage of college students who disapproved of open sexual liaisons of married couples (Cuber, 1972). If anything, the 1968 students were a little more conservative in their views toward marital infidelity, especially when it involved deception of the other partner.

As the author of the studies noted, however, the similarity in findings is somewhat deceptive because of the more liberal attitudes the 1968 students had toward a person's right to "do his own thing." There has been a significant change in the attitudes that the youth of today have toward traditional moral and religious rules. The older generation accepted unconditionally the moral and religious preachments of right and wrong, and cheated—sometimes with guilt and sometimes without guilt, but rarely without the belief of having transgressed a valid rule. The trend today is to view as "wrong" only that behavior that creates jealousy, distrust, or dishonesty, or that causes harm to others. People are also increasingly able to accept a particular behavior as wrong for themselves but right for someone else so long as it satisfies that individual's needs without involving deception of another (Cuber, 1972).

Today's generation eschews the traditional rules and asserts that every person has the moral right—and even the obligation—to develop his own code of behavior. Even if another's code is different from one's own, the trend is to accept it as valid for that person and to grant him the right to live by it, so long as no harm befalls another. Having rejected the traditional codes, this generation feels no guilt in formulating new ethics that are more relevant and valid for them. It is for this reason that the idea of sexual freedom in marriage will probably be increasingly accepted as a possibility for any who believe in it, even if it is not acceptable to others for themselves.

Some married couples who embrace the concept of sexual freedom may find that extramarital sexual experiences offer opportunities for the personal growth of both partners and an enhancement of the growth and satisfaction of the marriage itself. Others may find that the pain of jealousy and the feeling of exclusion is too great for one or both partners, and they may decide to confine their friendships with members of the opposite sex to psychic intimacy rather than sexual intimacy.

Certainly, any couple who contemplates making sexual freedom a part of their own marital commitment must take into consideration the rights and feelings of all parties concerned. Furthermore, couples should be aware that sexual freedom in marriage can be a destructive force if not handled with extreme care and maturity. Until the married pair has established a strong relationship that is free of doubt and unfilled needs, for example, sexual intimacy outside marriage may shatter the fragile marital bonds irreparably. Couples who want sexual freedom in marriage should therefore be very sure that their own relationship has matured to a secure, certain status in which both parties are self-confident and strong before they expand their interests and affections to include sexual relationships outside their marriage.

A problem may arise for older couples who have had sexual freedom in their marriages. As they grow older, the husband—especially if he is successful—will continue to be attractive to younger women, some of whom may be more attracted to his status than to him as a person. A husband who has fears of aging and death may be flattered by the attention of younger women and use them as a means of boosting his own ego. He may thus exploit his freedom—and the younger women—and put an unnecessary strain on his marriage. His wife may not be so likely to attract younger (or older) men as she ages, and she may feel that her husband's involvement with younger women is due to her own lack of sexual desirability, and the marital relationship may be strained to the breaking point. It should be emphasized that if a couple agrees to sexual relationships outside marriage, they must be open and honest and free of exploitation. Otherwise, sexual freedom in marriage can be simply selfishness that masquerades as liberality. When dishonesty, exploitation, and selfishness exist in any relationship, that relationship is faulty and should be corrected or dissolved.

One observer of modern marriage has stated the case against sexual permissiveness in marriage by an insightful and fair appraisal of sexual and psychic intimacy:

What is often desired in sex is an affirmation of the self by the other. It is no more logical to conclude that psychic intimacy must culminate in sexual intimacy than it is to conclude that sexual intimacy must culminate in psychic intimacy. A fair statement about the relationship of psychic and sexual intimacy seems to be this: sometimes and in some situations psychic intimacy progresses into sexual intimacy and in other situations psychic intimacy is destroyed by sexual intimacy. Sexual intimacy often creates only an illusory facsimile of psychic intimacy; that is, when one fails to experience psychic intimacy he deludes himself into believing that sexual intimacy will be an effective substitute. Significantly, a common manner of seduction depends on the manipulation of desires for psychic intimacy as a means of achieving sexual intimacy (Crosby, 1973, p. 114).

Advocates of sexually permissive monogamy, on the other hand, believe

. . . that if you achieve an open marriage, your marital relationship will be more vital, more fulfilling, and that you will be continually growing and discovering. Under these circumstances it would be only natural that you should wish to expand the circle of your love, to develop additional relationships in an open way, with or without sex. And that additional sharing can in turn make your marriage a still deeper, richer, more vital experience. Once you have achieved a true sharing within your marriage, there are no limits on its further development (O'Neill & O'Neill, 1972, p. 259).

Whether or not one accepts sexual freedom as an ethic for oneself, it is an issue that must be faced. The manner in which we resolve the dichotomy of sexual exclusiveness as a stated value of our society, while the number of adulterous relationships steadily increases, will have much to do with the future trend of marriage in our culture.

JEALOUSY

Whenever the concept of personal freedom in marriage—sexual or otherwise—is brought up, the inevitable question is, "But won't that cause jealousy?" The answer is yes, it probably will. There are some who optimistically and unrealistically claim that jealousy is a culturally learned trait and not one that human beings *must* feel. George and Nena O'Neill, the authors of *Open Marriage* (1972), for example, declare that there are some societies in which jealousy is virtually nonexistent. They cite as an example the Toda of India, a society to be discussed in Chapter 3, which favors fraternal polyandry—the sharing of one wife by brothers. That brothers might have no jealousy over the wife they share is perhaps understandable, particularly since there are not enough females to go around among the Todas. In this situation, one brother could hardly demand that his brothers "find their own women" since all the other wives are already taken. Furthermore, the economic deprivation of this and other polyandrous societies makes survival a far more pressing concern than either sex or love. Another society, the Marquesans, was cited by the O'Neills as having a minimal amount of jealousy. The Marquesans also practice polyandry as the preferred form of marriage.

Polyandry, especially fraternal polyandry, is probably the most unlikely of all marriage forms to create jealousy. Through **polyandry**—several men with one wife—each man is provided with a sexual partner who alternates among the husbands. Each man is therefore relieved of the burden of performing with great frequency, and the wife is provided with several different sexual partners, each of whom has no one but her. Jealousy may very well fail to raise its ugly head in such an idyllic situation.

In our own culture, however, women are as important to the economic system as men are. Furthermore, there are enough women to go around, and there is not the abject poverty that causes a people to relegate sex and love to lower-level needs. In our society, men and women marry for emotional, not sexual or procreational, reasons, and jealousy may therefore be almost inevitable when there is an expanding of affection or sexual attraction to include other people. The marital partner is very likely to feel rejected and abandoned in spite of an intellectual acceptance of the concept of individual freedom in marriage. The desire to be special, to be "Number One," to be wanted above all others, probably burns in all of us, especially in those who are not fully actualized.

"I don't even **like** him!"

An example of this desire was Karen, who was divorced and happily living with another man. She chanced to meet her former husband and the woman he was living with, and her reaction caused her to be disgusted with herself. "I don't want him, I wouldn't have him, I don't even *like* him!" she said, "but when I saw his girlfriend, I was so jealous I couldn't stand it!" Her jealousy was not because another person had something she wanted or considered her own, but from the knowledge that her former husband no longer preferred *her*.

Childish, you say? Or possessive or selfish or silly? It is all these things, but it is also very human, and we have all probably experienced the feeling.

In some respects, the kind of jealousy that Karen experienced is easier to defeat than the kind that erupts when one's spouse feels strong affection or sexual attraction, or both, for another person, while still vowing his love and commitment to his partner. Carl Rogers (1972) believes that jealousy may be a trait, like territoriality, that all human beings share in common. Jealousy in open relationships is more likely to be due to the feeling of ruptured or weakened intimacy between the partners than to an actual sexual jealousy. For example, in one sample (Knapp, 1975) of couples in an open marriage, a verbal agreement to keep each other first became more difficult to maintain and caused stress as other partners naturally assumed a greater and greater importance. Knowing that an equal intimacy exists between the spouse and another person may cause one to feel threatened and less important.

To suggest to married couples that they can allow one another the freedom to choose their own friends, and that they can accept without jealousy the fact that friendships may lead to sexual intimacy, seems both too optimistic and too unmindful of human behavior. True, there may very well be people who are secure enough within themselves not to be threatened by their spouse's openly having a sexual relationship with another person. But, as Gracie Allen used to say, "There are a lot of people like that, but not many."

Coping with jealousy. Instead of trying to convince ourselves that sexual freedom in marriage can exist without jealousy, it would be better to focus on our fear of jealousy and the significance we attach to it. We say, "He is eaten up by jealousy," or "I am dying of jealousy," as if the emotion of jealousy had some terrible power to destroy. "Jealousy killed their love," we say, and certainly we all know of relationships that seemed to be destroyed by the jealousy of one or both of the people involved. But the truth is that jealousy does not kill or destroy, any more than any other emotion does. The person who has the emotion of jealousy may, by his actions, cause himself or others unhappiness or cause the destruction of a relationship. But we should remember that it is the manner in which an emotion is handled that causes problems, and not the emotion itself. A man who feels anger toward his boss, for example, may suppress it and get ulcers, yell at his wife and children and be ostracized by them, get a gun and kill his boss and be imprisoned, or get a punching bag and take out his hostilities on the bag. In any case, the results of his actions are not caused by his anger, but by the manner in which he deals with his anger.

Similarly, a man or woman who intellectually accepts the right of his or her spouse to form close relationships with others, but who nonetheless feels the pain of jealousy when it occurs, has several choices. The jealous one can believe in the power of jealousy to maim, and proceed to suffer in grand and glorious style, all the while hoping that the other will notice his pain and prove his love by rejecting his outside relationship. In this way, jealousy can be used as a tool by which the other can be manipulated. "I know I promised you freedom, John, but I'm just so *jealous*!" If this is said with the proper amount of attempted self-control, letting the lip tremble *just* so, John is bound to feel like a complete heel if he continues to enjoy his close relationship with another woman, and he will probably terminate it. If the scene is replayed often enough, he may terminate the marriage.

The jealous mate can also try retaliation. If John develops an intimate friendship with Bernice, then Mary may begin to go to bed with all of John's friends. "I'm as free as you" becomes a weapon that clubs John and degrades Mary. A relationship that was begun on the assumption of mutual freedom to grow thus becomes a contest to see who can have more extramarital sexual activity. The result, of course, is an empty marriage and empty sex.

Another method of coping with jealousy is to deny it—vigorously. "I think it's wonderful that you've found a woman who can add to your happiness, dearest. Why don't you bring her home to live with us—better yet, she can sleep with us! I love her too, without even meeting her!" This method may be the least painful for all concerned, but it also removes the extramarital relationship from the realm of a personal friendship to a shared one. It is no longer a friendship that might contribute to John's personal growth and freedom, but one that Mary shares and controls. Triadic sex allows Mary literally to know every move John makes with Bernice, and Mary may even show John a thing or two by doing more for Bernice than he can.

The least popular method of coping with jealousy is to face it squarely and examine its basis. If a total relationship is good, if there is mutual respect and affection, and if there is openness and honesty between the partners, then the jealous party must carefully examine the reason behind the jealousy. If one is honest, the jealousy usually is found to stem from a feeling of abandonment during the time the spouse is with the other person. At those times, the spouse obviously *prefers* the other person, and it is the plain fact of being second choice at those times that causes the feeling of abandonment and anger that we call jealousy. Being Number One is important to our competitive society, whether it is in sports, nuclear armaments, education, or soft drinks. Winning is so important that we expect a consolation prize if we lose. We dare not lose, and certainly not in love. And for someone else to be preferred—even for a short while—seems tantamount to losing. It is as if one who is not preferred has lost, and once he has lost he is out of the contest forever.

The truth is that none of us is always the preferred one, not even to those who love us the most. And, as we all know, no one person is always our preferred companion. One friend may be the one we most like to have long, philosophical discussions with, another friend may be the one we want to be with when we feel silly and frivolous, and still another may be our choice when we feel like sharpening our wits by debate. All three friends may be liked equally, but we choose one over the others at certain times.

So it is in a marriage that has freedom as its foundation. Each partner chooses the other as the preferred mate in life—the person with whom he or she is most comfortable and contented. That preference does not change when one partner looks elsewhere for particular needs such as shared interests, excitement, or sexual variety. And the increased self-awareness and zest for living that one acquires from freely exploring every desired avenue is brought back to the preferred mate, thereby keeping the marriage a dynamic, fluid stream of happenings, rather than a static, enclosed pond of still stagnation.

So, if you accept that and believe that, and you are nevertheless faced with your own or your spouse's jealousy when outside relationships develop, what do you do? You accept it and use the jealousy as another growing experience. Jealousy can be another shared experience for the married couple, and it can be an opportunity for greater closeness and openness. There is no more reason for the jealous person to hide his or her jealousy and grin and bear it than there is to use it as a manipulative tool against the other. There is a world of difference in one partner saying to the other, "Hey, I'm jealous. *We* have to work it out," and in saying "It's making me jealous. *You* have to stop." If both partners can see jealousy as simply another emotion, and not as a killing, destructive force, they can both deal with it more objectively and more effectively.

The solution may be as simple as frequent reassurance of being loved and wanted; it may be in more frequent physical contact, in being cuddled and fondled; it may be that the two partners together can discuss the feelings of abandonment and rejection than are apparent. He or she may be reacting to childhood hurts such as a father who neglected his family for his work, or a mother who had no time for showing love to her children. If the married pair, together, can talk about the jealousy as a problem they share and can try to find a way to ease the pain, it can be a strengthening and growing experience for the marriage and for each partner.

The point is that we should not make jealousy a more important emotion than it is. Jealousy should be approached rationally and courageously and dealt with as sensibly as possible. If jealousy is dealt with by both partners, if it is not used as a club or as a tool by either, and if neither feels ashamed or resentful when it appears, it will in time cease to be such an ominous bugaboo. Jealousy should not be glossed over as an unnecessary and foolish emotion, nor should it be invested with mystical powers as a destroyer of people and relationships. Instead, it should be acknowledged as one of the many emotions that human beings must learn to accept in themselves and others and one which can be dealt with in an appropriate, growth-producing manner.

PARENTAL RESPONSIBILITY

In the rigidly structured societies of the past, the task of the family was to bring up obedient conformists who could fit into the roles assigned to them. Parenthood was then essentially a task of molding human beings into noncomplaining conformists who could accept their lot without resistance or complaint. In today's world, children are encouraged toward individualism and the strength to stand on their own feet and forge their own destinies. Living in today's world requires autonomy, self-reliance, and the capacity to be responsible in freedom (Mace, 1972). The task of the modern parent is therefore to create an environment in which the children can learn to use freedom with wisdom and restraint. It was much

easier to deal with children when a parent felt it was his or her obligation to enforce rules and to produce submission in them. To guide children in such a manner so that they are encouraged to make their own decisions within certain boundaries requires infinitely more patience and acceptance on the part of the parent. Allowing children to think independently also raises the uncomfortable possibility that they may disagree with the parents on vital issues. Being a parent in today's world is no longer merely a task that involves the providing of physical care and discipline; instead, it is now a task that involves helping a person grow into an individual with his or her own unique ideas and behaviors, even if these ideas and behaviors are contrary to those held by the parent. To be able to carry out the complex responsibilities of parenthood requires the parent to possess more than a modicum of maturity, honesty, and flexibility.

The change in the responsibilities of the modern parent is another factor that affects marriage and the growth of the marriage partners. And every person contemplating marriage, parenthood, and self-fulfillment must give this issue serious consideration before making a final decision. The issues involved in becoming parents will be more thoroughly discussed in Chapter 12, "Becoming Parents."

CONCLUSION

In this chapter we have explored some of the needs that individuals may have when they enter marriage, and how these needs may interfere with the self-actualization of both partners and with the growth of the marital relationship itself.

Certain issues that must be faced were also examined as they relate to the growth and self-fulfillment of marriage partners. In the next chapter, we will discuss marriage as it has evolved from prehistoric times to the present. Such an overview is not simply to provide a "history of marriage" but to provide the reader with a perspective on marriage as it has been in the past before pointing to marriage as it may be in the future.

CHAPTER 3

MARRIAGE
IN THE PAST

I have made a ceaseless effort, not to ridicule, not to bewail, nor to scorn human actions, but to understand them. SPINOZA

64 Marriage in the Past

The institution of marriage, as a legally and spiritually sanctioned monogamous relationship between two people who pledge permanent love and fidelity to one another, is a relatively recent development in the history of mankind. The marriage form that Americans tend to think of as traditional is actually only a few centuries old. To understand the interdependence of societal needs and marital forms, it is necessary to view marriage from a historical perspective—from our present monogamous, nuclear family form, back through the pages of history and polygamous, extended families, to the earliest relationships between prehistoric men and women. Earlier historical investigations tried to make a case for an orderly evolution from primitive promiscuity to monogamy. Historians now realize, however, that any account of the man-woman relationships and familial forms of prehistoric peoples is purely conjectural; no one can say with certainty anything about the form of marriage and family practiced by early humans. However, there is geological evidence of the environmental conditions of the times, as well as archeological finds that allow some educated guesses to be made about prehistoric family forms.

PHYSICAL SURVIVAL

For prehistoric people, sheer physical survival was of primary importance, and they therefore roamed the earth in search of food and game. The first human societies were most likely made up of females who were bound to one place by pregnancy, childbirth, and childcare. For these early people, the sexual act was probably not connected with subsequent pregnancy, and males probably mated indiscriminately with any available and willing (or unwilling) female. Early men and women struggled with the elements, and their consuming interest was undoubtedly the necessity of acquiring food for survival, although they were also concerned with fertility. Interest in both hunting and human fertility is evidenced by prehistoric art such as the cave paintings found at Altamira in northern Spain and at Lascaux, in France, as well as the painting of The Nude Woman, found in La Magdeleine Cave at Penne (Tarn), France, and the Venus of Willendorf, one of several fertility goddesses found in Austria (Janson, 1967).

With the Neolithic Age, when people first attempted to domesticate animals and food grains, they began to form villages and communities, and a new discipline and order entered their lives, probably along with the beginnings of a sense of tradition and of clan or family continuity. They were so concerned with keeping the spirit in its original dwelling place, in fact, that "spirit traps" were erected over the graves of the dead (Janson, 1967).

INCEST TABOOS

At some point in the evolution of the family, incest taboos were established, and probably constituted the single most important development affecting the structure of the family. **Incest taboos** prohibit sexual intercourse between close blood relatives or other kinsmen—especially members of the nuclear family—and have been found in all known societies. Except for a very few highly restricted exceptions, sexual intercourse and marriage between brother and sister, mother and son, or father and daughter are nowhere permissible. In some societies, the taboo is extended to secondary or tertiary relatives as well as to primary relatives. (A person's **primary relatives** are one's parents, brothers, sisters, one's mate, and one's children; one's **secondary relatives** are the primary relatives of his or her own primary relatives—grandparents, in-laws, aunts, uncles, et cetera; one's **tertiary relatives** are the primary relatives of secondary relatives—his or her sister-in-law's children, aunt's husband,

first cousins, and others along these lines.) Generally speaking, however, the incest taboos are less stringent for those kinsmen who are outside the nuclear family than they are for those inside it. Regulations governing the taboos vary from society to society and not only stipulate relatives who are denied as mates, but also those most desirable. In one society, for example, a first cousin may be a **preferred mate**, while he or she may be taboo in another society, which may, in turn, stipulate a third cousin as a preferred mate. Furthermore, many societies allow varying degrees of sexual freedom outside marriage, and the freedom may extend to sexual relations between a man and his stepmother, sister-in-law, aunt, mother-in-law, niece, and so on.

There have been many theories advanced to explain the establishment of incest taboos, but none of the theories is considered totally plausible. It was once believed that incest taboos originated because primitive people intellectually recognized the biological dangers of inbreeding. However, genetic studies have indicated that inbreeding in some cases is advantageous, its results being dependent upon hereditary factors. Furthermore, it is doubtful that primitive people had developed reasoning to such a degree that they would have been concerned about genetic inheritance.

Similarly, some authorities have attempted to account for the incest taboos by relating them to "instinct," but there is little or no scientific evidence for this contention, and considerable evidence against it.

Present-day authorities also reject an earlier theory (Westermarck, 1922) that incest taboos resulted from habits formed during childhood, and that avoidance of sexual contact is the result of dulled sexual appetites caused by prolonged association within a family. Later evidence, as well as common sense, indicates that incestuous desires do exist within the unit of the nuclear family, and that they are usually—but not always—held in check by individual control and by societal pressure. Almost everyone knows of instances in which adolescent brothers and sisters are sexually intimate, and it is probably only the censure of society that prevents marriage between brother and sister in many cases.

Freud believed that incest taboos were acquired or learned, rather than instinctive or inborn. He further believed that incestuous sexual impulses were controlled through repression and that they were allowed expression through the process of **reaction formation**—taking a strong stand opposite the one unconsciously held—and other related defense mechanisms. This theory is also lacking as an adequate explanation of the origin of the incest taboo.

While it is doubtful that any theory will satisfactorily explain all aspects of incest taboos, one common-sense theory is that man established taboos as he became aware that his own strength was increased through cooperation with others. Incest taboos allowed men to work together in cooperative endeavors without battling each other over the females in their group. If this is true, then the first incest taboos were probably agreed upon in the first simple social groups that were formed by primitive men. Males in the group would thus have been freed to band together and to support each other in fights with other groups and to work together for the good of their own group (Lederer & Jackson, 1968). This theory, of course, assumes that sexual jealousy existed among primitive men—an assumption that may be more a reflection of "civilized" emotions than of primitive ones. It also assumes that incest taboos were primarily for the peace of mind of primitive men, and that primitive women would have been able to work cooperatively together in their grain-gathering and childrearing duties without exhibiting or feeling sexual jealousy. For whatever reason, incest taboos became more defined as family forms became more prescribed, and certain taboos evolved in certain societies according to the spe-

"If we go to their orgy, I suppose we'll have to invite them to ours."

cific needs and circumstances of those societies. In all societies, incest taboos simplify and strengthen the social structure by allowing family members to live together in a unit that is not vulnerable to disruption by sexual jealousy.

Incest taboos are more intense and more emotionally laden than any other sexual restrictions found in any society. However, they are not absolute, and sporadic violations occur in all societies, including our own. In some societies, incestuous unions have been reserved as a privilege of those of exalted status, and forbidden only to the general populace. Marriage between brothers and sisters was common in the royal families of Egypt during the Ptolemaic period, among the royal families of the Incas of Peru, and among the Hawaiian aristocracy of olden days. The usual interpretation of this practice is that it provided a method for keeping power and property in the hands of the family (Leslie, 1967).

There are also exceptions to the incest taboo in present-day societies. Among the Melanesian Dobuans, for example, intercourse between a widowed mother and her son is not given any serious consideration since it is viewed as a private sin and not a public offense. Among the Balinese peoples of Indonesia, twins are allowed to marry on the basis of their undue intimacy in their mother's womb. In Africa, an important hunter of the Thonga tribe is permitted to have intercourse with his daughter in preparation for a great hunt. The nature and special circumstances surrounding these exceptions, however, serve to emphasize rather than to disprove the universality of the incest taboos (Murdock, 1949).

In all cultures, of course, incest is found in a variety of circumstances. In our own culture, incestuous unions between fathers and daughters, brothers and sisters, and, less commonly, between mothers and sons, occur more frequently than many people realize in spite of our strong incest taboos. It may be more accurate to say that incest taboos do not *prevent* sexual unions between members of a nuclear family, but that they may provide for the punishment of the offenders when incest occurs. Incest taboos restrict the nuclear family to a two-generation unit, and force most people to belong to two nuclear families within their lifetime—their own original **family of orientation,** and the family that they create with the person whom they marry—their **family of procreation**.

TRIBAL AND ECONOMIC SURVIVAL

At the time that incest taboos were being laid down, the family unit was a unit that functioned for physical survival. Procreation was

important because it insured a stronger family unit. As local populations grew beyond the available food supply, such strength became increasingly important. First in Egypt and Mesopotamia and later in neighboring areas, a group's capacity to survive was challenged by competition with other groups. The family structure, along with customs and mores, adapted to the needs of the people.

Many of the customs which originated in the Near East, the "cradle of civilization," remained somewhat static from one generation to the next, and were finally recorded in the books of the Old Testament. Ancient marriage and family customs are also described in such archeological finds as the recently discovered Nuzu texts in Mesopotamia. It is from these written records, plus the evidence presently existing in **primitive societies**—those rural and self-sufficient societies in which the social and political units are the village and tribe, rather than the city and state—that we gain an understanding and knowledge of early marriage forms and family relationships.

POLYGAMOUS MARRIAGE FORMS

As people were faced with the need for competition for land, marriages were arranged with the strengthening of the tribe or clan in mind. **Polygamous** marriages—one person with two or more mates—with strict rules of inheritance, served the clan needs best. A polygamous society might practice either **polyandry**—the marriage of one woman and more than one man—or **polygyny**—the marriage of one man and more than one woman. The type of polygamy practiced depended on the economic conditions of the society. Polyandry, for example, is quite rare, and is usually associated with extreme poverty that prevents a man from being able to support even one wife of his own. By joining other men in marriage to one woman, a man in a polyandrous society can be assured of sexual privileges and of a family. Many polyandrous societies stabilize the ratio of one woman to several men by practicing female infanticide. Polyandry has been found among the Eskimo, the Pawnee, and other Plains Indian tribes of North America. Murdock's study (1949) found only two societies, the Toda tribe of India and the Marquesan tribe of Polynesia, in which the practice was culturally sanctioned and actively practiced as the preferred form of marriage.

Polyandry may be either **fraternal** or **nonfraternal**. If fraternal, one woman marries two or more brothers. Fraternal polyandry is the preferred form of marriage among the Todas (Murdock, 1949), although occasional instances of nonfraternal polyandry can be found. The Marquesans of Polynesia prefer nonfraternal polyandry. If fraternal polyandry is practiced, the co-husbands usually occupy the same dwelling, and the wife has intercourse with each of them in turn. Co-husbands who are not brothers usually occupy separate living quarters, with the wife cohabiting regularly with each of them. The father of the children of such a union is apparently unimportant. During the first pregnancy of the wife, paternity is established through the performance of a rite. In this ceremony, one of the brothers gives a toy—usually a bow and arrow—to the wife. The same ceremony may be performed during succeeding pregnancies, and children are always assigned to the last husband to perform the rite, although, in some cases, he may have been dead for a number of years.

A special form of fraternal polyandry called **levirate** was stipulated

"My wives don't understand me."

for the ancient Hebrews as a means of perpetuating a man's lineage after his death (Deuteronomy 25:5). In the societies in which levirate is culturally approved, the preferred mate for a widow is a brother of her deceased husband. In cases where the brother is already married, the widow becomes a secondary mate to him as he is to her. For the Hebrews, it was a man's *duty* to marry his deceased brother's widow if she had not yet borne a son and to perpetuate his brother's name by impregnating his widow. If a woman conceived a son by her husband's brother, the child was legally considered her dead husband's and bore his name. It was for his refusal to follow God's dictate to impregnate his brother's widow that Onan was said to have been struck dead by God (Genesis 38:6-10), and not for the sin of "wasting his sperm" (onanism).

Polygyny is the most common type of polygamous marriage; it was practiced among the Navaho and was, in the past, the form of Mormon marriage. It has occurred in all parts of the word (Reichard, 1938).

In some societies, a man is expected to take his wife's sisters as his secondary mates in a form of marriage known as **concurrent sororal polygyny**. In other societies, a man may be expected to marry his wife's sister if his wife dies (Murdock, 1949), in a form of marriage known as **consecutive sororate marriage**.

Among the ancient Hebrews, sororal polygyny was a custom that developed around their rules of inheritance. According to the Nuzu texts, if a man had no sons to inherit his lands, he could either adopt a slave as a son or have sons through a slave concubine whom his wife was obliged by law to provide (Fritsch, 1960). Thus, the childless Abram adopted a slave and considered him his heir until he was told by God that his own flesh and blood was to be his heir (Genesis 15:3,4). Convinced that she was barren, the aged Sarai then gave Abram her Egyptian maid Hagar as a concubine to provide him with a biological son (Genesis 16:1-3).

A third method by which Hebraic law allowed a man to acquire a son to inherit his lands was through the marriage of his daughters. By law, a man's son-in-law took on the same status as an adopted son (Nuzu texts). The son-in-law paid for the privilege of inheritance by paying a bride-price or by working for his future father-in-law for a stipulated period of time. By his marrying all the daughters in a family, the inheritance was kept intact. If a son-in-law also married women from other families, he forfeited his inheritance rights (Nuzu texts). Such marriages to preserve or collect inheritance were not at all unusual in the past.

An example of these inheritance laws and of concurrent sororate marriage is the Biblical story of the marriage of Jacob to Rachel and her weak-eyed sister Leah. After Jacob bought the inheritance rights of his brother Esau for a meal of bread and pottage (Genesis 25:29-34), his father Isaac told him to marry one of the daughters of his uncle Laban (Genesis 28:1,2). Jacob obediently sought out his uncle and offered to work for seven years for his daughter Rachel. After seven years, Jacob was tricked into marrying Leah instead of Rachel, and he then worked another seven years for Rachel (Genesis 29:16-30). In all probability, Jacob knew from the beginning that he would marry both sisters, and the "trick" was the fact that Leah became the first wife, having authority over his preferred Rachel. While Jacob may indeed have loved Rachel more than Leah (Genesis 29:30), his fourteen years of work were for land and not for love.

There are adjustment problems created by polygynous unions, of course, that are not found in monogamous marriages or, apparently, in polyandrous marriages. The two that most often occur are sexual jealousy and disputes over economic duties and tasks, although most cultures have found satisfactory solutions to these problems. In most societies, plural wives occupy separate dwellings. The first wife usually has a recognized superior social status and is given supervision of the other wives concerning household duties. The problem of sexual jealousy is usually dealt with by requiring the husband to sleep with each wife regularly. Intercourse may not be actually required, but he must spend the night in each of their dwellings to keep his wives from being humiliated by public rejection and ridicule.

Fewer problems are usually found in sororal polygyny since sisters, having grown up together, usually have similar habits, attitudes, and values. In many polygynous societies, such as the Crow, Soga, and Sinkaietk, it is reported that sisters who are co-wives regularly occupy the same dwelling and those who are not sisters are given separate living quarters. Murdock found sororal polygyny practiced to some degree in 70 of the 193 societies he studied, and he believed the figure would be higher if the information had been more complete.

HOUSEHOLD AND EXTENDED FAMILY

While the nuclear family in our own society is a relatively isolated unit, in other societies nuclear families tend to unite into groups of various sizes and to occupy a single residence, a group of adjacent dwellings, or a specifically designated compound. Whatever the living arrangements, the grouping is referred to as a **household** (Murdock, 1949). This type of union differs from the communal organizations that exist in various forms in our own culture by virtue of the fact that in primitive societies the nuclear family combinations are almost always bound to one another through close ties of kinship as well as of common residence. Occasionally, households may be found that are composed of families that are distantly related, or even unrelated, like our own communes or the Israeli kibbutzim, but such forms of the household are exceptional and are contrary to common practice in all the primitive societies that have been studied (Murdock, 1949). When several nuclear families, such as the families of several brothers, live together or are otherwise bonded together, they form an **extended family**.

In all early societies, marriage forms and family arrangements continued to evolve and to be accepted according to the economic needs of the people involved. Interestingly, sexual moral codes were also intertwined in the particular marriage forms of a period. According to Hawks and Wooley (see Sherfy, 1966), women—at least in certain parts of the civilized world—were considered sexually

insatiable for the span of time from 1200 to 800 B.C., and were accorded a great deal of sexual freedom with many partners. With the transfer of property to blood relatives and a greater understanding of a male's role in conception, the image of women's sexuality became altered. Eventually, English common law made transfer of property to the eldest male a cornerstone, and there was a fear that sexual freedom for women would cause a mixing of lineage and difficulty in correctly transferring property. Laws were therefore passed to punish women who did not repress their formerly "insatiable" sexual needs, and women finally became viewed as having very few sexual needs or desires. Again, economics and property rights determined the moral code for female sexuality and for laws regarding adultery.

During the Middle Ages, marriage was contracted strictly for the purpose of transferring property. Two families who wished to join their property might thus arrange and solemnize the marriage of their children while they were still in the cradle. In these marriages, the husband and wife often grew up together, and were more like brother and sister or good friends than what we traditionally think of as lovers. Wives in the Middle Ages had equal rights with men, and often supervised large estates while their husbands were off crusading. (Some of them also found time for romantic dalliances with men who stayed home from the Crusades. It was from these affairs that the concept of **romantic love**—a relationship existing en-

Household and Extended Family **75**

tirely apart from marriage—emerged as an emotion between men and women.) In the large and bustling households of the Middle Ages, there was ample companionship and work, and each spouse found fulfillment in his own sphere of activity (Perutz, 1972).

THE NUCLEAR FAMILY

The discovery of the individual in the Renaissance little altered the extended family life. Children were educated in the home and were frequently apprenticed out to other families or sent to other families for training as pages at an early age (Perutz, 1972). Until the Industrial Revolution, the family remained an extended one that was more a public institution than a private one. Industrialization splin-

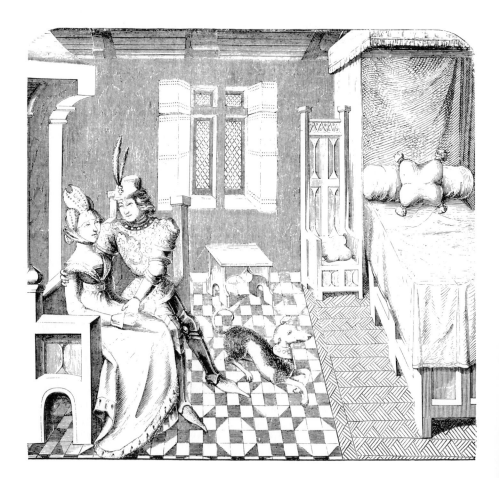

tered the self-sufficiency of the extended families, and nuclear families separated into isolated units, turning over the authority and duties of the extended family to the state and to society. Mass production took the place of personal fulfillment in work, and public education took the place of family authority. Thus, the isolation of the nuclear family served a need for society—that of perpetuating the industrialization of a people. By the end of the eighteenth century, marriage in Europe and parts of America had the structure of the present day form, but the sanctimony of marriage was not achieved until the Victorian era (O'Neill, 1967). Today, there is an increasing questioning of both structure and sanctimony.

THE AMERICAN FAMILY

In John Demos' (1976) writing on early American family life, he points out the influence of the earlier European traditions on American society and family organization. In the seventeenth and eighteenth centuries when the American colonies were being formed, there was a tight link between family and community. The community exercised control over family affairs, which was a means of preserving order in society. For instance, the community had the power to force a husband and wife to live together, and the responsibility for children's behavior was shared by the community with the parents.

The roles and functions of the family then were, in some respects, significantly different from what they are now. For example, the family was responsible for training their children in academic and social skills, for caring for the elderly, for orphans, and at times even for criminals (Demos, 1976).

But the nuclear family structure was operating even then. When a couple decided to marry, they were expected to set up their own household; gifts were provided for this purpose which had been formally agreed upon beforehand by members of both families. It was not expected that these marriages be solely for economic purposes, however, and with most couples there was affection present before marriage. Divorce was not unheard of, but was granted in a very few cases for desertion (seven years or more), adultery, and impotence (Demos, 1976).

Sex roles for men and women were much more clearly distinguished. Women were regarded as weaker and inferior, yet men were suspicious of them and even feared them. They were subordinate to their husbands, but they worked side by side with them. Thus, in many ways, women were not really set apart, but shared their everyday experiences. Many women, for instance, managed shops, inns, and taverns. According to Demos (1976), the many functional purposes that women served in production and economics, as well as their relative scarcity (the ratio of men to women was 3:2), contributed to a rise in their status.

This situation was altered in the nineteenth century when the American woman became idealized as the virtuous, pure figure who stood behind and supported her hard-working, dedicated husband. She was not permitted to work outside her home, but was charged with preserving the purity and sanctity of home and family life—always in subjection to her husband, of course, who was responsible for making major decisions. Demos (1976) writes, ". . . her central role was that of comforter." She did not live for herself, but for others in her family.

About the same time, men became more distant from their families. Work life was separated from home life, and the family was no longer informed about the nature of the work that produced money for their livelihood. While he maintained authority over family affairs, the father became less emotionally involved (Demos, 1976).

This historical account of the family was meant to illustrate the point that ". . . there is no Golden Age of the family gleaming at us from far back in the historical past. And there is no good reason to construe recent trends in terms of decline and decay." Indeed, more is expected of marriage now: "more intimacy, more openness, more deep-down emotional support" (Demos, 1976).

CONCLUSION

The history of marriage can be traced by identifying people's changing needs at various times. Early humans founded a form of marriage for physical survival. With civilization, marriage became a form for tribal survival and then one for economic survival—a means of transferring property. The economic development of a region dictated the form of marriage that was most economically advantageous for the particular culture. Marriages were rarely based on individual choice or romantic love, but were arranged by families and were given sanction by some public demonstration of the fulfillment of an economic arrangement (Reichard, 1938). The demonstration was either in the form of a bride-price, in which the husband's parents brought gifts to the bride's family, or in the form of a dowry, in which the bride's family brought gifts to the groom's family. Again, the custom depended on the economic structure of the particular culture.

During the twentieth century, our industrialized and democratic society has stressed equality. People tend to marry now not out of physical or economic need, but out of emotional need. Our marriage customs are a loose admixture of customs that were developed to serve the needs of former times. Instead of a dowry, the bride's parents pay the wedding costs, and instead of a bride-price, the groom gives his bride an engagement and wedding ring and takes on certain financial obligations, such as paying for the reception dinner. Both bride and groom expect to have romantic love in their marriage, as well as the fulfillment of their physical, economic, and emotional needs. All this is encapsulated in a package that is considered both a sacred union and the vital basis for our entire social structure! Our unrealistic expectations of marriage have resulted in a high divorce rate, an even higher number of unsatisfying marriages, and a general attitude of concern about the future of marriage and the family.

Thus, it can be seen that marriage and the family are structured according to the needs that exist within a specific culture. As the needs of that culture change, so the structure of marriage and family in that culture must change. And so it is with our culture and our marriage and family structure. Rapid changes have taken place in the needs of our society within the past few decades, and we are only now beginning to attempt to cope with the restructuring of our marriage and family forms that, of necessity, must also change or at least be modified considerably.

The following chapter will discuss some of the changes that are now taking place in our own marriage forms, and some of the ways that people are attempting to recapture some of the security and personal fulfillment that existed in the extended family. With every significant change in marriage forms, there are both benefits and drawbacks that can have an impact on the populace. It is to our distinct advantage to weigh carefully all aspects of the changes, keeping those that add to society and discarding or modifying those that hinder or subtract from our healthy growth and development.

CHAPTER 4

ALTERNATIVE MARRIAGE FORMS

When two people are under the influence of the most violent, most insane, most delusive, and most transient of passions, they are required to swear that they will remain in that excited, abnormal, and exhausted condition continuously until death do them part. GEORGE BERNARD SHAW

In our society, the married pair and their children live apart from their families of orientation, sometimes many thousands of miles away. A crisis such as an accident or a prolonged illness of a family member imposes strains upon the resources of the individual members of the family such as no other family structure has ever known. In the extended family of yesterday, there was always an aunt who could help care for an ailing child, or a wise old uncle who could help provide training for the children. If either parent was incapacitated by illness or injury for any length of time, other family members were always on hand to provide continuing care for the children. There was, in these extended families, a sense of security that our own isolated nuclear families cannot experience. By sharing the responsibility of the family's function, each family member was relieved of some of the stress and strain of daily living. Some of the new marriage forms that are emerging as alternatives to our monogamous, two-generation family are actually efforts to recapture the security and extended identity afforded by the extended family.

Theoretically, the actual form of the extended family could be revived in our culture. A group of relatives could live cooperatively, sharing either a common residence or living separately in adjacent dwellings. An apartment house, for example, could become the household of an extended family, each nuclear family having its own private apartment. Or a block of houses could be purchased by a group of relatives, with the individual families having regular meetings to discuss their needs and problems.

In theory, the idea has some attraction. In practice, however, it is doubtful that many groups of relatives could live so closely together without discord. Our democratic society is based on the premise that every individual can be whatever he chooses to be, that his limitations are only intellectual and physical. Thus, a family may produce one child who becomes a teacher, another who becomes a salesman, and a third who becomes an artist. Siblings from one family may become politically conservative, liberal, or apathetic. There can be wide divergence in the development of religious, sexual, or social values. An attempt to permanently mix individuals whose only common link is consanguinity is therefore likely to lead to more conflict than satisfaction.

Though rarely formally planned, there are groups of married couples who are related to one another not through blood ties, but through occupational or professional interests, such as artists' or writers' colonies. However, while these individuals who are united in a common interest and who live in close proximity to one another may also help one another in time of need, there is no obligation to do so as there is in the extended family. Some people who seek the genuine flavor of the extended family are therefore experimenting with various alternatives such as cluster marriages, group marriage, or communal families.

CLUSTER MARRIAGES

Cluster marriages, a cooperative relationship between a cluster of individual families within a community, has been advanced as an answer to the isolation and alienation of today's nuclear family (Mead, 1970; Stoller, 1973). In such an arrangement, there would be no common occupational or economic base. Most property would be privately owned, but some recreational or utilitarian features would be communally owned. The ideal cluster of families would include couples with children, couples whose children were grown, couples who were childless by choice, single individuals of different ages, and people who were retired. Intimate relationships would be shared whereby the fragile were helped by the strong, the young were enriched by the experiences of the old, and the old were kept alert and vigorous through contact with the young.

The clustered families would be in close physical proximity in a block of homes, a subdivision, or an apartment house, but there would be no long-term commitment to membership. The families would hold regular meetings in which they shared intimate secrets and influenced one another in terms of values and attitudes. They would also provide one another with a variety of services and thus extend the boundaries of the intimate family (Stoller, 1973).

While such an arrangement of clustered families would definitely offer opportunities for richer lives and more intimate relationships with more people, it is doubtful that very many people could create, organize, or sustain such an arrangement, simply because of the complexities involved. In the rare instances in which clustered families do exist, their arrangement has usually been an outgrowth of a happy combination of personalities in a subdivision or housing complex. As intimate friendships spontaneously evolved, they became a central value for the families involved and were sustained and nurtured (Crosby, 1973). It would be extremely difficult, however, to gather together in one area a group of families who already had such a level of intimacy, or who could develop it once they were living close together. Close friendships are treasured in part because of their fragility, and they can neither be willed into being nor maintained when too great a strain is placed upon them. Cluster

Cluster Marriages **83**

families are therefore not likely to attract a large percentage of the population in practice, although the idea probably finds much support in theory.

GROUP MARRIAGE

Group marriage, several people married to each other, is similarly an idea that appeals to many but will probably attract only a few. Although the term "group marriage" or "multilateral marriage" implies a communal living arrangement, not all communal living arrangements are group marriages. Earlier anthropologists devoted much time and thought to group marriage as a form of polygamous marriage, but it has never actually existed as a cultural norm in any society. Only sporadic instances of group marriage have been found, and anthropological investigation showed those were confined to a few tribes (Murdock, 1949).

In our own society, the small number of group marriages that have been reported can hardly be considered a trend, but they are indicative of a search for viable alternatives to our existing form of monogamous marriage. Today's group marriage is not the same as polygamy, since polygamy is a result of economic necessity. Group marriage in our own society is, instead, a response to psychic needs—those at the higher levels in Maslow's hierarchy of needs. In addition to seeking harmony and economic benefits, which are a part of polygamous unions, today's multilateral unions also seek psychological intimacy (Crosby, 1973). In contrast to the historical purposes of marriage, which were work and procreation, group marriage emphasizes more the goals of self-realization and sexual satisfaction.

Most group marriages form around a nucleus of one family, and the majority of those studied have contained four partners. If the group contains more than six partners, it becomes more like a commune than a marriage in which the partners are bound by deep ties of love and caring. People in group marriages come from a wide variety of occupational and income groups, and they frequently give as a reason for joining a group marriage a desire for "community" or "extended family." In actual fact, they seem to enter a group marriage for the same reasons that others enter **dyadic** (two-person) marriages—for love, security, sex, childrearing, companionship, and all the other needs that might be found in a sampling of conventional marriages.

In a group marriage, all the mechanics of daily living become more complex. Conflicts can arise over food preferences, budgeting, allocation of household duties, discipline of children, and the thousand-and-one other things that two-person marriages have disagreements about. Unless an individual has the temperament that would suit him for living in a large family or in a commune, he would likely find it extremely uncomfortable to try to adapt to the idiosyncrasies of three or five marital partners in an intimate relationship.

Economic and social advantages. There are economic and social advantages in a group marriage, since the marriage is maintained even if some of the adult members are temporarily out of work (Ellis, 1973). Group marriages also open up new dimensions of parent-child interaction. In most group marriages, all adults take on the parental responsibility of all the children, with the male members assuming much more responsibility for the physical care of the chil-

dren than is usual in conventional marriages. While the children are expected to regard all the adults in the group as parents, they know who their biological parents are and the character of their discipline is usually determined by the biological parents. This can pose a problem if two sets of biological parents have divergent modes of discipline for children within the same group marriage. In general, however, children in group marriages appear to adjust remarkably well to their parents' lifestyle, and there seem to be more positive than negative results for the children.

Sexual sharing. The aspect of group marriage that is most disturbing to the majority of people is the sexual sharing that goes on among the members. Members of group marriages tend to deemphasize the sexual aspect of their arrangement in public statements, but in actual fact they all appear to spend a considerable amount of time and energy deciding on who will sleep with whom and how often. Most groups have sexual involvements very early in their relationships, and all seem to have had some difficulties in achieving completely harmonious sleeping arrangements. If a formal rotation schedule is established, the feeling of spontaneity is destroyed, along with the excitement of feeling chosen. On the other hand, if no formal arrangements are made, one partner may be more frequently preferred than another, and since sexual rejection is tantamount to personal rejection in our society, jealousy and hurt feelings are bound to result.

Although sexual variety does not seem to be a driving force for initial entry into a group marriage, it emerges as a central element in the advantages of such an arrangement. No other form of marriage provides for a variety of sexual partners for both sexes *within* marriage. Since extramarital affairs are prevalent in conventional marriages, some believe that a variety of sexual partners is a distinct need of both men and women. Group marriages attempt to fill this need, while at the same time attempting to retain a depth of emotional commitment and involvement that is usually impossible in an extramarital sexual relationship. Proponents of group marriage therefore claim that it satisfies the need for sexual variety without exacting the cost of clandestine affairs or demanding the impersonal involvement of mate-swapping (Constantine & Constantine, 1973). It is unlikely, however, that a four-member or even a six-member group marriage would provide continued sexual variety, since each member would have not one but two or three sexual partners who would eventually become so well known that they no longer provided sexual excitement.

In most group marriages, the idea of group sex and possible bisexual activity is accepted as permissible or even desirable, but in actual practice it seems to occur infrequently. When it does occur, it is usually a triad of one man and two women. Multiple couple sex is rare among group marriages, as it has been found to be particularly conducive to jealousy. Furthermore, temporary impotence has been found to be an especially destructive element in multiple couple sex due to the competition aroused among the males (Constantine & Constantine, 1973).

The most significant difference between multilateral marriages and the conventional dyadic marriage is the potential for jealousy, possessiveness, and competition that must be dealt with as an intrinsic part of the marriage itself. The majority of the members of group marriages have outgrown or learned to deal with jealousy, and some appear never to have experienced it. No group that has been studied, however, has completely freed itself of problems related to jealousy (Constantine & Constantine, 1973).

Experiential advantages. For the exceptionally freedom-loving individual who can paradoxically adjust to the restrictions and self-discipline required by a group marriage, there are definite advantages. In addition to and equally or more important than the fact that frequent sex relations with more than one partner may serve to keep the members sexually alive, the members usually feel more fulfilled because of the possibility of experiencing intense love for several other people. There may also be the gratification of sharing family life with a large number of people, with the possibility increasing that some of those people will share one's own interests and absorptions (Ellis, 1973).

The most satisfying aspect of group marriage is the extended experiential quality that is not attainable in monogamous marriages. A member of a group marriage can come to know himself better and can find more self-fulfillment because of multifaceted sex, love, childrearing, and other human relationships that are intimate and reciprocal. Loving and living cooperatively with a large group is also intensely satisfying to those who are interested in gaining a sense of the brotherhood of man (Ellis, 1973).

Group marriage is only for a select few and, interestingly, more men than women find the idea attractive (Ellis, 1973). A large number of people are hostile to the idea, possibly because of guilt over their own extramarital involvements or resentment over the greater sexual freedom of others (Constantine & Constantine, 1973). In order for group marriages to become a viable form of marriage, the concept would have to become reconciled with contemporary society, and such a reconciliation is not likely to occur within our present climate.

Most members of group marriages consider themselves far ahead of the conventionally married who, if they are lucky, will have one fully trusted confidant, one secure relationship, and one intimate relationship with another person. The person in a group marriage feels that he has gained a sense of community, an extended sense of identification, and has expanded his intimate relationships without guilt. Regardless of the final outcome of such marriages, therefore, their members regard their involvement in them as worthwhile (Constantine & Constantine, 1973). As mentioned before, however, few people have the emotional stability or experience to permit them to participate successfully in group marriage.

COMMUNAL FAMILIES

The **communal family** is another form of the extended family and is one of the oldest forms of shared life. The first recorded communal living arrangement was that of the first Christians who "were together and had all things in common" (Acts 2:44). By the nineteenth century, there were at least 130 known communes (Haughey, 1972). Of these, the Oneida Community (1846–1880) was probably the most controversial, and the Israeli kibbutzim have been the most successful. A discussion of these two groups and the characteristics that caused their success or failure may shed light on the nature of present-day communes and their future.

The Oneida Community. The Oneida Community began with a Bible class started in 1839 under the leadership of John Humphrey Noyes, a lawyer turned minister. Noyes rejected the traditional theological belief that man was a depraved, sinful being who had to continually work toward being liberated from sin. Instead, he preached that Christ had already returned to earth and that the Kingdom of God was an accomplished fact for those who accepted Christ. The belief that man could therefore live in a sinless state was called **Perfectionism**, and for teaching his doctrine, Noyes's license as a minister was revoked. The followers of Perfectionism continued to meet and to discuss the idea of spiritual equality, however, and eventually that belief came to include the idea of both economic and sexual equality. The members believed that if, in the Kingdom of God, all beings were to love one another equally, then monogamy and sexual exclusiveness were manifestations of self-

ishness and not to be practiced by those who strove to attain the perfect state (Kephart, 1971).

In 1846, the Perfectionists founded the Putney Community in Putney, Vermont. All property, even personal belongings such as clothes, trinkets, and children's toys, was communally owned. All adult members practiced sexual communism; every adult considered himself married to every other adult of the opposite sex. The Community was thus a combination of group marriage and communal living, and while the term "free love" was coined by Noyes, he preferred "complex marriage" or "antogamy."

To Noyes and his followers, romantic love led to jealousy and hypocrisy and made spiritual love impossible to attain. The one requirement in the Community concerning sexual intercourse was that a woman had to give her formal consent before a man could have sexual intercourse with her. A man who wanted to have sexual intercourse with a woman had to appear before the Central Committee, who then conveyed his request to the woman in question. If the woman gave her consent, the man simply presented himself at her door at bedtime and stayed an hour or two in her room before returning to his own room for the night. (There were no provisions for women members who might wish to have intercourse with a particular man.)

In 1847, Noyes was arrested and charged with adultery, but he and his flock fled to New York State in 1848 and reestablished their community on old Indian lands along Oneida Creek. From that base, the most revolutionary of all American marriage systems flourished for the next 29 years.

In assessing the reasons for the longevity of the Oneida Community, one is tempted to attribute it to the charismatic personality of Noyes. He was a man of tremendous vigor and dedication, and he was able to put into practice his original ideas with perseverance and courage. He inspired tremendous loyalty in his followers, and it is possible that his group would have endured for no other reason than his dynamic leadership. It is more likely, however, that the group endured because of a combination of Noyes's leadership, their economic solvency, their dedication to their religious belief, and the satisfaction of their interpersonal relationships—both psychic and sexual.

The economic solvency of the Oneida group came about as a result of the invention of a steel trap by Sewell Newhouse, one of their members. The trap, still in use today, proved to be the best of its kind, and the Oneida economy was based on its manufacture. The Community members also became known for the quality of their garden produce, which they put in glass jars and cans and sold. As they branched out in their communal economy, they also engaged in silk spinning on a large scale, and in 1877 they began to manufacture silverware that became well known and is still manufactured today.

In the Oneida Community, various jobs were rotated from year to year in order to eliminate feelings of discrimination. Almost everyone took turns at the menial tasks, but no person was placed in a position beyond his innate capacities. Status came from how well a person did his work, and not from the type of job he held.

The members of the Community set themselves apart from the rest of the world not only by their style of living but also by their appearance. In an age when women were noted for their long hair and long gowns, the Oneida women bobbed their hair and dressed in short knee-length skirts over long, loose trousers. In further deviance from the norm of marital arrangements, all the Oneida Community members lived together in a spacious brick residence called the Mansion House. Built in the 1860s, it still stands today and houses some of the descendants of the original Community members.

Discipline was maintained by mutual criticism within the group. Whenever a member was believed to be deviating from the norms of the group, or whenever a personality or character weakness seemed to exist in a member, a committee would meet with the member to discuss his offense. Oneidans were willing to be the

"Fine. And do all you people on the left side over here take all you people on the right side to be your lawful wedded spouses?"

CHRISTIANSON

subject of penetrating, frank criticism, delivered in an impersonal matter, and the end result was often a spiritual cleansing or catharsis, which the members counted as one of the greatest rewards of membership in the Community. Whether due to the innate high character of the individual members, or to the system of mutual criticism, the Oneida Community had no crime, no alcoholism, and no desertion during its lifetime, in spite of the fact that there were no laws or law-enforcing officers.

In order to insure that children born into the Community would be given the best of care, the Oneidans delayed childbirth for the first 20 years of their union, by **coitus reservatus** (sexual intercourse up to but not including ejaculation.) Until they mastered the necessary control to stop short of ejaculation, younger males were limited to having sexual relations only with women past menopause.

In 1869, the Oneida group started a pioneer eugenics program whereby only couples who had superior physical and mental abilities were given permission to become parents. The eugenics program was called "stirpiculture" and parents were called "stirps."

In the decade during which the stirpiculture program was in effect, 58 children were born, a dozen of them fathered by Noyes, who enthusiastically practiced what he preached.

The children born to the Oneida stirps were remarkably healthy and had a significantly lower death rate than children born outside the Community. They were evidently well adjusted, and about 13 of them—all in their 80s and 90s—are still living; they all remember their childhood as a happy one. Until they were about 15 months old, they were in their mothers' care. They were then gradually transferred to a special section of the Mansion House and spent most of the remainder of their childhood in age-graded classes. Under Perfectionism, all adults were to love all children, and vice versa, and sentimentalism on the part of the biological parents was frowned upon.

The disintegration of the Oneida Community came about as a dual result of Noyes's resignation in 1877 and the intense pressure brought to bear by Anthony Comstock, the self-appointed defender of America's morals. Although the surrounding townspeople knew the Oneidans to be hard-working, devout individuals, the charges of "incest," "lust," and "animal breeding" aimed at the Oneidans' form of complex marriage were finally too great to combat. Had Noyes retained his youthful vigor and leadership, the Community might have survived the public onslaught against them, but his son and successor, Dr. Theodore Noyes, was not able to prevent the factionalism that emerged after Noyes's resignation. Rebellion on the part of some of the younger men at having to confine their sexual relations to older women, dissatisfaction on the part of some of the mothers at being separated from their children, and a general discontent among the Community members made their union easier to disrupt. Perhaps because he was unable to face the death of a dream, Noyes left the Community in June of 1879 for Canada and never returned. He sent a message to the Community a few months later, suggesting that they abolish their complex marriage and revert to the marital patterns that were acceptable to society. Soon after, the group disbanded, and many of the members became formally married. The members formed a joint-stock company with their approximately $600,000, and the stock was divided among them. No other experiment in communal living and group marriage has before or since been so successful for so long a time.

The kibbutzim. A kibbutz is an agricultural collective that emphasizes communal living, collective ownership of all property, and communal childrearing (Spiro, 1971). Of all communal living arrangements, the kibbutzim have been the most successful at maintaining their way of life. A group of Russian Jews established the first agricultural collectives in Palestine in the 1880s. By 1936 there were 47 kibbutzim in Palestine, and when the state of Israel came into being in 1948 there were 149. The number had reached 232 by 1968 (Shatil, 1971); it seems that the kibbutzim will endure in one form or another for some time to come, although they have been constantly changing and evolving (Crosby, 1973).

In present-day Israel, the kibbutzim are organized into three separate national federations. While there are differences among them, the basic structure of society is similar in all three. Since many are scattered along the Israeli border, some of the modern kibbutzim also may serve as part of the national defense strategy of the outnumbered and embattled Israelis.

The **family** has been defined as a social group characterized by common residence, economic cooperation, and reproduction (Murdock, 1949). According to this definition, the family actually does not exist within a kibbutz, since the economic, residential, and childrearing function of the family has been taken over by the kibbutz itself. Economic cooperation is among all kibbutz members and is not confined to the nuclear unit; children and their parents do not share a common residence; and the physical care, socialization, and education of the young are the responsibility of the kibbutz rather than of parents. Other than the function of reproduction, therefore, the kibbutz itself functions as a family, serving the economic, residential, educational, and socialization function of the family (Spiro, 1971).

In many of the kibbutzim, there are no sanctions against premarital sexual relations for those who have graduated from high school and who have been elected into the kibbutz, so the desire to establish a permanent relationship with one person is primarily motivated by a wish for psychological intimacy.

In the kibbutzim of one federation that was studied (Spiro, 1971), marriage is strictly a legal matter, serving merely to insure the legal rights of children born to a couple. Most kibbutz couples eventually do marry, usually just before or just after their first child is born, but becoming united with another person does not require the sanction of a marriage ceremony or any other event. Instead, a man and woman who wish to have a permanent relationship signify their commitment to one another by requesting a common room. When the kibbutz grants their request, their union is *ipso facto* sanctioned by society.

The legal and social status of males and females is probably more egalitarian in the kibbutz than in any other form of living arrangement. Both men and women work either in the agricultural branch or the service branch of the kibbutz. When a woman marries, she retains her maiden name and is a member of the kibbutz in her own right. In fact, her registration card in the kibbutz file is completely separate from that of her spouse.

A kibbutz couple live in a single room and eat their meals in a communal dining room. Their children are reared in a communal children's dorm, seeing their parents a few hours a day and possibly all day on Sunday. The kibbutz cherishes its children and lavishes care and attention on them, but the entire socialization and education of the kibbutz children are the responsibility of nurses and teachers, not the parents. However, the kibbutz children are, if anything, more attached to their parents than are children in our own society. Their parents are crucially important in their psychological development, as they provide the security and love that the kibbutz child—like the child of all nuclear families—usually gets nowhere else. In a very real sense the kibbutz, by providing the child with love, affection, and security from sources in addition to the nuclear family, often diminishes the severity of problems found in all cultures. For example, economic hardship, death, desertion, illness, and a host of other problems often decimate the American nuclear family to the extent that security for the child becomes a vaporous entity. The big success of the kibbutz is that it has overcome such extreme hazard through the very nature of its social structure.

As a kibbutz child enters preadolescence and adolescence, he or she is gradually inducted into the economic life of the kibbutz, thus gaining the feeling of importance and belongingness that children in our own society so often lack. Children in grade school work an hour a day, and high school seniors work about three hours a day, under the supervision of adults, in one of the economic branches of the kibbutz. Economic skills, therefore, like social skills and values, are taught by adults other than the parents.

In addition to performing the necessary functions of the family, the kibbutz atmosphere tends to be familial, and its members tend to regard one another as psychological kin. The bonds of psychological kinship within the kibbutz are so great, in fact, that individuals born and reared in a kibbutz tend to marry people from outside the kibbutz. Their feeling is that they are so intimately related to every other kibbutz member that marriage to a kibbutz kinsman would be tantamount to incest. It is interesting to speculate on the possibility that the first groups that primitive people formed may have engendered similar familial atmospheres that caused an aversion to choosing mates from within the group, thus creating the incest taboo.

In the kibbutz, therefore, the entire society has become a large extended family. The kibbutz' function as a family is probably dependent upon the members' perception of one another as psychological kinsmen, and this perception would probably diminish if the kibbutz population grew so large that interaction of its members ceased to be face-to-face. It is the very nature of the familial society of the kibbutz, therefore, that allows for the deemphasis of the family as it traditionally exists (Spiro, 1971).

The modern commune. While there have been other communal groups that have survived successfully, such as the Hutterites, Mennonites, Shakers, Mormons, and Bruderhofs, they were unified around religious principles (Schulterbrandt & Nichols, 1973). The kibbutzim and the Oneida Community, while also based on unifying principles, involve more complexities than these strictly religious groups and therefore serve as better comparisons for the modern commune, whose purpose is usually to find more meaningful forms of social and interpersonal relationships.

Most modern communes have in common a desire to withdraw from the traditional, regulated forms of society and to try to experience a new form of brotherhood with a group of people who have the same goals. A commune also can be formed because of negative reasons such as ostracism by society (Plath & Sugihara, 1971). In either case, there is no such thing as a typical commune or communard. Commune members may be irresponsible, lazy, exploitative individuals who open communes that soon close because of unsanitary conditions and discord among the members. Or a commune member may be a responsible, educated, hard-working individual who is emotionally stable and whose needs are for self-actualization in a setting that offers a broad range of human relationships. The communes opened by these individuals tend to survive, at least for a time, and their problems tend to center around economic survival rather than interpersonal relationships.

A commune may be in a rural setting where subsistence farming and welfare assistance provide the basic necessities of the members, or it may be in an urban setting in which all the members are gainfully employed. Drugs may or may not be used in a commune, sexual freedom may or may not be emphasized, and there may or may not be a strong leader around whom the members rally. Unfortunately, the sick and tragic example of the Manson Family, who were convicted and sentenced to life imprisonment for committing bizarre, ritualistic murders, has become the stereotype of the commune for many Americans, but this "family" was definitely not a typical commune.

In attempting to escape traditional society and to establish a subculture within a culture, commune members come face to face with an insurmountable dilemma. In order to become economically self-sufficient, it is necessary to do commerce with the outside world—an activity that violates their dream of living off the land in harmony with nature. Welfare benefits are therefore the principal source of income in most rural communes, and much discussion centers around their future when "the Man" will stop supporting them through welfare. There are occasional gifts from parents or other benefactors, but most rural communes lack the necessary machinery and tools to adequately work their land because of their reluctance to create economic arrangements with institutions outside their subculture (Berger et al., 1971).

In addition to the dilemma posed by their reluctance to engage in commerce with the outside world, there is another dilemma posed by the fact that rural commune members regard as central to their philosophy a commitment to the group and an abandonment of personal gratification. If a commune member possesses some special skill that might be salable and might contribute to the economic solvency of the commune, therefore, there is unspoken group pressure to ignore it in favor of jobs for the collective welfare of the commune, such as gardening or caring for domestic animals. To devote time and energy to a specialized skill or craft would be tantamount to a "side trip," which is seen by the commune members

as distracting from the "family trip" that is the major goal of communal living (Berger et al., 1971).

In most rural communes, subsistence farming is the principal occupation, but the work is usually not organized except for those tasks that must be done regularly, such as preparing meals and caring for the animals. The division of labor in most communes is sexual, with women usually assuming the traditional female roles of cooking and housekeeping. Occasionally, a woman may have a special skill and will escape kitchen duty, but rarely does one find a man in the communal kitchen. This is especially true in "hippie" communes, which tend to be very male-dominated. In the hippie commune, a woman may be accused of being a dyke, a bitch, or frigid if she tries to step out of the traditional female role (Estellachild, 1972).

Leadership in most communes is assumed rather than bestowed, and it may fluctuate in any one commune among several strong figures. In general, a commune leader is one who is able to speak compellingly and to kindle in his fellow communards a sense of love and fraternity when disputes and hostilities arise. Meetings are usually called when there are issues that need to be decided, and every commune member has a chance to speak his or her mind about the topic in question.

The American public generally assumes that sexual freedom is the rule in communes. This is true in some communes, completely false in others. Some communes are composed of strictly monogamous unions, others of celibate individuals, others of individuals who find their sexual partners outside the commune and who live together within the commune as brothers and sisters (Rogers, 1972). Still others have no definite rules regarding sex. Some members may practice sexual freedom while others do not.

The majority of communes are believers in sexual freedom, but the definition of "sexual freedom" varies from individual to individual, and from commune to commune. The most significant aspect of sexual freedom in the commune is that there can be sexual experimentation without guilt and without public knowledge, and without commitment to any one mode of behavior. Thus, a person can try a variety of sexual unions ranging from an extramarital affair to group orgies to homosexual relationships. An ever-present finding, however, is that those individuals who experiment with different sexual relationships and shifting of partnerships usually do so at a cost. Those involved experience loss, hurt, jealousy, self-pity, anger, and desire for retaliation again and again. The jealousy is not necessarily related simply to sexual behavior, but to a feeling of having lost a closeness with another. As one commune member said about sexual freedom:

There is a norm that you can sleep with anyone you want to here in the house. In fact, I can't think of anybody who at least intellectually speaking doesn't agree with that, but what makes me laugh so is that people think there won't be any problems about it. That you can take on a norm like that intellectually and say, "Oh fine, this is just what we happen to do." There is a problem every time. Someone feels hurt or someone feels threatened or someone feels less important. (Rogers, 1972, p. 138)

There are also curative elements in the commune that help to offset the hurt and jealousy of their sexual freedom. One member helps another in moments of pain, not by lecturing or consoling, but simply by understanding and being there, because that person too has experienced the same hurt. Frequently, these experiences of pain and loss of importance are also moments of potential growth, and the communard learns that permanent damage does not necessarily result from unpleasant pain (Rogers, 1972).

There is a slightly ambiguous attitude in many communes toward childbirth and childrearing. Natural childbirth without benefit of hospitals or doctors is usually emphasized. Many communes have a ritual celebration of childbirth in which the entire commune is present at the birth of a new child, chanting and offering encouragement to the woman in labor. By such a ritual, the commune signifies that the child being born is a member of the commune family, a child of all. Conversely, the father of the child is encouraged to assist in the delivery, symbolically establishing his paternal connection and emphasizing his unique relationship to the child

(Berger et al., 1971). Some commune members signify their rebellion against the state by failing to officially register the birth of the child (Rogers, 1972)—in such cases he therefore belongs to the communal family and not to the state (Berger et al., 1971).

The ambiguity in attitude toward the child continues as the infant matures. When he is nursing, he is considered the responsibility of his mother in all matters. As he gets older, however, the commune may adopt the attitude that the mother has no special rights over her child in discipline, guidance, or other traditional responsibilities of mothers.

Most communes that emphasize the idea of family are made up of nuclear units that strive for stability and fidelity, even if only for relatively short periods of time. The male adult in a nuclear family is regarded as a child's father, even though he may not be the biological father, and even though the child may have had many "fathers" due to his mother's shifting relationships (Berger et al., 1971).

The most pressing problem faced by the commune parent is that of discipline and guidance. The dominant ideology in the commune is that a child should be free to "do his own thing." Even communal parents find it necessary from time to time, however, to enforce necessary discipline and to encourage conformity to the norms of the community. They also naturally want to guide their children toward their own goals—which usually include the freedom to do one's own thing. Most commune parents, if faced with a real choice between training their children to be good commune members and allowing them to be completely free to express themselves in their own way would choose allowing freedom of expression, in spite of the problems it might pose for the community as a whole (Berger et al., 1971).

The most significant differences between today's communes and the group marriage-commune of the Oneidans or the kibbutzim of Israel are in the relative lack of structure and selectivity. The very aim of commune members—to withdraw from the "others' " world into a separate reality in which they can open themselves to living, loving, and learning in an accepting, open atmosphere—often becomes their nemesis. Without selectivity, a commune can be destroyed from within by psychotics, hedonists, drug addicts, and those who exploit their more accepting brothers (Keniston, 1970). Without definite structure with regard to daily routine and individual responsibility, the commune's unity is weakened by the irresponsible and the minimally committed. In their commitment to individual self-determination, many communes cease having any direction at all.

In addition, today's communes differ in their lack of definite sexual rules. Religious communes that have endured have either imposed celibacy on their members or, like the Oneidans, practiced a structured form of free love. Those communes that have been of short duration have no such imposed rules of sexual conduct. In most modern communes, sexual conduct is left to the self-determination of individual commune members, with the resulting jealousy that almost always accompanies shifting sexual relationships within a group. In their repudiation of the moralistic sexual taboos of society, commune members tend to underestimate the need of every person for a reasonably secure, continuing relationship with another person. The painful jealousy that occurs when such a relationship is threatened by another person may be a culturally learned response (O'Neill & O'Neill, 1972) or it may be a biologically based phenomenon, like territoriality (Rogers, 1972), but whatever its basis, it can undermine a group.

Because of the weaknesses inherent in their nonstructured, rel-

"This commune is just an excuse for sex, sex, and more sex. But I have to leave anyway."

atively nondiscriminating lifestyle, most communes are of the here-today, gone-tomorrow variety; only a few are more stable and permanent. Many of the more stable, responsible communes exist in urban settings and are peopled by mature married couples and their children who seek an involvement with others and a more viable lifestyle than that of the isolated nuclear family. For these communards, membership may mean greater opportunity for the women to pursue careers while being satisfied that their children have a family atmosphere. It also softens the impact of some of the harsher aspects of urban living by sharing them with others. Usually not a sexually open arrangement, the urban commune is an attempt to provide a more satisfying lifestyle within a traditional economic setting.

Both the failures and the successes of modern-day communes

provide information for the rest of society regarding interpersonal relations, sexual partnerships, and social organization. As a group of people who often absolutely reject all coercive forms of religious and governmental control, the experiences of commune members will undoubtedly affect the economic, ecological, educational, technological, and political framework of our country. In their endeavor to establish a new way of life, in which feeling experiences are vitally important and openly shared, today's communes actually constitute human living experiments (Rogers, 1972).

MONOGAMOUS ALTERNATIVES

Clustered families, communes, and group marriages are, as was said, forms of marriage designed to extend the boundaries of the family and to give individuals an extended sense of identity and community. There are other emerging forms of marriage that are designed to *preserve* monogamy—in an altered state—as a marriage form. These include monogamy with structured sexual permissiveness (such as found in swinging or mate-swapping) and trial marriage.

Swinging. Couples who are described as **swingers** are willing to swap partners with a couple with whom they are not acquainted and/or to attend a swinging party where both will have sexual intercourse with strangers (Denfeld & Gordon, 1973). They may also have sexual relations as a couple with at least one other individual (Bartell, 1972).

Couples who opt for mate-swapping or swinging as an alternative to sexual exclusiveness in monogamous marriage give as their reason the fact that sexual variety supports or improves their marriage. At the same time, they favor monogamy and want to maintain it (Denfeld & Gordon, 1973).

There are many societies, of course, in which wife-lending has been practiced. In some cultures a man's wife is expected to have sexual relations with various males, including her husband's friends, guests, and friends of the guests. In other societies there are times when the rules regulating sexual relations are relaxed, usually on special occasions, and there is extensive exchange of wives as well as other sexual freedom.

Modern **mate-swapping** differs from these primitive practices in that both mates must agree to exchange mates with another agreeable couple, so it is, therefore, not a matter of *wife*-swapping. As in the primitive societies, however, mate-swapping is conducted according to certain explicit and implicit rules and rituals, and it occurs only on specified occasions.

The number of swinging couples in the United States has been estimated at 8 million (Denfeld & Gordon, 1973), and 2.5 million couples are estimated to swing on a rather regular basis. Most studies of swingers have emphasized their overall normality, conventionality, and respectability. They tend to have some higher education (Denfeld & Gordon, 1973) and to come from all income groups, with the majority representing professional and white-collar occupational groups. The majority of female swingers have been found to be housewives who married young—between the ages of 17 and 21, or younger (Bartell, 1972). Swingers have been reported also to be predominately Protestant, with a slightly higher proportion of Catholics than would be found in the general population, but with the same proportion of Jews (Bartell, 1972). Most swingers do not regularly attend church, although their religious background does not differ from the nonswinger's (Rosen, 1971).

Although swinging is usually suggested by the husband, the wife has frequently planted the idea or promoted it before he suggested it (Bartell, 1972). After a couple have discussed the idea and agreed to try it, there are four methods by which they can become active in the swinging scene.

One method is to either place or answer an advertisement in one of the approximately 50 swingers' magazines that are nationally distributed (Denfeld & Gordon, 1973). These magazines range in price and quality from pulps such as the 25¢ *National Informer* to large slick-paged magazines such as *Swinger's Life* or *Kindred Spirits* that may sell for several dollars a copy. A secret language is used in the advertisements by which the swinger placing the advertisement describes sexual preferences. Terms such as TV (transvestite), S&M (sado-masochist), French Culture (cunnilingus and fellatio), Greek Culture (anal intercourse), Roman Culture (orgies), AC/DC (bisexual), gay (homosexual), and B&D (bondage and discipline) are sprinkled throughout the ads (Bartell, 1972), along with descriptions of the couple, who are usually "fun-loving," "attractive," "youthful," or "lusty." Physical dimensions of the female are frequently included—especially if she has large breasts.

A couple answering the ad does so by a letter in which they include descriptions of themselves that are designed to stimulate interest. Their ages are frequently minimized, and nude or seminude photographs of the female and sometimes also of the male are included. The answering couple may also say of themselves that they are "fun-loving," "friendly," "vivacious," and that they have unusual sexual talents.

104 Alternative Marriage

The letter, if it is sufficiently provocative, leads to a telephone call from the advertising couple. A meeting that is similar to a coffee or coke date is arranged between the couples, but no sexual involvement occurs at this meeting. If the foursome decide that they want to swap partners, they arrange to meet later at a motel or at one of their homes (Bartell, 1972).

Another way that neophyte swingers can meet other swingers is at a swingers' bar. These bars often are advertised openly in magazines or tabloids and may be reserved on certain nights of the week for swinging couples only. By their presence, a couple signifies that they are available for sexual swapping. Swingers' clubs are also frequently organized and may meet on certain nights of the week in a bar or hired hall. In metropolitan areas, these clubs may maintain a permanent meeting place with a bar and recreational facilities where members may drop by any night of the week. Swingers' clubs are frequently chartered, like a ski club would be chartered, and operate like any other social organization. Prospective members are screened, and couples who are known to be unmarried are usually denied membership. Some men pay prostitutes to pose as their wives in order to gain membership, but if the deception is discovered, there is usually an outraged denunciation from the rest of the members. The married swingers have a bond based on their double lives in society, and they feel that a prostitute or a single person has nothing to lose if his or her sexual involvements with many others should be discovered. They therefore resent their infiltration into the ranks of married couples who are flouting a societal norm (Bartell, 1972).

In general, no sexual activity takes place on the premises of swinging bars or clubs. Instead, members usually make plans to meet elsewhere, or they may leave the bar as a group and go to another meeting place for sexual intercourse.

Couples who want to swing also meet other couples through personal reference. If they answer an ad or go to a bar, for example, they will meet active swingers who are happy to give them the names of other couples to contact.

The least frequent method by which a couple is introduced to mate-swapping is through seduction by another couple. Such conversion to the swinging life occurs sometimes among couples who have known each other on a social basis for a long time, such as bridge partners or dance partners, and who mutually consent to exchange partners (Bartell, 1972).

For the "baby swingers" who have never been actively involved in the swinging life, there are many rules and regulations regarding swinging that they must learn. And the rules that are applicable and the behavior that is appropriate depend largely on the type of swinging they choose. Swinging may be either open or closed and may involve either two couples, large-scale parties, or a sexual triad (Bartell, 1972).

Closed swinging between two couples simply involves exchanging partners for an agreed-upon period of time and going to separate rooms for sexual activity that usually includes fellatio, cunnilingus, and coitus. Open swinging between two couples involves sexual activity in the same room, in the same bed, or as a sexual foursome. A swinging foursome frequently includes cunnilingus between the females, but rarely includes homosexual activity between the males. In some cases, the two males and one of the females will devote attention to the other female. It is unusual for the recipient of the attention of the other three to be one of the males in the foursome. Another group sexual practice is the formation of a "daisy chain" in which the members form a circle by alternating fellatio and cunnilingus (Bartell, 1972).

Large-scale parties, frequently held in private homes, are also organized along open or closed lines. If a party is of the closed type, the organizer of the party will enforce certain rules, such as allowing only one couple to occupy a bedroom at a time, setting definite time limits that a couple may spend in the bedroom, or forbidding nudity in the central gathering area (Bartell, 1972).

If the party is of the open type, it is considerably less structured. Nudity is permitted throughout the house, couples are free to participate in large-group sexual activity, voyeurism is openly allowed, and the party usually lasts until late the next morning, although many of the males become merely spectators to the females' continued sexual activity as the night wears on.

Of sexual triads involving swingers, the majority are composed of a married couple and a single female, with only a few involving a single male and a couple. When two males are involved, the married males report enjoying the voyeuristic qualities inherent in observing their partner have intercourse with another male. When a single female is involved, mutual cunnilingus between the females is almost always a part of the activity. Triadic relationships are usually of short duration, but some may last for a period of years. The quality that distinguishes such a triad from those that may exist in a group marriage is that the alternate female or male is not emotionally involved with the married couple. Instead, the involvement is strictly a sexual one.

A lack of emotional involvement is, in fact, the hallmark of the swinging scene. Swingers establish definite rules of behavior that are designed to prevent emotional involvement outside marriage.

Some swingers' clubs have rules forbidding telephone contact between members, for example, and social contact that does not involve sex is frequently taboo.

By avoiding emotional relationships, swingers circumvent the bugaboo of jealousy that so frequently causes pain and feelings of rejection in group marriages and communes. To the swinger, his marriage is of paramount importance, and he demonstrates his loyalty to his mate by willingly forgoing an attractive swinging opportunity if his mate is not interested or is opposed (Denfeld & Gordon, 1973). To the swinger, sex is sex and love is love, and the two meet only in the marriage bed. Extramarital sex becomes mutually acceptable to these married couples, therefore, because it is "just sex," and poses no threat of emotional abandonment or rejection.

The advantages of swinging seem to be the freedom to engage in a great deal of sexual activity with a large number of people without fear of damaging the marital relationship. Also, couples who swing usually find an increase in general sexual excitation as well as an increased sexual interest in one another that generalizes to a better total relationship. Women, especially, report a greater sense of personal freedom as a result of shedding their sexual inhibitions. There are also the positive benefits of engaging in a shared secret activity that must be kept hidden from their children, friends, employers, and neighbors. Becoming fellow conspirators in a socially disapproved activity that provides sexual excitement and satisfaction gives the swinging couple the feeling of being very avant garde. It also gives them a topic of discussion and an active social life. It may even broaden their horizons through travel, as many swingers go on weekend trips to other parts of the country in search of new contacts (Bartell, 1972; Rosen, 1971).

Swingers frequently report that they had unsatisfying sexual relations before they joined the swinging scene. They usually were bored with their marriages and few had any outside hobbies or interests beyond watching TV. It is interesting that almost every advertisement in a swingers' magazine lists hobbies such as movies, reading, dancing, sports, or travel, when in reality most swingers spend their leisure time either swinging or watching TV (Bartell, 1972). Swinging seems to have relieved their boredom, given them an outside interest, revived their flagging sexual interest in one another, and made them feel sexually desirable and socially popular.

The negative aspects of swinging are primarily in the self-doubts that such sexual opportunities may arouse—especially in the males. The fantasy of having an almost unlimited number of women who are sexually accessible and willing suddenly becomes a reality at a swingers' party where naked women are happily and freely engaging in all forms of sexual activity with any capable male. A man may discover to his dismay that he performs for a much greater duration in his fantasies than he does in reality. He may try to will himself to maintain an erection for a longer period, and his anxiety may cause him to lose his erection sooner than he would otherwise. While he is experiencing anxiety and erection failure, he sees the women around him continuing to satisfy each other over and over again throughout the night, and he may resentfully conclude that "women have the best time," and that swinging is unfair to men. Swinging women do, in fact, frequently find that they enjoy their relationships with other women more than they do those with the men.

Another negative aspect of swinging is the fact that a couple may encounter other couples who have sexual habits or attitudes that they find repulsive or objectionable. The fear of VD is also ever-present among swingers, as is the fear of discovery. Most swingers believe that their lives would be ruined if their mate-swapping was discovered. This is especially true of individuals who are professionals or state or federal government employees.

For couples who are insecure, swinging may create jealousy, in spite of the absence of emotional attachment to the sexual encounters. A man may resent his wife's responsiveness to other men, or she may feel that he enjoys other women more than he does her (Bartell, 1972).

More sensitive individuals object to the impersonal aspects of swinging and find that such mechanistic sex is unrewarding because of the absence of commitment and involvement. To individuals who find the greatest amount of sexual pleasure and satisfaction from an identification with their sexual partner and a deep emotional commitment to him, swinging is the antithesis of their sexual needs.

There is a growing trend among some couples who find that marriage cannot meet their needs for intimacy, stability, companionship, and personal growth to develop a circle of what are called intimate friends (IF). These are otherwise traditional friendships in which sexual intimacy is considered appropriate behavior. Essentially, these friendships develop as an outgrowth of practicing a sexually open marriage over an extended period of time. Participants believe IF to be more rewarding intellectually and emotionally than swinging.

In one study (Ramey, 1975) of upper-middle class couples involved in IF, important distinctions were made between IF and swinging. IF focuses on individual activity, rather than couple activity, with an emotional and personal involvement. There are no one-night stands as with swinging, and the relationships tend to be long-term. There is an intellectual sharing with the result that the interpersonal relationship is emphasized, not the sexual act. IF may even involve family interaction and business involvement with career ties. With swinging, there are no involvements other than the sex act, producing a strong emphasis on youth and physical attractiveness.

Some critics of group marriage claim that it is a rationalization for sexual variety and that its aim is not truly for community or extended identity. If this is true, then mate-swapping, through swinging or intimate friendships, may represent a more honest and viable attempt to deal with sexual monotony than group marriage does. A couple may achieve sexual variety—thus an increase in sexual interest and vigor—with a minimum of chances for jealousy, while keeping the nuclear family intact (Crosby, 1973). Theoretically, at least, the approach seems plausible.

Trial marriage. Another proposed method of maintaining monogamy while altering our traditional form of marriage is **trial marriage**. Trial marriages attempt to preserve monogamous unions by assuring a couple that they are psychologically and sexually compatible before they commit themselves to a permanent relationship. As an alternative to our present one-step form of marriage, a two-step form is more likely to gain widespread acceptance than are other alternative forms of marriage (Crosby, 1973). Young people, especially, are experimenting with the violation of social mores and openly living together for a time without a marriage ceremony. Many use this living-together period as a trial time of adjustment to the idiosyncrasies of the other, and if they find that their affection remains constant in spite of the irritations of daily living, they may formalize their union by legal marriage. They may, of course, also marry because they feel guilty about living together, or because their parents are outraged, or because they are expecting a child and want to legalize its birth.

Trial marriage has been practiced among some primitive people, such as the Peruvian Indians of Vicos in the Andes and the people of the Trobriand Islands, for centuries. The Trobrianders had "bachelors' houses" where pubescent couples were sent for sexual experimentation. In time, they formed exclusive sexual relationships and married, but they were not permitted to eat together or to share any other interest except sex before marriage (Malinowski,

Monogamous Alternatives **109**

1929). The Peruvians, on the other hand, shared their lives together in a true trial marriage that had as its purpose the testing of the woman's ability to work and her general compatibility. Most of their trial marriages lasted less than 15 months, and the majority ended in a formal marriage ceremony. For these people, trial marriage helped to ease the transition from adolescence to adulthood by giving to a young couple the social and sexual advantages of marriage without requiring them to assume the full responsibility of marriage (MacLean, 1941; Price, 1965).

In Staphorst, Holland, there is an old Teutonic custom that is still practiced today called **trial nights**. This custom requires that a man spend three nights a week with his intended bride until she becomes pregnant, but if she fails to conceive, she is regarded with suspicion and contempt by the community, and no marriage occurs (Gibney, 1948).

In 1927, Judge Ben B. Lindsey proposed trial marriage as an American concept, terming his proposal "Companionate Marriage." Bertrand Russell extended the concept of Companionate Marriage by favoring trial marriage for university students on the premise that it was ridiculous for a couple to marry for the purpose of raising a family when they had not first had sexual experience (Russell, 1929).

Society was not ready for either Lindsey's or Russell's theories, and both men were virtually ostracized. The concept of trial marriage remained relatively dormant until Margaret Mead revived it in 1966. Building on Lindsey's Companionate Marriage, Mead proposed a two-step marriage. The first step would be an **individual marriage**, with a simple ceremony, limited economic responsibilities, and an avoidance of conception. Divorce from an individual marriage would be easy to obtain. If a couple found that their relationship grew in mutual satisfaction and stability, they could then enter into a **parental marriage** by which they signified their readiness to take on the lifetime obligations of parenthood. A parental marriage would be significantly more difficult to enter than an individual marriage, and would also be considerably more difficult to end by divorce. Couples entering a parental marriage would assume a mutual continuing responsibility for their future children. The rationale for such a proposal was that many young people are driven into precipitous and unwise marriages by their sex drives. Many such marriages end in unhappiness and divorce, with children being the innocent victims. By insuring that unstable marriages end before children are brought into the world, the plan endeavors to assure that every child conceived is a wanted child and that every marriage that brings a child into the world is a stable marriage whose members are capable of fulfilling their lifelong obligations as parents.

Trial marriage is definitely not intended as an easy way to sexual access nor as an indiscriminate method for avoiding personal responsibility. Instead, it would result in a more responsible means for establishing permanent unions and families than now exists in our one-step marriages. It would demand more responsibility toward oneself, one's mate, one's children, and society than is now demanded of individuals contemplating marriage (Crosby, 1973).

As an alternative form of marriage, it will probably gain acceptance slowly, if at all, beginning with the college population and spreading to other segments of the population. Some believe that the trend will continue whether or not there is approval from the legal-ecclesiastical establishment, and that marriage in two steps will in time become a viable alternative to our traditional one-step marriage. Such a marital evolution may take five or six generations to provide an alternative form of marriage for 10 to 30 percent of our total population, but it seems inevitable that two-step marriage will appeal to more people than the other alternatives (Crosby, 1973).

Other plans have been proposed by those who regard sex as a questionable motivation for marriage. One proposal (Scriven, 1968) favors a three-step plan of **preliminary, personal**, and **parental marriage**. The first step would be simply legalized cohabitation, but would be a prerequisite for the other two steps and would require a year's trial relationship before it could be converted into a personal marriage.

Others have proposed contractual periods of marriage. Vance Packard (1968) has recommended a two-year confirmation period during which couples would work to stabilize their relationship. At the end of two years, the marriage would either become final and permanent or be dissolved. The rationale behind this plan is that the expectation of permanence would contribute to the success of the marriage as it would motivate the couple to adapt to one another and to marriage. Others have suggested apprentice periods of from one to five years' duration, with a renewable contract. Under this plan, partners would have a chance to find out if their fantasies matched the reality of living together (Cadwallader, 1966; Satir, 1967).

A premarriage contract, as opposed to contractual periods of marriage, may also be a solution to the prevention of specific problems that may arise within a marriage. Many people feel that marriage,

Monogamous Alternatives **111**

as any other voluntary human relationship, could benefit from a written contract that would force couples to think problems out in advance. Such contracts usually deal with financial matters, division of household tasks, children, leisure time, relationship with inlaws, place of residence, and so on (Wells, 1976). The possibilities of divorce, alimony, child custody, and support may also be covered but require more careful wording as the law does not allow agreements that encourage divorce or list property rights in the event of divorce. Premarriage contracts may become more important with the egalitarian attitudes spawned by the women's rights movement and as more couples choose to live together and establish a lifestyle that is outside the law's limited conception of a family (Wells, 1976).

Living together. Another alternative to traditional marriage is simply to remain unmarried. More and more couples today are choosing to live together without necessarily planning to have a wedding ceremony ever, even though in some states it is still against the law to have sexual relations without being married; the penalties for doing so include fines and/or imprisonment (Massey & Warner, 1975). A generation ago such a living arrangement was called "living in sin" or "shacking up." Today it meets with disapproval from fewer people and is almost disregarded in some areas of the country. For example, in 1977 almost two million unmarried adults were living together, representing an 83 percent increase from 1970 (U.S. Bureau of the Census, 1978). In contrast to marriage, in which a great deal of ritual is involved, living together often comes about spontaneously and nearly always informally. But some couples who choose to live together do so out of a deep conviction that there is something better than marriage. Some feel that living together is more adventuresome and that it is economically, emotionally, and sexually advantageous (Liddick, 1973). Most couples are well aware that it is much easier to get out of an informal living arrangement than it is a legally binding marriage, and it is probably not coincidental that most of these arrangements endure less than six months.

Unmarried couples who live together may share the philosophy that living in the present is important, that nothing is permanent, and that marriage vows of permanent love are unrealistic. They may believe also that marriage is an unnecessary, hypocritical institution because it is easy and popular to obtain a divorce. Such couples often emphasize the rights of the individual and freedom of self-determination (Liddick, 1973).

These relationships, as long as they endure, do appear to offer the kind of security that is engendered by each person's knowledge that the other is there because he or she *wants* to be and not because he or she *has* to be. They may then work harder at pleasing one another and at remaining faithful to the relationship. One of the advantages of living together without marriage would be in the emotional security of knowing that one's partner was there by choice and not because of duty. Another advantage is the opportunity for testing a relationship with a particular person before committing oneself to a permanent arrangement. One also may test the institution of marriage itself. Still another advantage is that it allows the couple more flexibility in defining their own unique relationship, since there are fewer customs and rituals associated with living together than with engagement or marriage (Schulz & Rodgers, 1975).

There are, of course, many reasons why couples choose to live together. Some may be surprised to find that sex is not always a factor, and it may not be part of the relationship at all. For example, a couple may want to live together for economic or emotional reasons.

The disadvantages of living together include its lack of acceptance by many people, so that a couple may have to deal with their disappointed and disapproving families. In addition, the woman has no legal protection and no community property rights. Children of such a union are illegitimate, and in most states are without inheritance rights.

There are precautions that people may be wise to take when living together unmarried. Massey and Warner (1975) advise couples to keep their financial affairs separate, for example, separate checking and charge accounts, separate savings accounts, etc. They should save all receipts for major purchases. If they decide to buy or rent a house together, take out insurance policies, etc., they should make explicit, detailed provisions for their disposal in the event of their separation.

With a change in our social structure brought on by greater affluence, the women's liberation movement, greater sexual permissiveness, and the changed meaning of marital vows, some see a new stage of personal development emerging. The period extends from the end of adolescence to sometime in the late 20s or early 30s, during which time men and women experiment with different lifestyles, search for careers they wish to pursue, and test educational goals. By keeping options open and by remaining flexible and prepared to change, people in this stage of development are able to minimize their responsibilities, maximize their personal freedom, and increase their self-knowledge, which better prepares them for adulthood and permanent commitments.

CONCLUSION

When one considers the hypocrisy, dishonesty, unhappiness, and restrictions on personal fulfillment that exist in all too many monogamous, sexually exclusive marriages today, it becomes glaringly apparent that marriage as it exists cannot continue indefinitely. But how is it to be changed? Will marriages in the future be unions whose shared interests consist almost solely of sexual intercourse with strangers? Or will future marriages be group marriages, with the opportunity for sexual variety and expanded intimacy in a framework that imposes great demands on a person to adapt to living intimately with several people without jealousy and discord? Will we try to maintain permanent monogamous marriages by requiring that couples live together for a prescribed period of time before they are allowed to establish a permanent union for the purpose of nurturing children? Or will we dispense with legal marriage contracts altogether? Can the family survive as a nuclear unit in a highly mechanized society, or should the function of the family be taken over by a collective aggregate? And, most important, are there any other alternatives? Can two people create for themselves a marriage form that allows them to satisfy their individual needs, while at the same time growing and expanding in awareness and fulfillment? (See the Appendix for examples of two contrasting sets of marriage vows.)

The answers to these questions remain to be seen, but one thing is clear: Society *must* face the questions and deal with them in an honest manner. Marriage is not dead or dying. Instead, it is metamorphosing into a new, more adaptive structure that will meet the needs of today. And whatever form it takes, it must be one that is meaningful and satisfying to the individuals who live it. No matter which path our future marriage forms take, some form of marriage and family will undoubtedly survive. Despite the present or future problems, shortcomings, and failures of the institutions of marriage and the family, no other forms of human interaction have served civilization so well as have these institutions, and it is highly doubtful that any ever will.

It is possible that the future will see a variety of marriage forms from which individuals can choose according to their own personal needs and preferences. Carl Rogers has half-seriously suggested a law making legal any partnership pattern between consenting adults, provided that there is no harm done to any others. Such a law, suggests Rogers, would be a legal illustration of the social philosophy of "We will not interfere."

Perhaps the concept of a society which allowed its individual members the freedom to decide for themselves how to find personal fulfillment in a loving, close relationship, while at the same time fulfilling their responsibilities to their offspring and to society, is the most revolutionary of all.

CHAPTER 5

THE CREATIVE MARRIAGE

*The art of living does not consist in preserving and clinging
to a particular mood of happiness, but in allowing happiness
to change its form without being disappointed by the change;
for happiness, like a child, must be allowed to
grow up.*   CHARLES LANGBRIDGE MORGAN

A marriage is like a tapestry, woven of the varicolored fibers of married life, some beautiful, some drab, some ugly. In a creative marriage, the form of marital experiences combines with the color of emotional responses, all fitting together in a meaningful, purposeful, satisfying design. As in viewing a tapestry, it is usually necessary to step back and get some perspective on a marriage in order to see it in its entirety and to judge its overall character. Viewed closely, one may see only the individual parts without seeing the overall design. Thus, small segments of a marital tapestry may appear to be creative, but when the marriage is viewed in its entirety, it may be revealed as a loosely woven fabric, full of holes and broken fibers, in colors that are random splotches rather than meaningful designs. A truly creative marital tapestry, on the other hand, is revealed as a grand design in which the neutral parts and the ugly parts add depth and contrast to the exciting, vibrant parts, expressing the philosophy and the soul of the marriage.

TRADITION AND CREATIVITY

In most marriages, the marital design is prescribed and planned by unseen authorities, and the couple attempt to produce a fabric that meets the approval of those authorities, rather than attempting to produce a creative work in which the goal is richness of emotional color and originality of marital design.

More and more couples want to break away from established, preplanned marital designs and create a uniquely personal life together, without attempting to copy other established marital forms. But like all behavior, marital patterns are learned through observation of models, and the goal of personal marital expression more often than not runs head-on into the need to copy some models, or at least into the need to have several models from which to draw in formulating a unique pattern of behavior for oneself.

Couples who seek to escape the traditional, conformist type of marriage may instead fall into the trap of becoming slaves to the nonconformist types, and find no more feeling of personal expression in them than they would find in the traditional type. We have been a society whose marital form expressed the credo, "If it feels good, it's probably a sin, so don't do it." Now some in our society seem to be experimenting with marital forms that express the "If it feels good, do it" philosophy without concern for the possible harm that may befall themselves or others. Neither the moralistic nor the hedonistic extreme allows for both personal fulfillment and growth as well as marital fulfillment and growth. In the overly moralistic approach, there is too little personal freedom; and in the overly hedonistic approach, there is too little marital commitment.

Married couples who want to make their unions richly satisfying, while pursuing individual interests and needs, are therefore faced with the dilemma of separating individuation from selfishness, of discriminating between social mores that are beneficial to individuals and to society, and social mores that are artificial and based on prejudice, guilt, and ignorance. In addition, they must be able to count the cost of nonconformity and decide when an action is nonconforming in a constructive manner, and when it is nonconforming in an infantile, rebellious manner. When is a marriage an expression of the philosophies, needs, and personal feelings of the people in it, and when is it an expression of contempt for society? When is a marriage a creative expression rather than merely a different marital form?

CREATIVE EXPRESSION—IN ART AND MARRIAGE

Creative expression is not simply *different,* whether it be in the arts or in marriage. Nor is creativity without discipline. In the art world, in fact, every new style of painting is rooted in some influence that imposes a particular kind of discipline on the artist. Renaissance artists, for example, assimilated the best of the Greeks and the Romans; the Impressionists recaptured the mood of the Magdalenian cave paintings; and the Fauvists were influenced by Egyptian, Greek, and Oriental artists. Cubism revolutionized artistic expression in its geometric concentration of form and color, while Abstractionism depended on objective composition, with each abstract artist interpreting reality in a different way, but always within a specific philosophical framework.

A parallel can be drawn between abstract painting and the emerging forms of marriage that rebel against the traditional marital form. When the abstractionist movement began, the public hooted, and common comments at art gallery showings of abstract collections were, "I could do *that!*" or "That looks like a child's finger-painting." Would-be artists soon learned, however, that there was more to producing creative abstract designs than simply throwing blobs of paint at canvases or smearing paint on canvases with their feet.

The difference between the poor imitations and the creative works of art was that the abstract artist painted with a statement in mind and with a firm grasp of artistic principles, while his imitators were merely concerned with superficial appearance and had

nothing they wished to communicate. The abstract artist applied paint in a balanced, meaningful design, while his imitators simply applied paint in a shallow, haphazard manner. When artist Jackson Pollock laid a canvas on the floor and walked around it pouring a continuous line of paint, the result was a harmonious pattern. But when his imitators poured, dripped, dribbled, or splashed paint on canvases, the results expressed neither experience nor feelings, and had no creative energy behind them. Abstract paintings that are creative works of art offer new perspective and fresh pleasure each time they are viewed. Imitations of creative abstract art are simply splotches of color that have no unifying balance or harmony. Rather than continuing to give the viewer pleasure, they quickly become boring and cause the viewer to feel irritable and uneasy. Both are *different* from classical paintings, but only one is *creative* and will have a continuing benefit for the populace.

Creative Expression—In Art and Marriage **119**

The same is true of marriages that attempt to break from the traditional yoked marital form without doing so as an expression of a particular philosophy. It is in the attempt to find new marital styles that many people become the counterparts of the dilettantes, the hangers-on who copy the style of the creative artist, without having the discipline or the understanding to ever produce creative ideas or works themselves. To the dilettante, that which is in vogue at the moment is the thing to copy. Thus, the movement away from the traditional, two-person, sexually exclusive, restrictive marital form has found many followers among those who simply see and copy the break with traditional lifestyles, rather than seeing and understanding the philosophies behind the changes.

True creativity and originality in marriage cannot be achieved without order, self-discipline and a philosophical framework to give meaning to the differentness. To imitate the appearance of creative marriages, without having the spirit and the discipline required for producing a creative marriage, will result in a meaningless, uninspired, chaotic marital form without soul or character. When married partners attempt to change the established form of marriage by each simply "doing his own thing," without regard to any rules of behavior or any inner self-discipline, they will create an infantile, superficial, chaotic design without structure or plan to give it meaning and character.

DEFINING CREATIVE MARRIAGE

Creative marriage, in other words, does not mean *undisciplined* marriage. It does not mean riding roughshod over the feelings, needs, and wishes of one's marital partner simply because he or she interferes with one's own momentary needs, wishes, and desires. It does not mean completely ignoring the mores of the society in which one lives and treating the other members of that society with contemptuous disregard. Nor does it mean drifting into marriages in the wistful hope that they will develop into meaningful relationships, without first giving close attention to the chances of marital success and without careful, cautious exploration of the relationship.

To have a creative marriage does not mean simply being a part of a group marriage, or of a communal family, or being a swinger, or having open extramarital sexual affairs. A creative marriage may embrace these changes from the traditional marital style, but a couple can do any or all of these things and still have a marriage that is distorted and meaningless because of a lack of self-discipline and a lack of coherence in the overall marital design. Or, a couple can do none of these things and still have a truly creative marriage.

For a creative marriage, a couple first must have maturity and self-discipline that will allow them to make sacrifices for the other person without developing a martyr complex, while at the same time expecting the other to make reasonable sacrifices also. They need the maturity and self-discipline to recognize that there are certain rules of society that must be followed for the orderly existence of a population that breathes down each other's necks.

There also must be discipline within each individual and within the marriage that resists the temptation to latch onto a movement, such as sexual freedom outside marriage, without understanding the spirit and the philosophy behind the movement. To view the concept of sexual freedom outside of marriage as simply sexual license, rather than as the need of a person to have an individual life that is not totally shared with his marital partner, *but which enhances the marital experience,* is to degrade the idea of individual freedom. It reduces it to the right to hurt and offend one's marital partner. A couple who enter marriage with the spoken or unspoken challenge, "I'll have sex with anybody I want to, anytime I want to, and you'd better understand that from the beginning," are not entering a liberated marriage or a creative marriage. Instead, they are entering an empty marriage, in which one's own immediate gratification is more important than the other's feelings or the marriage itself. There is a vast difference between the right to individual freedom and the right to ignore the feelings and needs of others. The knowledge of that difference spells the difference between a creative marriage and a marriage that simply goes against the traditions of society.

A lack of unifying philosophy, a lack of discipline, a lack of concern for the mores of society, do not result in creativity. No musician can create inspired music without knowledge of and adherence to fundamental musical principles, no artist can create inspired and enduring art without knowledge and application of artistic principles, and no marriage can be creative and meaningful to the partners in it unless the marriage is rooted in principles of fair play and integrity whereby the rights and feelings of each are equally important.

Without respect for the other, without concern for the other, and without honesty in dealing with the other, no marriage, whether a two-person traditional-style marriage or a six-person group marriage, can call itself a creative marriage. It is not the *form* of marriage that makes it creative, it is the skill of the marital partners in combining innovativeness with self-discipline, of blending individual freedom with social conscience, and their ability to insist on certain individual freedoms while being willing to sacrifice other individual desires in favor of the marriage.

Anyone can go against tradition, society, religion, and parental expectations in marital style, and many do. To do so takes no intelligence, courage, or skill. What does take intelligence, courage, and skill is the ability to creatively blend the needs of society with individual needs, to retain one's own sense of personal freedom while retaining one's own sense of personal integrity, and above all, to do so while maintaining a loving, intimate relationship with another person.

Just as an artist who breaks with convention first must have perfected his or her skills in traditional artistic expression, so must a person who hopes to have creative relationships first be able to find enjoyment in more restrictive relationships. Creativity is a fresh approach to an established order, and one who cannot cope with the established order will not be able to conceive of innovations and changes that are not chaotic. Before a couple can embark on creative innovations to traditional marriage forms, they first must have the ability to live within a traditional framework. If a lack of sexual freedom outside marriage will cause the marriage to fail, for example, then the marriage is in trouble anyway. If a two-person marriage cannot survive, adding two or four other marital partners will not solve the basic problem. The happiness and satisfaction that a person derives from a marriage is due largely to his own inner resources, and not to the particular form of marriage he has. Creative innovations should *add to* the marital satisfaction a couple find in each other, rather than being substitutes for deficiencies in the relationship.

Creativity is basically experimentation within an established order, with the flexibility to abandon an experiment that fails to provide greater rewards than were found before. Thus, a couple who are satisfied with their relationship together might experiment with adding new elements to that relationship to keep it workable and growing, but removing them should they detract from the relationship. Essentially, each partner accepts the other as an individual with needs and wishes separate from one's own, but within the partnership each attempts to fulfill one's own as well as the other's needs, without resorting to immature modes of interaction. It is within this context that one may provide for the other what he or she lacks.

It involves validation of the other by allowing differences in the other without attempting to disconfirm them. Invalidation or disconfirmation of the other may be attempted by denying what the

other person says is true of him or herself—"You don't *really* feel that way"—or by denying the other's accomplishments.

Sometimes creativity in a marriage simply means viewing the relationship in a different way and defining those aspects of the relationship that are most satisfying and those that are least satisfying. Once the least satisfying elements are identified, the couple may work to eliminate them. Is the materialistic, possession-acquiring aspect of marriage stifling the relationship? Then dispense with the struggle to keep up with the Joneses and adopt a simpler, less complicated life that emphasizes personal relationships as a criterion of success rather than the value of house and car and other possessions.

Is there a competitive spirit between the couple that causes both to struggle for a position of power? Introducing new sexual partners or moving to a commune will not eliminate the power struggle, and would not be a creative move. To get to the roots of each partner's need for power and to find ways that each can be the controlling partner in certain agreed-upon areas would be a more creative answer, and would allow the couple to have more trust in each other. In this way, their relationship could begin to grow together, rather than having each partner in competition with the other.

PSEUDOCREATIVE MARRIAGES

While it is possible to give broad suggestions for creativity in marriage, it is impossible to give a blueprint for a creative marriage. To attempt to do so would be to negate the concept of creativity itself. It is possible to demonstrate the imitations of creativity, however, and the imitations will be far more frequently found than the truly creative marriage will be. The following are some typical pseudocreative types of marriage.

The big dude and subdued chick marriage

"Keep 'em barefoot, busy, and obedient"

Mike and Jan are college drop-outs who decided that the irrelevance of college was too much of a drag to waste their time on. They lived together for several months before marrying, and they liked to tell their friends that they married simply to get their parents off their backs. For the first year of their marriage, they worked when they had to, and quit work as soon as they had enough money to pay their rent and buy groceries for a while. They never gave their employers notice, and when they moved, they simply slipped out after owing rent for a few weeks. They usually had two or three friends living with them, and they spent most of their time smoking grass and listening to music. The women did all the cooking, mostly beans and rice, and the men became quite angry if the meals were not ready on time. In time, both Jan and Mike found their marriage empty and meaningless, and they both were unhappy and irritable. Jan nagged at Mike, and Mike was rude and disrespectful toward Jan in front of the other people in the house.

The change in their marriage came one evening when Mike came home and announced to the entire household that they were all invited to an orgy in a neighboring town. The other couples responded enthusiastically. Only Jan demurred. She was shocked and hurt that Mike would consider their joining in such a party, and she was angry that he had not discussed it with her before announcing it. She told him in no uncertain terms that she would not accompany him to an orgy and that she considered his wish to go to one an expression of contempt toward her.

Mike's answer was succinct, "I am going to the party and I am going to ball other chicks. You can come or not, I don't care. But if you stay with me, you are going to have to expect me to have sex with other chicks from now on. I'm bored with sex with you, and I need a change. Take it or leave it." Jan spent the evening of the party in tears. She packed and unpacked her bags in an agony of indecision. Finally, the next afternoon when the rest of the household returned home, she greeted her husband with an apology and a promise to become more accepting of his needs. She blamed herself and said that she believed she had learned a valuable lesson. Mike accepted her apology and treated her with tenderness and consideration for the first time in months. The rest of the household warmly congratulated Mike on his firm stand and Jan on seeing the light.

This marriage is about as creative as a dime-store coloring book. Rather than being creative, it is exploitative. Rather than basing its marital interaction on mutual respect and consideration, it is based on the needs and desires of one, without any consideration of the needs and desires of the other. Rather than showing love for his wife, Mike shows selfishness; rather than showing love for her husband, Jan shows a masochistic need for subservience. Their marriage may appear "creative" to some onlookers, simply because it is contrary to traditional marital forms, but in truth it is simply a disguised paternalistic relationship in which the man is always right, and the woman is always wrong—and is praised for admitting it.

The absence makes the heart grow fonder marriage

"Who needs you, anyway?"

Tom and Julia have been married 13 years, and have two children, both of whom are in an excellent boarding school in the East. Tom maintains an apartment in Houston, while Julia lives in San Francisco. They have had this arrangement for a number of years, ever since Tom's company transferred him to Houston and Julia found it intolerable to leave her beloved San Francisco. At first, the children were small and needed her attention, but since they became old enough to send to boarding school, Julia has enjoyed an active social life in San Francisco, and she can imagine no other kind of life for herself.

Tom was lonely in Houston at first, but he soon regained his old expertise as a roving bachelor, and his bathroom sports the toothbrushes of several female friends. When Julia visits him, she teases him about the toothbrushes, and Tom sometimes reminds her, on his infrequent trips to San Francisco, that the brand of shaving cream in her bathroom is not his. They see each other about once every three months, and thoroughly enjoy each other when they are together. Julia has begun to expand her hobby of interior decorating, and is making a creditable income, so there is no strain involved in maintaining two residences. Tom and Julia tell their friends that their marriage is the only civilized form of marriage, and their friends sometimes envy their pioneering spirit. The friends sometimes ask the couple, individually, if they do not become lonely apart from each other, and both Julia and Tom are quick to answer that they actually rarely think of one another except when they are together.

This is an example of a pseudocreative marriage that appears on the surface to be the answer to all the ills of marriage. No jealousy, no demands, no boredom, no nagging, no sexual monotony, no silly togetherness. But no marriage, either. The fact that a couple has worked out a method whereby they enjoy each other's presence on an occasional basis does not mean that they have a creative marriage. It simply means that they have a system that works for them, without imposing the demands of a marriage. In effect, they are enjoying each other's absence.

The look how liberated we are marriage

"If you don't look, it's no fun"

Sam and Maurine are a middle-aged couple whose children are grown and married. They had quite a struggle while the children were young, and were able to afford a home in an affluent neighborhood only after the children were gone. Maurine felt useless for a while after the children left, and Sam was too busy with his business to pay much attention to her. Maurine joined a leaderless encounter group that aimed at helping the members of the group "find themselves," and after a while, she convinced Sam that he should join the group also. The group was composed of other middle-aged couples, and as their intimacy grew, so did their lack of inhibitions. Eventually, one of the members suggested a mate-swapping party, and Sam and Maurine enthusiastically agreed. Both were excited by the novelty of sex with someone else, but with knowledge and sanction of their spouse, and the group repeated their swapping on a regular basis.

Sam and Maurine enjoyed sex together more than ever for a while, and then they began to become bored with each other again. Sam suggested one day that they build a pool in the back yard, where they could hold nude parties, and Maurine became quite excited about the project, and personally designed the pool so that there would be interesting curves around which the couples could arrange themselves for aquatic games. Once the pool was built, the swapping parties were held regularly at Sam and Maurine's house, and they always started with the members swimming in the nude.

The houses on both sides of Sam and Maurine's are two-storied, with windows that look down into the fenced yard around the pool. All of the members of the mate-swapping group pretend not to notice the curtains moving on the upstairs windows when they are around the pool, but they whisper and giggle about it nonetheless. Sam and Maurine never mention their guests or their group to their neighbors, and their neighbors are too sophisticated to mention it to them. Sam tells Maurine that it would be a different story if any of their neighbors had children who would be offended by their nude bodies, and Maurine agrees. Each finds that their enjoyment of the swapping group is lessened if their party has to be held indoors because of inclement weather, but neither would admit that their enjoyment is enhanced by the knowledge that their neighbors are watching them. Sam and Maurine talk to each other of little else than the swapping group, and their recreational activity consists almost solely of the swinging parties.

Mate-swapping and exhibitionism, like the other examples of pseudocreative marriages, have in themselves little to do with creativity, or with marriage. They may be antidotes to boredom and indifference, but unless they enhance the marital bond, they offer no creative challenges. Furthermore, once the mate-swapping and

"I see a husband, two kids, a home in suburbia, two cars, a color TV set, credit cards . . . ."

exhibitionism become boring too, where are Sam and Maurine to go?

The liberated woman marriage

"Now I've got you in your own net"

Elliott and Joyce have a marriage that all who meet them regard as innovative, creative, and interesting. Elliott stays home and keeps house while Joyce works in an office. Elliott takes care of the two children, and Joyce pays the rent. Like the housewives around him, Elliott spends his days sweeping, mopping, cleaning toilets, and spreading peanut butter on bread. In the evenings, he has a hot dinner prepared when Joyce returns home from work, and Joyce reads the evening paper while Elliott does the dishes and gets the children to bed. Joyce tells her co-workers that Elliott is a much better housewife than she ever was, and Elliott tells the neighbors that Joyce is a more capable bread-winner than he ever was. The children always look to Elliott for help and for answers to questions, and they are sometimes shy and reserved with Joyce, who tends to be a very strict disciplinarian. At vacation time, Joyce decides when they will go, since it is she who must arrange her work schedule, and she also decides where they will go, since it is her money that pays for the vacation. Elliott accepts her decisions and makes the necessary preparations for their trips. He also accepts her decisions in matters pertaining to major purchases, since she earns the money to make the purchases. Both Joyce and Elliott agree, however, that it is unnecessary to bother Joyce with questions of minor purchases, and Elliott makes the necessary purchases of small items when the need arises.

Anyone who believes that this is a creative marriage flunks the "What's in a Sex Role?" quiz. Simply reversing sex roles does not make for a creative marriage. It matters little which partner is the dominant, authoritarian one, and which is the submissive, passive one; the point is that if either is unequal in the relationship, there is no chance for creativity.

The I'm your everything marriage

"You'll never guess what I've been up to"

Hazel and Royce are an attractive couple with two children. Hazel does a lot of community volunteer work, and Royce has an accounting firm.

Publicly, they present a united front as a loving couple, and they lead an active social life. Privately, each has sexual affairs, but each is convinced that the other is sexually faithful. Hazel tells her friends that Royce needs nobody else but her, and Royce tells his lovers (who are often Hazel's friends) that Hazel needs nobody else but him.

Both Hazel and Royce enjoy a feeling of power from the fact that they are leading a double life, and each is supremely confident that the other will never discover the truth. The only problems they have in their marriage stem from Royce's gambling tendencies, which frequently plunge them into financial crises, and from their children's problems in school and with their peers. They are especially concerned because their eight-year-old son is beginning to lie a great deal, and their six-year-old daughter frequently steals toys from neighborhood children and hides them under her bed. As Hazel and Royce tell each other, the children have certainly been given the proper examples, and they cannot imagine what has influenced the children to be untrustworthy. Except for the financial problems and the concern over their children, Hazel and Royce both say that they are perfectly happy, and that they would never divorce, and their friends and lovers consider their marriage a fine example of a creative marriage.

It is, of course, about as creative as warmed-over oatmeal, but it is a rewarding marriage, in which each partner's satisfaction is derived from a feeling of power over the other. Rather than deserving credit for creativity, they deserve Oscars for their acting ability (and for the entertainment they provide their friends). Their children will undoubtedly become more skilled in the art of duplicity as they mature, and they will probably continue to be models of togetherness to the public, while steadily losing the intimacy within their marriage.

The now marriage

"Will the real phony please stand up?"

Dede and Don are both college professors and have been married five years. In the beginning, they were engrossed in each other, but as their careers became more demanding, they have had less time for each other and their marriage has lacked its original excitement. Fellow faculty members asked them to join in a commune in which expenses and responsibilities would be shared, but there would not be sexual freedom between the members. Don was very enthusiastic about the idea, and Dede was less so, but she privately decided that the commune might hold their marriage together, and agreed to move into a house with three other couples.

Before joining the commune, Don and Dede had a small apartment with a weekly cleaning service. Their custom had been to leave for the university early and to eat breakfast in a little diner near the campus. They enjoyed the banter with the waitresses and the other diners. At the end of the day, they rode home together, and Dede would prepare a simple meal. If there was no work they needed to do in the evening, they might go to a neighborhood movie. On weekends, Dede liked to cook small gourmet dinners for a few friends, or she and Don might simply listen to records together.

In the commune, life is decidedly different. All the members eat breakfast together, and to leave before breakfast would be considered anti-social. In the evenings, there is much camaraderie and group discussion, with all the members cooperating in getting dinner and cleaning up afterwards. Although there are plenty of hands, Dede has the feeling that she is doing much more work in the communal kitchen than she ever did in her own, and she misses the quietness of her old apartment. She no longer cooks the gourmet dinners, because all meals are a communal affair, and because she feels no desire to prepare a special meal for all the people she lives with.

Although the commune members are able to spend their free time as they wish, Dede does not retire to their room in the evening as she would like, because she senses that the rest of the household enjoys the group's being together and she feels that she would offend them if she preferred to be alone. Don seems to have blossomed since moving into the commune, and he and the other members seem to have a special feeling for each other that Dede simply does not have. She misses her privacy and more and more looks forward to being at the university, and dreads coming home to the commune.

Dede loves her husband and is determined to pretend to be happy in the commune, but she feels depressed and confused. Her work is no longer as exciting to her, and she finds it difficult to concentrate when writing or preparing lectures. Her students all know that she is a member of a commune, and they approach her with eager questions about the way her commune operates. Dede answers their questions, but feels artificial and trapped.

Again, this is a marriage that appears to be creative, because it is found in a form that departs from the traditional form of marriage. However, a creative marriage is one in which the partners can be themselves without having to pretend that they are otherwise. Communal living is not for everybody, and all who live in communes are not satisfied with the arrangement. To conform to nonconformity is as restricting as conforming to traditional forms, and no more creative.

The sexually un-hungup marriage

"Sex is everything, isn't it?"

Rita is a receptionist in a stockbroker's office, and Charlie is a city policeman. They each consider their marital style creative and totally superior to the marriages of their friends. They have been married three years, and they are both bright, attractive people who are seldom still. Charlie has a very strong sex drive, while Rita's is considerably less than his. Charlie says that unless he has at least two orgasms at each sexual encounter, he is not satisfied, and the frequency of his need for sexual intercourse is increasing. He wants to have sex in the morning, in the evening before dinner, and again at night after bedtime. Rita finds his demands exhausting, but she is afraid he will look to other women if she does not cooperate, and so she has sex with him as often as he wants it. She does not often have orgasms, even though Charlie is skillful and experienced in pleasing women. Curiously, she does have orgasms when she has sex with other men.

She only has sex with other men because Charlie tries to remove her sexual inhibitions by letting his friends have intercourse with Rita while he watches. Lately, Rita's job has become more demanding, and she is less willing to comply with Charlie's sexual demands. Charlie is now suggesting that they ask a girlfriend of Rita's, Toni, to move in with them and share their bed. He has watched Rita and Toni bring each other to orgasm, and he was more excited than he is when he watches Rita with other men. Rita feels some jealousy because she fears that Charlie will find her friend more responsive than she is, but she feels that having another woman in their bed is the only solution to Charlie's insatiable sexual needs, and that it will keep their marriage together.

Like many marital partners who look at the form of innovation rather than the spirit, this is an example of two people who have a marriage held together with sexual myth rather than one that is creatively growing. They both confuse sexual quantity with sexual quality, so that Charlie needs more sex as the quality of sex with Rita declines. Rita acquiesces to his demands out of fear rather than love, and withholds sexual responsiveness because of her resentment. Charlie counters by degrading their own sexual union through staging sexual intercourse between his friends and his wife. The plan to introduce a third party into their marriage is a move of desperation rather than of creativity.

The Siamese twins marriage

"I'm nowhere without you"

Carmen and Jason have a marriage that appears to be the epitome of marital perfection. Jason is an insurance agent with an office in his home, and Carmen is his secretary. They are a smoothly operating team, and each feels a strong sense of unity of purpose and accomplishment. When their children were young, Jason's office was away from home, and they did not share their lives so much; but now that the children are grown, Carmen and Jason are seldom separated except for the time that Jason is calling on clients. Even then, Carmen frequently accompanies him.

When they are not working together they are enjoying their stamp-

"You know why we're so compatible, Harvey? Because
you're blind and I'm deaf."

collecting hobby together or listening to their favorite classical music
together. For entertainment, they go to concerts or the theater, and if
one is unable to attend a performance, the other insists on staying
home also. Carmen and Jason get up at the same time, go to bed at
the same time, eat together, watch TV together, read together, and cook
together. They rarely have arguments, and they seem to agree on almost
everything. They occasionally have sex, but it is of little importance to
them now that they are middle-aged.

The only problems they have are various physical complaints. Carmen
suffers from a wide range of allergies, and has to be extremely careful
about what she eats, the fabrics that touch her skin, and the scents she
smells. In addition to her allergies, she has frequent pelvic discomfort
that she attributes to some malfunctioning of her ovaries, although
gynecologists have been unable to make a definite diagnosis of her
problem. Jason has frequent gastric problems and has to watch his diet
carefully, and he has suffered for several years with chronic headaches
that he and Carmen refer to as "sinus attacks." Jason and Carmen are

sure that if it were not for these nagging physical complaints, their marriage would be perfect, and they always remind their children that they have parents who are models of marital compatibility.

As a model of togetherness, this marriage is perfect. As a model of creativity, it is a failure. Where is the growth of the two individuals? What are they learning from life and from each other? And, other than companionship, what are they giving to each other? Rather than relating to one another as significant beings with individual opinions and needs, they express their frustration and boredom with psychosomatic symptoms that further obstruct the free flow of life in their marriage.

Carmen's pelvic congestion may be related to her sexual deprivation, which is related to the lack of honest communication in the marriage, which is related to the effort to live up to some unrealistic ideal of marital harmony, ad infinitum. Similarly, Jason's "sinus attacks" may be traced to muscular tension, which can be traced to frustration, which can be traced to the effort to act out the stereotype of the perfect gentleman with rational, unemotional orderliness. (On the other hand, Carmen may simply have a physician who discounts all female complaints as hysterical and therefore fails to give her a thorough medical exam, and Jason might be suffering from polluted air!) If both Carmen and Jason could allow themselves to be individuals, they might indeed have a creative marriage. As it is, they have a business partnership. So long as they have medical insurance, they can be reasonably comfortable, but their heirs may collect their life insurance without their ever having really lived.

The mixed-careers marriage

"We'll make beautiful music together—someday"

Ginger and Clark are both successful professional people, and their lives revolve around their careers. Ginger is a psychiatrist, and Clark is a psychologist. Both work long, tiring hours, and both are extremely conscientious in dealing with their patients. They frequently discuss their patients' problems when they are together, and each values the suggestions and observations that the other makes as to therapeutic techniques and diagnostic possibilities. On weekends, they both read professional journals and books, and each often attends or conducts professional workshops with colleagues. They each have publications of their own, and each is almost always working on some article to submit to a professional journal. They manage to have dinner together

Pseudocreative Marriage **135**

once or twice a week, but otherwise they meet only in bed, where they are often too exhausted for anything but an affectionate kiss.

Since both Clark and Ginger are insightful, sensitive people, they both recognize that their marriage is being short-changed, and they sometimes discuss it, vowing to spend more time together as soon as they can find the time. But new patients crowd into their already busy schedules, new professional obligations arise, and the planned vacation together has to be postponed, the leisurely evening together is interrupted, or the fun weekend together is dampened by emergencies, telephone calls, or consultations. On the rare occasions when they make time for each other, they find themselves with little to talk about but events and situations relating to psychiatry and psychology. They both deplore their ignorance about current best-sellers, the latest movies, plays, and current music, but the truth is that both derive so much satisfaction from their professional accomplishments that they begrudge time spent doing anything else. Each is in demand as a speaker on marital problems, and each is a competent, successful marriage counselor. To the rest of the world, their marriage seems to be highly creative and successful, because each has so much respect for the other and because they share the same philosophies and beliefs. Only Ginger and Clark know that they are more roommates than marriage

partners, but neither is dissatisfied enough with the relationship to change it.

Like the shoemaker whose children had no shoes, the lives of psychologists and psychiatrists are sometimes lacking in the intimate interpersonal relationships that they help their patients to achieve. This marriage is satisfying to the people in it, but, like the other examples of pseudocreative marriages, it cannot be termed "creative" simply because it involves a couple who each have demanding careers. Perhaps because they derive so much emotional satisfaction from their relationships with their patients, both Ginger and Clark are avoiding a closer relationship with each other. By putting their professions above their marital relationship, they escape the necessity of meaningful communication and, perhaps, the realization that they are incapable of deep involvement with another person. Vicarious relationships through their patients' lives may substitute for sustained intimacy in their own lives, and they may thus be using their professional obligations as a means of escaping involvement with each other.

The separate but equal marriage

"I've enjoyed as much of you as I can stand"

Sheila and Max are a vivacious, outspoken couple in their early 30s who have been separated for two years. Max is a wealthy man, and most of his wealth has materialized since his marriage to Sheila. Neither he nor Sheila wants to take the financial loss that divorce would involve, and neither wants to remarry. They, therefore, live apart but remain good friends. Max supports Sheila and the children, and Sheila sometimes serves as hostess when Max entertains. Both date other people, but neither has any emotional entanglements. They enjoy each other's company and often go on trips together in spite of the fact that they were miserable living with each other. For Sheila and Max, being separated keeps them friends, while living together makes them enemies.

Again, this is a marriage that serves the needs of the people involved, and therefore should be no skin off anybody else's nose. It is again an example of a marriage that may appear to some to be creative because of the lack of friction between a married pair whose marital form is unorthodox. The fact is, however, that while it may be a creative solution to a marital problem, it is not a creative marriage in itself. The separation provides enhancement for the lives of the individuals, but not for the marriage, and to be creative, marital innovations must enhance the marital relationship as well as the lives of the individuals in the marriage.

All of these examples are of marriages that have attempted to solve the problem of marital boredom and individual needs in new ways. In all cases, the marriages are more pleasing to the partners than are most marriages, and therefore may seem enviable to those whose marriages are bogged in the quicksand of stale marital ties. In some cases, the solutions solve the problem of boredom, and in other cases the solutions keep the marriage together. In no case, however, do the solutions *provide greater individual growth, while strengthening the marital bond and enhancing the joy the partners find in one another*, and therefore they are not *creative* marriages.

EXAMPLES OF CREATIVE MARRIAGE

As was said earlier, it is impossible to give a blueprint for a creative relationship, and it can be dangerous even to give examples of creativity because of the tendency of many people to try to imitate the examples, thus negating the entire concept of creativity. However, the following two examples are presented in order to give the reader at least some suggestion of the spirit of creativity in marriage.

Change and growth within marriage

"What shall we become?"

Martha and Bob are in their mid-40s, and their youngest son is 15 years old, while their oldest daughter has just made them grandparents for the first time. During the years that their five children were young, Martha busied herself in Girl Scouts, church work, PTA, Little League, and the like, while Bob gave as much time to the children as he could manage, while building a small plumbing business. The two slipped away from the children as often as possible, doing simple things like having a quiet picnic in the park and talking about their feelings and problems, or exciting things like a canoe trip down a rapid river, or crazy things like checking into a motel with a bag of chocolate-covered peanuts and alternately making love and eating candy. When the youngest child was in school, Martha enrolled in the nearby university and completed four years of college and two years of graduate school in social work. While she was in college, the children and Bob pitched in and shared the housekeeping chores, and they all cheered wildly when she received her diploma. For the past two years, she has been employed in a family service agency as a social worker, and she loves her work and the people she sees.

Their marriage has been enhanced by the new awareness she has brought to it, and by the stimulation of new ideas and new friends made through her job. She and Bob have found a heightened enjoyment in each other, and their weekend escapes together are more fun and satisfying than they have ever been. Neither has ever had any extramarital sexual affairs, and they each feel that to do so would weaken and possibly destroy the quality of their close communication and intimate lifestyle together.

Through the years, both Martha and Bob have had emotional downs during which they wished that they had never met, never married, and, particularly, never had children. Bob has morosely contemplated the disintegration of his income after paying for the needs of seven individuals, and has sometimes thought wistfully of a lovely South-sea island where he could take up beachcombing. And Martha has occasionally had to go off by herself and have a good cry, or get completely away from her family for a weekend or a day because of all the different personalities, different needs, and different demands on her time and

emotions. They have also learned that their relationship has changed from wildly exciting to warmly glowing—with an occasional exciting flash—and they can laugh over the change in their response to one another. When they were first married, for example, they loved showering together and soaping one another's bodies, now they prefer showering solely for the purpose of getting clean, and only shower together occasionally when they are feeling playful. Through it all, they have maintained their sense of humor, and they find their lives together primarily satisfying in spite of the small annoyances and irritations. Bob has recently decided that he is ready to move to another experience, and he has enrolled in the same university from which Martha got her degree and in which one of their sons is a student. To the amazement of his children, Bob has bought a motorcycle to save both gasoline and money. He jauntily straddles it every morning and zooms off past his neighbors, while they watch him with envy and some perplexity. Martha is very happy that Bob is actively involved in the process of "becoming," and she is willingly shouldering the major part of the family's financial responsibilities while her husband gets a college degree. Neither has any clear-cut plans of what he will do when he graduates, but both are confident that he will find a path to follow that will be exciting and rewarding. In the meantime, the world of books and ideas is exhilarating and challenging, and is an end in itself.

This is truly a creative marriage, in that each partner has always grown independently of the other, but at the same time has supported the other in the growth process. All of their change and growth has enhanced their marital relationship and has brought them closer together as companions and lovers. Thus, they have grown individually *and* as a marital unit, and they have done so through a creative use of their talents, through courage and faith in their own and each other's abilities, and by maintaining a sense of commitment to one another.

Creative open marriage

"Shall we give it a try?"

Jennifer and Chuck are in their late 30s, and each has been married once before. Chuck has a daughter from his first marriage who lives with her mother, but Jennifer has never had a child. They met each other at a church-sponsored singles' party, and soon became good friends as well as lovers. They lived together for about six months before their marriage because both were apprehensive of legal entanglements. They married when they were both comfortable in the relationship and when they realized that marriage offered certain social advantages and career advantages. Chuck is an electronics engineer and Jennifer is a medical secretary, and both felt that their employers would be disapproving if their living arrangement were to become public knowledge.

Throughout their six-year marriage, they have shared the same interests and activities, and their sense of companionship has been a very satisfying part of their lives. Their church is important to both of them, and they have taught young people's classes together and sponsored youth groups within the church. For the last few years, they have both become involved in the drive for equal rights for women, and with groups that are searching for greater personal and marital fulfillment. They have attended many church and community-sponsored workshops devoted to marital enrichment, consciousness raising, sexual enhancement, and the like, and their views and attitudes toward themselves and their values have altered because of their exposure to new ideas and philosophies. Their communication has become even freer and more open due to their involvement in these groups, and they are comfortable with their honesty with each other about their feelings.

For about a year, each admitted to some feelings of sexual boredom, and they attempted to inject excitement and interest into their sex life. For the most part, they were successful in enhancing their sexual relationship, but they both still felt some interest in the idea of sexual variety. They discussed their feelings with another couple whom they met in one of the workshops, and the other couple admitted to having similar feelings. With both excitement and apprehension, the two couples discussed the possibility of exchanging partners simply for sexual variety. For many weeks, their discussions always ended with the agreement that they were not yet ready for extramarital sex because all feared that their feelings of jealousy would be too painful. By the time they arrived at a comfortable acceptance of the idea, they had discussed their jealousy, their fears of rejection, their fears of losing their mates, and their fears of personal inadequacy so many times that they all felt extremely close to one another and their sexual jealousy was therefore lessened to a large extent.

They have since exchanged partners several times and have enjoyed their extramarital sexual encounters very much. All four have gained in their feeling of being desirable to another person, and their sexual responsiveness has increased in their marital sex. There were problems when they first began their mate-swapping activities. Jennifer experienced a painful attack of jealousy and antagonism toward the other woman in the foursome, and Chuck went through a period of suspicion because he feared that Jennifer would prefer the other man to him. The four talked about their feelings, relieved their anxieties and most of their jealousy, and agreed that they found the benefits to their marriages

Examples of Creative Marriage

greater than the detriments. They are now toying with the idea of joining a few other couples from their church who are planning a communal living arrangement. They feel the same mixture of fear and excitement that they felt when they first discussed the possibility of mate-swapping, but they are moving forward in their acceptance of the idea, and they will quite likely give it a trial.

This marriage is also creative, because each partner is growing individually, and yet they are enhancing their marital relationship through their outside growth and freedom. Their marital style would be distasteful to Martha and Bob, as would Martha and Bob's be to them, but each is nonetheless an example of a marriage that is creative in its style.

Jennifer and Chuck's marriage would be viewed by a sizable majority of the population as being better described as "sick" than as "creative." However, when one considers the growth and fulfillment they have gained individually and as a couple from their marriage, and when their happiness is compared with that of many more traditional people, the term "creative" seems quite appropriate, as do "happy," "satisfied," "exciting," "understanding," and "accepting."

As should be well known, many people place blanket condemnation on almost any idea or behavioral pattern that does not fit into their own framework of what is "right" or "wrong," and this is especially true when such ideas and patterns are related to sexual and religious matters. Sexuality and religiosity have been so bonded together over the years that it is easy to understand that when one's traditional rules of sexual attitudes or behavior are violated, one's religious and moral structure is threatened. Such bonding is not accepted by the Jennifers and Chucks of today, however, who seem to base morality more on humanism and situational ethics that evaluate the "rightness" or "wrongness" of a particular act according to the particular circumstances under which it occurred and by the end results of the particular act.

CONCLUSION

All too often, people who are free to find individual growth and freedom are single, and those who find joy in one another are newlyweds or live together without marrying. It seems as if the marital bonds themselves stifle the joy of the couple as well as their individual growth. To have a combination of individual growth, a strong marital bond, and joy in one another may be an unattainable ideal, like perfect love, beauty, and truth. And it may be the *striving* for such a marital relationship and not the *achievement* of the ideal that constitutes the creativity in a marriage. In these cases, to have arrived at such an idyllic marital state is to cease the process of *becoming*. One learns, like Faust, that "he only earns his freedom and existence, who daily conquers them anew." A creative marriage, then, is an adventure shared by two people who believe that individual freedom and growth are possible within a marriage, and that it is possible for that marriage to grow as a third entity that spins off greater satisfaction to the individuals in it, who in turn strengthen the marriage by their greater resources, strength, and courage. Each couple will find their own solutions to the problems involved in such an endeavor.

To embark on a creative marriage requires faith in oneself, in one's mate, and in the possibility of coming close to the ideal of actualized people in an intimate, joy-filled relationship. Strength of character, flexibility, a sense of humor, and an acceptance of the weaknesses in oneself, one's mate, and the marriage itself are necessary, as well as a strong commitment to the idea of a creative marriage. It is quite probable that creative marriages are only for a lucky few, and that the majority of marriages will have to struggle along as best they can, either remaining in the restrictive confines of a yoked relationship, plodding down a well-marked road, or blindly going off on new, rebellious paths in the desperate hope that they will find a world that is more bearable.

The lucky people will be those who first find themselves and know themselves and like themselves, and then find someone with an equal amount of enjoyment in life. These two will not enter a marriage out of loneliness or fear or desperation, but because each enhances the other's enjoyment of life. They will, therefore, be free to approach their marriage in a creative spirit, always with consideration and regard for the other, always open to new ideas and willing to try them, but always with a sense of personal integrity that prevents their degrading themselves, their partner, or their marriage with experiments that would be based on selfish desires or on exploitative motives. Their love and trust in one another may extend to others, with the resulting enhancement of their lives and their marriage.

Similarly, they may try adding novelty to their sex life by mate-swapping. Or they may decide that the life and love they have can be expanded by a group marriage or by living in a communal family. Or they may prefer to enhance their relationship by expanding their circle of friends, or by periodically retreating from their jobs and responsibilities for a time of meditation and study.

Conclusion **143**

Whatever they choose to do, however they choose to live, their goals will be mutual growth and marital satisfaction, and they will sidestep gratification of momentary desires if that gratification would be defeating to the individuals in the marriage or to the marriage itself.

The creative marriage, then, is a union of self-discipline and flexibility, of well-defined values and a spirit of adventurousness, of a willingness to make personal sacrifices for the good of the mate and of the marriage, and a willingness to experiment with new ideas and new behavior.

The creative marriage has as its primary concern the growth of the marital partners and the marriage, while maintaining a sincere concern for the stability of society. The creative marriage is based on the premise that the marital partners are free agents, with individual rights and privileges; it is also based on the premise that those free agents have voluntarily made a commitment to each other whereby each will safeguard the emotional vulnerability of the other. The creative marriage is, in short, a relationship between two mature, disciplined individuals, each striving for personal fulfillment, and each careful to do no harm to each other or to society.

CHAPTER 6

THE NATURE OF LOVE

Being in *love isn't ever* really *loving, it's just wanting. And it isn't any good. It's all aching and misery.*   JAMES LEO HERLIHY.

"I love you." The words have been said countless times by countless people. Love has been the subject of a multitude of films, plays, books, paintings, sculpture, songs, and poems. Yet there is probably no other word used to express so many different feelings. "I love you," says John amorously to Mary, who wants to believe him. "I love you, too," she breathes, and they proceed to have sexual intercourse. It would be more honest for each to say "I desire you," but both John and Mary need to justify sexual desire with love. "I love you but I'm not *in* love with you," says Kathy as she leaves Bob. He, watching her go, says resentfully, "You never loved me. If you had loved me, you would have helped me and stood behind me." Again, if both were more aware of their actual feelings she would say, "I have affection for you, but you don't satisfy enough of my needs." And he would say, "I wanted someone to take care of me and you have disappointed me."

What is **love**? Is it an emotion that can be put on a continuum? Can it be measured and compared by degrees? If you love more than one person, does that mean that you love one more and the other less? Or does it mean that your commitment to one person is different from your commitment to another? Your commitment to your parents is of a different nature from your commitment to your spouse, for example, and that commitment is different from the one to your children, which is still different from your commitment to your close friends. And you may feel an entirely different kind of commitment to each of those friends. Different still is the sense of love one may have for his country, his hometown, his land, or his fellowman.

The attempt to define and identify love has occupied human beings for centuries. In the Middle Ages, several paintings by Ter Borch, Van Ostde, Dou, and many Dutch and Flemish painters portrayed a long-robed physician peering solemnly at a flask of urine to determine whether a woman patient was in love or pregnant (Menninger, 1942). If one asked the average American to define love, he would likely get a mixture of popular sociology, psychology, and religion.

The word "love" comes from the Sanskrit word *lubhyat*, "he desires." It is often said that love is different things to different people, but the fact is that love is a common experience that is more or less recognizable to oneself and to other people (Udry, 1974). Some of the many definitions of love are that it is "an illusion like every search for human perfection but . . . a necessary illusion" (Reik, 1944, p. 194); "a state of consciousness which accompanies the urge to do something with someone else" (Richardson, 1956, p. 339); and "a process of projections of one's own ego-ideal based upon narcissistic attitudes. Ultimately the lover loves only himself . . ." (Bergler, 1946, p. 32). Other concepts of love are that it is ". . . a cooperative behavior, a working together, which is the continuation and development of the maternal-offspring relationship" (Montague, 1953, p. 247), or "a strong emotional attachment, a cathexis, between adolescents or adults of the opposite sexes with at least components of sexual desire and tenderness" (Goode, 1959, p. 41). Still another definition of love is that it is "the positive emotion experienced by one person in an interpersonal relationship in which the second person either (1) meets certain important needs of the first or (2) manifests or appears to manifest personal attributes (beauty, skills, states) highly prized by the first or both" (Winch, 1963, p. 579). These definitions are not likely to be the ones that the average person would give, but most people believe that they know what love is (Kephart, 1966). Meerlo (1952) probably best captured the complexity, variety, and confusion about the meaning of the word "love":

I love you. Sometimes it means: I desire you or I want you sexually. It may mean: I hope you love me or I hope that I will be able to love you. Often it means: It may be that a love relationship can develop between us or even I hate you. Often it is a wish for an emotional exchange: I want your admiration in exchange for mine or I give my love in exchange for some passion or I want to feel cozy and at home with you or I admire some of your qualities. A declaration of love is merely a request: I desire you or I want you to gratify me or I want your protection or I want to be intimate with you or I want to exploit your loveliness. Sometimes it is the need for security and tenderness, for parental treatment. It may mean: My self-love goes out to you. But it may also express submissiveness: Please take me as I am or I feel guilty about you. I want through you, to correct the mistakes I have made in human relationships. It may be self-sacrifice and a masochistic wish for dependency. However, it may also be a full affirmation of the other, taking the responsibility for mutual exchange of feelings. It may be a weak form of friendliness, it may be the scarcely even whispered expression of ecstacy. "I love you," wish, desire, submission, conquest, it is never the word itself that tells the real meaning . . . (p. 83).

Not only are there differences in what we mean by the word "love," but there are differences in what we expect *others* to mean by the word. When John says, "I love you" to Mary, she *expects* him to mean, "I want to marry you, and I will never be sexually attracted to another woman." And when she says "I love you," he expects her to mean "I will create an atmosphere of total acceptance for you, and I will never complain or criticize you." That each has unrealistic expectations of how the other will show love is obvious. Mary might summarize her feelings by saying, "If you should ever show an interest in another woman, I'll leave you," which, translated, means "I hereby proclaim my ownership of you. You are to do only *my* bidding from now on." He, on the other hand, may feel that his wife's total loyalty and activity should be expended toward making his life more pleasant, which is making the same claim to ownership that Mary makes. Is love, then, a form of mutual ownership? How can two people own each other? Obviously, one has to be the owned and the other the owner, but in this kind of relationship each is determined to enforce his own definition of love in order to be the owner.

One must obviously think of love in terms of the person or persons receiving or giving the love. Altruistic love, for example, is one type of love and is expressed through concern and active endeavors for the general well-being of others. It has become a part of radical chic in recent years to sneer at those who give large donations to char-

"How do I love thee? Let me count the ways."

itable institutions and to accuse them of being motivated solely by a need for tax write-offs, social status, and acclaim. The accusation is usually followed by the cynical suggestion that the money is "blood money" earned from the exploitation of the working poor. While such accusations sometimes may be justified, they are not always so, and a person may express altruistic love by endowments to hospitals or to universities out of a genuine concern for the health or education of others. The same person, however, may not be capable of expressing any other form of love.

Friendship, or liking, another form of love, may be very intense and meaningful to the persons involved, yet they may not think of it in terms of "love." A close friendship between two men is expecially unlikely to be described by either party as a loving relationship, yet their affection and concern for one another may be intense and permanent. The overemphasis in our society on the sexual overtones to any relationship and the prejudicial attitudes that many people have about homosexuality cause our society to look askance at a relationship between people of the same sex, even though the notion that love cannot exist apart from sex (or sex apart from love) is nonsensical. It is also difficult for many people to believe that homosexuals can experience love as intensely and profoundly as heterosexuals can. Our society wants to believe that homosexual relationships are devoid of love and that they are always purely sexual. The fact is, of course, that homosexual love can be as genuine and lasting as heterosexual love.

When a feeling for another person is more sexual than emotional, people are likely to mask their true feelings of sexual attraction by convincing themselves that their emotion is "pure" and thus, love. When their sexual needs are not met, they may look at each other in dismay and say, "I don't love you any more!" If their sexual needs *are* met, but their intellectual or emotional needs are not, they may say to someone else, "I love my wife (husband), but she (he) doesn't understand me." And the implicit perceived message in this statement is "I don't love him (her) enough; perhaps I will come to love you more than him (her)." Thus another relationship based on unrealistic expectations and definitions of love is begun. Certainly sexual attraction is a part of love between a man and a woman, but far too often it is mistaken for love itself. Those who claim to have fallen in love at first sight actually were sexually attracted to each other at first sight. Love may grow from such an attraction, but it is certainly not the first emotion felt, in spite of the fact that more than a third of men and women seem to believe in the concept of love at first sight (Kephart, 1966; Landis & Landis, 1973).

The Nature of Love **149**

INFATUATION

There are actually three aspects of love: infatuation, romantic love, and mature love. Almost everyone has experienced **infatuation** and can recognize it, especially with hindsight. Infatuation is an emotion that is almost always spoken of in the past tense, and one rarely hears someone saying that he *is* infatuated with another person, but that he *has been* infatuated. Infatuation is more object- than person-oriented, with the infatuated person unrealistically idealizing another, without any real interaction between them.

Some people have infatuations before the age of 10 (Burgess & Wallin, 1953) and a majority of college women have had infatuations between the ages of 12 and 18 (Ellis, 1949). Most people distinguish between infatuation and being in love in their past relationships (Burgess & Wallin, 1953; Kephart, 1966), and some

people classify as infatuations relationships that lasted as long as a year or two (Burgess & Wallin, 1953).

Romantic love is similar to infatuation, because it too is based on an idealization of another person and of the emotion of love itself. However, romantic love is a step closer in the direction of marriage, and it includes more of the total personality than infatuation does. While romantic love operates on the assumption that love is mysterious and elusive, infatuation operates on the premise that love is totally unknowable. In a sense, infatuation is a situational experience that may be triggered by feelings of loneliness or boredom. Boredom with one's marriage, or feelings of alienation while away from home for the first time may be relieved by a quick, heady love affair that temporarily fills a void. Sometimes a new experience, such as moving to a new city, brings feelings of anxiety that are also filled in part by the excitement of an infatuation.

This aspect of infatuation may explain the preponderance of "crushes" that adolescents form for clay-footed idols as they attempt to deal with the newness of puberty. The sudden, powerful attraction felt during adolescent infatuations may be directed toward a teacher of either sex, a movie star, a famous personality, or someone in the person's peer group. Infatuation does not continue when elements of reality begin to filter into the perception of the infatuated, so this experience is somewhat like taking a ride on an amusement park roller coaster. First there is the exhilarating, heady thrill of the ride, and then the abrupt jolt when the ride stops. In some cases, the person recovered from an infatuation feels a powerful hatred for the recently idolized other because the other failed to live up to his imagination.

The mature person is certainly not immune to infatuations, and they sometimes add spice to life, but they are seldom mistaken by the mature for real love. Romantic love, however, especially in our society, is frequently mistaken for and accepted as "real" or mature love.

ROMANTIC LOVE

Romantic love has several distinguishing characteristics. The first is the belief that in all the world there is only one "soulmate" who is predestined for another person. It is this belief that leads to the belief in "love at first sight." Supposedly, when one meets his soulmate, he immediately knows that this is the one, and love and marriage swiftly follow. Perhaps this aspect of love has appeal because it is ego-satisfying; it makes one feel important and worthy to know that somewhere there is one just right, predestined person. Furthermore, the search for this soul-mate is exciting, and while it may take years—or a lifetime—to find the right one, the chase detracts from much of the monotony of everyday life.

If a person finds and marries the person he considers his soulmate, and the marriage turns out to be unhappy, the only logical explanation is that this was not his soulmate at all, but an impostor. If one strictly adheres to this belief, little need be done to save the marriage since obviously this was the wrong marriage partner to begin with, and divorce is the only solution. The aspect of romantic love has caused romance to be blamed in part for the large divorce rate in the United States, and the charge has been made that romantic marriage is one of the most pathological experiments of civilized society (DeRougemont, 1959). Too often the romantically inclined person goes on his way after a divorce again looking for his true, predestined soulmate. This belief may account in part for the serial monogamy that is often observed in our society.

Romantic love tends to idealize the loved one rather than viewing him in realistic terms, and such idealization has been found to be widespread among engaged college couples, with less than half being realistically oriented (King, 1961). Women tend to be more idealistic than men are about their loved ones, although men tend to become attracted to a woman quicker than a woman does to a man (Burgess & Wallin, 1953).

Romantic idealization is expressed in the cliche, "Love is blind." Since romantic love places little emphasis on social position, success, or other conditions, the personal characteristics of the individual become most important. However, because romantic love is so exciting and so important to the person, he may ignore or misinterpret many of the loved one's qualities. In addition, the courtship experience with its dates and pleasurable aspects is not conducive to seeing the real, everyday side of a person. Daily routines and ordinary tasks do not enter to mar the perfect picture. When the couple marry, they may find that their love diminishes as reality settles in.

People who rely on romantic love to give them a feeling of importance frequently believe that love must be "put to a test." This idea is especially prevalent in popular literature, movies, and radio and television soap operas. In Romeo and Juliet fashion, there must be obstacles to the course of true love, such as the partners coming from different social, religious, or racial groups, or having disapproving, unconsenting parents. By overcoming the obstacles, the lovers prove their love and leave their critics astonished and apologetic. Some authorities believe that this idea is so prevalent in the

American concept of romantic love that young people may even look for obstacles or overexaggerate minor situations. This may be due to the fact that romantic love usually originates during the adolescent period when individuals often have conflicts over dependency. By disobeying, at least to some degree, parental wishes or society's dictates, the adolescent is able to exert his individualism and his independence. Therefore, in a romantic love relationship that includes obstacles, the individual is able to conform to the social pattern as well as prove his independence.

Romantic love is also characterized by a very brief courtship before marriage. Despite the prevalence of romantic ideals in our society, however, it seems that most people postpone marriage until they have known each other for a year or more.

In spite of the criticism leveled at the prevalence of romantic love in America, the idea of romantic love is beginning to spread to Eastern cultures, which up until recent times have regarded love as an unruly emotion that could be very dangerous to their accepted institutions (Mace & Mace, 1960). In Japan, romance as a basis for mate selection is very much on the increase (Landis, 1965). Furthermore, America has never had a monopoly on the romantic concept of love. In Stephens' (1963) review of data on 19 cultures, romantic love occurred sometimes in 7, seldom occurred in 5, and was completely absent in 7 others. Even in America, the idea of love is rejected in some cultures. The American Navaho reportedly had little investment in the idea, and one woman would do as well as another for a wife if she was healthy and industrious (Leighton & Kluckhohn, 1947).

Over the past fifty years, American society has come to think of the word "romance" as a term applied to the pleasurable aspects of love in a man-woman relationship. The meaning of the word "romance" is actually "excitement," or "adventure," which explains the almost mystical attraction of romantic love. This short-lived emotional experience is too often the basis for marriage in our modern society. This is not to say that romantic love should be banished from our relationships. Through romantic love, people can examine potential marital partners for characteristics suitable in a mate, and from this base a mature love can be launched.

Romantic love has been described as camouflaged physical attraction that hinders the development of more permanent kinds of relationships (Peterson, 1964), and as a relationship of remoteness and adoration that is characteristic of persons who are emotionally adolescent and insecure (Winch, 1952). One writer (Folsom, 1934) called romantic love "cardio-respiratory love" because of the excited reaction of the heart and the breathing difficulties that individuals experience during their romantic encounters. This cardio-respiratory love is based largely on novelty, and in this respect is similar to infatuation.

While romantic love has been blamed for much of the ills of marriage in the United States today, some believe that its influence is exaggerated and that more people are concerned with mature love than are concerned with romantic love. Others are more tolerant of the influence of romantic love and believe that it can provide a basis for a mature love, and in fact may have saved the institution of marriage (Beigel, 1951). While the excited, cardio-respiratory nature of love usually does not last, a relationship built upon such love has a chance of establishing the qualities necessary for a mature, lasting love.

HISTORIC DEVELOPMENT OF ROMANTIC LOVE

The concept of romantic love arose from a schism in the early Greek culture between sexual and spiritual love. The Greeks distinguished between **eros**, carnal love associated with the sensual, physical, and sexual aspects of life, and **agape**, spiritual love associated with pure emotions. Neither of these concepts was related to marriage, because the function of marriage was to produce offspring. Spiritual love was an idealized love between men, and was considered an emotion so pure that women could not attain it. The ideal of Greek love was therefore homosexual, since the female was regarded as too lowly and imperfect for the emotion of love. The essence of beauty and the realization of love were found only in the male, and therefore usually existed between an older man and a young boy (Hunt, 1959).

While Greek love is usually considered homosexual love between males, the poetess Sappho on the Greek island of Lesbos penned erotic poems to and about her female students, thus giving to female homosexuality the name Lesbianism. In the Greek culture, homosexuality was preferred and heterosexuality was the second choice.

Christianity, following the Jewish tradition, condemned homosexuality, but idealized the purity of love apart from sex. Love of God was the only "pure" love, and celibacy became a means of proving one's love for God. As the influence of the Church spread, virgin nuns were wedded to Christ in a spiritual marriage that was believed to be far superior to the physical unions of men and women. As sexual expression was suppressed by the Church, the idealization of women was promoted, reaching its zenith in the doctrine of the Immaculate Conception and its idealization of Mary.

Near the end of the eleventh century, the nobles in the south of France—the only group strong enough to oppose the Church (Bell, 1971b)—combined the concepts of chivalry and the idealization of women into so-called "courtly love," in which chastity was the rule and chivalry was the basis of honor.

In many respects, courtly love was like the adolescent phase of love when sexual desire is denied satisfaction (Beigel, 1951). Just as the adolescent male strives for recognition and approval from

the female of his choice, so the medieval knight participated in
tournaments and jousts while his lady looked on, his efforts dedicated to her.

Generally a relationship between a knight and a lady whose husband was off crusading, "love" at this time was understood to mean
a spiritual, romantic relationship with someone other than one's
spouse, and "Courts of Love" sprang up in which medieval ladies

formulated rules and regulations governing their love affairs. An example of one such code, formulated by a group of women in 1174, follows:

1. *Marriage is no good excuse against loving.*
2. *Whoever cannot conceal a thing, cannot love.*
3. *No one can bind himself to two loves at once.*
4. *Love must always grow greater or grow less.*
5. *There is no savour in what a lover takes by force.*
6. *The male does not love until he has attained a complete manhood.*
7. *A widowhood of two years is prescribed to one lover for the other's death.*
8. *No one, without abundant reason, ought to be deprived of his own love.*
9. *No one can love unless urged thereto by the hope of being loved.*
10. *Love is always exiled from its dwelling by avarice.*
11. *It is not decent to love one whom one would be ashamed to marry.*
12. *The true lover does not desire embraces from any but the co-lover.*
13. *Love that is known publicly rarely lasts.*
14. *An easy conquest renders love despised, a difficult one makes it desired.*
15. *Every lover turns pale in the sight of the co-lover.*
16. *The lover's heart trembles, at the unexpected sight of the co-lover.*
17. *A new love makes one quit the old.*
18. *Probity alone makes a man worthy of love.*
19. *If love lessens, it dies speedily and rarely regains health.*
20. *The man prone to love is always prone to fear.*
21. *Real jealousy always increases the worth of love.*
22. *Suspicion and the jealousy it kindles increase love's worth.*
23. *Whom thought of love plagues, eats less and sleeps less.*
24. *Whatever a lover does ends with thinking of the co-lover.*
25. *The true lover thinks naught good but what he believes pleases the co-lover.*
26. *Love can deny love nothing.*
27. *The lover cannot be satiated by the delights of the co-lover.*
28. *The least presumption compels the lover to suspect evil of the co-lover.*
29. *He is not wont to love, whom too much abundance of pleasure annoys.*

30. *The true lover is haunted by the co-lover's image unceasingly.*
31. *Nothing prevents one woman from being loved by two men, or one man by two women.*

We pronounce and decree by the tenour of these presents, that love cannot extend its powers over two married persons; for lovers must grant everything, mutually and gratuitously the one to the other without being constrained thereunto by any motive of necessity; while husband and wife are bound by duty to agree the one with the other and deny each other nothing. . . . In the year 1174, the third day from the Calends of May. (Langdon-Davies, 1927, pp. 266–267)

Sexual intercourse was not a part of these love affairs, but a considerable amount of physical intimacy was encouraged (Beigel, 1951), and the "purity" of the relationship was sometimes put to the acid test by going to bed nude together and making love, but stopping short of sexual intercourse (Bell, 1971b). Thus, the married ladies and their knights enjoyed the excitement of an artificial, transitory relationship that allowed the ladies to retain their feelings of purity and the knights to be chivalrous. Marriage at that time was contracted for reasons of familial benefits, property rights, personal protection, and procreation, but courtly or romantic love was devoid of burdens and responsibilities. Thus, romantic love and marriage were two separate entities that fulfilled entirely separate needs. So long as the lovers remained sexually "virtuous," the husband's marital rights were safeguarded and the rules of chivalry upheld. As knighthood declined, however, so did the sexual inhibitions of the knights and ladies (Sirjamaki, 1955), and in the court society of the Baroque and Rococo periods, the brave deeds of gallants were rewarded with sexual favors, and so began the fusion of sex and love. And perhaps, too, began the confusion of sex with love.

The Renaissance period denied the existence of love in marriage, except by accident, as did the nobles of the seventeenth and eighteenth centuries in Spain, France, Austria, and neighboring countries. In fact, in Spain in the seventeenth century the nobleman usually had three principal women in his life. There was his wife for representative purposes, his lady friend for sex, and a mistress for esthetic conversation. However, the idea of love in marriage was taking root during this time, and the English novelist Samuel Richardson (1689–1761) is credited with being the first to say that love was necessary for marriage (Beigel, 1951). Too often this has

been interpreted as meaning love is the *only* thing necessary for marriage.

Around the turn of the nineteenth century, courtly love was transformed into romantic love in marriage by the common man who could not afford to be both married and romantically involved. Since the masses imitated the elite classes as best they could, romantic love and marriage gradually blended, with love becoming a prerequisite for marriage. In many ways it was a social and psychological necessity, for social and technological changes had created massive

Historic Development of Romantic Love **159**

insecurity and had diminished the importance of individual contributions. Exposed to the tensions of the modern world and its progressing materialism, man found an antidote and emotional satisfaction in love (Ogburn & Nimkoff, 1955).

To the Puritans in America, marriage was a civil contract alone, and ministers were forbidden to solemnize the institution of marriage. Romantic love and sex between young people were also acceptable to the Puritans, as long as the sanctity of the family was not violated. The practice of "bundling," which ostensibly included the practice of a young unmarried couple's spending the night together in the same bed but not indulging in sexual intercourse, is similar to the practice of the knights and their ladies in medieval times who were expected to be in the same bed nude together without having sexual intercourse. If a couple was not able to abstain from temptation and a pregnancy resulted, no particular censure was imposed by society, and the excitement of forbidden pleasure made the long New England winters less cold and miserable.

The transitional phase between Puritanical familial holds and our modern conception of romantic love came with the Industrial Revolution. Women went to work and met a much wider array of prospective mates. Mass production furnished more leisure time in which people could become involved in more heterosexual activities. Sexually integrated public meeting places sprang up, such as dance halls, movie houses, and recreational groups formed by companies for their employees. The family lost its authority over youth, and romantic love flourished. Movies and literature seized on the subject and made a large profit by portraying the strange, apparently irresistible attraction between lovers. Like every new generation, the youth of the Industrial Revolution retained more of their parental influence than they would have liked to believe. Also, the religious emphasis on the Madonna story fostered the concept of romantic love by placing women in an idealized position and by demanding sexual abstinence until marriage (Winch, 1963). Sexual attraction that did not have marriage and family in mind was therefore unacceptable to them, so they cloaked their physical attraction with the mysterious emotional experience they called love. In the United States, especially, an attempt was made to combine sex, love, and marriage into one unique experience between one man and one woman.

With the conquest of the American frontier, new qualities were required of young people if they were to survive in an unfamiliar world. Strength, ambition, and ability, as well as independence, ingenuity, and individuality, became the hallmark of the American ideal. The personality of the individual became more important than his family ties—a poor but bright child could gain greater wealth than his parents had ever dreamed of. Thus evolved a new kind of hero—a new kind of knight—who could not only woo his lady by displaying himself in combat, but win her for his wife as well. This form of chivalry was not restricted to the wealthy, and it did not exclude sex.

Taming the American frontier also demanded new qualities in women, and American females rose to the occasion and acquired independence and strength that brought them closer to equality in their relationships with men. Women made their own decisions, for the most part without parental interference, about the marriage partner they wanted, and they made their decisions based on the personality traits of the prospective mates and their own emotional responses to these traits.

There was not only a departure from the traditional European traditions governing man-woman relationships, but a departure from the hold of the Church regarding such matters. On the frontier, ministers were few and far between, and a marriage might be formalized long after a couple's first child was born. Expediency came to replace tradition, and the pleasures of romantic love made a hard life bearable.

Romanticism has continued to flourish in the Western world. English-speaking people listened in rapt silence as the King of England gave up his throne "for the woman I love." Millions followed with avid interest the later courtships and marriages of his nieces, the future Queen of England and her Princess sister. And when the present English Princess married, more millions watched the wedding ceremony on television. In our own country, a presidential candidate put his political future on the line by divorcing his wife of many years and marrying another woman. And the daughters of recent American presidents have captured the romantic interests of the population when their courtships and marriages were followed by the news media.

Although our divorce rate reflects, in part, the greater economic freedom of women and the greater stress placed on individual happiness in marriage, it also reflects the romantic idealism with which many enter marriage. Young people remain as romantically naive as they have been in any age, and it is perhaps because of this romanticism that they are able to embark on the sometimes painful journey through life. If there were no romantic illusions, people might find life and human nature too ugly to endure. But if romanticism is not modulated with realism, life and individuals never are seen as they actually are, and disappointment and cynicism may easily result. The mature person can therefore enjoy romantic love, while all the while being aware of objective reality. By being a little blind to another's imperfections, the romantic enjoys relationships more than otherwise, and by slightly exaggerating another's virtues, excitement and interest are added to life.

MATURE LOVE

Mature love, the interation between two emotionally mature individuals whose relationship is based on individual creativity, mutual esteem, and erotic fulfillment (O'Neill & O'Neill, 1972), grows as the relationship unfolds, and is not diminished by aging, physical infirmity, loss of looks, or changing situations. Communication in mature love is completely free and honest, with no restrictions or inhibitions placed on the relationship or on the individuals in it. Unlike the concept of romantic love, into which people "fall," mature love demands an ever-constant process of personal growth and awareness of the other's feelings and needs. In such a relationship, the individual can reach optimum potential as a human being through individual strivings, and also reap the rewards of the partner's personal achievements.

Obviously, mature love is infinitely preferable to elusive romantic love, but the question that troubles most young people is how one distinguishes one from the other. How can one be sure that the romantic love felt for another person at the age of 21 will remain through the years? Our soaring divorce rate indicates that it seldom does. Is the answer, then, to have a continuing series of romantic involvements that never culminate in marriage, or to have a form of serial monogamy by multiple marriages and divorces? Only the immature individual would prefer the brief excitement of superficial romantic involvements to a more lasting, growing, deeply fulfilling relationship, but many are unable to define for themselves what qualities in an individual make that person capable of mature love.

Mature love can only be experienced by a mature person, and the mature personality has components of self-worth, self-love, and self-respect. Love for others can only be achieved when one feels love for one's self (Fromm, 1956). Rather than seeking strength in another to compensate for weaknesses, the mature person is able to feel and project love from within. Instead of *taking* in order to complete one's own self, he or she is *giving* from a complete source—one's self. The mature individual knows himself and knows his own needs. He feels comfortable within and seeks a partner with complementary needs. While immature needs are centered around the need to shrug off responsibilities and neurotic needs, mature needs facilitate growth and are oriented in reality (Lantz & Snyder, 1969). Mature needs arise from the intellect and the fully developed emotions, whereas immature needs are more directed from deficiencies in the personality structure of the individual. Mature people are tolerant in their love. A person who can understand and overlook minor matters over which he or she has no control is far more capable of a mature relationship than one whose temperament is prone to explode over matters that cannot be changed.

The mature person has integrated within his or her personality a view of sex as an intensified pleasure in a relationship, but not as an activity around which to build the relationship. He or she feels no guilt over sexuality, most often because of a good understanding of human sexuality generally. Sex is not viewed as either a perversion or as a way of rebellion. In sex, as in all other matters, he or she is willing to accept the full consequences of his or her actions. Sexual attraction is not allowed to influence the selection of a marriage partner as much as sound judgment based on character analysis. The mature person may retain personal objectivity in a situation, but he or she can also empathize with the beloved and see the other side of the picture. Whereas being loved romantically may be attractive because the ego responds to flattery, mature love allows for freer interaction between partners, for less game-playing, and less striving toward living up to imaginary ideals.

In a sense, mature love exists in moderation. Whereas romantic love is a series of incredible highs and lows, mature love is evenly balanced and temperate. Where romantic love is hot, mature love is warm. Mature love is not an extreme, but a way of life.

DEVELOPMENT OF THE CAPACITY TO LOVE

The capacity for love is within every individual, but this capacity must be nurtured and developed. The only experimental evidence readily available on the development of love comes from studies on baby monkeys. In these experiments (Harlow, 1958, 1966), eight baby monkeys were raised alone in cages with equal access to a surrogate "mother." Although each mother was equipped with a baby bottle to dispense milk to the babies, one mother was merely a wire frame while the other was cloth-covered and heated by an electric light bulb. It was found that the monkeys had little contact with the wire mother except to get milk, and did not seek the wire mother out when frightened. On the other hand, the monkeys had frequent contact with the cloth-covered, warm mother; when frightened they would run to it, and in general they showed a preference for this "mother." As the monkeys grew, they ventured out from this mother, returning when something frightened them, and showing affectional responses to the surrogate. It was Harlow's conclusion that love was triggered by physical warmth and body contact. This conclusion, empirically based, is quite compatible with what is known about the growth of love in human infants.

During the first two to three years of life, a baby expresses and comprehends love almost strictly in physical terms. A baby smiles and coos when it is fed and fondled gently. This sensation of pleasure is associated with the person who is feeding or fondling it. When a baby is hungry or wet, tension increases and when the caretaker reduces the tension through care, the baby responds. Gradually, pleasure becomes associated with the particular person who provides the care. As the child grows, it comes in contact with more people and comes to love them as they provide pleasure. Gradually, the child will learn to associate other things with the loved persons and begin to view them in terms other than simply gratification. In early development, however, love is largely related to self-satisfaction and self-gratification. This inward-directed love usually reaches its climax between the ages of three and five (Cavan, 1953), and after this time more attention is turned to outwardly expressed love or "companionship love" (Landis, 1965).

During childhood, love is based largely on mutual satisfaction.

"This one is the love potion, and this one is the pill."

CHRISTIANSON

However, the degree to which a child can express love outwardly depends upon how amply love has been received at home during the infancy stage. As work with feral children (children reared without human companionship and care) and children in institutions has shown, love is essential to normal growth and development. Some authors connect juvenile delinquency with denial of love in the home during the early years (Landis, 1965).

The foregoing discussion about the development of love in humans reflects generally accepted theories of child development. Some theorists have slightly different views on the development of love. Reik (1957), for example, holds that for persons to love later in life, they must have been loved by the mother or mother substitute, and also must have felt somewhat insecure in this love so that there is a need to be loved. Since they need love and have not been totally satisfied, people will then act out this need throughout life. They will search for someone to love them and will be anxious about keeping this love. According to this theory, the usual mother-child relationship provides for some insecurity in love.

While these theories may account for the capacity of human beings to love, they do not account for the perpetuation of the con-

Development of the Capacity to Love **165**

cept of romantic love. Instead, our society seems to provide training in the idea of romantic love (Udry, 1974). Beginning at the nursery school age, there are fairy tales replete with ideas of romantic love. Always there is a beautiful girl and always there are barriers to the love of this beautiful girl (a slippery glass hill, thorn bushes, a cruel stepmother) and always the obstacles are overcome and everyone lives happily ever after.

Today's child is barraged by commercial symbols of romantic love. The dolls a little girl plays with are no longer cuddly baby dolls but slim, curvaceous adolescent dolls with swinging long hair and well-stocked wardrobes. These female dolls have male counterparts, so the little girl can play that they are on dates and obtain more preparatory training for the love-saturated adolescent period. (These dolls are equipped with very realistic bodies, but their genital areas are neuter, another reflection of the sexual repression in our society.) The young child is always fascinated by older children, and shows his onward striving by emulating them. Little girls learn quite early to speak about their boyfriends, and there are frequently parties given by beaming matchmaking mothers where young people can begin early to learn proper romantic behavior.

Movies, television, and popular songs are all full of the romantic love idea, and all these are readily accessible to the under-12 set as well as to older individuals. One report (Horton, 1957) is that 90 percent of popular songs are about romance. A sample of short stories in popular magazines covering two five-year periods revealed that the stories dealt mainly with romance, and that the physical characteristics of lovers were close to beauty stereotypes—tall, dark, and handsome (England, 1960). Over 45 percent of the stories had romantic chance encounters, and 41 percent had short courtships: furthermore, 57 percent of the stories had love occur in a flash with no courtship at all. Certainly, the mass media available to the American public are thoroughly saturated with the idea of the all-consuming power of romantic love.

The dispensation of the romantic myth during the adolescent period is even more intense. The wonder is that it takes the adolescent so long to fall in love in this climate of saturated romantic love (Udry, 1974). The adolescent in our society is almost bound to have an overwhelming need to fall in love, and usually does. In fact, most writers feel that adolescence is the proper time for love to begin. Often the adolescent is accused of being in love with love, for to be in love is so expected of the teenage girl or boy that many literally convince themselves that they are in love. Reik (1944) has used the expression "jumping" into love rather than falling in love to illustrate the overpowering need to be "in love" that so many

people in our culture have. Usually this first love has many of the qualities of infatuation or cardio-respiratory love with its blindness and idealization. In many ways, though, adolescent love can be a stepping-stone to mature love. It can also become a style of love that continues as long as adolescence does, which, psychologically speaking, can be throughout life (Richardson, 1956).

Development of the Capacity to Love **167**

Nothing has been said yet about sex entering into this romantic training process, although it certainly does. However, the way sex enters is in a rather repressive, negative way, again quite characteristic of our American culture. In some ways the attempt is made to divorce sex and love, especially in the early training of an individual, but on the other hand, sex is considered evil without love. Our attitude, at least during the first decade of a child's life, is that sex is evil and love is good (Winch, 1952). During the second decade, sex is strictly forbidden fruit, but love is still good. Then during the third decade, sex becomes good under the prescribed condition of marriage that supposedly results from love. What this means is that early sexual expression in young children is often quite disturbing to parents, and frequently children are severely reprimanded for masturbating or showing interest in sexual matters. Presently some of the early sexual repression is becoming less severe due to the enlightenment of parents through books on child development that regard early sex expression as natural and acceptable.

In adolescence, when an individual becomes sexually mature, sexual activity is even more a taboo area. Teenage boys and girls often suffer extreme guilt and anxiety over their masturbatory activity, but heterosexual sexual activity is even more severely condemned. Despite the fact that all the skills of giant advertising agencies are directed toward selling products by using sex appeal, which necessarily influences youthful ideas on the subject, having sexual intercourse is still considered taboo unless one is married. Of course, there is always a discrepancy between the mores of society and individual practice, and a considerable number of individuals no longer wait for the social sanction of married love to enjoy sexual gratification. (This topic is discussed in detail in Chapter 8, Human Sexuality.) More adolescents, especially girls, are justifying premarital sex on the grounds that they are "in love." In a culture that places such a premium on love and has such a thorough teaching process in it, it is little wonder that such a belief has become widespread. It is somewhat unrealistic for American society to believe it can exist in the midst of a sex-saturated, "love is the epitome of existence" atmosphere and continue to retain the old traditional restrictions against sex outside of marriage when it weds love and sex.

CONCLUSION

One more thing should be pointed out in connection with romantic love. Several theorists believe that the romantic love ideal taught in American society serves useful purposes. The effect of romance may help to free young people from their family attachments, thereby substituting for the interlocking kinship roles found in other societies and motivating the individual to conform to marital role expectations (Parson, 1949). Some authorities believe that love, usually a prelude to marriage, is too important to a society to be uncontrolled (Goode, 1959). The emphasis placed on romantic love in the United States is one means of controlling and channeling love before it appears. Other cultures control love through childhood marriages, a kinship system to prescribe eligible mates, or extremely close supervision or isolation of marriageable-age youths. By encouraging love relationships and sanctioning free love choices, American society influences social contacts, and control lies in peer groups and parents. The romantic ideal means that only certain people, probably those in one's own social group, are likely candidates for romantic love attachments, and such people are more prone to be acceptable to one's parents and friends than if there were no romantic love myth.

In summary, while the capacity to love presumably exists at birth, the relationships one has in the early years and the culture in which one grows up play vital roles in the actual development of love.

CHAPTER 7

DATING AND
MATE SELECTION

Some marry in haste, and then set down and think it careful over.
JOSH BILLINGS

Recently in the news was a report of an Australian psychologist-matchmaker who was in the United States recruiting brides for 1000 potential bridegrooms in Australia. Because there are 15 million more single women than men in the United States, and 163,000 more males of marriageable age in Australia than there are women, the United States provides good hunting ground for his clients. Updating the custom of mail-order brides, the matchmaker said that his clients are tested for emotional stability and that they must submit sworn affidavits concerning age, marital status, children, and other data that are of interest to a prospective mate.

For many of America's 46 million single adults, 14.6 million (Statistical Abstract of the United States, 1977) of whom are between the ages of 20 and 34, the idea of having the services of a professional matchmaker is undoubtedly intriguing. Not only would the difficulties encountered in dating be sidestepped, but the responsibility for the choice of a marriage partner would be transferred to another person. If the marriage failed, the matchmaker could be blamed.

If mate selection were done on a scientific, systematic basis, there would not be the possibility of having the experience, such as one woman reported, of having a date who, upon being served the first course in a posh restaurant, said loudly, "That looks like belly button lint floating in my soup." Neither would there be the possibility of spending an evening racking one's brain trying to think of something to say to a date who responds in monosyllables—if at all—to one's every attempt at conversation. In short, there would be no reason for dating, no painful experiences encountered in dating, and no reason for discussions such as this one about dating.

FUNCTIONS OF DATING

Dating is variously described as exploitative (Waller, 1937), pleasurable (Burgess & Locke, 1940), educational (Lowrie, 1951), and sometimes dissatisfying (Albrecht, 1972). Women date a little more than six years, on the average, while men average more than eight years of dating. One-half of a person's dating years are before college (Albrecht, 1972). Although a large majority (three-quarters) of college students feel a lack of confidence in their associations with the opposite sex (Landis & Landis, 1973), most young people continue to date even when they are apprehensive about dating and even when they know that dating is not always fun (Albrecht, 1972).

Through dating, young people acquire social and personal competence, extend their range of cross-sex interaction as well as gain valuable learning in the form of feedback from other people about their own habits, attitudes, and behavior. In addition, they learn to distinguish between the traits or qualities in others that they could never live with and those that are the most satisfying to them, thereby increasing their chances of making a sensible decision when they choose a mate.

From early adolescence to marriage, certain functions are served by dating. In the first awkward contacts with the opposite sex, a young adolescent begins the process of learning how to relate in a different way from before. There is increased awareness of the self as male or female, and there is a chance to gain more understanding of the adult roles of oneself and of significant others (Bell, 1971a).

Dating also provides pleasure and recreation for young people, and it is an interlude between childhood, when one is told what to do by adults, and adulthood, when one has to consider responsibilities before pleasure. In dating, adolescents choose their own entertainment and are free to enjoy themselves without having heavy responsibilities. In addition to the pleasure of the recreation and entertainment, adolescents also have the pleasure of discussing their dates with their friends, thereby further extending their own sociability. Furthermore, young people acquire prestige through dating when they meet the standards of their peer group, and they often achieve a certain status if they date frequently or if the person they date has a lot of prestige (Bell, 1971a).

As a person enters late adolescence and early adulthood, he or she begins to have marriage more consciously in mind when dating, and dating becomes increasingly important. The frequency of dating increases, as does the number of different people dated, as dating as an end in itself becomes secondary to dating in order to find a mate (Bell, 1971a).

The high school years are a time when differences among people in terms of race, social class, religion, and ethnicity become more distinct. Whether or not the student plans to go to college, the academic curricula chosen, and the extracurricular activities engaged in will separate the student from some groups and bind him or her to others. The intention of going to college is a particularly dominant factor in high school relationships. As Gagnon and Greenblatt (1978) point out, it creates a major "cleavage" between young people, although in some cases it has a homogenizing effect in that it may make it easier for a couple from different backgrounds and social classes to date, since it is expected that after college they will both have a social status that is similar.

As recently as the late 1930s and 1940s, dating was a relatively new phenomenon on high school campuses, and it only began to be common on college campuses in the 1920s. The trend for the past several decades is for youngsters to start dating at younger and younger ages. The average age for beginning dating is around 13 years for girls (Bell & Chaskes, 1970), although many youngsters begin to date as early as 10 and 11 (45 percent of boys and 36 percent of girls) (Broderick & Fowler, 1961).

Girls start dating at slightly younger ages than boys and show romantic interests at younger ages. Girls who date much earlier than their peers are more likely to marry at younger ages, frequently while still in high school (Burchinal, 1964b), but no relationship has been found between the age of first dating and premarital pregnancy (Lowrie, 1965).

Girls whose parents are highly educated tend to begin dating at earlier ages than girls whose parents are less educated, and girls from small families begin dating earlier than girls from large families. Southerners begin dating earlier than people from other geographical areas do. Not surprisingly, girls who begin dating late in adolescence tend to be less discriminating in their choice of mates than are girls who begin dating at an earlier age (Lowrie, 1966).

CATEGORIES OF DATING

Five categories of dating have been described by college students (DeLora, 1963), and these five are probably practiced on most college and high school campuses. Each type of dating appears to have its own function and to be characterized by recognizable behavior. The types of dating are casual dating, steadily dating, going steady, engaged to be engaged, and engagement.

Many relationships that culminate in marriage have had a sequential development of the five forms of dating, although certain stages or combinations of stages may be skipped. These forms of dating illustrate the fact that dating is a series of steps like the education process. It is a learning experience leading to maturity, understanding of oneself and others, clarification of the roles of the sexes, and to the final socialization of the individual.

Casual dating. Casual dating usually begins when a person is about 12 to 14 years old. Less a pairing up than dating within a group as a whole, casual dating provides the first close contact with a person of the opposite sex who is outside the family. Through casual dating, a person can begin to learn what members of the opposite sex are like.

As a person becomes more confident and experienced, he or she begins a kind of random casual dating whereby he or she pairs off with various others, but has no permanent commitment to any particular one. The primary purpose of this form of dating is to get acquainted, and it often involves double dating with another couple. Sexual behavior varies, but it usually is confined to a goodnight kiss.

Casual dating provides an opportunity for a great deal of personal growth and development. Through random casual dating, a person can learn to understand oneself and others in his social circle. There are certain dangers in casual dating, however, that can cause pain to the persons involved, especially if only a very few different people are dated.

The most common harmful aspect of casual dating occurs when one person becomes considerably more involved in a relationship than the other is. Young people should thoroughly understand the fact that *the person who is least involved in a relationship controls that relationship.* There is always the possibility of the least involved person exploiting the other person, and this possibility must be guarded against. If one person is much less emotionally involved than the other and uses that advantage against the involved person, he or she may gain sexual gratification, social advancement, or material gain by making insincere statements and promises. The more insecure and inadequate the involved person is, the more likely he or she is to be a victim of "a line," and to allow herself or himself to be selfishly used by the other. Only through emotional maturity and self-control can dating people avoid one-sided relationships in which one person is exploited.

The words "exploit" and "use" are words that may need defining, since they are so frequently used. Women maintain that men **exploit** their bodies; men maintain that women **use** them as money trees or as status racks on which to hang. The fact is that if a woman wants the status of being the steady of the campus idol or the town's best catch, and if he **wants** to have sex with her, neither is exploiting the other if each realizes the exchange taking place. She achieves her goals through him, he achieves his through her; neither is being used since each is aware of all the ramifications involved. On the other hand, if the woman wants marriage, and the man wants sex and falsely promises marriage, that is exploitation since the woman

CHRISTIANSON

failed to get what she had expected and had been promised. The point is that nobody can be exploited by anybody—sexually or otherwise—if they always make sure they are doing what they *want* to do and that they clearly realize all the ramifications of their actions. To jump into bed with an attractive, exciting acquaintance with the anticipation of a satisfying sexual experience is a gamble. If it is not satisfying, there has still been no exploitation, there has simply been a disappointment. Interestingly, there are far fewer accusations of sexual exploitation when the activity has been mutually enjoyable than when it has not.

If a young person does experience the painful and humiliating realization that one has been used by another person, there is an opportunity for growth even from such a negative experience, and he or she can go on to other relationships, sadder but wiser, and be more wary of becoming entangled in a one-sided relationship in the future. In this manner, young people learn to deal with many different kinds of people and with various sorts of problems.

Steadily dating. If a boy and girl become acquainted through random, casual dating, and begin dating each other more than anyone else, they are **steadily dating**. There is no formal agreement in this kind of relationship, and each is free to date anyone else. The boy usually initiates each date, and the two are more concerned with entertainment and having a good time than they are with companionship. Sexual activity usually is confined to necking and light petting.

According to a 1966 survey of adolescent dating behavior (The teenagers, 1966), the trend is toward dating steadily rather than going steady. Dating steadily represents a compromise between the lack of emotional involvement in casual dating and the intense emotional commitment of going steady (Bell, 1971a).

Going steady. When two people begin to go with each other exclusively, they are **going steady**, and the companionship, especially for precollege students, may be the most important aspect of their relationship. Couples who are going steady usually take equal responsibility for initiating the interaction, and heavy petting is usually a part of their relationship.

According to one study of college students, 68 percent of the women and 72 percent of the men had gone steady at least one time, and the males had gone steady more often than the females (2.2 to 1.6) (Bell & Blumberg, 1959). Young people who begin dating at an early age tend to play the field for a longer time before settling down to a steady, while people who wait longer to begin dating tend to rush into emotional involvements and begin going steady without having dated a great number of individuals (Lowrie, 1966). Among young people under the age of 16 or 17, going steady has become popular only since the end of World War II (Bell, 1971a). Two types of steady dating have been found among high school students. One is marriage-oriented, and the other is maintained simply for fun, recreation, or other reasons (Herman, 1955). At least one-half of all middle-class youths probably go steady at least once before the age of 17 (Bell, 1971a).

Going steady is especially attractive to younger adolescents because it gives them a feeling of security. They are assured of having a date for all important occasions, and there is much less possibility of being either rejected or ignored than there is in a competitive open dating situation. Furthermore, the younger peer groups exert pressure on their members to go steady, and a person may strive to meet peer group expectations in order to avoid individual frustration (Bell, 1971a).

176 Dating and Mate Selection

Going steady may help to ease the transitional stage between adolescence and adulthood, as it allows young people to take on adult role-playing without having adult responsibilities. There is also value in going steady in that it helps the adolescent to shift the center of commitment away from his home and parents and to another person who is important. Going steady may also provide a sense of being significant to another person—a need we all have—at a time when the adolescent's relationship with parents may make him or her feel less significant to them (Bell, 1971a). Since adolescent rebellion against parents usually results in less parental approval, the adolescent may feel anxiety at the decrease in positive regard from parents, and may turn to going steady as a means of recapturing the feeling of being unconditionally accepted by someone important to him or her.

The disadvantages associated with going steady are primarily concerned with the person who goes steady for long periods of time and therefore limits the opportunities for interaction with a wide variety of people. The fewer people a person dates, the more limited he or she will be in the ability to know oneself and to know how his or her needs are related to others. That person will, therefore, be at a greater disadvantage in choosing an appropriate mate than will the one who has had a variety of dating experiences (Bell, 1971a). There is also a possibility that steady dating may be harmful to the people involved when younger adolescents are pushed into commitments before they have developed the skill and maturity to deal with such an intense personal relationship (Stroup, 1966).

Engaged to be engaged. If a couple is **engaged to be engaged**, or pinned, they are not only going steady, but have discussed plans for the future involving marriage and educational and occupational goals. There is increased sexual intimacy, and usually the couple exchange some personal objects or the woman is given the man's fraternity pin.

Engagement. Engagement, of course, involves actual preparation for marriage, with possible professional counseling from physicians, counselors, or clergymen about various aspects of marriage. Having a good time is less important than companionship, and either party may initiate the interaction. There is usually increased sexual intimacy, and there is equal authority in the relationship.

Rather than being considered a *promise* to marry, such as a betrothal is, an engagement is an *intention* to marry, and carries with it no contractual implications. Young people today break off engagements with relative ease, and they view the engagement period as a time of testing their relationship. Up until 1935, however, a woman could bring a breach of promise suit in the United States courts if a man who had been engaged to her broke their engagement. (A man could file a similar suit, but was less likely to.) Early German custom appears to have influenced the concept of betrothal as a contract in English common law, from which American law derived. The contractual view of an engagement was based on the premise that if a couple promise to marry one another, they may behave in ways that could be harmful to the woman if they did not eventually marry. The woman's family might lose money spent on wedding arrangements or on a dowry. The woman might give up opportunities for an education, a career, or another husband, or she might have sexual relations because she was confident that her lover was to be her husband. To protect the woman, therefore, the possibility of court action persisted from the thirteenth to well into the twentieth century.

Since women are no longer dependent on men for their survival, and since few modern women have the time to languish with a broken heart, gaining recompense because an engagement period fails to end in marriage is unnecessary and unfair to the man. Betrothal, therefore, has given way to a time of testing of the relationship.

Traditionally, there is an official announcement of a couple's engagement, either through a newspaper announcement or by an engagement party to which friends and relatives are invited. Among today's college students, however, official engagement announcements are less commonplace, as the prestige attached to such announcements is less important than it was to their parents.

Also traditional is a diamond engagement ring, which not only announces that a girl is "taken," but also (symbolically at least) announces the financial status of her prospective bridegroom—the larger the diamond, the more affluent the man. The fact that a ring having significant monetary value is customarily given to the prospective bride, whether or not her fiancé or his family can afford it, is reminiscent of the bride-price paid in some primitive societies, and is an example of how traditional our marriage customs are.

All of the traditions surrounding an engagement are designed to enhance the prestige of the woman. *Her* picture appears with the newspaper announcement, *she* receives an expensive piece of jewelry, *she* is the object of wedding showers, and large sums of money are spent for *her* wedding gown and trousseau. The groom remains in the background, simply a necessary accessory to the wedding plans, and many a man has had the uncomfortable feeling that his prospective bride found her wedding plans more exciting and rewarding than she found her future husband. For many women, their engagement period is the most prestigious of their lives. For a short while, they ride on the heady wave of excitement that surrounds a bride-to-be. They are photographed, fitted, admired, and envied, and they have the fun of selecting furnishings for their new home. Unfortunately, there are many women who become engaged and marry precisely for that reason—for the excitement of being the center of attention and of being envied by their friends. Those who do so find to their sorrow that an engaged girl is glamorous and admired, but she soon loses her glamour when she joins the unromantic ranks of married women who spend a considerable amount of time in front of the kitchen sink.

Many women who reject the traditional engagement trappings find that their mothers react with outraged indignation. "I've given gifts to hundreds of brides, now *their* parents are going to give to *you!*" or "I've planned your wedding since you were a baby. You're not going to deprive me of it now!" are frequently the reactions of the mother of a bride-to-be who wants to slip off and quietly be married in private. Many women, therefore, find themselves caught in the confusion and tiring preparation of a big wedding when their mothers are the only ones who are enjoying it. Mothers who insist that their daughters have elaborate weddings when their daughters would prefer private ceremonies should remember that a wedding is a personal affair, and not a spectacular performance for friends and relatives.

DATING FAILURES

Rarely does a person progress smoothly from casual dating to marriage without encountering some failures in one's dating experiences. A date is considered a failure if neither person enjoyed the activity or the company of the other, or if only one person had a good time. Sometimes failures occur because one or both lack social skills, are lacking in self-confidence, or are insecure. About 80 percent of dating failures, in fact, have been attributed to behavioral factors (Albrecht, 1972).

Either a man or a woman may turn off his or her date by drinking too much, for example, or by being sexually exploitative. Similarly, if either talks too much about oneself, or fails to introduce the other to acquaintances,or is sarcastic or intolerant, the date may well end in failure. A date may also go sour because one partner lacks social skills that are important to the other, such as dancing. And every man has probably had the unhappy experience of dating a woman who ordered too much to eat or asked to be taken to a place that was too expensive, and every woman has probably had a date with a man who had no plans for the evening and seemed permanently unable to suggest any activity.

There can also be circumstantial or personal factors that can cause a date to be a failure, and each accounts for 10 percent of dating failures (Albrecht, 1972). If it rains on a couple's first date, when they had planned a picnic, for example, the date may be unsatisfying to both because they are not well acquainted enough to alter their plans to something equally pleasurable.

Similarly, if plans have been made to attend a concert or play and the couple discover that tickets are not available, disappointment on the part of one or both may be so great that the date is considered a failure. About two-thirds of all dates that fail occur on the first date, but even couples who are engaged or going steady may have an occasional date that is frustrating for one reason or another (Albrecht, 1972).

Blind dates seem to be particularly fraught with peril for college men and women, accounting for about one-half of the dating failures of college men and one-fourth of the failures for college women. Blind dates are not so often disappointing for high school students, as they account for less than one-fourth of all dating failures in that group (Albrecht, 1972).

On the college scene, fraternity parties to which men bring blind dates may go sour, especially on a big football weekend or homecoming, because of the length of time that the couple spend together. A man and woman may exhaust their conversational topics in the first half-hour, but they are stuck with each other for many more hours. The main complaint that women have in relation to dating failures associated with fraternity parties is that the men drink too much alcohol and then are unable to function socially. Men more often complain that their blind date to a fraternity party was unattractive or not dressed properly. Fraternity parties are probably the setting of so many dating failures because of the pressure that fraternity brothers put on each other to bring a date, even if a man has a steady girlfriend at another college or back in his hometown and is not dating women on his own campus (Albrecht, 1972).

In spite of the fact that a dating failure can be embarrassing, disappointing, or emotionally painful, fewer adjustment problems are encountered in young people who have experienced dating failures than in those who have not. Failure may therefore be an aid in becoming mature and in learning about oneself and one's reaction to others. The person who has had a dating failure is able to select more appropriate partners, and can decline unsuitable social opportunities with more confidence than the person who has never experienced a failure. Furthermore, a dating failure makes a successful date more appreciated and enjoyed (Albrecht, 1972).

It should be mentioned that a failure on a first date may not mean that no future relationship is possible. It is entirely possible for a first date to be a miserable failure, and for the couple to eventually become good friends or to marry each other.

SCIENTIFIC MATE SELECTION

With the advent of computers and other electronic devices, dating has been subjected to electronic and scientific scrutiny. Computer dating services have appeared in most major cities, some of which are exploitative of the lonely and the socially inept, others of which may serve as introduction services after careful screening of the applicants. One such introduction club was established and maintained for a period of ten years for research purposes alone (Wallace, 1972). A correspondence club with a total of 6033 members, the club electronically matched selected people by assessing 35 characteristics that were reported by the members in questionnaires. The members were more educated than the general population, and their occupational levels corresponded to their educational levels. More males joined the club than females, a finding that is probably universal among introduction clubs, since the public usually thinks of women members of such clubs as sex-starved and exploited by undesirable males, so that women are therefore reluctant to join introduction clubs.

When the members of the research introduction club were evaluated as to neurotic tendency, sociability, conformity, attitude toward sex, and religious orthodoxy, they were found to be slightly less neurotic, more conforming, more religious, and less inhibited in their attitudes toward sex than was true of a comparison random sample. The differences in these traits were so slight that they could have been explained by chance, but there were significant differences in the sociability rating of the club members and the comparison group, with the club members being considerably less sociable. The club members were more likely to be quiet, nonaggressive, and shy, and therefore unable to compete effectively in the dating-mating system of our society (Wallace, 1972). For the middle-aged single person, the problem of meeting eligible mates is particularly acute, and legitimate introduction clubs appear to offer promise as a method of intelligent mate selection.

WHO DATES WHOM

In our male-dominated society, the responsibility of initiating a date is usually that of the man, causing men to fear rejection and women to fear being undesirable. Whether or not a woman dates is almost completely dependent on her attractiveness to men, and a man's attraction to a woman may depend—among other things—on whether or not he believes she is attracted to him.

There is an age-old question of whether a man prefers a woman who is hard to get or one who is easy to get. Women frequently base their behavior and responses to men not on their actual feelings but on their belief in either remoteness or easy availability as the way

to dating popularity. Needless to say, success in such cases depends upon good judgment *and* good luck.

A University of Wisconsin research team reported that most men prefer a woman who is discriminating, but not *too* hard to get. Their study reported that the easy-to-get woman may be undesirable because men may fear that she will be too possessive and demanding and that she may be too sexually promiscuous. The hard-to-get woman, on the other hand, is frequently seen as possibly frigid, standoffish, and selfish. The choosy woman was seen as responsive but not promiscuous and was therefore most attractive. Rather than being hard-to-get or easy-to-get, therefore, a woman probably will be more desirable if she seems hard for *other* men to get (Walster, Piliavin, & Walster, 1973).

Attraction between men and women is probably a mystery to almost everyone. The question, "What in God's name does he see in *her?*" or "That cute girl is going with *him?*" is frequently heard from both men and women. What causes someone to like another person? Why is one person attracted to a person when another person is completely turned off by the same person? While nobody knows all the answers to these questions, there are important antecedents to attractiveness. The most important of these is simply propinquity—physical closeness. Obviously, we will like those who are nearby more than we will like those who are far away from us, because we will receive more rewards from those who are close by, and we will have to exert less energy to receive the rewards.

Similarly, we tend to like those who think the way we think and whose attitudes, opinions, and beliefs are the same as ours. The person who holds values and beliefs similar to our own is considered much brighter and more worthwhile than a person whose values and beliefs are contrary to our own. Furthermore, we like people who are similar to us in personal traits. Fun-loving people seek out other fun-loving people, and quiet, studious people seek out other quiet, studious people.

We also like people with whom we have complementary needs. When people can satisfy our needs and when we easily satisfy theirs, we will be more comfortable and the relationship will be more rewarding.

In addition to these features of attraction, we tend to like people who are competent and capable, rather than helpless and incompetent. We also like people best whose behavior is pleasant and agreeable. And perhaps most important of all, we like people who like us (Aronson, 1970).

All these antecedents would imply that we like people who bring us maximum gratification at minimum expense. However, re-

184   Dating and Mate Selection

search has shown that we also like people for whom we have suffered. Furthermore, while we like people who are competent and able, we like most the person whose competence is laced with some manifestations of human fallibility. The person who never makes a mistake is therefore less attractive than the one who occasionally errs. This may account for the fact that a Gallup poll found that President John F. Kennedy's popularity increased immediately after the Bay of Pigs fiasco. It is possible that he became more likeable when he appeared to be less than perfect. Before the Bay of Pigs incident, he had been an idol to many. His youth, good looks, intelligence, wit, charm, and courage, coupled with his wealth, athletic interests, expert political strategy, beautiful wife, charming children, and powerful, close-knit family were an awe-inspiring combination. To be revealed to the world as having human failings may have made him more likeable (Aronson, 1970).

Interestingly, we seem to like best the people whose liking for us progressed from lukewarm to warm, rather than those who appeared to like us immediately on first meeting (Aronson, 1970). It is possible that the fact that we change a person's initial negative opinion of us to a positive opinion gives us such a feeling of competence or effectiveness that we feel more ego-involved with that person. According to a theory called the **conversion effect**, a missionary would probably feel more warmth toward someone he has converted to the faith than toward someone who has always been a loyal member, since conversion would be more rewarding to the missionary's ego (Aronson, 1970). Research lends support to this theory, and everyone has probably had the experience of meeting someone whose friendliness was overwhelming and toward whom one felt no particular attraction. And we probably have all experienced a feeling of satisfaction when one who was neutral toward us in the beginning seemed to warm toward us as time passed.

The line "You always hurt the one you love" may be true, because those who are constant sources of reward have the ability to hurt by withdrawing their approval, but they cannot supply greater reward. The stranger, however, has the power for new reward, but not the power to hurt by withdrawing approval. We are therefore inclined to be indifferent to the rewards offered by those who love us and seek the approval and admiration of new people.

We also hurt those who are closest to us by displacing onto them hostility felt toward others. Since we know that our loved ones will accept us even when we are hostile, and since we fear that those toward whom we really feel hostile will reject us if we openly express hostility toward them, we unfairly "take it out" on the persons who love us.

When we hurt those who love us by being indifferent to their approval, however, they almost always are inspired to react in a kindly way rather than in a retaliatory manner because they wish to reestablish the intensity of the relationship.

Couples who fail to give honest feedback—both negative and positive—are more likely to reach a plateau where neither has the ability to provide greater reward to the other any more. If two people remain honest and open, rather than falsely approving one another's every move, their relationship will be less likely to become dulled by indifference and frustration (Aronson, 1970), and they will remain attractive to one another.

SEX APPEAL

No matter how often psychologists and other researchers report the factors that go into making up one's feeling of liking for another person, it is commonly known that the factor which most frequently determines whether or not a woman is asked for a date or whether a man is accepted by a woman is not propinquity, similarity of values, or any of the other factors that go into making a person like another person. The determining factor is often simply sex appeal. A man may *like* the woman who is his lab partner, who shares his views and opinions, and who likes and agrees with him. Unless she has some physical characteristic that is sexually appealing to him, however, he may not consider her a possible romantic interest. Sex appeal is almost synonymous with physical attractiveness (Byrne, 1971), and the physical characteristics that are sexually arousing depend largely on cultural dictates. For example, the artificially distended lips of African Ubangi women or the deformed "lotus" feet of Chinese women of the past would not excite sexual passions in American men, but they do and did in African and Chinese men (Gadpaille, 1971). Similarly, the buxom women of Lillian Russell's time were found highly desirable by men, while men of today desire women who are slim and trim. While most people are influenced by cultural standards, every person forms views of what is and what is not sexually appealing from relationships during childhood with his parents and other significant adults in his life (Gadpaille, 1971). A man whose mother was tall and willowy, and who had a close, loving relationship with her, is more likely to be attracted to tall, willowy women than he will be to short, rounded women. Conversely, if his relationship with his tall, slim mother was full of discord and unpleasantness, he will probably be attracted only to short, rounded women, and may be turned off by tall, slim women.

Similarly, a favorite aunt or uncle or close family friend may become an unconscious prototype of what a sexually attractive person looks like (Gadpaille, 1971).

It would make life much less complicated and frustrating if every person were sexually attracted to a person who shared one's own sexual values and who wanted to engage in sexual activity with the same frequency. Unfortunately, this is not the case, and a person may be sexually attracted to another person who is completely turned off by him.

To make matters more complicated, a person tends to approach only those people by whom he believes he has a chance of being accepted. Men and women who become couples are usually about equal in physical attractiveness since highly desirable men do not often approach unattractive women—the prize seems undesirable—and undesirable men do not approach highly attractive women—they do not feel that they can be interesting to them (Murstein, 1971). Unfortunately, many men who consider themselves undesirable may be quite desirable but their low self-concepts prevent them from making the approaches.

While a discussion of what turns a person on and why applies to romantic or sexual involvements that may or may not lead to marriage, there are also other relationships, usually marriage or a long-term affair, that are based solely on greed. A woman who has an ideal man in mind, therefore, may jump at the chance to be the wife or mistress of a bandy-legged, bald, fat millionaire, reasoning that she can take her ideal man as a lover, or, more likely, that what she gets by way of financial security and such things as a fine home, clothes, servants, and travel, will more than make up for the physical attractiveness and other qualities on which she is closing the door. Or a young man with a healthy response to young women may cheerfully become the companion or husband of a rich older widow. The average person, however, has neither the opportunity nor the willingness to barter body for bounty, and will instead try to marry someone who comes as close as possible to his or her physical ideal.

FALLING IN LOVE

Let us assume that our hero is tall and broad-shouldered, and that he has been blessed with a flawless complexion and seductive brown eyes. Let us further assume that he is turned on by short, dark-haired, large-breasted women, and that there is a woman who answers that description who sits next to him in his Ceramics II class. She is friendly, obviously likes him, shares his opinions and beliefs, has a similar religious background, and is turned on by tall, broad-shouldered, brown-eyed men. Will they "fall in love"?

Research indicates that they will do so only if certain conditions exist. If each could be injected with adrenaline at the same time, for example, causing palpitations of the heart, nervous tremor, flushing, and accelerated breathing, the experience of falling in love would occur if both identified their feelings as passionate love. Physical arousal, then, is a precondition to love, and an aroused person is more likely to respond with affection than an unaroused person is (Walster & Berscheid, 1971).

Some researchers believe that the emotion that people label "love" can be excited by either positive or negative feelings, and that the crucial factor is simply that the emotion be an intensely felt one. According to this theory, it matters little whether a person is agitated because of anger or because of sexual frustration—the important factor is that the person himself labels his feelings as passionate love (Walster & Berscheid, 1971). It is perhaps for this reason that the hard-to-get woman frequently arouses passion in a man, and that the famous love affairs of real and fictitious people usually have been marked by some barrier that frustrated the lovers and kept them apart. Lovers such as Heloise and Abelard, Romeo and Juliet, Tristan and Iseult, and Charlie Brown and the Little Red-Haired Girl all experienced some form of frustration that may have kept their love kindled.

Vassilikos (1964) told the story of a little fish who was a bird from the waist up and a little bird who was a fish from the waist up. The two were madly in love, and the Fish-Bird would moan, "What a

pity for both of us," while the Bird-Fish would sagely answer, "No, what luck for both of us. This way we'll always be in love because we'll always be separated."

It appears, then, that passionate love can be aroused by fear, frustration, or rejection, as well as by sexual gratification, excitement, companionship, or joy in each other's presence (Walster & Berscheid, 1971). Therefore, emotions such as sexual gratification and jealousy may erroneously be considered love by the person who wishes to dignify sexual or insecure feelings by lofty terms. Furthermore, if a person believes oneself to be a romantic, he or she will label the intense emotions as love more often than the person who considers himself or herself nonromantic, even though their emotional responses may be the same (Walster & Berscheid, 1971).

Whether or not a person falls in love with another person also depends to a large extent on the recipient's self-confidence and self-image. Even if all other conditions are perfect for a man to label his emotions as love, his esteem for a women will be lowered if she is insecure or demanding, or sets forth the reasons why she believes that her boyfriend doesn't love her. He may label his feelings as love, however, for a woman to whom he ordinarily would not be strongly attracted, but who has a great deal of self-confidence and considers herself sexually attractive (Walster & Berscheid, 1971).

CHOOSING A MATE

The reasons most often given by people as to *why* they marry usually include love, companionship, security, sex, and children. Under ideal conditions, people progress from casually dating as many people as possible to narrowing their field to a more limited set of partners to whom they are especially attracted, then falling in love with one of those persons and marrying. Nothing in life is ideal, however, and a person may fall in love with another person who is ideal in every way except as a marriage partner. A man may have all the physical and intellectual characteristics that attract a woman, for example, and he may be strongly attracted to her. They may progress to the point that their emotions lead them to believe they are "in love." It is at this point that each must evaluate the relationship and the other person, and decide if the other is a person with whom one can have a successful and satisfying marriage. If the woman in question has strong financial security needs, and the man she loves has little ambition for material success, they would do well to question the wisdom of marrying. Among the million other unfortunate facts with which people must live is the fact that we may love many people, but there may be relatively few with whom we could have a satisfying marriage.

Theories about how mates are chosen state that there are elements of both conscious and unconscious motivation operating. Murstein (1976) proposes that Americans' approach to marriage is a relatively conscious, bargaining one, in which there is an "exchange principle" that is based on profit, rewards, costs, assets, and liabilities.

In addition to the personal factors that may prevent a couple from marrying, there are societal rules that must be considered. There is no known society that allows an individual to marry any person he might choose, even though that person is of the opposite sex. Every society has established elaborate rules and regulations for marriage and for specifying the categories of people who may or may not marry.

The two general rules regulating the choice of a mate are endogamy and exogamy. **Endogamy** simply means marrying a person within one's own nationality, race, religion, community, tribe, social class, or other similar group. Religious endogamy is practiced in varying degrees in various parts of the world but is becoming less a rule in our own society. A generation ago, marriages between Jews and Gentiles or Catholics and Protestants (or even Baptists and Methodists) were unusual enough to cause dismay among the families and the churches involved, but such marriages are much more common and accepted now.

Racial endogamy is also becoming less firmly enforced in our society, and black-white marriages are more acceptable, though still uncommon. Until fairly recently, there were legal sanctions in the United States against interracial marriage, particularly between blacks and whites. As of 1960, 29 states had laws prohibiting interracial marriages between whites and blacks, Chinese, Japanese, and Filipinos. Some states also prohibited marriage between whites and American Indians. By 1967, only 16 states retained statutes prohibiting racial intermarriage when the United States Supreme Court declared that ethnic or racial background could not be made a condition for marriage (*Loving* v. *State of Virginia,* June 1967).

Even in societies with tribal forms of government, **tribal endogamy**—members of one tribe forbidden to marry members of another tribe—is rarely found. It is most common in India, where the caste system is prevalent and members of one caste cannot marry outside their caste. However, in some parts of India there are variations that allow people in different levels of the same caste to marry.

Exogamy requires an individual to marry outside one's own group—usually the nuclear family or other kinship group—and is an extension of the incest taboo. A person therefore rejects those who are different socially, racially, and religiously when choosing a mate, but is not allowed to marry those who are most like him—close relatives (Rodman, 1965). Restrictions also have been imposed on the selection of a suitable mate by the state on the premise that some unions would be detrimental to the future of society. These restrictions prevent the marriage of persons below legal age of consent, those who live in other states, and those who are mentally incompetent or who have a venereal disease. To control mate selection, the state has set up impediments such as delays for premarital examinations and required waiting periods for the remarriage of divorced persons.

In the United States, most states require both men and women to have a physical examination for venereal disease before they can be married. The examination has to be from 7 to 40 days before the marriage ceremony, and if the wedding is unreasonably delayed, the examination must be performed again. In addition to venereal disease examinations, 2 states require a physician's statement certifying that both prospective mates are free of infectious or advanced TB, and in 17 states marriage between epileptics is prohibited, although epilepsy is not genetic (Landis & Landis, 1973).

In most "civilized" nations, there are laws regulating the age at which males and females can become married. In many Central and South American countries, boys of 14 and girls of 12 are allowed to marry, and more than half of the states in the United States allow men of 18 and women of 16 to marry if their parents give their consent. Without their parents' consent, the minimum age of legal marriage is usually 21 for men and 18 for women. Most people who marry when they are between 14 and 17 are female, and the largest percentage of them come from the South. Generally, there is a trend toward fewer marriages among females aged 14 to 17. In 1975, there were 68 per 1000 females who were 14 to 17 at the time of their first marriage. This compares with 83 per 1000 in 1970, and 88 per 1000 in 1960 (Statistical Abstract, 1977). Many of these early marriages are probably the result of premarital pregnancy, as the proportion of women with a first child born shortly after marriage is highest for brides aged 14 to 17 at marriage (U.S. Bureau of the Census, 1976).

The tendency to marry within the same class, rank, or profession is almost an unwritten law that is universally practiced in primitive as well as in civilized societies, and is accounted for in large part by the influence of social class and family on the mate selection process (Hollingshead, 1960; Reiss, 1965). A person's parents have

a great deal to do with the person he chooses as a mate (Bates, 1942) because of their influence on the persisting value system that a child develops before maturity (Davis, 1940; Sussman, 1963). It is within the framework of this value system that a person chooses a marriage partner (Hudson & Henze, 1972).

The influence of parents upon their children's dating pattern can be seen by the fact that parents usually insist that their children date people from their own age and social group when they begin dating. A person's dating pattern is thus structured by these initial dating experiences. Since he chooses a mate from the circle of people whom he dates, his early conditioning limits his choices of marital partners (Coombs, 1962).

In view of the changes in lifestyles and attitudes during the last decade, one might expect today's young people to have different sets of values than those their parents had when selecting mates. Studies have found, however, that there was very little difference in the traits that college men and women valued in a marriage partner in 1939, 1956, and in 1967 (Hill, 1945; Hudson & Henze, 1972; McGinnis, 1959). In the three studies, college students ranked 18 characteristics according to their importance in a mate, and there was surprisingly little difference across the time span of 28 years in the weights attached to the traits being ranked. Among the women, in fact, there was no trait consistently evaluated as more important in 1956 or 1967 than in 1939. In each time period, emotional stability and dependable character ranked first and second in importance to women. The least weight was given by women to good looks and similar political background of prospective marriage partners.

Similarly, males ranked dependable character as the most indispensable personal characteristic in a mate in all three time periods. There was a difference in the emphasis that men put on good looks, with good looks being more important to the men in the 1967 survey than to the males in either the 1957 or the 1939 study. For both males and females, chastity declined in importance to a greater extent than any other characteristic. The double standard continues to exist, however, as men evaluated virginity as more important for wives than women did for husbands. The authors of the study concluded that young people of today have not departed from the traditional values of their parents as much as they would like to think they have (or as much as their parents fear they have). The values of the youth of today—at least regarding mate selection—appear to be much the same as they were a generation ago (Hudson & Henze, 1972).

"Wow! Did you see the eyes on <u>that</u> one?"

PREDICTING SUCCESS IN MARRIAGE

To return to our mutually attracted hero and heroine, suppose they each evaluate the traits the other possesses and decide that each embodies all the characteristics that the other wants in a mate. Can they then assume that they can marry and live happily ever after? Does it matter that he thoroughly enjoys television and she hates it, or that she "loves" to go to parties and social functions while he prefers quiet evenings at home. When their sexual passion is reduced from a roaring blaze to a warm glow, will there be anything else to interest them and hold them together?

While there are no hard and fast rules of thumb to predict happiness in marriage, there are some general findings that should be taken into consideration by any couple who are in love and considering marriage. The more mature a couple is and the longer they have been acquainted, for example, the better their chance of marital adjustment. Couples in their late 20s or 30s and 40s and older, therefore, have a better chance of marital bliss than do couples in their early 20s. If our hero has previously experienced divorce, he is less likely to remain married when problems arise than a man who has not been divorced. (The same is not true of women who have been divorced.) Other factors that enhance a couple's chances of marital success are similar religious faith, advanced education, and parents who were happily married, although a man whose parents were divorced is a poorer marital risk than a woman whose parents were divorced (Stephens, 1970). Factors that are indicators of probable marital difficulties are premarital pregnancy, social class differences, parental disapproval, and unsociability on the part of either or both partners.

It is frequently said that common interests are basic to a successful marriage, and research has tended to confirm that well-adjusted couples more frequently have the same interests (Burgess & Cottrell, 1939; Kirkpatrick, 1937). It may be important, however, to consider what interests the couple share. If a couple's main interest in common is drinking and dancing, for example, they are more likely to divorce than they are if their interests are in romantic love, sexual relations, owning a home, children, or religious activities (Burgess & Cottrell, 1939; Locke, 1951). Good adjustment is also associated with having several friends in common and having an equal interest in sex (Locke, 1951). Obviously, it goes without saying that good mental health is a vital component in a successful marriage.

Poorly adjusted couples are frequently interested primarily in fame or success, drinking, money, travel, commercial entertainment, and companionship to escape loneliness. The women in poorly adjusted marriages are more likely to have married in order to escape their families than for love (Locke, 1951). It does not appear, therefore, that mutuality of interests alone is the crucial factor in predicting good marital adjustment. Instead, the type of mutual interest is important. Furthermore, almost as many happy couples had no common interests at the time of their engagement as those who did (Locke, 1951).

As has been mentioned before, it is also important that prospective marriage partners share similar views on sex roles after marriage. A man and woman who are considering marrying each other might consider the following quote from the Reverend Billy Graham: "In the sight of God there is equality between men and women but when it comes to governmental arrangements in the home, the husband is the head. God says he cannot answer prayers which come from a woman who doesn't take her God-given place in the home" (Landis & Landis, 1973). Does that start an argument? Does it lead to outraged mutterings on the part of either? Or does it result in nods of agreement? If only one partner finds the idea of God-given subordination of a woman in the home unacceptable, there will be discord in the marriage unless one or the other changes his views. (Today, most people would not be so likely to portray God as a "male chauvinist.")

The most salient factor in considering mate selection might be simply the motivation behind each person's desire to marry. There has been so much social pressure—especially in the recent past—on young people to marry that many begin to hunt a mate simply because they feel that it is expected of them, and not because they are educationally, emotionally, financially, or sexually ready for marriage. In Tripoli, Libya, recently, the People's Committee of Tripoli declared bachelors a "menace to family life" and ordered the evacuation of all bachelors from apartments and shops in any areas of the Libyan capital.

While few in America would actually banish all unmarried men or women from their midst, there is much reward given to those who decide to marry and little reward given to those who remain single and put forth no effort to find a mate. Marrying "because one's friends are all married" and "it seems the thing to do" are poor motives and poor predictors for marital happiness. Certainly a person should not marry because his mother or aunt or employer exerts pressure on him to do so. Marrying because one wants a regular sexual partner readily available is an equally poor reason to marry. Even if two people are sexually attracted to each other, like each other, share common interests and backgrounds, and are ideal marital risks insofar as the predictors of marital adjustment are concerned, these are not sufficient reasons to marry unless they also have a strong desire to establish a home and to commit themselves to one another.

THE MARRIAGE RITUAL

Billions are spent annually in this country on weddings and wedding gifts. The traditional wedding ceremony, with the bride floating down the aisle in a cloud of white lace and tulle, followed by her attendants in their pastel gowns, is so firmly fixed in the minds of the public that no department store doll display would be complete without a bride doll with an elaborate bridal costume. Wedding showers, formal wedding invitations, the wedding rings, the photographer, and the wedding reception with all its fixed procedures make up the ritualistic stamp of approval that society gives to a marrying man and woman. By giving the bride a pristine, virginal appearance, society divests the marriage ceremony of sexual overtones, and by showering the couple with gifts and congratulations, friends and relatives deny the fallibility and dissatisfactions that abound within marriage, thus temporarily recapturing for themselves the illusion of the "so they were married and lived happily ever after" myth.

Our marriage rituals are an outgrowth of the rituals of primitive societies, in which marriages are either contracted with consideration or without consideration. If the marriage is **with consideration**, the groom supplies a bride-price, or he may exchange a sister or other female relative for a wife. He may also perform services for the bride's parents in exchange for her.

A marriage **without consideration** may involve an exchange of goods of similar value between the parents of the bride and groom, or the bride's parents may give the groom's parents a dowry. In the absence of economic transactions, primitive marriages may be contracted by wife-capture, elopement, or an initiation period of cohabitation. (Elopement and living together before marriage, of course, are also practiced in our own society.)

Wife-capture is exceptionally rare as a means of marriage, and most elopements are later solemnized through the performance of the rites and customs of the particular society involved. Some form of ceremonial fighting or sham struggle and capture are part of wedding rituals in a large number of primitive cultures. The purpose of these forays appears to be that of emphasizing the loss of a valued member of the family. Supposedly, these customs are survivals of the past when the battles were genuine, although no real evidence has been brought to light to substantiate this theory (Westermarck, 1922).

A bride-price may be symbolic, such as the shell money still used as a symbolic exchange of gifts between two families on the isle of Yap, or it may be in the form of an actual sum of money paid to the bride's family. In Afghanistan, for example, a woman's worth is judged by her potential as an earner, in spite of a recently enacted law that prohibits bride-buying. In the Afghanistan countryside, an accomplished carpet weaver may fetch as much as $2500, but a usual fee is about $100. Since the average per capita income is somewhat less than $100, this represents a considerable sum.

Societies that exact a bride-price appear to expect a child to be delivered as repayment (Perutz, 1972). In primitive societies in which there is no bride-price, such as in some parts of Melanesia and Papua, contraception, abortion, and infanticide have traditionally been freely practiced by women, with no interference from men (Bunzel, 1938), but in societies in which men pay a bride-price, a

man may be allowed to demand his bride-price back and to repudiate his wife if she does not produce a child (Perutz, 1972).

Murdock (1949) found that some sort of consideration was usually demanded in cases where rules of residence required the bride to leave the home of her parents. This is especially common if the bride leaves not only her home but also the locale in which her family lives. An exception to this rule is found in cases in which a family has only daughters. In such cases one daughter is married without the usual bride-price and her husband resides with her family and assumes the role of a son. A bride-price is not only a form of compensation for a daughter who leaves the home of her parents when she marries, but a guarantee that she will not be mistreated in her new home. In most cases, if she is mistreated she can return to her parent's home and her husband forfeits the bride-price. This fee is almost never construed as equivalent to that given for a slave or a chattel.

Among the Kwakiutl of British Columbia, the bride-price has also been involved in their matrilineal rules of descent by which family names descend through the female line. When a man married, he gave a gift to his bride's parents. When she had a child, her father

The Marriage Ritual **199**

gave her husband a name and a rank and property that was of greater value than the bride-price. The marriage debt paid, the woman was free to return to her original home. If her husband elected to keep her, he had to pay another bride-price. With the birth of their next child, he was given another name and higher rank. A woman could marry the same man as many as four times, and each time a new transaction was made. With the birth of each child, the man's rank in the family was increased (Bunzel, 1938).

In societies in which mutual consent is not practiced, marriages are arranged by parents for social, economic, political, and other reasons. There are some cases in which the bride and groom do not meet until the day of their wedding. In some societies, infant betrothal—and even infant or child marriage—is still practiced. There may be an exchange of property involved in order to make the agreement binding.

Despite the custom of arranged marriages in some societies, mutual consent, or free choice, seems to play an important role in most marriages. Often prearranged unions have been broken by one of the members directly involved. Freedom of choice in selecting a mate has been so predominant in our culture that it can be difficult to picture a marriage that does not involve such freedom, but this choice has been quite restricted in other societies (Linton, 1936). Modern ethnographic research shows that love and freedom of choice in mate selection are increasing throughout the world and are found in many geographic areas. Some societies are enacting laws forbidding former customs that allowed parents to arrange marriages for their children without their consent—in Libya, for example. Also, the new Libyan law provides that a couple may marry against their parents' wishes.

In other parts of the world, changes in the ritual of marriage are also being noted. Mass marriages are becoming popular in many Asian countries as a means for couples to avoid beginning their marriages in debt. In a mass wedding, several hundred brides and grooms exchange their vows at the same time and then share the expense of a single banquet. Each couple may be allowed to invite one table of family and friends. By combining the wedding ceremony, banquet, and honeymoon trip, the couples are able to reduce considerably the expense of their wedding.

LAWS REGULATING MARRIAGE

In the United States, laws regulating marriage vary from state to state. Unless the marrying couple are Quaker or members of certain other religious groups, they must get a marriage license before they can be married. A license allows a couple to be married by a minister or a civil authority, but it does not obligate any official to perform the wedding ceremony. If any official has personal objections to performing the ceremony, he or she may decline to do so. To prevent hasty marriages, there is in most states a waiting period of about five days between the issuance of the license and the time that it is requested or the time that it becomes valid. However, in most states, couples may apply to a judge to have the waiting period waived if there are extenuating circumstances, such as pregnancy or a soldier groom-to-be who is about to be shipped overseas. In all states, couples have a choice of being married by either religious or civil authorities. Those who are married by civil authorities most often choose a Justice of the Peace, but the majority of marriages are performed by a minister, priest, or rabbi (Landis & Landis, 1973). In many states, Quakers and other denominations who have special methods of solemnizing their marriage are exempted from the laws requiring an officiant.

If a couple marry without the legal right to do so, their marriage is void and it is not necessary to have it annulled to end it. It simply never existed. A man who marries more than one woman, for example, has only one valid marriage, and his children by his invalid marriage may or may not be considered legitimate, depending on the laws of the state in which he lives. However, despite the fact that he has only one legal spouse, he has committed bigamy and may be prosecuted for it.

Other marriages may be voidable because one or both partners is below legal age, or because of insanity, fraud, impotence, or other factors, but marriage in these cases must be dissolved through an annulment. When a marriage has been annulled, the marriage is legally considered never to have existed, and neither party is entitled to further rights of support or to property that belonged to the other before marriage. Children of an annulled marriage have the same status as children of a void marriage. One-third of all annulments occur within the first year of marriage, and at least a quarter of them are due to one or both parties being under legal age. In most states, however, a voidable marriage between underage persons is usually considered legal unless some action is taken to have it annulled. In certain states, if a man and woman agree to live together as husband and wife and present themselves to the world as such, without obtaining a license or having a ceremony, their union is as legally binding as if they had married with all the legal and ritualistic traditions. Called common-law marriage, such unions are valid in 14 states and are recognized as valid in 10 more. If

there are any legal reasons why a couple cannot be married with a license and ceremony, a common-law marriage is invalid, but otherwise a common-law marriage must be dissolved through divorce before either can remarry, and property and inheritance rights apply as if there had been a regular marriage.

In many parts of the world, there are indications of a move toward reform of laws pertaining to marriage. In Finland, a proposed government reform of the marriage laws would make civil weddings compulsory for all marrying couples. Although 90 percent of Finnish weddings are now held in a church, the committee submitting the proposed marriage reforms suggested that a church wedding could be held after the civil ceremony, but that only the civil wedding would be legally recognized. The committee was formed after the Nordic Council, comprising Finland, Sweden, Norway, Denmark, and Iceland, recommended that its member governments achieve similar matrimonial laws.

In the United States, there have been expressions of protest from women who object to the custom of taking their husband's surname when they marry. Legally, women have the right to retain their maiden name, but the custom of adopting the husband's surname is so entrenched that women who do not do so are relatively few—although there will probably be more and more who will go against custom. Some women have chosen to use both their own and their husband's name, inserting a hyphen between them. Women's groups have asked for adoption of the custom of retaining their own names and giving their children both the mother's and the father's surname, as is the custom in Latin American countries. Another suggestion is that a woman have the option of retaining her maiden name or taking her husband's name when she marries, as is the custom in Russia, Denmark, and France. In many states, a married woman cannot change her name as a single woman can, and if she divorces, she must retain her former husband's name unless she brings suit to resume her maiden name. If she remarries, of course, she adopts the name of her new husband (Perutz, 1972).

CONCLUSION

Although it may seem a giant leap from the point at which John asks Mary to the movies to the point at which either is concerned with the inequalities in the law regarding marriage or the rights of married parties, it is actually not a great leap at all. We marry those whom we date, and our laws both reflect and determine our attitudes toward marriage and toward sex roles in our society. Neither the marriage laws nor the institution of marriage can exist without the other, and both result from the fact that men and women are sexually attracted to one another, get to know one another because of that attraction, develop an emotional as well as physical intimacy with one another through dating, and become legally joined according to the laws of their particular geographic location. Which is to say that every time a John invites a Mary to a movie, the possibility exists that someday they may marry and become subject to laws and established customs regulating marriage in our society.

CHAPTER 8

HUMAN SEXUALITY

Sex is never an emergency.   ELAINE C. PIERSON

Different types of dating are characterized by different forms of sexual behavior, ranging from a goodnight kiss to heavy petting or sexual intercourse. It is perhaps a reflection of the genital obsession of our society that the words "sexual activity" generally are thought to convey the meaning of sexual intercourse. But, of course, the term "sexual activity" embraces many forms of physical contact between two people who are physically attracted to one another, or by one person alone who desires release from sexual tension.

FORMS OF SEXUAL EXPRESSION

There are five common methods of sexual expression: masturbation, nocturnal orgasm, heterosexual petting, homosexual relations, and heterosexual intercourse, with the vast majority of people engaging in at least one of these forms of sexuality during their lifetime, and most engaging in more than one. A sixth form, sexual contact with animals (**bestiality**) is usually confined to boys who live in rural areas and lack available sexual partners. About half of all farm boys have had some sexual contact with animals, but it usually constitutes an experimental activity rather than a sexual pattern.

Masturbation. Masturbation is a sexual outlet that is common among both men and women, whether they are unmarried or married. Youngsters discover masturbation at an early age and usually enjoy the practice in spite of dire (and erroneous) warnings from their elders that they will go crazy, get acne, lose all their hair, or some other fallacious myth. Many young people believe the warnings given by their elders and peers, but they doggedly continue to masturbate anyway. Masturbation, if continued long enough, leads only to orgasm, and not to any of the unpleasant and fearful consequences that parents frequently hold up to children in order to frighten them into ceasing their masturbatory activity. In contrast to our own society, Micronesian mothers pacify irritable baby boys by caressing their penises, and children therefore learn early to enjoy the pleasure of sexually stimulating themselves.

As American youngsters reach adolescence, they continue to masturbate as a substitute for sexual intercourse. For young people who have no sexual partners, masturbation is the most sensible alternative to sexual intercourse. Also, through masturbation boys and girls can discover their own sexual responses and can develop their own sexuality. By becoming familiar with their own bodies and their own preferences in sexual arousal, they can develop the self-awareness and self-confidence that lead to open and frank communication with future sexual partners. Furthermore, a person who is able to touch and stimulate his or her own body in a loving and erotic way will be better able to give pleasure to another person through stroking and touching. Masturbation is therefore not only a substitute for sexual intercourse, it is a learning experience that can enhance one's own sexual experiences with other people as well as one's ability to give sexual pleasure to others. Practically all authorities in the area of human sexuality state freely not only that masturbation is not harmful, but that it is a beneficial as well as pleasurable act for both males and females (McCary, 1971).

Although many fathers become upset when they discover their sons masturbating, about 95 percent of all men admit to having masturbated to orgasm at some time in their lives (and psychologists believe that the other 5 percent may be lying about it). Each generation apparently must discover masturbation on its own, however. Most boys learn how to masturbate by being told about it by another boy, while girls usually learn about masturbation from bodily experimentation and through accidental stimulation. Even the most sexually uninhibited parents rarely instruct their own children in the act of masturbation.

There is no such thing as a "normal" amount of masturbation. Boys are frequently warned against "excessive masturbation," but if the person doing the warning is asked to define the normal amount of masturbation, his answer will do little more than reveal his own masturbatory habits. If an adult male tells an adolescent male that it is normal to masturbate about twice a week, but no more, you can be sure that he masturbated about twice a week in his youth. If he says that seven times a week is allowable, then seven times a week was probably his norm. If a youngster is lucky, he will find an adult who masturbated at a prodigious rate in his youth, and who uses that figure as a ceiling on the amount of "normal" masturbation. The truth is that the human body has its own sexual capacity, and that capacity varies from individual to individual. When a given person's sexual needs are completely satisfied, his body will refuse to respond to further sexual activity. Just as there are individual differences in the amount of food people want to eat, there are individual differences in the amount of sexual activity they require. One person may masturbate one time a week and be perfectly contented with that amount. His next-door neighbor may masturbate fourteen times a week. Neither is either undersexed or oversexed, and each develops his own individual norm.

As a man ages, he may continue to masturbate, but the incidence declines steadily. The more education a man has, the more likely he is to masturbate, at least on a sporadic basis, throughout his life. About 70 percent of married men who are college-educated masturbate occasionally. Orthodox Jews and devout Roman Catholics masturbate less frequently than do Protestant men, and Protestant men who are religiously inactive masturbate more frequently than any other group (Kinsey et al., 1948).

Although the incidence of deliberate masturbation to orgasm is lower in women than it is in men, a majority of all women masturbate at some time in their lives, even if they are not aware of it. Any activity that produces a pleasurable stimulation of the genitals is a form of masturbation, even if the stimulation is indirect, such as that from horseback riding. It is probably no accident that so many teenage girls have a passion for horses and horseback riding at a time when their budding sexuality is just awakening. While they are still fearful of heterosexual contact, horseback riding provides pleasurable stimulation of the erogenous zones around their vulva and inner thighs, while at the same time allowing them to experience a feeling of mastery over the animal beneath them.

While men tend to masturbate with less frequency as they grow older, women tend to masturbate more frequently up to middle age, and then the frequency remains fairly constant. About 63 percent of college-educated women, 59 percent of high-school-educated women, and 34 percent of grade-school-educated women masturbate at some time in their lifetimes. Again, there is no norm in female masturbation. One woman may masturbate once or twice in a lifetime, and another woman may have as many as 100 orgasms in a single masturbatory session. Women who masturbate to the point of orgasm, however, usually do so about every two to four weeks, regardless of age or marital status, although there are, to be sure, many women who masturbate more frequently than this (Kinsey et al., 1953). Recent research has found an increase in frequency of masturbation among single women and men in the mid-20s to mid-30s age group since the Kinsey studies (Hunt, 1973a).

Most women prefer to masturbate by manipulating their genitals manually or with an electric vibrator, while others may masturbate by directing a stream of water on their vulva, or, less frequently, by thigh pressure, muscular tension, or fantasy without physical stimulation. Women who cannot achieve an orgasm through sexual intercourse rarely fail to be orgasmic during masturbation—a climax is reached 95 percent of the time in masturbation. Women also reach orgasm more quickly through masturbation than they do through other forms of sexual stimulation. Three-fourths of all women reach orgasm in less than 4 minutes through masturbation, while the average woman requires at least 16 minutes of vaginal penetration during sexual intercourse to reach orgasm and many require intromission to last as long as 20 minutes (Gebhard, 1966; Kinsey et al., 1953).

Women frequently fear that their masturbatory activity will cause them to be unresponsive to the "real thing" when they marry. The fact is that women who have experienced masturbation to orgasm are far more likely to reach orgasm through sexual intercourse during their first year of marriage than are women who have never masturbated to orgasm before marriage.

Nocturnal orgasm. Although both men and women experience **nocturnal orgasms**, men have evidence of their "wet dreams" in the form of ejaculation, while women simply have the memory of their dreams. Like masturbation, the frequency of nocturnal orgasm is greater in young men and middle-aged women, with the frequency declining as a man ages and increasing as a woman approches her 40s. Kinsey found that 100 percent of the men he sampled had experienced erotic dreams and 85 percent had experienced dreams ending in orgasm. About half of all married men continue to have occasional nocturnal emissions, especially if they are college-educated. Almost all of the college men in Kinsey's study had had dreams to orgasm at some time, but only 75 percent of the grade-school-educated had done so. Young men who are still in college experience more frequent nocturnal emissions than do men their age who are not in college, probably because college men do more petting that does not culminate in intercourse, causing them to have sexual tensions that are at a higher pitch at bedtime. While only about 35 percent of the women in Kinsey's study had experienced dreams ending in orgasm, a good 70 percent had had sexual dreams. There is no correlation for women between their educational background and the frequency of their nocturnal orgasms. Unlike other forms of sexual activity, the incidence of nocturnal orgasms is not influenced by religious or educational background in women, and is not related to religious devoutness or affiliation in men (Kinsey et al., 1953).

Heterosexual petting. Any sexual contact between a man and a woman that does not culminate in intercourse is considered heterosexual petting, and is a form of premarital sexual activity that almost all married couples have experienced. Educational level and religious commitment influence both the form of premarital heterosexual petting that a person engages in, and the frequency with which he engages in it. The more formal education a person has had, the more petting he has experienced, and the more varied are his methods of petting (Bell, 1971b; Kinsey et al., 1948, 1953).

Of the total male population in the Kinsey studies, 55 to 87 percent had engaged in deep kissing; 78 to 99 percent in manual manipulation of a woman's breasts; 36 to 93 percent in mouth-breast contact, 79 to 92 percent in manual manipulation of a woman's genitals; and 9 to 18 percent (unmarried) and 4 to 60 percent (married) in oral stimulation of a woman's genitals (Kinsey et al., 1948, 1953).

There has been a significant increase in the number of single men and women who have engaged in oral-genital petting. A recent survey (Hunt, 1973a) found that 72 percent of high-school- and college-level males had experienced fellatio with a woman, in contrast to 33 percent of the males of the same age group in Kinsey's study. Although only 14 percent of the single males in the Kinsey group had engaged in cunnilingus, 69 percent of the 1973 group of males had done so.

The 1973 study also found that half of the white single women between the ages of 18 and 24 had petted to orgasm, while only about a fourth of the single women in Kinsey's group had done so by the age of 20. Similarly, two-thirds of the males in the recent study had petted to orgasm by the age of 25, while only a little more than a fourth of Kinsey's males had done so (Hunt, 1973b).

College-educated women are more likely to have experienced heavy petting than are women with less education. From 60 to 90 percent of college women have engaged in genital stimulation in an unclothed state, with more than one-fourth having these experiences with three or more partners. More than half of college-educated women have engaged in heavy petting with a partner for whom they felt no love (Davis, 1971; Kinsey et al., 1953). Heavy petting is also more prevalent than is generally supposed among high school girls. One study reported that almost 60 percent of the college women sampled reported heavy petting while still in high school (Davis, 1971).

Men usually have more petting partners than do women. More than a third of men who have petted have had 21 or more partners, while only about one-fourth have had 5 or fewer partners. The number of petting partners a woman has varies from only one to more than 20. Over one-third of all women have experienced premarital petting with more than 10 men (Bell, 1971a; Kinsey et al., 1948, 1953).

Homosexual relations. Although homosexual relations are usually not considered a part of premarital sex, there are, nevertheless, many men and women who do have homosexual relations before marriage. The incidence of homosexual experience appears to be about the same in the 1970s as it was in the late 1940s and early 1950s (Hunt, 1973a). More than one-third of all men and nearly one-fifth of all women have had some experience with homosexual relations to the point of orgasm (Athanasiou et al., 1970; Kinsey et al., 1948, 1953), while only about 4 percent of all men are exclusively homosexual all their lives (Kinsey et al., 1948), and very few women are exclusively homosexual. Most female homosexuals—**lesbians**—are actually bisexual, and only 33 percent of them are exclusively homosexual (Bieber, 1969). About one-tenth of all men continue to have some homosexual relations after marriage (Kinsey et al., 1948). The fact that an individual has experienced homosexual relations does not make him a **homosexual**—one who prefers a member of his own sex for sexual activity—any more than exceeding the speed limit on the freeway makes one a race driver. One may be done out of situational expediency, experimentation, thrill-seeking, foolhardiness, or for some similar reason, while the other is a way of life.

Premarital heterosexual intercourse. As was said earlier, heterosexual intercourse is commonly thought of as occurring in the marriage bed, but anyone who is not comatose knows that hetero-

sexual intercourse also occurs outside marriage, before marriage, and after marriage. For purposes of this discussion, only sexual intercourse occurring before marriage will be considered.

For men, the incidence of premarital intercourse has not changed appreciably since the Kinsey studies in the 1940s when it was reported that 98 percent of men with grade school education, 84 percent of men with a high school education, and 67 percent of men with a college education had had sexual intercourse before marriage. There has been a change in the age at which young men begin to be sexually active. Kinsey's studies found that about two-thirds of the noncollege men had had intercourse by the age of 17. Today nearly three-fourths of noncollege men have had intercourse by the age of 17, and more than half of those with some college have done so, in contrast to the quarter of those who had in Kinsey's sample (Hunt, 1973a). For women, the incidence of premarital intercourse is increasing, particularly among college women. Less than a third of college women were estimated to be sexually active between 1945 and 1965, while current studies indicate that the rate is now about 35 to 50 percent (Bell, 1971b; Kaats & Davis, 1970). The most significant change in the sexual behavior of college women is that their sexual partners are no longer necessarily men whom they plan to marry. A study comparing sexual practices of college women in 1958 and 1968 found that in 1958, most women who had premarital coitus were engaged to their partners. In 1968, a greater number were merely dating or going steady with their partners. Furthermore, there was less guilt among the 1968 college women about premarital intercourse than there had been a decade before (Bell & Chaskes, 1970). A 1973 study found that there has been a significant increase in the incidence of premarital sexual intercourse among women at all educational levels. Half of the married women sampled had had premarital intercourse by the age of 25, and three-fourths of the single women had done so, while only a third of the women in Kinsey's study had had premarital coitus by the same age. Less than a tenth of the 1953 sample had had intercourse by the age of 17, but twice that many have done so today. However, most of the casual intercourse seems to be among women over the age of 25. Younger women are still more likely to have had intercourse only with a man they love and plan to marry, just as their mothers did (Hunt, 1973a). Another recent study showed that of the 2372 married women sampled, 65 percent had had premarital coitus, with the younger women more likely to have engaged in premarital coitus than the older women (Bell & Balter, 1973). Most other recent studies on this aspect of human sexuality show similar results.

Unlike other forms of sexual activity, the more education a man has, the less sexual intercourse he is likely to have. Kinsey found that of men between the ages of 16 and 20, the grade-school-educated had intercourse with seven times greater frequency than the college-educated man of the same age. The less-educated males also experienced first intercourse five or six years earlier than the unmarried college-educated man did, and the man with less education continued to have more frequent coital activity than his better-educated brother did. In the Kinsey study, from 40 to 68 percent of the grade-school-educated man's total sexual outlet was from sexual intercourse, while the high-school-educated man obtained 26 to 54 percent of his total sexual outlet from intercourse, and the college-educated man only 4 to 21 percent (Kinsey et al., 1948). Those figures have increased only slightly since Kinsey's studies, although men are beginning their premarital sexual experiences at an earlier age (Hunt, 1973a).

There are changes in the emotional attitudes of college men toward premarital sex. While women are beginning to move toward the view traditionally held by men, of enjoying sex for its own sake, men are beginning to move toward the view traditionally held by women, to desire sex with women for whom they have an emotional attachment. Most studies have found that college men are now less likely to visit a prostitute than their fathers might have been, and they are less likely to exploit women from lower classes or to use trickery to seduce a woman (Davis, 1971), although one study (Frede, 1970) found a higher percentage of men having visited a prostitute than was found in the Kinsey studies.

Depending on his educational status (and his stamina) a man may have premarital intercourse only one time, or he may have as many 35 or more coitions a week. Similarly, a man may have premarital intercourse with only one woman or with as many as several hundred (Kinsey et al., 1948).

Among women in the Kinsey studies, those under the age of 20 who had premarital intercourse usually did so on the average of once every 5 or 10 weeks, while women between the ages of 21 and 25 did so about once every 3 weeks. Today, single women between 18 and 24 who have intercourse do so more than once a week (Hunt, 1973a). Only about 20 percent of women in the Kinsey study had premarital intercourse as often as 7 times a week, and 7 percent had it 14 times a week. That figure has undoubtedly increased.

Of all women who have premarital intercourse, about half still have only one partner (Hunt, 1973b). In the Kinsey study, 13 percent had 6 or more, while about one-third had from 2 to 5 partners. That finding seems to still hold true today (Bell & Balter, 1973). A

"With you, Marvin, sex always seems dirty. I guess
that's why I like you."

woman's coital activity is related to both her educational level and
her attractiveness. Those with little education tend to begin premarital intercourse at an earlier age than women with more education, and the attractive woman is more likely to become involved
in premarital sexual intercourse and to have more sexual partners
than the unattractive woman (Kaats & Davis, 1970).

THE PHYSIOLOGY OF SEX

While a complete discussion of the endocrinological, hormonal, and
anatomical aspects of human sexuality cannot be included here,
there are some basic physiological facts that every person who contemplates marriage or who has any interaction with members of
the opposite sex should know.

214 Human Sexuality

Perhaps the most significant fact about the human sexual system is that male and female systems are counterparts of one another. Until about the fifth or sixth week of prenatal life, all embryos appear to be structurally female, and the sexual characteristics of both male and female are undifferentiated. When the male hormone **androgen** is released, external male sexual structures differentiate from the embryonic cell mass into penis, foreskin, and scrotum. Since females need no such hormonal addition for the development of external female characteristics, they continue to develop sexual structures that are counterparts to the man's: clitoris, clitoral hood, and the labia minora and majora. In the rare instances in which the male embryo fails to receive androgen, he will form the same external sex organs as a female embryo, although testes and other male internal organs will be present. At birth, these male infants are identical in appearance to females and are reared as such, with the error only becoming apparent at adolescence.

Male genitalia. The first sexual structures to develop in the male are the testicles or testes. The testicles are housed in the **scrotum**, a pouch of skin that hangs just under the base of the penis. It is in the testicles that **sperm**—the fertilizing agent of the male—are produced. Each testicle contains several small chambers that contain several hundred tightly coiled seminiferous tubules, each measuring one to two feet in length. These tubules are lined with germinal tissue in which sperm are produced in a process called **spermatogenesis**. Since sperm production requires a temperature that is lower than the body's, the scrotum and testicles are supported by muscles and tissues that can raise or lower the testicles, according to the outside temperature. In cold weather, the testicles draw up closer to the warm body, and in warm weather they relax and hang farther away from the body. Spermatogenesis does not begin until the time in pubescence when the pituitary gland secretes the follicle-stimulating hormone (FSH), which, coupled with the interstitial cell-stimulating hormone (ICSH) that allows the sperm to mature, marks the beginning of sexual maturity in a male. The interstitial cells of the testes also produce the male hormone testosterone (Lloyd, 1964). It is this hormone that is responsible for a male's facial and body hair, his voice change, his muscular and skeletal development, his attraction to females, his mental attitudes, and the development, size, and function of his penis, scrotum, prostate, and seminal vesicles.

Sperm are produced in a never-ending cycle through the process of **mitosis**. When a cell divides, one of the daughter cells is a sperm-

atogonium, ready to split again and perpetuate the formation of future spermatogonia. The other daughter cell undergoes **meiotic** cell division, producing two secondary spermatocytes, each containing 22 similar (autosomal) chromosomes, and one containing an X chromosome and the other a Y. In this way, X and Y chromosomes are produced in equal numbers, and there is always a spermatogonium ready to begin the meiotic cell division process (McCary, 1978). From the testicles, the sperm are emptied into the **epididymis**, a swelling attached to each testicle, and there they mature for as long as six weeks. From the epididymis, the sperm are transported into the **vas deferens**, a small connecting tube about 18 inches long that provides passage to the **seminal vesicle**, a pouch that flanges from the end of the vas deferens as the vas enters the top of the **prostate gland** behind the bladder. Since there are two testicles, each of the accessory structures comes in pairs, but there is only one prostate gland. It is primarily the prostate gland, along with the seminal vesicle, that produces the milky secretion known as the **ejaculate** that spurts from the man's penis at the time of orgasm. Sperm are mixed with the ejaculate to form **semen**, but the sperm are so microscopic that they add no bulk or weight, and the consistency of the ejaculate is not changed if sperm are absent.

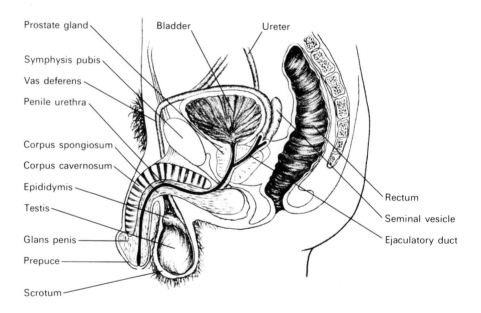

Prostate gland
Bladder
Ureter
Symphysis pubis
Vas deferens
Penile urethra
Corpus spongiosum
Corpus cavernosum
Epididymis
Testis
Glans penis
Prepuce
Scrotum
Rectum
Seminal vesicle
Ejaculatory duct

The male reproductive system

Between 500 million and 600 million sperm are present in each ejaculation, and in the average man about 100 million become mature every day.

The consistency of seminal fluid varies from man to man and from time to time in the same man. Sometimes it is a thin, watery discharge, and other times it may be a thick, gelatinous substance. Usually, the more frequent the ejaculations a man has, the thinner is his ejaculate. Men frequently are concerned about the force of their ejaculation, which also varies among men and in the same man. Sometimes discharged semen squirts three feet or more beyond the penis, and other times it may simply ooze out of the urethra. The force of ejaculation usually diminishes as a man becomes older, although the pleasure and frequency of the sex act may not decrease at the same rate, if it decreases at all.

Along with all the other myths about sex, men are frequently told that ejaculation will weaken them and leave them unable to compete successfully in athletic events. The fact is that the average ejaculate contains about 36 calories, weighing about 4 grams, and its loss cannot in any way weaken a man. Usually no more than about a tablespoonful, the ejaculate is a highly alkaline fluid that contains proteins, calcium, citric acid, cholesterol, and various enzymes and acids. The alkalinity of the fluid allows sperm to move through the highly acid vaginal canal without being destroyed.

The vulnerable sperm are further protected by the secretions of the **Cowper's glands** located just below the prostate. During sexual excitement they secrete an alkaline fluid that lubricates and neutralizes the acidity of the male **urethra**, the canal through which urine and seminal fluid flow through the male penis. (The seminal outlet joins the bladder outlet within the prostate.) After prolonged sexual excitation, a few drops of fluid from the Cowper's glands (called **precoital fluid**) can frequently be observed at the opening of the penis. Ordinarily, the fluid does not contain sperm, but it is possible for some sperm to have spilled into it. For this reason, the practice of withdrawing the penis from the woman's vagina just before ejaculation does not always prevent pregnancy, although pregnancies resulting from precoital fluid are extremely rare.

The **penis** is both a man's most sexually sensitive sex organ and the one about which most men are the most emotionally sensitive. Almost every man worries about the size of his penis, comparing it unfavorably to the penises of other men and believing that the bigger the penis, the better a man is in sexual performance. Much of their concern is due to the fact that as children they observed the size of adult or post-pubertal penises and concluded that their own were inadequate in comparison. Believing that sexual prowess can only be attained by an inordinately large penis, many men find that that their own never quite measures up to their unreasonable standards. Since a woman's vagina has few nerve endings, the size of a man's penis has very little to do with the pleasure experienced by either partner, and the size is far more a matter of concern to a man than it is to a woman.

The penis is composed of erectile tissue that lengthens and increases in diameter during sexual excitement. Three hollow bodies of erectile tissue, two on top and one below, form the shaft of the penis, and it is when these bodies become engorged with blood during sexual excitement that the penis becomes erect. The average adult penis measures from 2.5 to 4 inches in length when limp, or flaccid. It is slightly over 1 inch in diameter and about 3.5 inches in circumference (McCary, 1978). There is very little relationship between the size of a flaccid penis and its size when erect (Masters & Johnson, 1966). During erection, the average penis extends to 5.5 to 6.5 inches in length, becomes 1.5 inches in diameter, and about 4.5 inches in circumference (McCary, 1978).

The size of a man's penis is purely hereditary, although a pathologically small penis may be enlarged during childhood or early adolescence through the application of hormones (Raboch, 1970), and bears little relation to his general body size. Women sometimes try to guess the size of a man's penis by the size of his feet or his hands, but the fact is that there is no method of accurately determining the size of a man's erect penis when it is limp. A six-foot man may have a 3-inch-long penis, and a shorter man may have a 5-inch penis. The 3-inch penis may stretch to twice its size, while the 5-inch penis may increase less in size, so that both penises may be 6 inches long when erect. Whether the man's penis is 2 inches or 10 inches, one is no less capable of coital performance than the other, and neither is a guarantee of sexual pleasure in a woman.

The most sexually sensitive and excitable part of the penis, and of the man's body, is the **glans** of the penis—the smooth, conelike head. At the back edge of the glans, the rim where the glans and penile shaft meet, is the **corona**, which is especially sensitive to sexual stimulation. The thin tissue on the underside of the glans, called the **frenulum** or **frenum**, is a particularly sensitive area. A woman who is manually or orally stimulating a man's penis would do well to remember that direct stimulation of the corona or frenum is likely to bring him to a climax. Unless that is her intention, she should instead concentrate on the **shaft** of the penis, which is covered by loose skin to allow for erection and free movement. The skin is not attached to the tip of the penis but hangs loosely. The flap of overhanging loose skin is called the **prepuce** or **foreskin**. Through **circum-**

cision, the surgical removal of the prepuce covering the glans, a man is frequently left with a smooth, even continuation of penile skin and glans.

In men whose foreskin has not been circumcised, a smelly, cheeselike substance called **smegma** may collect under the loose skin and emit an unpleasant odor. Smegma is a combination of a lubricant material secreted by the **sebaceous glands**, located just behind the glans at the frenulum, and the cells shed from the glans and the corona. It is for prevention of this condition, as well as for religious purposes in some cases, that circumcision is performed.

No discussion of the male penis would be complete without a comment on the persistent myth that human beings can become "hung up" as dogs do. Everyone knows someone who knows someone who knows someone who has required the services of a physician to be uncoupled because of becoming "hung up" while having sexual intercourse. While it is possible for a woman's vaginal muscles to contract severely during sexual intercourse (**vaginismus**), with a momentary tightening around the man's penis, the pain and fear that the man might experience would immediately cause a loss of erection and easy withdrawal. There are no scientifically verified cases of **penis captivus** among humans, and the notion results, as stated, from the observation of dogs who may become "hung up" while copulating. Unlike the human male, the male dog's penis contains a bone which allows for penetration of the bitch's vagina before complete penile erection. As the bitch's vagina swells and the male dog's penis becomes more erect, a knot forms on the base of the dog's penis and traps it in the vagina until ejaculation and a return of the penis to its nonexcited state. If the copulating dogs are interrupted by outraged humans before the male ejaculates, the two may become trapped, or "hung up" (Dengrove, 1965).

Female genitalia. While a man's sexual organs are more outside than inside his body, a woman's are more internal than external. Ovaries, fallopian tubes, the uterus (or womb), and all but the opening of the vagina are hidden from sight. The **ovaries** are homologous to the testes in the male and are the source of ova or eggs. In each ovary of a newborn girl are some 200,000 to 400,000 follicles, each housing the earliest form of an ovum, the **oocyte**. At puberty, that count has diminished to approximately 10,000, a number far in excess of the approximately 450 that a woman will discharge during her reproductive life (McCary, 1978). The ovaries also manufacture the hormones estrogen and progesterone that prepare and maintain the uterus for the implantation of a fertilized ovum. Although the male hormone testosterone is responsible for a man's sex drive, the

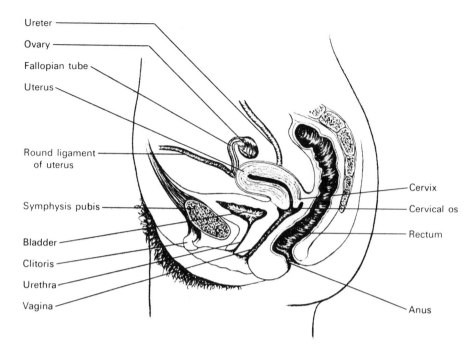

Ureter
Ovary
Fallopian tube
Uterus
Round ligament of uterus
Symphysis pubis
Bladder
Clitoris
Urethra
Vagina
Cervix
Cervical os
Rectum
Anus

The female reproductive system

same is not true of female hormones and a woman's sex drive. In fact, a woman's sex drive is largely controlled by her adrenal glands, which produce the male hormone androgen. Removal of a woman's adrenal glands diminishes her sex drive far more than removal of her ovaries does (Rubin, 1965). Ovulation may occur alternately in each ovary, or one ovary may discharge several times in succession. Although a single egg is usually released during ovulation, two or more can be discharged. Ovulation usually occurs once a month, but an additional egg may be discharged during the month, especially at a time of sexual excitement (McCary, 1978).

The use of drugs to increase fertility may also cause several ova to mature and be discharged during the same ovulation period. It is for this reason that the incidence of multiple births among women taking such drugs has become almost commonplace.

The **fallopian tubes** cup over the ovaries, and the discharged ovum enters the open end. It is in the **ampulla** portion of the fallopian tubes—that portion nearest the ovary—that fertilization usually occurs. The fertilized ovum, or **conceptus**, is then moved, during a journey of several days, to the **uterus** (womb), a hollow, thick-walled muscular organ shaped somewhat like a pear. In a nonpregnant state, the cavity of the uterus is only a slit about 2.5 inches long that narrows to a tiny opening near the center and then continues through the **cervix**—the lower narrow end of the uterus—in an even smaller opening.

The cervix protrudes by somewhat less than an inch into the **vagina**, a muscular tube whose walls are usually touching in a non-stimulated state. The vaginal vault serves four purposes: Facilitated by a "sweating" process of its walls, it receives the penis in sexual intercourse; it acts as the passageway to the uterus and fallopian tubes for ejaculated sperm; it serves as the canal through which the fetus is expelled from the uterus in childbirth; and it serves as a passageway for the discharge of menstrual fluid. With sexual stimulation, the walls of the vagina dilate and elongate to receive the penis. The walls also "sweat," providing lubrication for easy penetration of the penis. The female vagina is about 3 inches long on the front wall and about 3.5 inches long on the back wall, and extends upwards at a right angle to the uterus.

Although the vagina contains few nerve endings that give sexual pleasure, women usually experience a distinctly pleasurable sensation from penile containment during vaginal penetration. While such containment, by itself, does not lead to an orgasm, it affords psychological as well as physiological pleasure, and is probably the reason why so many women enjoy penetration, even though an orgasm is no different, physiologically speaking, whether it is attained by penetration, manual manipulation, or some other technique.

At the external opening of the vagina is the **hymen**, or **maidenhead**, a fold of connective tissue that partially closes the opening. It is not true that a broken hymen means that a woman is not a virgin. In most women, the hymenal tissue is broken during masturbation or through some injury to the vulval area in childhood. It is also not true that an intact hymen means that a woman is a virgin. In many cases, the hymenal tissue is so pliable that it does not obstruct the vaginal opening, and repeated intercourse or even childbirth may take place without tearing it.

If a woman's hymen is intact when she marries, it is wise to have it surgically incised, with a mild anesthetic, by a physician before her wedding night. By doing so, any pain that might accompany its rupturing is eliminated, and there is no difficulty in first penile penetration after marriage. Pain that may accompany first intercourse is usually due to the result of the hymen's being torn at that time. Such discomfort can both dampen a couple's sexual ardor at the moment and can also lead to future negative feelings toward sex in the woman.

The Physiology of Sex **221**

It might be mentioned here that even a sexually inexperienced woman is usually capable of having completely painless and enjoyable first sexual intercourse if she is relaxed and unafraid and if her partner is gentle and considerate. With adequate stimulation, the woman's vagina will be well lubricated and even the largest penis can be accepted by a virgin with comfort and pleasure. If a woman is frightened or under other emotional stress, however, she can experience painful muscle spasms (**vaginismus**) that make penetration very painful or even impossible. Under such circumstances, an insensitive husband who attempts to force penetration by using his penis as a battering ram can cause his wife untold pain and future resistance against any part of the sex act.

The female genitalia that are external are collectively called the **vulva**, and consist of the mons veneris (or mons pubis), and the labia majora (outer major lips), the labia minora (inner minor lips), the clitoris, the vestibule, and the outer one-fifth of the vagina.

The **mons veneris**, or **mons pubis**, is that mound of fatty tissue that is covered with pubic hair. There are nerve endings in this area that produce sexual excitement when stimulated by pressure. The **labia majora**, two longitudinal folds of skin that are covered with pubic hair on their outer sides but are smooth on the inner sides, continue from the mound of the mons veneris. The **labia minora** are smaller lips that lie within the larger labia majora. The labia minora are rich in nerve endings and blood vessels and are major erogenous zones. They form the border of the vestibule—the opening of the vagina—and fuse at the top to form the prepuce that encloses the clitoris. Under sexual excitement, the labia minora may flare out to expose the vestibule, but in a nonstimulated state the lips are together, sealing off the inner vaginal opening from view.

The **clitoris** is the most sexually sensitive part of a woman's body, and is a homologue to a man's penis. Unlike the penis, however, the clitoris is enclosed under the juncture of the labia minora and only the clitoral glans is exposed.

The average clitoris is less than an inch long, but sexual excitement may cause it to enlarge to twice its flaccid size or more. The enlargement, however, is primarily in the diameter of the clitoral shaft, because the length of the clitoris is not increased significantly.

Like the glans of the penis, the glans of the clitoris is especially sensitive to sexual stimulation. It is through clitoral stimulation that a woman usually reaches an orgasm, whether it is by masturbation, petting, or intercourse. Clitoral stimulation during sexual intercourse is either indirect, through pulling and tugging of the minor lips as the penis moves in and out of the vagina, or direct, through contact with the man's pubic bone as it rubs against the clitoris. During masturbation, women usually stimulate to one side of the clitoris rather than directly on the glans. Smegma that accumulates under the foreskin of the penis also collects under the prepuce of the clitoris. If left undisturbed, it may become granular and can cause abrasions and adhesions between the prepuce and the glans. If such granulated smegma exists there will often be pain when the clitoris enlarges during sexual excitement. If the smegma is not extremely hardened, a woman can gently remove it herself with a dull probe such as an orangewood stick, until the surrounding skin pulls back freely from the clitoral glans. In stubborn cases, hardened smegma must be removed by a physician. After the smegma is removed, it should be kept away by thorough cleansing of the clitoral region each day. In almost all cases, problems with smegma can be avoided by careful cleansing of the clitoris by pulling back the foreskin and gently soaping and rubbing away, with washcloth or fingernail, the daily accumulation of secretions. Furthermore, by working a washcloth-covered finger in and around the folds of skin and mounds of tissue of the vulva, the woman can prevent daily accumulations of vaginal and vulval secretions that may produce offensive odors.

Within the lips of the labia minora is the **vestibule**, within which are the openings of the vagina and the urethra. Rich in nerve endings and blood vessels, this area is highly responsive to stimulation. At each side of the vaginal opening are the **Bartholin's glands**, which secrete a drop or two of lubricating fluid during sexual excitement. This fluid is not for the purpose of vaginal lubrication, as was once believed, but is instead too insignificant to aid in vaginal penetration.

Puberty. Before adult sexual functioning is possible, certain anatomical, sexual, and endocrine changes must take place. This physiological transition is accompanied by "sexual awakening," and typically begins when a girl reaches the age of about 10 years, and a boy about 12 years. This period of change and growth, which transforms a child into a male or female capable of reproduction, is called **puberty**.

During puberty, secondary sexual characteristics commence their development. A girl's ovaries begin to secrete female sex hormones, and these hormones prompt additional ovarian growth and other body changes. The first signs of puberty in a girl are changes in her breasts; the small conical buds increase in size, and the nipples become larger and project forward. The body contour becomes

more rounded at this time, and the pelvic area begins to broaden. Fatty pads develop on the hips, pubic and axillary (underarm) hair growth appears, and the vaginal lining thickens. With time, the pubic hair coarsens, thickens, becomes curly and darker in color, and grows in the inverted triangular shape unique to women.

At approximately 13 years of age, or two to three years after the onset of puberty, menstruation begins. Even though a girl has reached the menarche (the beginning of menstruation), she cannot become pregnant until ovulation—the process whereby the ovaries release mature ova—commences. Ovulation ordinarily trails the menarche by a year or two. Changes within the female genital structure continue into adolescence. The mons pubis, the fatty pad just above the rest of the external genitalia, becomes prominent. The labia majora, or larger outer lips, thicken, hiding the vaginal opening, which was previously visible. The labia minora, the thin inner lips, also develop to form an additional shield for the vaginal opening. The mucous lining of the vagina thickens further, turning a deep red color, and its secretions now become acid. The clitoris grows rapidly as its extensive blood system develops, and the uterus doubles in size by approximately 18 years, although 60 percent of girls have mature wombs by the age of 15.

A boy's pubic growth curve is similar to that of a girl, but lags behind hers by a year or two. At about the age of 12, his testicles are stimulated to a rapid growth because of pituitary gland secretions. Under the influence of the pituitary, the testicles also commence to secrete testosterone, the male hormone that has a marked effect on primary and secondary sexual characteristics. The penis and scrotum begin to increase significantly in size.

When a boy is about 13 years old, pubic hair appears, soon to be followed by the growth of underarm and facial hair. The testicles commence secreting sperm, and ejaculation is possible; the boy may now experience nocturnal emissions. As in the case of ova produced by a girl of this age, a boy's sperm are rarely mature. Approximately a year later, the boy's voice changes, and although his total body growth is rapid, he may not reach his adult stature and full sexual maturity until he is 20 years old.

Menstruation. A woman's reproductive capacities begin with, or about a year after, the onset of menstruation, or the **menarche**, and end with the **climacteric**, or menopause, when menstruation ceases. Between the menarche and the climacteric, the average woman menstruates from 300 to 500 times.

The menstrual cycle is measured from the onset of one menstrual flow to the day before the next one, and varies considerably in women—anywhere from 21 to 90 days is considered normal, and the average for women in their 30s and 40s is about 28 days.

In each cycle, the menstrual flow commences when progesterone, the hormone that prepares and maintains the walls of the uterus for the implantation of a fertilized ovum, is withdrawn. The withdrawal causes the lining of the uterus to break down and slough off, as it is no longer needed for nourishment of a possible fertilized egg. The amount of blood and other fluids and debris discharged from the uterine wall during a menstrual period is about one cupful, but the amount of actual blood loss on even the heaviest day is rarely more than one tablespoon.

After the menstrual flow stops, usually from three to seven days after its onset, the secretion of estrogen gradually increases, and the maturation of an ovum-containing follicle in an ovary is begun and completed. The follicle ruptures, discharging the mature ovum on about the fourteenth day of the menstrual cycle. This discharge of the ovum, or **ovulation**, occurs at the time of maximum concentration of estrogen in the blood, and it is the time when pregnancy can occur.

Following ovulation, the hormone progesterone is secreted, and the preparation of the uterus for a fertilized egg begins again. If conception does not occur, the concentration of both estrogen and progesterone decreases sharply, leading to the breaking down of uterine tissue and the beginning of another menstrual cycle.

Ovulation gradually begins to cease when a woman is about 45 or 50 years of age, usually stopping altogether by the end of two years. The time interval during which the woman's ovulation and menstrual cycles gradually cease to exist is the climacteric or menopause. During this time, ovulation and the menstrual flow are erratic, but as long as any menstrual periods occur at all, the possibility of pregnancy remains. A woman cannot be reasonably sure that ovulation has completely ceased until she has gone a year without a menstrual period.

Only about 25 percent of all menopausal women have any sort of distressing side effects, and generally speaking, the better the mental health of the woman before the climacteric, the fewer unpleasant symptoms she will have when it occurs.

THE SEXUAL RESPONSE CYCLE

Both men and women become sexually excited when stimulated by either psychological or physiological methods. Stimulative techniques are many and varied, and may deviate considerably from the more commonplace ones without suggesting abnormality. With sufficient stimulation, almost all men and about 95 percent of all women are capable of reaching an orgasm, although undoubtedly because of stringent sexual controls that are imposed upon girls throughout childhood, only about 70 percent of women are able to achieve orgasm during their first year of marriage (Kinsey et al., 1953).

An orgasm is the ultimate goal of sexual stimulation, whether or not that goal is actually reached. **Orgasm** is a short-lived, highly pleasurable, intense, seizure-like response that is tension-relieving. Lasting usually from three to ten seconds, it is the peak of physically and emotionally gratifying sexual activity.

The course of sexual excitation, orgasm, and subsequent return to a normal state is a cycle that has four stages (Masters & Johnson, 1966). The first, or **excitement phase**, which is the beginning of sexual arousal, may be a brief episode or last for hours, depending upon such factors as the type and intensity of sexual stimulus, and the absence of fear and guilt feelings. A man's penis usually becomes erect during this phase, the scrotal tissue thickens, and the testicles

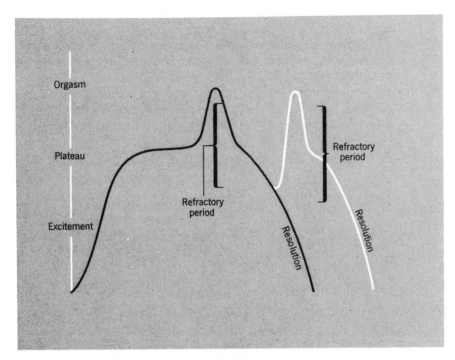

Male sexual response cycle (Masters & Johnson, 1966)

are pulled closer to the body. In the woman, the breasts enlarge and the nipples stand out; the labia majora and minora thicken and flare away from the vaginal entrance as they become engorged with blood; and the vagina begins the "sweating" process that serves to lubricate it for easy penile penetration. In both men and women, muscular tension, blood pressure, and heart rate accelerate during this phase, and about three-fourths of women and one-fourth of men experience a rash, the **maculopapular sex flush**, which spreads from their abdomen and throat to cover much of their bodies.

In the second or **plateau phase**, tissues in the genitalia of both men and women continue to enlarge, and muscular tension, blood pressure, and heart rate continue to climb. Muscular strain of the hands and feet, the face, and especially of the cords of the neck becomes apparent. The outer one-third of the vaginal canal becomes markedly constricted because of vascular congestion; the muscles involuntarily contract and tighten around the inserted penis. The inner two-thirds of the vagina balloons as it enlarges and is drawn upwards by the uterus. From its usual glans-exposed position, the clitoris pulls back deeply beneath its hood.

The Sexual Response Cycle **227**

The **orgasmic phase**—orgasm itself—is very short, but brings with it the most highly pleasurable sensations of a sexual act. The orgasmic experience varies little from man to man, but the variations of response among women can be considerable. A woman's orgasmic response may be so mild that she is not sure that she has had an orgasm, or it may be extremely intense. In a case of multiple orgasms, a woman's later orgasms are generally more intense than the first one. The same is not true, however, for those few men who are capable of multiple orgasms. Contractions of the prostate and

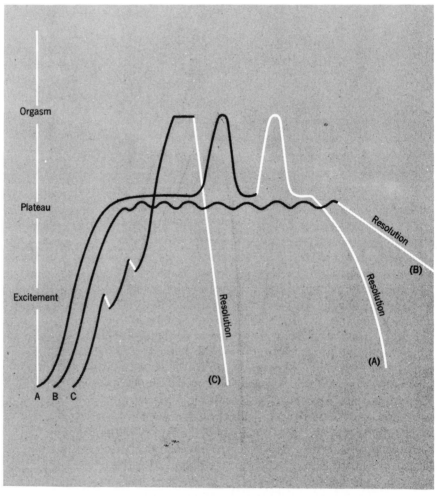

Female sexual response cycle (Masters & Johnson, 1966)

related structures bring about a man's ejaculation. Both men and women experience contractions in the genital and anal regions during the orgasmic phase, and a woman experiences strong uterine contractions.

During the **resolution phase**, the sexual systems of both men and women return to their normal nonstimulated state. The time required for the involution to take place is directly related to the length of the excitement phase; the longer the first phase was, the longer the last one will be. A large percentage of both men and women exhibit a perspiratory reaction in the resolution phase—a film of perspiration spreads over the chest, back, forehead, or other parts of the body. This perspiration is not related to the physical exertion of intercourse.

During the last phrase, men enter a **refractory period**, a temporary state during which time they find further sexual stimulation unpleasant or at least ineffective. Women do not usually experience the refractory period; and if the same sexual stimulation that produced the initial orgasm is continued, they may again and again go through the four phases of the sexual response cycle.

ATTITUDES ABOUT PREMARITAL SEX

Much has been said and written in recent years about the sexual revolution that is supposedly taking place. A true sexual revolution involves a dramatic change in the attitudes and ethics governing sexual behavior as well as in the behavior itself. Conclusive evidence of such a change does not as yet exist (Davis, 1971), but there are signs that the trend is in that direction. There has been an increase in sexual *activity* among young adults, both in heavy petting and in sexual intercourse, but the most pronounced changes have been in a growing liberalization of sexual *attitudes* (Hunt, 1973a, b; McCary, 1978).

Among adult young women particularly college women, there are pronounced changes in premarital sexual behavior and sexual attitudes. Today's college woman is having more sexual experiences, earlier and probably with more partners, than was true of women students before 1960 (Davis, 1971). One study of the premarital sexual attitudes of unmarried university students (Bauman & Wilson, 1976) found that, in comparison to a past study made on the same campus, students had (1) more permissive attitudes toward premarital sexual behavior, (2) fewer differences in attitudes between men and women, and (3) less adherence to the double standard.

There is also a liberalization of sexual attitudes in the general populace—at least insofar as talk is concerned. Talk and action are not necessarily one and the same, however, and attitudes and the ease of discussing them are not to be confused with behavior. Rather, inconsistency between sexual attitudes and behavior is still very much a part of the American culture.

There are various conflicting American premarital sexual standards. Among them are **abstinence** (premarital intercourse is wrong for both men and women, regardless of circumstances); the **double standard** (premarital intercourse is acceptable for men, but unacceptable for women); **sexual permissiveness when affection exists** (premarital intercourse is right for both men and women under certain conditions—in a stable relationship involving engagement, love, or strong affection); and **permissiveness without affection** (physical attraction alone justifies premarital intercourse for both men and women) (Reiss, 1960b).

The double standard is the ethic that has prevailed in our culture more than any other, but it seems to be collapsing, at least among younger Americans. A Gallup poll revealed that 75 percent of men and women on 55 separate U.S. college campuses think that virginity in a mate at the time of marriage is unimportant (In the News, 1970). There are vestiges of the double standard, however.

One study found that more than half of the college men sampled expressed approval of premarital coitus, but three-fourths of them nevertheless preferred marrying a virgin (Christensen & Gregg, 1970). Many women, too, continue to believe that sexual conquests in a man are an indication of masculinity and prefer that their husbands be nonvirginal at the time of marriage.

A person's attitudes toward and involvement in sexual behavior are affected by many factors such as age, religion, race, and culture. Conservatism concerning sexual attitudes is often found to become stronger with advanced age (Snyder & Spreitzer, 1976). A logical prediction would be that there will be a wider range in sexual attitudes among the older population of the future as a more egalitarian generation grows older. In considering the effect of religion, a recent investigation (Ogren, 1974) has shown that it is not religion per se that affects sexual behavior, but sex-related guilt built up in the individual as a result of his or her religious training and experience. Among whites, the more devout and frequent a churchgoer, the more conservative an individual's attitudes and behavior are likely to be. This tendency has not been found to a significant degree among blacks (Reiss, 1964).

Premarital intercourse is more likely to be viewed as acceptable behavior by black males and females than it is by white males and females (Reiss, 1970), and there is therefore a higher frequency of sexual activity among blacks. It was previously believed that this finding was due to the disparity between socioeconomic levels, but the most recent studies have indicated that the finding holds even when socioeconomic and education factors are matched between the two racial groups, as well as the incomes and occupations of the fathers (Rainwater, 1966). The differences in attitudes between the two groups can thus be attributed to differences between the two subcultures, just as there are wide differences between cultures throughout the world in sexual attitudes and behavior.

In addition to the external influences exerted by culture, race, religion, and other environmental factors, there are also internal influences exerted on the individual in the formation of sexual attitudes. Self-esteem, for example, has been related to sexual behavior in women. Women who rate high in self-esteem, or dominance feelings, are self-confident, self-assured, and display feelings of superiority. Women who rate low in dominance feelings, or who have low self-esteem, show the opposite personality characteristics, while middle-dominance women fall about midway between the two extremes. High-dominance women are much more likely than low-dominance women to masturbate and to have premarital sexual intercourse. An exception to this finding is in Jewish women, who are generally found to be higher in dominance feelings and behavior than Catholic or Protestant women; they are nonetheless more likely to be virgins than either of the other two religious groups (Maslow, 1966b).

A high-dominance woman is attracted only to a high-dominance man and wants him to be straightforward, passionate, and somewhat violent in their lovemaking. The middle-dominance woman prefers gentle, loving words, tenderness, soft music, and low lights (Maslow, 1966b). (The low-dominance woman apparently prefers to be left alone.)

The most satisfactory marriages are those in which the husband equals or is somewhat (but not markedly) superior to his wife in dominance feelings. High-dominance couples appreciate sex for its own sake and wholeheartedly approve of it. They are more likely to engage in and to enjoy oral-genital activity and to find the external genitalia of the sexual partner attractive. In marriages of high-dominance people, the couples frequently have experimented with almost every form of sexual activity known to sexologists. These sexual acts would likely be considered pathological by low-dominance people, but they have no pathological connotation for high-dominance people (Maslow, 1966b).

Of all the emotions that distort and inhibit healthy sexual expression, guilt is probably the most significant. Interestingly enough, however, most young people minimize their guilt over premarital sexual behavior by increasing their sexual involvement (Reiss, 1960a, 1971). For example, a couple might begin with only kissing, but feel some guilt about it. When they next involve themselves in kissing behavior, they do not feel the same degree of guilt. They then continue the kissing episodes until the guilt disappears altogether. Next they move to a level of greater sexual intimacy, such as petting. Again they feel guilty, but they overcome it by repeating the same behavior over and over again until the guilt disappears. They then move to another level of intimacy, and so on. In new dating situations, furthermore, they may quickly progress to the level of sexual activity they had reached in earlier relationships.

The decision of whether or not a person is to engage in premarital sexual intercourse should be based on his or her own maturity, values, beliefs, and needs, and not on the values of any other person or any group. It makes no more sense to have sexual intercourse because of peer pressure than it does to abstain from intercourse because of societal pressure.

All too often, young people believe that it is better to let sexual intercourse "just happen" in a spontaneous manner, without previous thought and decision. Letting sexual intercourse "just happen" without forethought and planning makes as much sense as "just happening" to wander into the rain forests of South America without protection from the dangers there.

The risks associated with premarital sexual intercourse are pregnancy and venereal disease. Many young people, believing that premarital sexual intercourse is a sin, refuse to purchase or to use contraceptives because to do so would require planning and, therefore, committing a "planned sin." One study found that an astonishing 75 percent of sexually active girls failed to use contraceptive measures (Teen-age Sex, 1972). The increasing number of premarital pregnancies and abortions attests to their foolishness. A total of over 1,034,000 legal abortions were obtained in 1975 alone. Three out of 10 pregnancies end in abortion with the greatest number being sought by unmarried women and women under the age of 20 (Statistical Abstract, 1977).

Sadly, many young women punish themselves for their premarital sexual intercourse by forgoing contraceptives. By creating a situation in which premarital pregnancy is highly probable, they provide for themselves a time of fear and anxiety each month before their menstrual period. If no period occurs, and if they are indeed pregnant, many women feel a secret sense of relief; they have believed their activity to be a sin that should be punished, and they are receiving the punishment they believe they deserve. They no longer have to live with the anxiety of fearing pregnancy because their fears are realized. Furthermore, they have the satisfaction of believing that their pregnancy-punishment absolves them of their guilt.

The question of morality or immorality of premarital sexual intercourse should be decided on the basis of each person's conscience and own beliefs. Obviously, if a person believes that premarital intercourse is wrong, then he or she should not engage in it. If, however, it is acceptable to one's own philosophy and value system, the person should take the responsibility of making sure that no pregnancy results from the activity, and every precaution should be taken against contracting or disseminating venereal diseases. The following discussion is directed to those individuals who wish to prevent conception and venereal diseases in themselves or their sexual partners.

BIRTH CONTROL

Birth prevention—which is usually referred to as birth control—involves considerably more than contraception, although the terms are frequently used as if they were synonymous. Contraceptives are devices or techniques that prevent conception. Methods of birth control include not only contraceptives, but abortion, abstinence, and sterilization as well. Since unmarried people are usually more concerned with postponing conception, rather than permanently preventing it, only contraception, abortion, and abstinence will be included in this discussion.

Abstinence as a means of birth control implies a total avoidance of coitus. It is, obviously, the safest form of birth prevention. For reasons equally as obvious, it is the least popular one.

Contraception encompasses a variety of techniques, some considerably more effective than others. Contraceptives that are available only with a doctor's prescription include the diaphragm, oral contraceptives, and intrauterine contraceptive devices (IUDs).

A **diaphragm** is a thin, rubber, dome-shaped cup stretched over a collapsible metal ring, designed to cover the mouth of the womb (the cervix). Having the correct size and shape in a diaphragm is of vital importance for both the wearer's comfort and for its effectiveness as a contraceptive. The device in no way interferes with the conduct or pleasure of intercourse for either partner. Used with contraceptive cream or jelly, the diaphragm seals off the cervix and prevents sperm from entering the womb and has a fairly high success rate. When the diaphragm is used with contraceptive foam, its effectiveness improves significantly, making it one of the safest of all birth-control techniques.

Oral contraceptives, commonly called "the pill," are a combination of synthetic progesterone and estrogen that prevents ovulation by mimicking the hormonal state of the body during pregnancy. Since no ovum is released, pregnancy cannot occur. If taken as prescribed, "the pill" is virtually 100 percent effective—a level of success that is unequalled by any other means of contraception.

Any side effects of the pill, such as nausea, weight gain, headaches, and irregular bleeding, usually disappear as the cycles of pills are repeated. In cases where the discomfort persists, a change in strength or brand of pills usually eliminates the problem.

The most serious side effect associated with the pill is that its estrogen content increases the coagulatory action of the blood, thereby increasing the risk of thromboembolic (clotting) disorders. In spite of these risks, women using other forms of birth control have 3.5 times greater chance of dying from complications of pregnancy, childbirth, and the postpartum period than do women who use the pill. Among women who use no method of birth control at all, the risk of maternal death is 7.5 times greater than it is among women taking the pill. Furthermore, there is no evidence that the

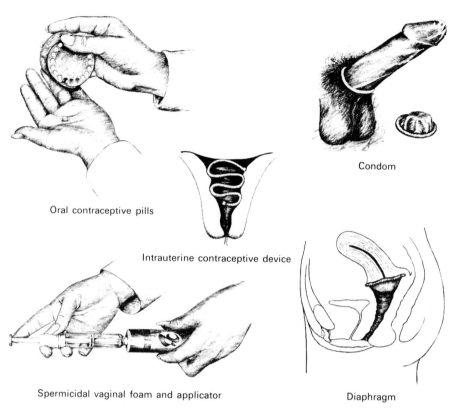

Oral contraceptive pills

Condom

Intrauterine contraceptive device

Spermicidal vaginal foam and applicator

Diaphragm

Various common contraceptive devices
19

pill causes cancer, and endocrinologists and gynecologists alike have proclaimed the pill eminently safe for most women, especially when its advantages are weighed against its risks.

In the future, the new **mini-pill** will probably replace the presently used contraceptive pills because it contains no estrogen and little progestin. The danger of thrombogenic complications and most other unpleasant side effects are virtually eliminated, although it is not an aid in cases of vaginal bleeding or menstrual irregularity, as the present pill is. Taken every day of the month, the mini-pill prevents pregnancy by causing the cervical mucosa to become thick and sticky, rather than thin and watery, as it becomes during ovulation, thereby preventing the passage of sperm into the uterus (Westoff & Westoff, 1971).

Intrauterine contraceptive devices (IUDs) are small plastic devices of various sizes and shapes that are designed to fit into the womb. It is thought that the IUD in some way acts as an irritant to prevent the implantation of the fertilized ovum in the uterine wall. A new T-shaped or 7-shaped IUD has recently been developed that is much smaller and easier to insert than the more conventionally shaped IUD. Wrapped with copper—which appears to be an additional deterrent to conceptus implantation—the polyethylene T has proved, in the initial stages of its use, to be approaching 100 percent effectiveness. Its cost is minimal, and its effectiveness lasts several years. There is no evidence that the IUD increases the chance of cervical cancer, nor is there evidence of any other adverse physical effects from its use.

Contraceptives available without a doctor's prescription include the condom and chemical methods. The **condom**, still one of the most popular contraceptives in the United States, is made of thin rubber or of sheep's intestine and measures about 7½ inches in length. About 750 million condoms are produced each year in the United States, and their effectiveness as a contraceptive is fair. In addition to its contraceptive usage, the condom is the best method of preventing the spread of venereal disease.

Chemical methods include **creams, jellies,** and **vaginal foams**, which block the entrance to the uterus and which are toxic to sperm. The foam is somewhat more effective than creams and jellies. **Vaginal suppositories**, another chemical method, are less effective than creams, jellies, or foams, and the use of **vaginal tablets** is the least effective of all chemical methods.

Other methods of birth prevention that are still less effective than contraceptives with or without a doctor's prescription include douching, coitus interruptus (withdrawal), and the rhythm method. **Douching** fails miserably as a contraceptive method because sperm move too quickly for a douche to reach them in time and flush them from the vagina. **Coitus interruptus** requires precision timing on the part of the male to withdraw his penis from his partner's vagina just before he ejaculates. An added risk is the fact that sperm may be present in the coital fluid that is secreted before ejaculation.

The **rhythm method** requires that a couple abstain from sexual intercourse during the period of a woman's menstrual cycle when she is capable of conception—just before, during, and just after ovulation. The major problem with the rhythm method is that only about 30 percent of women have sufficiently regular menstrual cycles that they can correctly pinpoint their "safe" period.

A variation of the rhythm method is the **temperature method**, which is based on the belief that a woman's temperature changes according to the changes in her menstrual cycle. The primary difficulty with this method is that many women do not have pronounced or consistent changes in temperature. Both the rhythm and temperature methods, furthermore, are risky since many women ovulate more than one time during a menstrual cycle, with the possibility existing that sexual excitement itself can trigger ovulation. Under these circumstances, ovulation and pregnancy may actually occur during the menstrual flow itself.

Any woman who does not wish to become pregnant should equip herself with the most effective contraceptive she can obtain. However, the effectiveness of any contraceptive technique depends on how well the user follows prescribed directions and how consistently the method is used. Carelessness in the use of even the most effective contraceptive increases the chance of pregnancy.

Scientists are constantly working on improved contraceptive methods for both men and women. Birth-control methods designed for men have been less successful than those for women, however, and at the present time birth prevention remains largely the responsibility of women.

Abortion is spontaneous or induced expulsion of an embryo or fetus from the uterus before it has developed sufficiently to survive. Before the 1973 Supreme Court decision that eliminated state laws prohibiting induced abortion, millions of women who had not used contraceptives or whose contraceptives had been ineffective sought illegal, often unsterile abortions annually. The death rate in such abortions was understandably high, and infections and other complications were frequent because of the crude and nonsterile methods so frequently employed by illegal abortionists. Performed in sterile conditions by trained medical personnel, however, an abortion poses less hazard to the life of a woman than childbirth does.

The standard method of abortion until quite recently was the procedure of dilation and curettage (**D and C**) in which the cervix is gradually dilated and the fertilized ovum is scraped from the uterus with a curette, a spoonlike instrument.

A newer and more popular method of abortion, **vacuum curettage**, is a procedure whereby a tube is inserted into the uterus and a vacuum pump is used to suck out the uterine content. The technique is safe and is easier and faster to perform than the D and C, and it causes the patient less trauma. It may be performed in the doctor's office, and the woman may well be able to resume her activity after an hour or so of rest and observation following the procedure.

Both the D and C and the vacuum curettage methods of abortion are performed before the twelfth week of pregnancy. A new and valuable use of the vacuum technique has recently been developed whereby a woman whose menstrual period is no more than two weeks late may have the menstrual content removed on an out-patient basis in a two-minute procedure without medication. Called **menstrual regulation** or **menstrual extraction**, the process ends a delayed menstruation without pain or bothersome side effects. It involves inserting a thin, flexible tube into the uterus, without the necessity of cervical dilation, then sucking out the month's menstrual lining, including a fertilized egg if one happens to be present. Since the procedure is performed within two weeks of a woman's missed period, there is no way for existing laboratory tests or for the woman herself to make an accurate diagnosis of pregnancy. The woman who might be bothered by a known abortion can thus free herself of the possibility of the burden of pregnancy without positive knowledge that she is pregnant.

After the twelfth week of pregnancy, methods other than a D and

"Not <u>another</u> one, Professor! Remember Zero Population Growth!"

Birth Control **239**

C or suction techniques must be utilized. One method is a **hysterotomy**, which may entail a minor caesarean section, or removal of the fetus via slits in the uterus and vagina. In another method, **saline injection**, about 200 cc of amniotic fluid are withdrawn through the wall of the abdomen. The fluid is then replaced with an identical amount of salt solution of a specified strength. Abortion occurs spontaneously, usually within 24 hours. Obviously, the later abortion is done, the more severe the technique, and the more dangerous it is for the woman.

VENEREAL DISEASE

There are many diseases, infections, and inflammations that affect male and female genital organs. The most prevalent of these is **gonorrhea**, which can cause painful complications in both men and women. A man who has contracted gonorrhea has a thin watery discharge from his penis that begins from 2 to 7 days after his infectious sexual contact. The discharge becomes thicker and greenish-yellow in a day or two, and there is usually a frequent and urgent need to urinate. Urination causes a burning sensation at the swollen and inflamed penis tip.

About 80 percent of infected women have no symptoms of gonorrhea, and they therefore are more likely to have serious complications of gonorrhea than are men. Certainly they are dangerous carriers of the disease when they are not aware of their infection. If they do have symptoms, they are in the form of a vaginal discharge beginning 2 to 7 days after infectious contact, and then an irritation of the vulva that causes it to become red and raw. There is a frequent and urgent need to urinate, and urination causes pain and a scalding sensation.

Treatment of gonorrhea consists of a single injection of 2.4 million units of penicillin for men, and 4.8 million units for women. For women, the penicillin is usually given in two separate injections during a single visit to a clinic. If a patient is allergic or resistant to penicillin, one of the tetracycline drugs may be successfully substituted.

The second most prevalent venereal disease is **syphilis**, which has a dangerously deceptive latent period, lasting for as long as 30 years, during which the disease causes irreversible tissue damage. If detected during the first two years following infection, syphilis can be easily cured. The **primary stage** of syphilis is recognizable by a lesion or a **chancre** (sore), usually in the anal-genital area, that appears from 10 to 40 days after infectious sexual contact. There is also a painlessly swollen lymph gland near the site of infection—in the groin, for example, if the chancre is on the penis or labia minora. The sore heals in 4 to 10 weeks, and the infected person may mistakenly believe that all danger is passed.

Secondary stage symptoms appear after 6 weeks and usually within 3 months of infection in the form of a nonitching rash on the trunk of the body. It may be so indistinct as to escape notice, and other syphilis-related symptoms, such as glandular enlargement, throat infection, headache, malaise, and a low-grade fever, may also be overlooked as symptoms of syphilis. These secondary symptoms heal, usually within a few weeks or months, and the only indication of syphilis is in a blood serum test.

After 6 months to two years of untreated syphilis, a person enters the **third stage** or **latent period**, during which time there are no symptoms, except those in a blood serum test, and the syphilitic cannot infect sexual contacts. Without treatment, the disease can now progress to the destructive stage of late spyhilis.

During the **fourth stage**, or **late syphilis**, symptoms may appear as late as 30 years after the initial infection, in any organ, in the central nervous system and the cardiovascular system and, particularly, on the skin. About 25 percent of untreated cases of syphilis develop into **neurosyphilis** and about 3 percent develop into **general paresis**. Both of these conditions are severely disabling disorders.

There are other venereal diseases that can be contracted by sexually active individuals, three of which are chancroid, granuloma inguinale, and lymphogranuloma venereum. It cannot be stressed too frequently that an individual who develops a urethral or vaginal discharge, or who has any inflammation or irritation of any kind of the urethral or genital area should immediately consult a physician for diagnosis and treatment. Most venereal diseases respond readily to penicillin or other antibiotics, but if left untreated they may cause complications that can result in considerable pain and possible sterility or death.

There are also various nonvenereal diseases such as **moniliasis** (yeast infection) and **trichomoniasis**. Both of these are common in women, and while they are not seriously disabling disorders, they can cause maddening itching and inflammation of the genital area, as well as a smelly, unpleasant vaginal discharge. An infected woman's sexual partner is likely to harbor the disease too, although he may not experience symptoms. Treatment is quick and simple, and a woman who suspects that she has either of these conditions should consult her physician at once.

CONCLUSION

Just as human beings do not exist in a vacuum, neither does human sexual expression exist apart from psychological and societal influences. People often say of sex, "It's just a physical urge," or "It satisfies a physical need, like eating does." The truth is, of course, that the manner in which people express themselves sexually depends upon both psychological and sociological influences and not merely on physiological needs. Furthermore, these same influences will determine the extent to which people enjoy their sexuality and how responsibly they use it. Before marriage, during marriage, or after marriage, all men and women are sexual beings, and sexual expression plays a large part in efforts toward self-fulfillment.

CHAPTER 9

SEXUAL
PRACTICES
AND PROBLEMS

The thing that takes up the least amount of time and causes the most amount of trouble is sex.   JOHN BARRYMORE

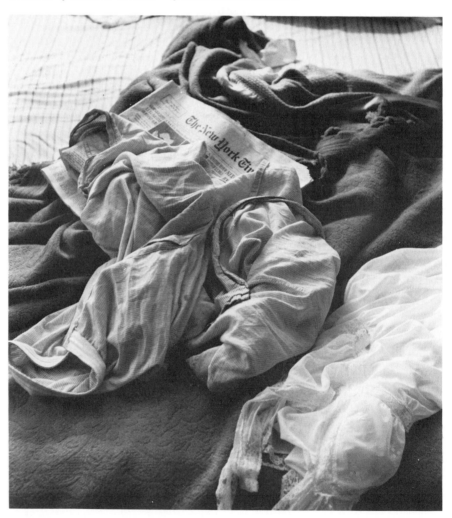

Of all areas of adjustment in marriage, sexual adjustment requires the greatest amount of effort and usually takes the longest period of time. A conservative estimate is that about 33 percent of all married couples have an unsatisfactory sexual relationship (Bell, 1971a; Burgess & Wallin, 1953; English, 1957); Masters and Johnson set the percentage at 50 (1966). Unsatisfactory sexual relationships in a marriage usually generate other marital problems, which, in turn, add to the sexual problems. From one to twenty years are required for many couples to achieve mutually satisfying sexual relations, and a sizable percentage never achieve sexual adjustment (Landis, 1946).

SEXUAL ACTIVITY OF MARRIED PEOPLE

Marital sexual intercourse, the most widely approved type of sexual activity in our society, is engaged in by almost all married couples. Marital sexual activity provides 85 percent of the total sexual outlet for married men, the remaining 15 percent being derived from masturbation, nocturnal emissions, petting, homosexual activity, extramarital coitus, and, in some rural areas, animal contact (Kinsey et al., 1948).

Among married women between the ages of 21 and 25, 89 percent of their total sexual outlet is derived from marital coitus. After the age of 25, there is a gradual decline, so that by the time a woman reaches the age of 70, only 72 percent of her total sexual outlet is provided by marital coitus (Kinsey et al., 1953). The cause of the decline is probably the fact that her husband's sex drive declines as he ages, but a woman's sex drive peaks in her 30s or 40s and remains at that level, with only a slight decline, into old age.

During the first year of marriage, 75 percent of all women attain orgasm during coitus at least once. After 20 years of marriage, 90 percent attain orgasm during coitus. The more education a woman has, the more likely she is to reach orgasm in marital intercourse (Kinsey et al., 1953).

For many women, the need for cuddling and closeness is of greater importance than the need for coitus itself. Some wives, in fact, lure their husbands into sexual intercourse in order to satisfy this very real need to be held and cuddled. They therefore barter coitus for close body contact, because such contact tends to reduce their anxieties and to promote relaxation and feelings of security (Hollender, 1971).

The frequency of marital coitus decreases with age, dropping among men from an average of 3.9 times per week during the teens to 2.9 times a week at the age of 30, 1.8 at the age of 50, and 0.9 at the age of 60 (Kinsey et al., 1948).

Kinsey's study found that women who married in their late teens had intercourse on an average of 2.8 times a week in the early years of marriage, 2.2 times a week at the age of 30, 1.5 times a week at the age of 40, once a week at the age of 50, and once every 12 days at the age of 60 (Kinsey et al., 1953). A more recent study (Bell & Bell, 1972) reported that of the 2372 married women sampled, those aged 26 to 31 had sexual intercourse 9.4 times a month; those aged 31 to 40, 7.4 times a month; those aged 41 to 50, 6.1 times a month; and those over 50 reported sexual intercourse 4.1 times a month.

Almost 15 percent of all women respond regularly with multiple orgasms (Kinsey et al., 1953; Terman, 1938), and many more do so occasionally. More women would do so if it were not for sexually ignorant or indifferent sexual partners or if there were not misconceptions held by women concerning their sexual capacity and what is "normal" in sexual behavior.

The average college-educated man will spend from 5 to 15 minutes—sometimes an hour or more—in precoital petting. After sexual intercourse commences he is more likely than a man of lower education to attempt to delay orgasm (although three-fourths of all men reach orgasm within 2 minutes of intromission). About 90 percent of college-educated men prefer to have intercourse in the nude, while only half as many of the grade-school-educated have ever engaged in intercourse without being at least partially clothed. The reason for the difference is that college-educated men are capable of a higher level of abstraction, and therefore can be more easily excited by external erotic stimulation. Consequently, they derive greater pleasure from intercourse if it is in a lighted room where they can observe both the nude body of their partner and the act of coition itself (Kinsey et al., 1948).

Highly educated men are much more sensitive to the sexual needs of their wives than are men with less education. Of men with some college education, 82 percent express concern for their partner's satisfaction, in contrast to a mere 14 percent of men with no college education (Masters & Johnson, 1966). College-educated women are consequently more satisfied with their sex lives than their less-educated sisters are.

Surprisingly, the frequency of marital intercourse is lower among religiously active Protestants than among inactive Protestants, in spite of the fact that marital coitus is totally sanctioned by all religious groups. Early puritanical training undoubtedly carries over into marriage and continues to inhibit sexual expression, despite

the couple's conscious acceptance of the "rightness" of marital coitus (Kinsey et al., 1948).

Although most marriages include sexual intercourse, there are a surprising number of marriages in which sex is almost or totally absent. In some marriages coitus may occur between husband and wife no more than one or two times a year, and may be accompanied by feelings of disgust and dissatisfaction. In many of these marriages, affection is present between the couple, but they relegate sex to an extremely unimportant or negative area of their lives. So long as both partners have an equally low sex drive, they may enjoy a satisfying sex life together, but if one partner has a stronger sexual appetite, there is inevitably stress and dissatisfaction in the marriage. If the couple remain together, the one with the stronger sex drive may turn to affairs to satisfy his or her sexual needs. Prostitutes, of course, gain many of their customers from the ranks of men whose wives have low sex drives or who insist on sex being performed in a way that they deem "normal" rather than allowing any variation in their sex lives.

Sometimes there are physical disabilities that render a marriage virtually sexless. Certain heart conditions require sexual absti-

"It was a nice idea, John, but the truth is that no,
the bunny outfit does not turn me on."

nence, for example, and some cases of diabetes in men result in impotence. More often than not, however, abstinence from sexual intercourse in marriage is due to emotional problems such as guilt or sexual ignorance.

Even in marriages that include regular sexual intercourse, there are frequently sexual problems that interfere with completely satisfying sexual relations. These problems include sexual ignorance, with its usual accompanying guilt, shame, and fear; fear of pregnancy; and some form of sexual dysfunction in husband or wife or both.

MYTHS ABOUT SEXUALITY

Ignorance about human sexuality accounts for the greatest percentage of unsatisfactory marital sex and points to the overwhelming need in our society for a sound sex education for every individual. Many times, couples are the victims of some of the more damaging sexual myths that abound in our society.

Sexual stimulation. One of the most dangerous myths is that oral-genital contact is a homosexual act (McCary, 1971). Oral-genital contact is in fact enjoyed by both homosexuals and heterosexuals and is not the exclusive domain of either. A large majority of college-educated men and women enjoy oral sex, and it is probably the most satisfying activity, next to sexual intercourse, for both sexes. Many women who cannot achieve orgasm during sexual intercourse readily climax during oral-genital contact and find it intensely satisfying.

If a man's penis is stimulated by a woman's mouth and tongue, it is called **fellatio**. During fellatio, a woman sucks on the man's penis while moving her tongue in alternately slow and fast movements. If a man should ejaculate during fellatio, it should be remembered that the ejaculate is merely a milky fluid containing protein, calcium, enzymes, citric acid, and cholesterol, is in no way harmful should it be swallowed, and should not be considered repulsive or offensive.

The act of orally stimulating a woman's clitoris and labia is called **cunnilingus**. By a man's licking, sucking, and kissing this region, a woman experiences the pleasure of moist genital stimulation. Using alternately fast and slow tongue strokes, a man licks on and around the clitoral shaft, inside the inner and outer lips, and around the outer and inner edges of the vaginal opening.

Oral-genital sex is particularly important at times when one partner is unable to have sexual intercourse. During the last few weeks of pregnancy, for example, oral sex allows sexual release for both husband and wife at a time when sexual intercourse may be contraindicated.

Another sex-inhibiting myth is that anal intercourse is exclusively a homosexual act. While anal intercourse is a preferred form of homosexual behavior, it is also practiced as a form of sexual variety by many heterosexual couples and in no way implies homosexual tendencies. Couples who engage in anal sex should be sure that there is ample lubrication in the form of a commercial lubricant such as KY Sterile Lubricant before the man's penis is inserted into the woman's anus. The couple should be aware that there is danger of transmitting, via the penis, certain organisms from the anus to the vagina and causing a vaginal infection if the couple have vaginal intercourse soon after anal intercourse. Appropriate cleansing of the penis is therefore required if vaginal penetration is to follow anal intercourse.

Another source of tension among married couples is the fact that many men become concerned that they have homosexual tendencies when they discover that they enjoy having their nipples stimulated. Nipples are erogenous zones in both men and women, and a man can enjoy manual or oral nipple contact as much as a woman can. Again, this is neither a homosexual nor a heterosexual practice. Instead, it is simply a sexual practice.

Orgasm. In addition to these myths, many couples also fall prey to the erroneous belief that every act of sexual intercourse should end in orgasm for both the man and the woman. Married couples particularly become obsessed with the woman's achieving orgasm at each sexual union, and each may feel a failure if one fails to occur. Sexual activity can and should be engaged in for its own sake, because it provides pleasurable stimulation and ego-satisfying feelings of being desired by the other, and not as a means to an orgasm. A man or a woman may enjoy manual stimulation, oral-genital contact, or sexual intercourse without an orgasm. Some women are capable of orgasms while masturbating but not during intercourse. The sensible solution is for them to relieve their own sexual tension as often as necessary through masturbating to orgasm, or by manual or oral stimulation by their sex partner, and then entering into sexual intercourse with their husbands for the erotic and emotional pleasure it gives them. Similarly, some men require few orgasms but enjoy frequent sexual contact. For their wives to feel cheated at their infrequent ejaculation is senseless. Most important is for both husband and wife to be sexually and emotionally satisfied after each sexual encounter, whether or not each has achieved an orgasm.

A related myth is that simultaneous orgasms of husband and wife are the most satisfying sexual climax. The truth is that simultaneous orgasm is both a physically difficult achievement as well as one that does not necessarily provide the utmost in emotional satisfaction.

An orgasm is essentially a solitary experience. Up to the moment of impending orgasm, a person is extremely involved with his sexual partner, but at the moment of orgasm, he is caught up in his own physical responses and is not inclined to be as concerned with his partner's well-being. If both partners are engaged in experiencing their own orgasms at the same moment, it is much like two people who climb two different mountain peaks and then tell each other about the experience. If one climaxes first, however, the other can enjoy his partner's orgasm and then give himself up to his own while the other experiences the added thrill of helping him have a thoroughly satisfying one. Since women are capable of several orgasms at one sexual session, it is most sensible to bring the woman to as many orgasms as she needs before the man has his. In this way, the sexual pleasure of each is further enhanced by the pleasure of the other.

Male and female sexual patterns. A lack of understanding of the differences in male and female sexual patterns also frequently leads to dissatisfying marital sex. A man has his greatest sex drive in his teens, while a woman's sex drive peaks in her 30s or 40s (Kinsey et al., 1948, 1953). While a man's sex drive is gradually slackening, therefore, a woman's is gradually increasing. After a woman reaches her peak of sexual interest and capacity, she maintains that level until her late 50s or 60s, when a slight decline in sex drive begins. A woman remains capable of multiple orgasms until her very late years and often has the same physical potential for orgasm at age 80 as she had at age 20. In fact, it may well be higher. In most cases, when a healthy woman in her fifties and beyond has a significant decrease in coital frequency, the cause is more likely related to her partner's loss of sexual interest than to her own.

If married couples are unaware of this cruel trick of nature, they will be unable to understand the sexual changes in their mates and may become resentful and bitter, with each nagging the other, to the further detriment of their marital sex life. Young men frequently feel rejected because their young brides are not ready for intercourse with the same frequency as they are, while their weary

brides may tearfully decide that they are married to a sex maniac. As a husband's sex drive declines, and a wife's increases, the wife may believe that her husband no longer finds her desirable, and she may suspect him of having affairs with other women. He, on the other hand, may wonder why his wife is so sexually demanding when she was formerly sexually "rejecting," and may conclude that the milkman or the postman has "turned her on." In their frustration and confusion, they may turn away from each other; he turning to less demanding younger women for nonthreatening sex, and she seeking out more sexually active men to satisfy her sexual hunger. Ideally, couples should understand each other's sexuality and make the necessary adjustments to provide each with sexual pleasure at all stages of their marriage.

FEAR OF PREGNANCY

Second to sexual ignorance as an inhibition of satisfying marital sex is the fear of pregnancy. Improved contraceptive measures

Sexual Practices and Problems

have removed that fear for many couples, and even the majority of devout Roman Catholics are ignoring their church's ban of "artificial" contraception and employing one of the methods discussed in Chapter 8. Some women, however, cannot tolerate either the pill or an IUD, and distrust the other methods (with good cause). For them and their husbands, sexual intercourse is always accompanied by the nagging fear of an unwanted pregnancy.

Sterilization. For couples who have as many children as they can afford, or who realize that population control is imperative if our world is to maintain a satisfying standard of living, sterilization removes both the possibility and the fear of pregnancy but does not remove the pleasure or interest of sex. On the contrary, both sex drive and sexual pleasure are usually increased for both husband and wife when the fear of pregnancy is removed.

Sterilization entails one of several surgical methods to render an individual incapable of reproduction. In men, the procedure usually involves cutting and tying the ends of the small tubes of the vasa deferentia in an operation called a **vasectomy**. Performed in a doctor's office under a local anesthetic, it results in some soreness in the scrotum for a few days, but a man may usually continue his near-normal activities with only a few hours' interruption. A vasectomy in no way affects a man's sex drive, his sexual functioning, the consistency of his ejaculate, or the production of sperm. By the surgical procedure sperm are prevented from being transported via the vas deferens to the ejaculatory ducts and are absorbed into his body.

Until recently, the most common method of sterilization in a woman was an operation called **tubal ligation**, in which the fallopian tubes are cut and tied. Despite the fact that a tubal ligation requires hospitalization and is considered major surgery, many men insisted that their wives undergo tubal ligations rather than having the relatively minor operation of a vasectomy performed upon themselves. The reason for this puzzling fact lies both in the double standard by which women have been given the entire responsibility for contraception, birth, and childcare, and in the irrational fear that many men have that a vasectomy will affect their sexual vigor.

A newer method of sterilization for women is that of **laparoscopy**. Under general anesthesia, two tiny incisions are made in a woman's abdomen and the fallopian tubes are severed and cauterized by an electrical instrument. Only very small bandages are needed to cover the incisions, causing the procedure to be called the "Band-Aid Operation," and the patient need remain in the hospital only until she is fully awake.

Other methods of sterilization for women, usually performed for the purpose of correcting abnormalities rather than for sterilization alone, include the surgical removal of the ovaries (**oophorectomy**), the uterus (**hysterectomy**), or the fallopian tubes (**salpingectomy**). These are, of course, major surgical procedures and should never be considered solely for the purpose of sterilization.

SEXUAL DYSFUNCTION

In addition to the causes of sexual dissatisfaction already discussed, there are conditions that may interfere, either temporarily or for an extended period of time, with sexual satisfaction and performance. In the male, such interference is usually from impotency or premature ejaculation; in the woman the problem is usually orgasmic dysfunction.

Erectile dysfunction (impotence). Erectile dysfunction, or impotence, is the inability of a male to attain or maintain an erection of sufficient firmness to enable him to have sexual intercourse. Impotency may be organic, functional, or psychogenic (Kelly, 1973). **Organic impotence**, a relatively rare problem, is caused by an anatomical defect in the reproductive or central nervous system. **Functional impotence** may be due to a nervous disorder, excessive use of alcohol or certain drugs, deficient hormonal functioning, circulatory problems, or physical exhaustion. **Psychogenic impotence**, by far the most frequently encountered type of impotence (Harper, 1965), is usually caused by emotional inhibition or by blocking of impulses from the brain that act upon the neural centers of the spinal cord that control erection.

A man with psychogenic impotence who has never been able to achieve or maintain an erection of sufficient firmness to engage in coitus is considered to have **primary impotence**. If a man has had at least one successful coital experience, but is now incapable of it, he is considered to have **secondary impotence** (Masters & Johnson, 1970). Such men usually have become fearful and apprehensive because of failing to achieve an erection during one sexual encounter, or because of several failures occurring within a short period of time. Virtually all men at one time or another—particularly when they have had too much to drink, are upset or very tired—are unable to attain an erection or to maintain it long enough for penetration (Ellis, 1963), but some men become so frightened by normal failure that they can no longer function sexually. Fear of failure then becomes a self-fulfilling prophecy, with a pattern of erectile failure being established. A man is diagnosed as having secondary impotence when he fails to achieve penile erection in 25 percent of his sexual attempts (Masters & Johnson, 1970).

Aging men may erroneously convince themselves that they are too old to function sexually and actually become impotent because of their belief, in spite of the fact that they continue to have morning erections and erections during sleep. A man with a morning erection is capable of having an erection for sexual intercourse; any failure to do so has psychological rather than physical causes (Harper, 1965). Just as sleeping women develop vaginal lubrication every 60 to 80 minutes, almost all men have erections at about the same time intervals, whether or not they are capable of erections during the waking state (Fisher et al., 1965; Masters & Johnson, 1971).

Secondary impotency can be caused by anxiety and overconcern about a long-standing problem of premature ejaculation, by excessive alcoholic consumption, excessive maternal or paternal domination in childhood, inhibiting religious restrictions, homosexual conflicts, faulty sex education, and certain physiological inhibitors. Fortunately, secondary impotence is amenable to treatment by trained therapists, and there is a success rate of 73.8 percent (Mas-

CHRISTIANSON

Sexual Dysfunction **255**

ters & Johnson, 1970). If the success achieved through the prescribed treatment is not maintained for at least five years, the therapy is considered a failure.

Ejaculatory dysfunction. Premature ejaculation is a condition in which there is "the absence of voluntary control over the ejaculatory reflex, regardless of whether this occurs after two thrusts or five, whether it occurs before the female reaches orgasm or not" (Kaplan, 1974, p. 290). It is a condition causing anxiety and stress for many men and women; it frequently bedevils a marriage or seriously impairs a sexual relationship. Although the Kinsey group found that 75 percent of all men ejaculate within 2 minutes after intromission (Kinsey et al., 1948; Mozes, 1963), a woman's ability to have an orgasm through coital stimulation and a man's pleasure in prolonged penile containment is enhanced when his staying power is closer to 15 minutes. Certainly, sexually aroused partners will both feel cheated if ejaculation occurs within mere seconds of penile insertion. Repetition of this sort of bad timing can understandably spell quick death to what might otherwise have been a thoroughly satisfactory sexual relationship.

The causes of premature ejaculation are many and varied. In most cases, there are historical incidents that have conditioned the man to hurry his ejaculation. Anxiety and fear over the aspects of the sex act are also prominent causal factors in the problem. There may be an element of revenge toward the particular partner or toward women in general. Or the man may be unduly tense, tired, or lacking in self-confidence in his sexual abilities. An overlong period of sexual abstinence or a prolonged period of sexual excitement before intromission can also lead to premature ejaculation. It was once theorized that premature ejaculation could be due to abnormal sensitivity of the penis due to circumcision. Neurological and clinical testing of tactile discrimination has failed, however, to reveal any differences in the sensitivity of a circumcised and an uncircumcised penis. Control of ejaculation, or lack of it, is related far more to self-training and to emotional factors than to such physical conditions as an overly sensitive penis (Mozes, 1963).

A man with a history of premature ejaculation can be trained to withhold orgasm until both he and his partner want it to occur. There is a success rate of 97.8 percent in the treatment of premature ejaculation (Masters & Johnson, 1970).

Orgasmic dysfunction. Female orgasmic dysfunction is a condition in which a woman fails to go beyond the plateau phase in sexual response (Masters & Johnson, 1970). The term "orgasmic dysfunction" has replaced the meaningless word "frigidity," which has been used unfairly to describe women whose sex drive was less than what some subjective report termed "normal." A husband who desires coitus seven times a week may label his wife "frigid" if she desires it only three times a week, for example. (If the situation is reversed, the wife may well be called a "nymphomaniac" by her complaining husband!)

If a woman has never in her life achieved an orgasm through any method of sexual stimulation, she is considered to have **primary orgasmic dysfunction**. If she has achieved at least one orgasm in her life, whether by coitus, masturbation, or some other form of stimulation, but no longer does so, she is considered to have **situational orgasmic dysfunction** (Masters & Johnson, 1970). A few women are nonorgasmic because of organic factors—injuries to or constitutional deficiencies in the sexual system, hormonal imbalance, disorders of the nervous system, inflammation or lesions of the internal or external genitalia and surrounding areas, excessive use of drugs or alcohol, or old age (Ellis, 1961). More women are nonorgasmic due to relational factors—a woman may be filled with revulsion or distaste for her sexual partner either because of his sexual selfishness or because of her inability to accept him as a sexual partner for other reasons (Coleman, 1972).

By far the most common causative factors in female orgasmic dysfunction are psychological (Coleman, 1972; Ellis, 1958, 1960, 1961), and these are typically such emotional problems as shame, guilt, and fear. Our society indoctrinates women from an early age, either directly or by implication, into a warped sexual attitude (Ellis, 1961). Taught to suppress sexual feelings, many women formulate a negative sexual value system that is based on the premise that sex is bad, wrong, and dirty. Even after a woman knows intellectually that sex is good, right, and healthy, she may still be unable to respond orgasmically because of emotionally inhibitory factors or because of her lack of orgasmic experience.

Stimulative methods, such as oral-genital contact and especially the use of mechanical vibrators, are frequently successful in producing orgasmic responses in a woman. Once she achieves orgasm by one method, she is better able to achieve orgasm during other forms of sexual activity. After orgasm is attained and the woman gains confidence in her ability, subsequent orgasms are usually more easily and more frequently reached. If this method does not make a woman orgasmic, professional sexual treatment should be obtained.

Other conditions. Two other conditions which interfere with marital sexuality bear mentioning. One is **dyspareunia**, painful coitus, and the other is **vaginismus**, powerful and often painful contractions of the muscles around the vaginal tract. Dyspareunia can occur in either men or women, but is more common in women. In men, the condition is marked by a severe, jabbing pain during orgasm, and is usually caused by some congestion or inflammation of one of the sexual organs. In women, dyspareunia more frequently is caused by tension, fear, or anxiety over initial sexual intercourse. Coitus may also be painful for a woman because of lesions or scar tissue on the vaginal opening, because of an accumulation of hardened smegma under the clitoral foreskin, because of a displaced or prolapsed uterus, or because of polyps, cysts, or tumors of the reproductive system. Chemicals contained in contraceptive creams, foams, jellies, or suppositories may also be irritating to the vaginal passage in some women, and other women react painfully to the rubber or plastic that condoms and diaphragms are made of, or to excessive douching. Still other women—especially those who are postmenopausal—produce insufficient vaginal lubrication during coition, so that coital movements produce a painful or burning sensation. This latter discomfort can be readily avoided by using a commercial lubricant such as KY Sterile Lubricant, or, in the case of postmenopausal women, by using vaginal creams containing female hormones (Clark, 1965; Rubin, 1966).

In about 85 percent of the cases of persisting dyspareunia, small undetected lesions in the vagina are the cause (Kleegman, 1959). In other cases, infections of the vagina, uterus, bladder, or surrounding areas can obviously make intercourse painful for a woman. In cases where dyspareunia continues for a period of time, a woman should consult a physician for its cause. If there are no physiological disorders, psychotherapy can help overcome the emotional blocks and fears that led to the condition.

Vaginismus is almost always due to emotional factors. It can be caused by the anticipated pain of first penile penetration, feelings of fear or guilt about sexual intercourse, or frustration due to a sexually incompetent partner. In severe cases, an attempt even to introduce the penis into the vagina will often produce such agonizing pain, or such severe contractions of the ring of muscles encircling the vaginal opening, that penile penetration is impossible. In less severe cases, the vaginal spasms merely delay intromission or make it more difficult. Physical treatment, such as the use of dilators that are graduated in size, for a three- to five-day period sometimes relieves the involuntary spasms of vaginismus (Shaw, 1954). However, because the dysfunction usually has its roots in the psychological quagmire of fear, guilt, and shame, physical efforts at overcoming it may be unsuccessful and psychotherapy is therefore indicated.

Success in the treatment of vaginismus is near the 100 percent level. Furthermore, the vast majority of women are able to achieve orgasm after treatment for their vaginismus (Masters & Johnson, 1970).

KEEPING EXCITEMENT
IN MARITAL SEX

While much is made of the tendency for marital sex to become boring and stale after a number of years, the fact is that boring people have boring sex and that interesting people have interesting sex, whether they have been married one month or one decade. A woman who always serves dinner at six o'clock, who always prepares the same dishes week after week, and who always sets the table with the same dreary dishes is probably the same woman who always expects sex in the same position and never varies her approach or response in any way. She's both a boring cook and a boring bed partner. By the same token, a man who performs his duties on the job in the same endless pattern, week after week, without imagination or variety, probably bores his co-workers on the job as much as he bores his wife in bed. When these types of people attempt to inject excitement into their sexual life, they usually attempt some mechanical, external change rather than making real changes within themselves to become more exciting people. The boring cook may purchase a pair of black lace bikini panties, and her boring husband may splash on some cologne he got for Christmas two years ago, but unless the new panties and odors signify significant changes in their own attitudes toward life, they will still be boring and their sex life will be equally boring. Exciting and interesting marital sex is related to a favorable attitude rather than to gimmicks. Such an attitude holds that sex is fun and exciting and comforting, that dinner can be turned off while a couple makes love on the dining room floor, and that an overcooked casserole is more palatable than half-baked rules about the proper time and place to have sexual intercourse. A couple who trust each other in sex can express to each other their fantasies, their desires, and their dislikes without inhibition, and they can experiment with sexual activities they read about, hear about, or think about without fear that the other will be repulsed or frightened. Sexual failures may provide a couple with as much fun as their most monumental suc-

cesses. If a novel position or technique proves uncomfortable or unrewarding, it is a shared experience about which they can laugh and joke later as they move on to other experimentation.

One couple who have a very satisfying sex life told of an experiment with an alleged Oriental practice of the woman inserting a string of beads into the man's rectum and pulling them out at the moment of his orgasm. "The damn beads got hung on a hemorrhoid," said the husband ruefully, "and I thought I was going to die." While the experience was painful, the memory of it causes the couple to go into fits of laughter when they speak of it, and it obviously is a memory that binds them closer together.

Another couple told of having contorted themselves into a particularly complicated position for sexual intercourse. As they struggled to maintain the position, the wife looked her husband in the eye and said wonderingly, "What if we got locked in this position and had to stay this way the rest of our lives?" "Well, we could just act natural, and maybe nobody would notice," replied her husband, and their resulting hysteria delayed the completion of their intercourse for several minutes. It was both a complete failure as a sexual experience and a wondrously intimate moment that they treasure.

Exciting and satisfying sex is therefore a matter of openness of mind and a willingness to experiment with the new and novel. It is not, however, a matter of trying to make every sexual experience a novel one, or of trying to interject something new and exciting into every act of sexual intercourse. Sometimes there is a need for the comfortably familiar. Experimentation and sexual variety can become as boring as no experimentation and variety. There must be a combination of both surprise and predictability in sexual encounters to make them satisfying. One must not be so tiresome as to make identical movements and say identical words at each encounter, but there should also be enough similarity in each experience that each feels comfortable and secure. Armed with a knowledge of the basic techniques and positions of sexual activity, the imaginative couple can add stimulating and exciting fillips to their sexual repertoire and prevent staleness and dullness in marital sex.

Techniques of sexual arousal. Sexual arousal consists of both indirect stimuli, such as the sight, smell, and sound of another person or of the couple's surroundings, and of direct stimuli, such as touch and taste. Arousal may be felt by both men and women many times a day as they go about their work and is not confined to one's sexual partner or to a particular situation.

Cleanliness and attractiveness are the most important factors in initial arousal, with pleasant odors and tastes being the important factors in more intimate encounters. Both men and women are sensitive to unpleasant odors. Interestingly, there is a substance called **exaltolide** that has a chemical constitution similar to that of civet—presumably conveying the essence of maleness—that a woman can readily smell during her reproductive years. She cannot smell it as a child or after menopause, but only during her estrogen-producing years. A man, however, can never smell the odor unless he is given an injection of estrogen (Morgan, 1972). This ability to detect male odors may account for a woman's "finickiness" when there is too much of a good thing about the way a man smells. A man who wants to be sexually appealing should therefore keep himself scrupulously clean and free of odor, especially when he is about to engage in sexual activity, although some women enjoy the "musty" smell associated with slight perspiration.

While men are less particular about a woman's body odor than women are about a man's, they are nonetheless turned off by offensive urine or smegma odors in the vaginal area. Douching is not necessary to be free of offensive odor, as the vagina is a self-cleaning structure, but regular bathing is necessary to keep the smelly accumulation of smegma and other secretions from becoming offensive.

When a man and woman are confident of their own cleanliness and sex appeal, they are free to give themselves up to enjoyment of stimulation of their own bodies and to exploration of the other's erogenous zones. **Erogenous zones** are those areas of the body that are the most sexually sensitive. For both sexes, the most sexually sensitive areas are the genitals, the inner and outer thighs, the breasts (especially the nipples), the buttocks, anal region, and the abdomen. In addition to these areas, men and women are sexually sensitive on their armpits, small of the back, shoulders, neck, earlobes, scalp, eyelids, and especially the mouth, tongue, eyes, and nose. Actually, any area of the body can become a conditioned erogenous zone if it is stimulated during pleasurable sexual activity (Williamson, 1961).

During the first stages of sexual arousal, both men and women are excited by gentle, slow, sensual stroking that becomes more specific as sex play progresses (McCary, 1978). Rather than moving directly toward the genital area, stroking should be over the entire body, with occasional brushing of the genitalia. Interspersed with the stroking motions should be gentle squeezing, pinching, and massaging of the other's breasts, nipples, and other body areas. Kissing, nibbling, and licking are also important during sexual arousal, again with the emphasis constantly moving and varying in pressure and intensity.

As movement progresses to more specific attention to the genital area, both men and women should be conscious of the delicacy of the tissues there. While a woman's vulval region is somewhat more delicate than a man's genital region is, a woman who is too rough can cause pain to the penile skin or to the scrotum. She should be particularly careful during fellatio not to scrape her teeth along the penile shaft, and if she takes the testicles into her mouth she should be very gentle, as this is an especially pain-sensitive area. Similarly, a man should not manually manipulate a woman's clitoral region unless his fingernails are smooth and unless the region is well lubricated, either with the woman's own secretions or with a commercial lubricant.

Both men and women are frequently ill at ease and unsure of themselves when they caress their partner's body. From early childhood, boys and girls are taught not to touch each other, particularly in the genital or breast area. Many nursery schools, in fact, have as a category of evaluation of their toddler students "keeping hands off others." Touching the body of another child is frowned upon by teachers and parents on the grounds that it is "unsanitary" or "bad manners," but the truth is that it conveys sensual pleasure to the toucher and to the touched, and adults are extremely uncomfortable in the presence of childhood sensuality—however innocent. As children grow older, they continue to avoid close physical contact with one another, and by the time they marry, they may have a firmly ingrained attitude that touching another person's body is somehow distasteful or offensive to the other.

By training themselves to take pleasure in touching and being touched, a husband and wife can add to their sexual pleasure immeasurably. Called **sensate focus** by Masters and Johnson (1970), the technique of learning to pleasurably touch is actually a form of nonverbal communication between husband and wife. Lying between her husband's legs and leaning on his chest, as he leans back against the head of the bed, a woman can learn to receive pleasure without feeling called upon to respond in any way. Her husband's hands are free to explore all areas of her body, and to caress, fondle, stroke, squeeze, and massage her inner thighs, breasts, abdomen, and vulval area. If he touches her in a way that is not pleasurable, she can gently guide his hand away from that spot, or change the pattern of his stroking, but without speaking. To indicate to him what is most pleasurable, she can again silently guide his hands into the areas and patterns of movement that are most pleasurable

to her. Her only responsibility is to signify what is pleasurable and what is not pleasurable. Beyond that, she is to simply give herself up to the enjoyment of the sensations. Her husband's only responsibility is to respond to her nonverbal communications of what she prefers and what she dislikes, and to enjoy the feeling of his wife's body under his hands. By aiming solely at the enjoyment of the sensation of touching, without having intercourse as the goal, a couple can thus learn to communicate through touch alone.

To learn her husband's likes and dislikes in touching, the wife sits facing him, while he lies on his back with his thighs over hers. She can thus fondle, stroke, and manipulate his genitals, stroke his inner thighs, run her hands up his body and fondle his nipples, and reach his shoulders and arms. By guiding her hands, her husband can indicate to her his dislikes and likes as she indicated hers, while he enjoys the sensation of being stroked and caressed.

Each couple may vary the sensate focus according to their own preferences. They may prefer to use it as a prelude to intercourse, or they may use it simply as a form of pleasuring one another. Some may add total body massage to their nonverbal communication. Whatever a couple does in this respect, the goal should always be to become better acquainted with one another through touching, and to learn the sensual pleaures both of being touched and of touching.

Coital positions. There are an endless number of coital positions that a couple can adopt, but almost all are based on one of the four basic positions of face-to-face, man-above; face-to-face, woman-above; face-to-face, side position; and the rear-entry position.

No one position in sexual intercourse can correctly be considered to be more "normal" than another, although a particular position may be more desirable or appropriate than others under certain circumstances. Uninhibited experimentation with sexual positions permits a couple to work out their own variations of the four basic positions. This achievement, along with other spontaneous sexual activity, adds an extra measure of spice to the sex lives of most couples. Such additions to the amatory techniques of couples can add to the pleasure, comfort, and fulfillment of the two people involved, all of which may be quite instrumental in expanding or maintaining the joys of marriage.

The **face-to-face, man-above position**, called the "missionary position" by amused people in other cultures where the position is relatively rare, is the most common in our own culture. Indeed, it is considered by some the only "normal" position, and anything else

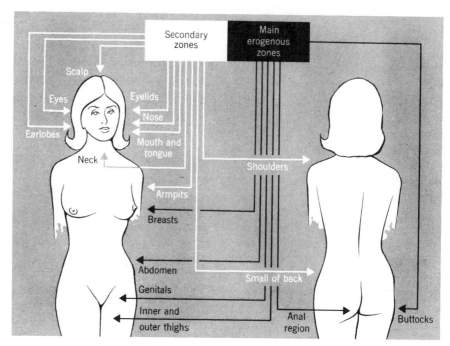

Erogenous zones

is considered deviant. Probably reflecting the passivity traditionally assigned to women, the position requires the woman to lie on her back with her legs apart and her knees bent while the man lies between her legs. In this position, the man has the greater control of the couple's body movements, but the woman can vary the position of her legs by closing them, pulling her knees to her shoulders, or locking them around her partner's back or neck. If the man puts pressure on the upper part of his partner's vulva, he will be more likely to keep contact with the clitoris and increase the possibility of an orgasm in his partner.

When the woman is astride the man, in the **face-to-face, woman-above position**, she is in control of the tempo of movement and the depth of penetration. Clitoral contact is easier and the friction is more intense as the woman either sits or lies on her partner. She is frequently more likely to be orgasmic in this position since she is free to make the pelvic movements she needs for her own stimulation. This position also enables the man to "hold off" his ejaculation because he experiences less muscular strain than in some other sexual positions.

In the **face-to-face, side position** each shares control of pelvic movements, and neither is supporting the weight of the other. A variation of this position is the **lateral coital position** in which the woman lies against the man's inner thigh, with her upper leg over his upper hip. The man is best able to control ejaculation in this position, and the woman can engage in pelvic thrusting of her own choice. It is therefore a position that allows most flexibility of free sexual expression for both partners.

The **rear-entry position** is usually achieved when the woman is kneeling, lying on her side, or assuming a knee-chest position while facing away from her partner. She may also sit on a man's lap with her back to him or lie on her stomach, although the latter position is usually unsatisfactory to both.

Couples who want to keep their marital sex life pleasurable should engage in all of these positions, as well as in their variations. Whatever the position employed, it should allow freedom of movement for the woman to allow her to have an orgasmic response. If she is sandwiched between the man and the bed, or if her buttocks are clasped too firmly by the man, she will be unable to move freely and thus will be less likely to have an orgasm during intercourse. Most important is that the position be mutually pleasurable to both the husband and the wife.

Aphrodisiacs and anaphrodisiacs. Certain foods have long been thought to have sexually stimulating properties, especially those foods that in some way resemble a particular sex organ. The superstitious belief that eating such foods results in increased sexual strength is called the **doctrine of signatures**. One example of the doctrine of signatures is the idea that the oyster—resembling a testicle—contains sexually arousing properties. Any aphrodisiac effects of oysters or any other food, of course, are due to the *belief* in their powers, and not to any chemical component of the food itself.

Alcohol is probably the most famous of the alleged sexual stimulants, but the truth is that alcohol is a depressant. In sufficient quantities, it narcotizes the brain, thus retarding reflexes, and dilates the blood vessels, thus interfering with the capacity for erection. In small quantities, alcohol acts to remove a person's inhibitions, so that sex drive and sexual enjoyment may be increased by alcohol consumption in persons who are sexually repressed by shame, guilt, or temporary stress, such as that sometimes caused by one's job. Again, however, the increase is due to temporary removal of psychological barriers rather than to an increase in physical prowess.

Of the drugs commonly associated with increased sexual drive, the most popularly known has been **cantharides**, or "Spanish Fly."

Actually dried and powdered beetles, the powder causes an acute irritation of the genito-urinary tract, with an accompanying dilation of the associated blood vessels. While penile erection can result due to the increased blood supply to the irritated tissue, there is no increase in sex drive and there is considerable discomfort. Taken in excessive doses, "Spanish Fly" can cause violent illness or even death.

Another drug long believed to have aphrodisiac qualities is **yohimbine**, used by African natives as a diuretic. Since it stimulates the nerve centers that control erection, yohimbine is generally conceded to be the most widely used drug for increasing sexual drive, although there is some question of its effectiveness. It has not gained recognition or approval as an aphrodisiac by the national food and drug authorities.

The popularity of drugs such as "Spanish Fly" and yohimbine has been largely replaced by the mystique that has grown up around the drug culture of modern times. Various addicting or illicit drugs such as opium, morphine, cocaine, LSD, hashish, and marijuana have been touted as aphrodisiacs. Like alcohol, these drugs release inhibitions, but also like alcohol, they tend to have the opposite effect of an aphrodisiac if taken in large enough quantities.

Marijuana has probably gained the most popularity as a sexual stimulant. Its effect, however, appears to be that of enhancement of the enjoyment of sexual activity rather than increasing the sex drive. Because marijuana heightens sense perception and distorts time perception, orgasm is subjectively prolonged and more pleasurable. One study showed that, among unmarried college students, marijuana users tend to be more sexually active than their non-marijuana-smoking counterparts, but there is not a direct cause-and-effect relationship. Instead, marijuana users and the sexually active tend to be more responsive to all forms of bodily stimulation (Stewart, 1972). The other side of the coin, however, is that heavy marijuana users tend to lose their ability to discriminate between a "high" and a new sensory experience, and may become temporarily impotent. Their potency returns, however, when they discontinue using marijuana for a period of several weeks. This dual effect of marijuana, to both heighten sexual enjoyment and cause impotence, has led to marijuana's reputation as both an aphrodisiac and an anaphrodisiac (a sexually deterring agent).

Other drugs that may have possible aphrodisiac effects, but that also may have undesirable side effects, are PCPA and L-dopa. Sniffing amyl nitrite during orgasm has also been claimed to enhance the pleasure of orgasm. Side effects of the use of this drug include dizziness, headache, fainting, and, in rare cases, death. None of these drugs has been approved as an aphrodisiac, and, at best, all are still in the experimental stage. Any sensible person recognizes the danger of using such drugs without medical sanction.

Some people depend on erotic pictures, songs, literature, or recordings of sounds suggestive of sexual activity to act as aphrodisiacs for them. While new sexual excitement can occur when exposed to erotic stimuli, immunity to such stimulation rapidly develops if the exposure is overdone.

The most effective aphrodisiacs remain good health, plenty of rest and sleep, adequate diet and exercise, and freedom from emotional tension. The opposites of these, of course, are the most effective anaphrodisiacs. The best known reputed anaphrodisiac, however, is **saltpeter**, or potassium nitrate. It is an almost completely neutral chemical and is an absolute failure as an anaphrodisiac, although it is a fairly effective diuretic.

Some ancient recipes for aphrodisiacs

From *The Perfumed Garden* by Sheikh Nefzawi (translated from the Arabic by Richard Burton): He who makes it a practice to eat every day fasting the yolk of eggs, without the white part, will find in this aliment an energetic stimulant for coitus. The same is the case with the man who during three days eats the same mixed with onions.

He who boils asparagus, and then fries them in fat, and then pours upon them the yolk of eggs with pounded condiments, and eats every day of this dish, will grow very strong for coitus, and find in it a stimulant for his amorous desires.

From the *Kama Sutra* (translated from the Sanskrit by Richard Burton):
Drinking milk with sugar, and having the testicle of a ram or goat boiled in it, is also productive of vigour. . . .

[A man will be able to enjoy innumerable women if he] mixes with rice the eggs of a sparrow, and having boiled this in milk, adds to it ghee [clarified butter] and honey, and drinks of it as much as necessary. . . .

If ghee, honey, sugar and liquorice in equal quantities, the juice of the fennel plant, and milk are mixed together, this nectar-like composition is said to be holy, and provocative of sexual vigour, a preservative of life, and sweet to the taste.

SEX IN THE MIDDLE YEARS

As the years go by in marriage, the husband is usually intent on making a success of his career, and the wife is usually caught up in the duties of a mother. Each may be too preoccupied and too fatigued to give sex the important place it deserves in their lives. When the children are grown and the career is well-launched, husband and wife may discover that there are differences in their sexuality that are disturbing to them. Furthermore, at a time in their lives when they both may have regrets about their accomplishments, they may focus all their feelings of inadequacy onto their sexuality and create a problem where none needs to exist.

Menopause. For a woman, menopause may cause her to feel that she is no longer a woman, simply because she no longer menstruates or is capable of bearing children. She might become alarmed if she should actually become pregnant, but she would like to be *able* to become pregnant because it signifies youth and desirability at a time when she is acutely conscious of being older and less desirable than she was. Our culture subtly conditions women to look upon menopause as a time when feminine desirability ceases. Sexuality is present in terms of youth—the younger and more nubile, the more tantalizing, to some—and fecundity, while sexual deprivation and ugliness are associated with aging and barrenness. Lolita is far more sensuous than her grandmother, in spite of the fact that Lolita's grandmother is experienced and knowledgeable while Lolita's seductiveness depends largely on her lack of experience. The only person who admits to wanting to share a bed with Grandmother is her toddler grandchild, while Grandfather undermines his wife's self-confidence by ogling young girls who might be the same age as his own grandchildren. Thus, cultural conditioning has more to do with a woman's dread of the menopause as signaling an end to sexuality than does actual physical reality. Many of the symptoms of menopause are simply symptoms of depression concerned with being older and are not physiologically related to menopause at all.

Unfortunately, women who are actually approaching years of relatively free time during which they can pursue their own interests and activities all too often feel that their years of usefulness are over and that they will no longer be sexual beings. Menopause, literally meaning a pause in the menses, is in no way an end to a woman's sex life. It is simply an end to her childbearing life, and is caused by a decrease in estrogen production by the ovaries. Contrary to popular belief, menopause does not signal the *end* of estrogen production, but a reduction in the amount produced, so that ovulation ceases. Even if monthly bleeding is prolonged artificially by the use of the pill, the ovaries will stop producing ova sometime between the ages of 40 and 55 just as if no hormones had been given (Kaufman, 1971).

A sad commentary on our emphasis on youth and youthful sexuality is that only about 30 percent of women pass through menopause easily, continuing to enjoy life and sex as they did before (Kaufman, 1971). To be sure, physiological changes occur due to estrogen deprivation, but a woman's estrogen production does not end overnight; it is a gradual process that varies from woman to woman and can be detected by periodic medical evaluation. If symptoms of estrogen deprivation occur, such as thinning of the vaginal lining, hot and cold flashes, night sweats, insomnia, or fatigue, any one of several estrogenic preparations may be administered to relieve the symptoms quickly (Kaufman, 1971).

The truth is that most women who experience sexual difficulties during and after menopause do so because of emotional and cultural factors and not because of estrogen deprivation. Female sex hormones, in fact, have no direct influence on sexual desire, sexual performance, or sexual response, although the male hormone, androgen, found in both women and men, does have such an influence. Psychological factors more than hormonal factors govern sexual functioning. A woman who has never enjoyed sex may use

menopause as an excuse to reject it by complaints of headaches, fatigue, and other vague discomforts. She also may reject sex because she believes she is *supposed* to lose her sex drive after menopause.

In addition to the above concerns, there are physical problems that may occur at the same time, further undermining a woman's confidence in herself as a sexually adequate woman. Due to various common pelvic disorders in middle-aged women, hysterectomy—the surgical removal of the uterus—is not uncommon. If a woman believes that her womb or ovaries are the main source of her sexuality, she will be likely to react to their removal with depression and a loss of sexual interest and responsiveness. She should be assured that her uterus has little to do with her sexual pleasure, and that if her ovaries are removed, ovarian hormones can be replaced. Whether a woman's hysterectomy involves removal of ovaries and fallopian tubes as well as uterus, or removal of only the uterus, she should be informed that her libido is more cerebral in origin than hormonal.

Women who have borne children frequently find that their sexual enjoyment diminishes with the years, and their husbands also find that intercourse is less pleasurable than it was, because of relaxed vaginal muscles. As the vaginal muscles relax, there is less friction during penile penetration and less pleasure for both husband and wife. There also may be some embarrassing loss of urine during orgasm due to relaxed sphincter muscles.

By exercising the muscles, a woman can restore the muscle tone to her vaginal walls and sphincter muscles and provide a snugger vagina for her husband's penis and more clitoral stimulation for herself when the penis moves in and out of her vagina. She should practice the same muscular control that she would use to stop urination in midstream, and repeat that action as many as 100 times a day until she can hold the contraction for as long as three seconds at a time. She should continue the exercises for life, doing at least 25 a day to maintain vaginal muscle tone. Within a few weeks after beginning the exercise, both she and her sexual partner should be able to tell a difference in muscle tone and in sexual enjoyment.

Sex and aging in men. Although men do not cease sperm production as women cease ova production, they do undergo a climacteric of sorts that is more psychological than physiological. A man may experience discontent and frustration at having failed to realize all his goals at a time when he feels that there is too little time to do so. He may also feel older and more fatigued when he looks at his depressed, menopausal wife, and he may feel a need to restore his sexual self-confidence by having affairs with younger women.

There are also physical problems that may plague a middle-aged man and indirectly affect his sexual functioning. Prostate problems, for example, frequently occur at this time of life, and many men fear that they signal an end to their sexual activity. **Prostatitis—** an inflammation of the prostate gland—sometimes leads to painful or inadequate erections, premature ejaculations, or impotence. Medical treatment usually clears up the infection with no permanent loss of sexual functioning. Many men, however, who have experienced impotency as a result of prostatic infection have so much fear of the problem recurring that they may indeed become impotent. The impotence is due to their fears, however, and not to their prostate.

The same is true of men who have suffered cardiac seizures. In a large majority of cases, a man can continue to enjoy his sex life, but many men become so preoccupied with fears of another heart attack that they are unable to function sexually. They then conclude that they are impotent and channel their sexual energy into their jobs or professions.

The most notable effect on men of a decrease in testosterone production with age is that their peaks of sexual tension grow farther

apart. Sexual tension peaks about every 48 hours in a young man, but with diminishing testosterone, the peaks occur every 3, 4, or even 5 days (Lief, 1971).

A corresponding hormonal effect in aging men is that there is a decreasing need to ejaculate. There is no decrease in the capability for erection, but the ejaculate decreases in amount and there is a decrease in the capacity to ejaculate. Since he will have a greater capacity to maintain an erection prior to ejaculation, an older man should become a better lover, more capable of satisfying his wife than he was when he was younger and quicker to ejaculate (McCary, 1973).

Whether or not a man and woman continue to have an enjoyable sex life in their late years seems to depend on how their sex life was in the 30s and 40s. If it was satisfactory then, and if they successfully coped with the physical and situational changes in their lives, the chances are that they will continue to enjoy pleasurable sexual relations well into later life (Lief, 1971).

CONCLUSION

As the foregoing chapters on human sexual behavior have indicated, human sexuality begins at birth and ends at death. It is not
a facet of humanity that exists solely during the years from 16 to
60, as some would like us to believe, but is rather as much a part
of being a person as breathing is, and lasts just as long as breathing
does. The important factor in human sexuality is not *when* but *how*.
If one's sexuality is expressed with respect for oneself and one's
partner, with regard for the rights of others, and with full knowledge and acceptance of one's responsibilities, it can be one of the
most rewarding aspects of a person's life.

CHAPTER 10

ADJUSTMENT IN MARRIAGE

He drinks because she scolds, he thinks, She thinks she scolds because he drinks, And neither will admit what's true, That he's a sot and she's a shrew.   OGDEN NASH

276   Adjustment in Marriage

When a man and a woman marry, each brings into the marriage a lifetime of learned values, philosophies, attitudes, beliefs, and styles of coping with life. Since each has a unique background and unique experiences, there will be differences in the set of values and goals that each marital partner possesses, and clashes are inevitable. The good life to Harry may mean owning a flashy automobile, living in an expensive home in the best part of town, and regularly frequenting the most popular night spots. To Beth, the good life may mean having three children, belonging to a church and actively working in it, and planting a garden behind a modest home and canning the vegetables produced there. A visit with family or friends may constitute her favorite entertainment, and she may consider nightclubs a frivolous bore. One might legitimately ask the question, "Why would two such people ever marry in the first place?" But legitimate question or not, such marriages do occur, and occur, and occur. And unless such a marriage is to be one that lacks any of the interdependence that accompanies an intimate relationship, with each partner living independently of the other in every way, each must make adjustments so that his own and the other's needs and expectations are met satisfactorily. This is certainly not an easy task and it is not something that even the best adjusted partners can accomplish without expending a considerable amount of emotional sweat and tears.

Marital adjustment has been described as a state in which "the individual or the pair has a good working arrangement with reality, adulthood, and the expectations of others" (Waller & Hill, 1951, p. 362). Obviously, since everything in life is in a constant process of change, there is no such thing as a state of absolute adjustment in marriage. Neither is there a static achievement that successfully married people possess once and for all. Rather, adjustment is a process, an ongoing process, that is achieved for a period of time in some areas of living and is perhaps only an ideal to be striven for in others.

Specific adjustments in marriage are usually demanded at different stages of the natural sequence of marriage: early marriage, the childbearing and childrearing years, the time in middle life when the children leave home, and the time of retirement. Adjustments are also called for in times of crisis (Landis & Landis, 1973).

Marital adjustment almost always means that one or both partners give up something in one area in order to satisfy a need in another area. A good adjustment is one in which each derives more satisfaction than deprivation and in which the interlocking needs of each are usually met. It is the satisfaction of the marital partners themselves that determines the relative success of their adjustive efforts. What one couple might consider a well-adjusted pattern of marriage might be unacceptable to another couple.

ATTEMPTS AT ADJUSTMENT

Attempts at adjustment may be either defense-oriented or reality-oriented (Saxton, 1968). **Defense-oriented** behavior aims to reduce tension rather than seeking to fulfill a more basic need. Heavy drinking is an example of defense-oriented behavior that temporarily reduces a person's tension and so becomes a repeated pattern. The drinking causes increased stress and deprivation in the marriage, however, and is therefore an inadequate adjustment. In fact, alcoholism has been named as a cause of divorce by one in three semi-skilled workers, one in five clerical and sales workers, and one in seven professional workers (Kephart, 1954).

A person also may attempt to escape or reduce tension in a marriage by emotional withdrawal or by substituting anger and frustration in one area for another area. A wife who bitterly resents her husband's autocratic control over the family's money, for example, may make no mention of it and instead criticize the way he drives or his expertise as a lover.

Tension-reducing efforts also may take the form of rationalization, fantasy or some other mode of repression, displacement, or similar defense mechanisms. Through these defense mechanisms a person may seek to escape tension by excessive sleeping, for example, or by converting anxiety and anger into physical illnesses. All of these defense-oriented modes of adjustment become unconscious patterns of behavior because of their immediate alleviation of tension and thus are very resistant to change (Saxton, 1968).

Reality-oriented adjustive behavior is directed at the conflicting needs of the partners. They recognize their own and their partner's abilities and limitations and attempt to work within those limits. For reality-oriented behavior, the partners must be fully aware of their own feelings and needs. They must be able to rank their needs in order of importance and be able to fulfill important needs without denying the spouse fulfillment of *his* or *her* important needs. When two people each have their important needs satisfied at the loss of some less important needs, and their adjustive methods are carried out in a spirit of good will and mutual affection, then they have a well-adjusted marriage.

The most successful patterns of adjustment seem to be in marriages in which each spouse is equally emotionally dependent on the other (Peterson, 1964) and in which each is equally dominant in the relationship (Kirkpatrick, 1955; Poponoe, 1940).

Some couples reach a state of marital adjustment through compromise, whereby each can give in on points that are not essential to self needs, while understanding the partner's wishes and their importance to him or her. A wife may have very strong feelings about the importance of a family's attending church together, for example, and feel that her marriage is lacking in fundamental areas if her husband stays home from church. He, on the other hand, may enjoy spending Sunday morning with the newspaper and a coffee pot, but he may recognize that his wife's need for his participation with her in church services is more important to her than his own preference for leisurely Sunday mornings is to him. They may work out a compromise whereby the husband attends church with his family on Sunday morning, and the wife allows him the enjoyment of Sunday afternoons spent in front of the TV, without reminding him that the yard needs mowing or that the shrubs need pruning, because she recognizes his need for some inactivity.

In other cases, a couple may not be able to reach agreement on a particular issue, and compromise may be impossible for either. In these cases, adjustment consists of simply accepting their lack of agreement and living with it, without antagonism, in the interest of their commitment to their total relationship. A husband may feel neglected and rejected, for example, if his wife is not at the door to greet him when he comes home. His wife may understand his need and be willing to arrange her schedule so that she can be at home whenever possible, but she may also need to pursue her own interests and to have activities outside the home that sometimes overlap with her husband's homecoming. Disagreement may then arise over the obligations that a wife has to her husband and to herself. The husband may be adamant in his belief that a wife's first duty is to her husband, while the wife may feel strongly that she is first a person, with needs and rights of her own, and then a wife. If neither is able to accept the other's position, they may decide that the only point of real friction lies in the question of whether or not the wife is at home when the husband arrives home, and they may be able to overlook that point of friction because the rest of their interaction is fairly smooth.

Schulz and Rodgers (1975) point out the importance of *feedback* in resolving conflicts realistically. Its importance comes from contributions it makes to our self-image. Feedback that is positive and consistent may be helpful by serving as a guide to our position in a relationship.

But sometimes feedback we receive is contradictory or is divergent from our own view. What we may interpret as progress on our part may be threatening to our partner's own self-image. A typical example is that of a wife going back to school to continue her education. She sees the progress she makes as enhancing her self-image and contributing to her growth as a person. The husband may see her growth and progress as a threat to his own self-image, thus creating a conflict. Their ability to communicate adequately with each other and to use the feedback each gives the other will determine how the conflict is resolved.

In addition to feedback, self-disclosure is another important factor in conflict resolution. Nowadays it is generally assumed that "openness" is always good. It is true that self-disclosure affects the way others regard us and it is sometimes through this means that we gain their understanding. But the effect of self-disclosure may not always lead in a positive direction. It could undermine authority and power, or be used against the "confessor" years later. Thus, in a family the rest of the members may not be able to handle well one person's sharing of negative or weak points about himself or herself. Sometimes, therefore, a person may think it wiser to conceal, rather than reveal such information about oneself.

... many people, in urging more communication with their spouses, are really urging more positive *communication, rather than full communication of both positive and negative. The conventional wisdom is that most disturbed marriages are afflicted with misunderstandings and misconceptions; what may be more dismaying in an intimate relationship is the existence of bitter* understanding, *when what is bitter is also true (Gagnon and Greenblatt, 1978, p. 255).*

A more thorough analysis of couples and how they may arrive at a positive adjustment in marriage through conflict that is openly expressed follows in the next chapter, "Dealing with Conflict Creatively."

DIFFERENCES BETWEEN WOMEN AND MEN

Most studies have come to the dismal conclusion that marriages become less satisfying as time goes by, and that satisfying companionship in marriage occurs only during the early years of marriage (Pineo, 1961; Rollins & Feldman, 1970). A more optimistic viewpoint comes from studies that indicate that as many as one couple in four *improve* their relationship between the early and middle marital years (Dizard, 1968; Pineo, 1961). Couples who were most likely to report decreases in marital satisfaction during this time period were those in which the husband had risen to the top of his profession or occupation and had become increasingly involved in community affairs. This finding would seem to suggest that men who focus the greater part of their attention and energy on their careers rather than on their marriages are likely to create an unhappy marital situation. (Or, that unhappy marriages cause men to concentrate on their careers.) Another study (Uhr, 1957) reported consistency of the husbands' personalities and great changes in the personalities of the wives in marriages that were happy, while unhappy marriages were characterized by great change in the personalities of the husbands and little change in the personalities of the wives.

Women are usually called upon to make more adjustments in marriage, possibly because they often have a greater investment in marriage than men do, and because they are often economically dependent on their husbands. For many women, marriage is the most important role they ever adopt as an adult, especially if they have a family soon after marriage and shift quickly from a wife role to a mother role, without ever having an occupational role (Bell, 1971a). Women are also slower to become disillusioned with marriage, although both men and women are likely to have some postmarital disillusionment, particularly concerning personal freedom, marital roles, having children, in-laws, control of money, the value of neatness, and attitudes toward divorce. There is some evidence of a direct relationship between the degree of romanticism prior to marriage and disillusionment after marriage (Hobart, 1958a). At the time of marriage, almost all women feel that their husbands are just the right men for them. After 2 years of marriage, only 65 percent of women maintain that opinion of their husbands, and after 20 years of marriage, only 5 out of 100 women believe they have made the proper choice (Sex around the world, 1974).

Whereas men tend to become disenchanted with the romantic relationship in the early years of marriage, women tend to retain their romantic illusions until sometime between the early and middle years of marriage (Bell, 1971a). Perhaps for this reason, the husband's role definition and expectations have been found by one study to be more important to the early success of a marriage than are the wife's role expectations (Stuckert, 1963). This also may be because our society exerts more pressure on a wife to adjust her marital role than it does on a husband to adjust his. It will be in-

teresting to observe whether or not this trend continues during the next decade or so.

While women tend to make more adaptations to their roles than men do, they receive less satisfaction from them during the child-bearing and childrearing years. There is an increase in marital satisfaction for both men and women after their children leave home, although there may be a temporary setback just before the husband's retirement (Rollins & Feldman, 1970).

There are also sexual differences in the manner in which a husband and wife react to problems in their marriage. Husbands are more likely to take a "wait and see" attitude, while wives are more likely to openly express their reactions when their expectations and needs are not met. The one area in which husbands are more likely to talk openly about the violations of their expectations is in money matters. They are least likely to be open about their disillusionment in the area of sexual intimacy (Cutler & Dyer, 1969).

As a couple's romantic idealism is disillusioned, changes occur in their relationship. On the one hand, they are less likely to maintain pretense with each other, and each becomes more able to predict the other's behavior. Their method of communication changes, with facial expressions and gestures becoming more important and verbal communication becoming less used (Brownfield, 1953). This intimacy of behavior is counterbalanced by the fact that the marital partners may become less dependent on each other as audiences. While young wives turn to their husbands for sympathy and to vent their anger, they gradually turn to other outlets as time goes on (Blood & Wolfe, 1960). It may be for this reason that most marriages count their happiest years their earliest years, when the most marital adjustment problems occur (Bernard, 1964), and when there is more husband-wife interaction than there is later.

ROLE EXPECTATIONS

In the rural, extended families of the past, people married other people from within the same community, whose experiences and backgrounds were similar and whose values and goals were also similar. The role expectations of each spouse were clearly defined, and there was far less chance of role conflict. With urbanization and industrialization, however, came a more heterogeneous population, and people from dissimilar backgrounds and experiences married and role definition became more complex.

The marital expectations of a married couple are based largely on the marital relationships of their parents. The way children see the marital role of their same-sex parents and that of the opposite-sex parents will determine the expectations they have of their own marital role and that of the spouse. The only son of a widowed mother will, for instance, fail to see his parent in a marital role and will view the rights and obligations of a wife in a different light than will the person who had two parents and several brothers and sisters (Kirkpatrick, 1955). If two people with such dissimilar backgrounds marry, there will almost certainly be conflict in how each defines the appropriate roles of self and partner.

"He's a robot," "She's a pig"

When Elaine and Herbert married, they were both convinced that theirs would be a perfect marriage. Yet they came for marriage counseling within three months.

"He's absolutely a robot!" charged Elaine. "He used to be fun, but now he's completely unemotional and dull."

"She's a pig," said Herbert, "You need a steam shovel to get through our apartment. She starts undressing when she opens the front door and leaves her clothes lying everywhere."

"He," said Elaine scathingly, "is so neat that he hangs his short-sleeved shirts separately from his long-sleeved shirts, and each group is divided according to color!''

Because of their conflict about neatness, this couple's entire relationship was deteriorating. Elaine was one of two daughters of a youthful working mother whose husband traveled a great deal. The three females enjoyed each other's company and spent a great deal of time planning their wardrobes and discussing hair styles and makeup. On the weekends, the three worked together cleaning and straightening their home as quickly as possible, but housekeeping was otherwise kept to a bare minimum and fun was more important than neatness.

Herbert, on the other hand, was the only son of a dominating, perfectionistic mother and a withdrawn, passive father who displayed his hostility toward his wife by leaving a trail of clutter behind him for her to pick up. Herbert had enjoyed Elaine's casualness before they were married, but his idea of a wife's role was a woman who valued a neat home. When his wife failed to immediately live up to his expectations, he assumed his mother's role himself, and viewed Elaine's clutter as a sign of her disrespect for him, as if his wife were enacting his father's role.

Since Elaine's mother had stressed fun over neatness, and since her father was absent most of the time, she had no views of a husband's role and thought of her husband as a friend and companion as her mother and sister had been. Their conflict was almost inevitable and could have destroyed their marriage if they had never gained the ability to view their problem objectively.

The fulfillment of role expectations is important to marital happiness; and if these expectations are not met, marital discord can result. Marriages in which there is congruence in the views of the correct roles for each mate are far more likely to succeed than marriages in which there is significant conflict in role expectations. Divorced couples, in fact, have been found to be four times farther apart in their views of appropriate marital roles than are married couples (Baber, 1953). Furthermore, both partners in a successful marriage find satisfaction in fulfilling their own roles and also in their partner's meeting their role expectations (Bell, 1971a). If a husband believes that he satisfies his wife sexually, for example, when in truth he rarely or never satisfies her, the wife is unlikely to find satisfaction in either her own or her husband's role as a sex partner, and the marriage is less likely to succeed. It is on an especially hazardous path if the wife does not quickly find ways to communicate her dissatisfaction to her husband, and in a manner that is not threatening to his ego.

In regard to the role of women in marriage, career-oriented

women of today face a troublesome dilemma. The lines of development toward marriage and toward a career are still not as convergent for women as they are for men. For example, many women in college encounter a considerable degree of conflict between academic demands and the pressure to socialize and find or keep a mate.

In preparing for the role of wife and mother, even now the pressure is toward being nonassertive, compliant, and supportive. These are qualities that are in almost direct contradiction to those required to succeed academically and professionally: assertiveness, self-confidence, competitiveness, and advancement toward self-serving goals. The pressure and tension created by this conflict is keenly felt by women, most particularly those who are already wives and mothers.

The difficulty lies, not only in women's self-concept, but also men's expectations of women. While women are becoming aware of their potential for a more complex, equal role, the man who continues to maintain a traditional attitude would rather marry a more acquiescent woman than a feminist (Komarovsky, 1973).

The uncertainty of the implications of these discrepant attitudes for men and women in the future is acknowledged by Gagnon and Greenblatt (1978, pp. 156–157):

> *To the degree that women make their feminist interests explicit there will be additional conflict in the partner selection process. Women who express these views strongly may indeed find some difficulty in finding partners. On the other hand women who conceal their desires may be setting up relationships in which conflict is deferred to the future rather than resolved at the present. What is difficult to predict for the future is the degree to which such values will be acted upon in real marriages. As more women enter the labor force as a permanent commitment . . . the real need to reallocate household and marital roles will become greater.*

The degree of disruption to a marriage from unsatisfactory role fulfillment depends in large part on the area of dissatisfaction, and on how specific the frustration is (Bell, 1971a). A husband may dislike his role as home repairman, but his frustration will probably not be intense enough to cause him to feel negatively about the total marital relationship. If he strongly objects to his role as the family breadwinner, however, his frustration will be much more pervasive and far-reaching.

In modern marriages of today, in which the emphasis is on each individual in the marriage achieving emotional satisfaction, each marital partner has the additional strain of fulfilling the marital role seen as appropriate for him or her by the spouse, while at the same time fulfilling his or her own needs and desires. If there is lack of agreement on what the appropriate roles are, there is likely to be even more conflict between marital roles and individual needs and wishes (Bell, 1971a).

RELATIONSHIP ROLES AND POWER

The parties in a relationship define the nature of that relationship either overtly or covertly, and they agree in some way upon what has been defined and the boundaries of power for each. ". . . in healthy relationships there are role expectations in common and individual motive disposition that allow the mates to agree on how the marriage will operate" (Goethals et al., 1976). As these authors point out, the one who contributes the greater resources is the most powerful. "Resources" includes such things as job and social status, income, occupation, education, etc.

In immature relationships partners attempt to sabotage the other's efforts toward control, rather than agreeing upon the areas where each one has control. Continually sabotaging the other's efforts results in either an imbalance of power with one retaining too much control over the other, or instability in which power struggles are frequent but unresolved. In an unsatisfactory relationship, there is no explicit or implicit agreement reached about who is in control of the relationship or areas within it. "It is characterized by the need to redefine the relationship the moment it becomes defined so that stable periods are brief, and unstable periods are long" (Jackson, 1959).

Dependency needs of the partners are not met, nor is either allowed to be independent. Dependency is an accepted part of a mature relationship and need not be feared, because each partner can trust the other not to reach for complete control at vulnerable times, and each partner knows that the other will gratify certain dependency needs that are part of the individual's makeup.

PREDICTORS OF SUCCESSFUL MARRIAGE

While it is tempting to try to predict future marital adjustment on the basis of the personality characteristics of the couple, it is impossible to do so with exactitude. In general terms, some predictors of marital success include: a stable, happy childhood with good relations with one's parents; informed attitudes about sex and discipline; marriage later in life (after age 20) after self-identity is more firmly established; establishment in an occupation; emotional maturity and the ability to give emotional support to the other; mutual interests and values; and a lengthy engagement period (six months to two years) (Saxton, 1977).

In successful marriages, there is the opportunity for individual expression for each partner. Having individual interests, engaging in separate activities, and expressing one's own personality are important to the success of a marriage, because each partner achieves individual growth in this manner and because some separateness allows each mate to retain some illusions about the other. For example, a husband who proudly acclaims his wife's artistic talent, may be less impressed if he attempts to help her market her work and discovers that it has no commercial value.

Another common pattern in successful marriages is that each mate remains the focus of the other's affection, thereby allowing each to continue to feel wanted and important. If either spouse transfers affection to another person or simply loses interest in the mate, the withdrawal of affection is a severe loss for the one who continues to want affection (Bell, 1971a).

From studies conducted to determine the main components of happy marriages, it would appear that the best insurance for a satisfactory marriage is for both husband and wife to have as much education as possible, and for the husband to have a high income. This analysis is based on the findings of studies such as that of Bumpass and Sweet (1972) who concluded that a wife's educational level was not significantly related to marital stability, but that the husband's was. However, when husband and wife are similar in educational level, they are more likely to have a mutual enjoyment of marriage (Burgess et al., 1963), and better educated women are more sexually responsive, as well as more satisfied with love and affection in marriage (Blood & Wolfe, 1960; Kinsey et al., 1953; Terman, 1938). A final argument in favor of higher education for both husband and wife is that, generally speaking, a man's education determines his earning power, and the husband's income has been found to greatly affect marital stability (Cutright, 1971). Perhaps it should be mentioned that a highly educated man whose particular specialty is not in demand in the job market, or who has personality problems that keep him from earning an adequate income for his family will probably have a far less happy marriage than the less well-educated man who has a skill that is well rewarded monetarily. Furthermore, it is becoming less a truism that education equals monetary success, and there is a trend toward a return to the prestige of the craftsman who commands full value for his skill. While it is true that marriages in which the wife has a higher education than the husband more frequently end in divorce than marriages in which the husband has an equal or greater amount of education (Scanzoni, 1968), the crucial element in these cases may be the wife's higher earning power. Many men, and many women, endorse the idea that the person in the marriage who earns the greater income is the most important person in that relationship. Such persons become uncomfortable with a relationship in which the wife has the greater income, and tensions may arise simply because of the difference in earning power. Men with less education than their wives probably would be far less threatened by their wives' greater education, and their wives would probably be more satisfied in the marriage, if they had equal or greater intellectual capacities, and equal or greater incomes. Hopefully, the day will come when couples are no more uncomfortable with a wife's earning the greater income than they are now with the husband's earning the greater income. A woman may happen to have a more marketable skill than her husband, and it is ridiculous for the husband to feel that her higher earning power places him in an inferior position, just as it is ridiculous for women to feel that their husbands' greater earning power places them in an inferior position. The belief that earning power is synonymous with superiority is one of the reasons why women are so poorly paid in the working world. Many men have the irrational fear that women will become "uppity" if they are paid an equal or greater amount of money than men, and therefore they perpetuate the lower salaries of women in order to retain their feeling of masculine superiority.

SOME COMMON PROBLEMS

A problem that is frequently encountered in marriage arises from the fact that both boys and girls, but most especially boys, are taught from childhood that open demonstrations of affection are "forward" or "sissy." With such background learning, both men and women frequently enter marriage with only an abstract knowledge that warm emotional interchanges are vital in a marital relationship. Men especially are likely to be unable to freely express their positive, warm, affectionate feelings. When they feel moved to express emotion, such men will express negative emotion—the only emotion with which they are familiar—rather than positive emotion. Instead of expressing tenderness, therefore, a man may show anger toward his wife, or he may make belittling remarks about her. An example of this kind of negative-for-positive substitution is the man who reacts with anger when his wife burns her finger while cooking. He may inwardly feel concern and even alarm, but his childhood conditioning may have taught him that to show sympathy and tenderness is to be less than a man. With "manly" strength, therefore, he may exclaim, "How could you do such a stupid thing?" or "My God, can't you even cook without making a mistake?" His wife, who needs some affectionate sympathy, will very likely fail to interpret his angry outburst as an expression of love, and will feel rejected, humiliated, and despised.

A similar misunderstanding frequently occurs in sexual matters. When an undemonstrative man does show affection and his wife is responsive, they may end up having sexual intercourse. Since a wife may receive only occasional demonstrations of affection, she may therefore accuse her husband of showing affection only when he wants sex. He may have felt like showing affection just for the sake of affection, but her responsiveness led to further response on his part, and so on to sexual intercourse. Both husbands and wives

can add immeasurable satisfaction to their marriages by cultivating the habit of spontaneously expressing their affectionate feelings when they occur. A touch, a smile, a glance of secret understanding, a word of sincere praise, a warm hug, or a warm touch can make a gray day seem brighter, and a frustrating situation less dismal. For those who have failed to learn how to express the warmth they feel toward another, psychotherapy can help them to learn the joy of experiencing a close, loving relationship with a spouse.

Couples who reach compatibility between their own needs and the roles that each fulfills are more likely to place the major emphasis on their relationship rather than on their respective roles (Bernard, 1964). Furthermore, the happiest couples tend to stress their relationship as their major source of happiness, while less happy couples tend to stress other aspects of marriage, such as home, children, or social life (Gurin, Veroff, & Feld, 1960). In order

"Do you realize that the only thing holding their marriage together is us?"

for a couple to maintain their satisfaction in their personal relationship, it is necessary for each to make some adjustments in his or her expectations of the other's role. Such adjustments are usually not conscious, and a couple may be surprised when they realize how much each has adjusted to the other (Bernard, 1964).

STYLES OF ADJUSTMENT

A 1965 study of the marriages of 211 prominent people who were considered by society to exemplify good adjustment as individuals and in their marriages revealed five distinct lifestyles that reflected methods of adjustment (Cuber & Harroff, 1965). The lifestyles were categorized as either "utilitarian" or "intrinsic." Utilitarian marriages are "conflict-habituated," "devitalized," or "passive-congenial," while intrinsic marriages are either "vital" or "total."

Marriages classified as **utilitarian** are characterized by avoidance behavior on the part of both partners. Husbands and wives work far away from home, accept travel assignments, are active in hobbies, club or civic work, or church activities, and may have separate bedrooms. Their mode of marital adjustment is rational and satisfying to the people in it, as it provides a comfortable framework for adult living, childrearing, and discharging civic responsibilities (Saxton, 1968). Most utilitarian marriages are **conflict-habituated**, meaning that the tensions and pervasive incompatibility between the couples are well controlled and concealed.

Utilitarian marriages that are not conflict-habituated are either devitalized or passive-congenial. The now **devitalized** marriages were originally important sources of deep personal expression, but have lost their intrinsic value to the partners. The partners spend little time together, they no longer share interests and activities in a meaningful way, and their sexual relations are less satisfying than they once were. Their interaction tends to be apathetic, and the time they spend together is primarily occupied with their children, with guests, or with community activities. People who have devitalized marriages frequently believe this to be the most appropriate form of marriage during the middle years.

In the **passive-congenial** utilitarian marriage, there has never been any deep emotional commitment, and neither has ever wanted to invest any personal involvement in a male-female relationship. From the beginning, these couples have stressed common sense, common interests, and emotional and physical comfort. Their creative energies are directed toward their careers, community service, or their children.

In contrast to the utilitarian marriage, the **intrinsic** marriage is characterized by intense feelings on the part of each partner for the other. Partners in intrinsic marriages find the other indispensable to their own satisfaction in any activity, and each depends on the psychological and physical presence of the other. In intrinsic marriages, serious arguments are reserved for important matters, and they are settled as quickly as possible to the satisfaction of both. Of most importance to the partners in an intrinsic marriage is the relationship they share, and not who is right or wrong. Sex is usually important for the partners in an intrinsic marriage, and it often pervades the entire relationship. Partners in an intrinsic marriage frequently find so much ecstacy in their relationship that they hide it from their friends who have utilitarian marriages, lest they be considered deviant. Their vital marriages are reflected in better physical and mental health, as well as in increased creativity. It is these marriages that sometimes become devitalized in middle or late years.

The fact that these divergent lifestyles are satisfying to the people in them reflects the fact that there is no one mode of adjustment that is right for all people. Each marriage and each individual must adopt the style of adjustment that provides for the utmost satisfaction and the least dissatisfaction.

Another helpful categorization of modes of adjustment is that worked out by Karpel (1976): In the mode of **unrelatedness**, rejection and denial form the basis of the relationship; thus close relationships to others is not possible, and there is an attempt to deny any dependency.

In **pure fusion**, the relationship is one of infantile dependence. There is a high degree of identification taking place between the two persons with only minimal differentiation. One sees the other as essential to one's own existence, and any indication of separateness is met with anxiety.

Ambivalent fusion is a transitional period in the development toward mature relationship, and is characterized by conflict between regression and progression, dependency and self-support; thus, it is an unstable relationship. There are five patterns of functioning in this mode:

1. One partner distances; the other pursues.
2. Alternate distancing by one and then the other partner.
3. Cycles of fusion and unrelatedness on the part of both.
4. Continual conflict, an "uneasy compromise between fusion and unrelatedness."
5. One partner is defined as independent, the other as dependent.

The patterns are not mutually exclusive; relationship may involve more than one, or move from one to the other.

In a **dialogue**, there is a mature relationship between two well-differentiated individuals. There is encouragement toward further individuation by acceptance of difference and change. Each accepts responsibility for one's own life. The success of this type of relationship is attributable to trust, trust that allows oneself to be used by another without feelings of being taken advantage of. However, permanence is not necessarily implied, since change is an inherent part of the relationship, but it is free from the anxiety and ambivalence characteristic of ambivalent fusion. There *are* features of the dialogue relationship that are conducive to permanence, however—the continued satisfaction when the partners' needs are met, the advantage of continuity and stability, and the rewarding sense of commitment.

ADJUSTMENT DURING EARLY MARRIAGE AND THE CHILDREARING YEARS

The pattern of living that a couple establishes at the beginning of their marriage usually becomes their lifelong pattern together. It is for this reason that married couples should begin the process of adjustment early, when each is strongly motivated to make the marriage succeed. Adjustment should actually begin during the engagement period. The more adjustments that are made during this period, the fewer that are necessary after marriage (Burgess & Wallin, 1953). Certainly, the earlier adjustments are made, the more successful the marriage is apt to be (Landis & Landis, 1973).

In the early stage of marriage, the most important factors to a couple are love and affection, satisfactory sexual relations, emotional interdependence, and temperamental interaction (Burgess & Wallin, 1953). Later in marriage, the factors that are most important may change. Companionship becomes of primary importance to wives (Bell, 1971a; Blood & Wolfe, 1960), and the husband's expression of love and affection may be of less importance than his understanding of her problems and feelings (Blood & Wolfe, 1960).

Sexual adjustment is a primary factor in a marriage and has been treated separately in Chapter 9 (Sexual Practices and Problems). Other important areas requiring adjustment in the early years are finances, the in-laws, recreation, and marital roles.

The role of the wife. Since wives have traditionally assumed the roles of housewives, they have borne the greater burden of adapting to marriage and to their mates' needs. The husband's role has always remained essentially the same, while the wife's has changed to that of homemaker and has required greater commitment to the marriage (Burgess & Wallin, 1953). Modern women are less likely to restrict themselves solely to the role of housewife, and they are therefore less likely to be more totally committed to the marriage than their husbands are. For married women in the past, and for those who now opt for solely a housewife's role, four role possibilities exist: primarily husband-oriented, sometimes husband-oriented, children-oriented, and home-oriented (Lopata, 1965). Traditionally, these orientations have frequently been seen as concomitants of the sequential stages of marriage. In the early part of marriage, women have frequently found their identity through their husbands. When children arrived, they divided their identification between husbands and babies, and as the children grew older, they began to live through them and to see their husbands merely as providers. After the children left home, they often gained their feeling of identity from their homes and material possessions.

Fortunately, this dismal process of vicarious existence is ending for many women, who recognize that they can find ego-satisfaction through their own accomplishments and not through those of their husbands or children, or through the value of their possessions.

Whether a woman intends to make a career of being a housewife, or to assume that role only during her children's preschool years, she usually will feel isolated and will dislike the monotony of housework and childcare (Baber, 1953). In fact, the majority of married women cite housework as the least satisfying part of their lives (Bell, 1971a). This is particularly true of the modern woman who does not choose housekeeping as a role in life when she chooses marriage and motherhood, but finds that it has been thrust upon her anyway (Hunt, 1962). One study found that of the 90 percent of high school girls who wanted to marry, only 15 percent wanted to be housewives (Bell, 1971a). (The other 75 percent would be wise to steer clear of men who expect their wives to be content in the kitchen or the nursery all their lives.)

Adjusting to the role of housewife, then, and finding satisfaction in it, requires a strong sense of personal identity apart from the wife-mother-housekeeper identity. Furthermore, a woman should be secure in her conviction that her particular role in life is necessary and important. Many women believe that their children's preschool years are a time when they particularly need their mother's presence and guidance. For them, the decision to be a full-time mother and housekeeper during those years is one of personal commitment, and they find genuine satisfaction in their roles because

294 Adjustment in Marriage

of their sense of purpose. Even for these women there is a need for some other aspect of life with which they can identify and which serves to remind them of their individuality. One mother of small children presented herself to the store manager of a suburban dress shop and said, "I don't have any experience but I love fashion. I can only work one night a week from six to nine. Will you hire me?" He did, and she found her three hours of employment a week just what she needed to keep herself feeling a part of the outside world. Her interest in her appearance increased, she earned enough money to buy herself some unnecessary, frivolous clothes, and she had something to talk and think about besides babies, formulas, and potty-training.

While the idea of freeing oneself of the sticky morass of Zwieback, pediatricians, nursery school, and Sesame Street by spending time thinking about frivolous clothes may be offensive to some women, such a release may be all that a tightly chained woman can manage, in terms of time or effort. A stop-gap measure only, it at least serves the purpose of letting her retain the feeling that she is something other than a mother, and frivolity may be easier to take after a 12-hour day than more intellectual pursuits.

A house-bound woman can also keep in touch with the world of adults and maintain her intellectual capacities by enrolling in a class in a university or high school extension program or by becoming involved in the promotion of a favorite community project or political party. Whatever she chooses, she should make finding outside outlets and interests an important part of her own life so that her individual growth is not stifled by the monotony of housework and childcare.

The working wife. Young wives today are more likely to work than their mothers were. Women 20 to 24 showed the greatest growth in the labor force between 1976 and 1980 as they increased by about three quarters of a million (U.S. Bureau of the Census, 1976). However, married women are less likely to be in managerial or professional positions than unmarried women are—partly because business and industry tend to promote single women more readily than they do married women—and they are likely to earn less money than unmarried women. Indications from research are that the more money a young woman earns, the greater her reluctance to marry, while the opposite holds true for men.

When women do marry and maintain a career, the degree of adjustment required of the couple is increased. Issues of responsibility for child care and division of labor in the home are the two major areas for potential conflict. But jealousy of the other's accomplishments and outside interests are often important issues as well.

Interestingly, while more and more women are rejecting the role of being solely a housewife, many working women continue to believe that their *responsibility* as a wife is to see that the traditionally feminine chores are done, while the husband sees his *responsibility* as providing the family with status and income (Poloma & Garland, 1971). Even dual-professional couples tend to have this attitude, and the woman is more likely to do the majority of household chores than is the man. The working wife, then, is the one most likely to interview and oversee domestic help and babysitters, and to arrange for repairs to household appliances. Furthermore, a recent poll found that the majority of women polled did not want complete equality with their husbands, even if they wanted more than a husband and children in their lives. Only 31 percent of the women polled believed that a woman's ultimate fulfillment was the realization of her own personal goals, while 67 percent believed that ultimate fulfillment for a woman came from marriage and motherhood (Overholser, 1973).

Thus, more than any other factor, the presence of children and the desire for the best possible care for them has kept women from pursuing careers with the same degree of enthusiasm as men. Traditionally, and still to a great extent today, child care has been per-

ceived as the woman's responsibility. When both partners in a marriage work and children arrive, one of them will have to interrupt a career, at least for a time, since good childcare centers are difficult to find and most people feel that the beginning of a child's life is important and demanding enough to require the presence of a parent. For various reasons—economic and cultural—it is usually the wife who devotes full-time attention to the child while the husband supports them. If the wife's income is greater, or if her career will suffer from interruption more than the husband's, the sensible approach would be for the husband to care for the infant, but this actually occurs very rarely. In many cases, when adequate and reliable childcare is available, both parents choose to continue working, with only a short maternity leave for the mother. If she continues her career with only temporary interruption, ideally both she and her husband would share responsibility for the children and for providing them with satisfactory nurturance. Some industries are beginning to allow maternity leaves for both mothers and fathers so that the husband may be better able to do his share of childcare.

Childrearing is especially demanding, for it requires a fair degree of subordination of oneself and one's own wishes and desires to provide the unconditional love an infant needs. These heavy demands are often overlooked by those not directly involved, and even when a parent chooses to postpone career or job activities to devote full time to the task, some kind of relief from the day-to-day demands of the household should be devised.

Objectively speaking, while household work can be tedious, it is no more boring and monotonous than many jobs that both men and women hold. The difference seems to lie more in attitudes toward it, that is, its status relative to other jobs, and the rewards for its achievement. There are no direct, tangible rewards, and the tendency for the family to take the housewife for granted is common. In addition, there is little relief from it. How does a woman go home from *home*?

Another factor relevant to whether a wife works or not is the attitude of her husband. Several studies have shown that the degree of support and encouragement that the husband has for his wife's working is decisively important in her choice to work (Arnott, 1972; Ginzberg, 1966). It seems important for most husbands and wives that the husband not be threatened by or neglected as a result of his wife's achievements.

A wife's work outside the home sometimes has a positive effect on marital adjustment. If she is working because she wants to, there is likely to be more companionship and less tension in the marriage than if she stayed home. If the wife is working to supplement an inadequate income by her husband, there may be conflict, but the higher socioeconomic level created by the wife's income tends to balance out this conflict through its positive effect on marital adjustment.

Unfortunately, many working wives whose motive is to add to the family income find that the second income dwindles quickly. One financial consultant has estimated that extra costs and hidden expenses may eat up as much as 70 percent of a wife's income. An example is the wife with preschool-age children who takes a job with a base pay of $177 a week. After $23 is withheld for federal income tax and another $5 for a typical state tax, $9 for social security, and $2 for group health and life insurance plans, she has a remainder of $138 a week. However, she will have to pay approximately $25 a week for childcare, $15 a week for housekeeping help, $10 a week for lunches and coffee breaks, and $3 a week for bus fare. In addition, there are the costs of new clothes, more frequent trips to the hairdresser, more expensive convenience foods, the cost of more dry cleaning, and similar expenses for which the working wife now has to pay. Her $177 a week dwindles to $70 a week, or $3,640 a year. At tax time, her withholding enters into the total family income, and if her husband earns $14,400 annually, the family will owe an additional $818 in federal income taxes. State and city income taxes also may take another bite, so that the wife may end up with only 30 percent of her annual salary. An outside job may also mean that a second car is needed, or that dues and licensing expenses are involved in the job itself (Second income: It dwindles quickly, 1972). Of the 31.5 million women who hold jobs, therefore, those who are married and/or have children actually keep only a fraction of their income, and the more than 35 million women (the latest count from the U.S. Department of Labor) who are housekeepers may contribute as much to the family income by judicious money management and money-stretching procedures.

For many working wives, therefore, working may bring more emotional satisfaction than actual income, in spite of the fact that their skills are needed in the economy for the development of new industries and the expansion of others. If women earn salaries based on their skills and not on their sex, their incomes would be substantially greater, as would be their motivation to improve their skills. A highly skilled secretary does not receive a salary that is proportionately higher than that of an incompetent typist, and the incompetent typist may therefore feel little incentive to improve her skills to try for a more responsible position. The discrepancy between the salaries of the two positions is far less than, for instance, the discrepancy between the salaries of a corporation executive and that of a beginning sales trainee.

Marriage and money. The problem of family finances is probably most often mentioned in regard to marital adjustment at all stages of marriage. Since our society believes in romantic marriages instead of marriages arranged by parents, money and property matters are not considered until later, when they sometimes become major problems. Values formed in childhood through early adulthood are brought into marriage by each partner, and the two therefore may differ sharply in their opinions of how money should be handled. The necessity of choosing between the values of the newly married spouses frequently causes difficulties. The question of how the couple's money is to be handled and who is to handle it is laden with issues such as domination, submission, insecurity, and inferiority. For this reason, it usually takes longer to work out problems centering around family finances than problems in any other area except sexual relations (Landis, 1946).

While wealthier couples may argue about money in more comfortable surroundings, wealth is certainly no guarantee of marital adjustment, although couples who are financially secure are more likely to be satisfied with their marriages than those who are not (Williamson, 1966).

Difficulties over money are generally not due to a lack of management know-how, but rather to basic psychological needs and patterns of problem-solving. A husband may accuse his wife of being irresponsible in spending money, for example, because he feels guilt over his own impulsive spending. In other cases, a man who has married a strong, competent wife because he wanted someone to make decisions and assume responsibility for him may begin to resent her control of the purse-strings because her competence in financial matters highlights his own incompetence.

A frequent bone of contention between husbands and their non-employed wives stems from the attitude that the husband is the sole source of income for the family, and therefore has the right to make all decisions regarding its distribution. As stated earlier, however, a housewife may contribute substantially to the amount of money that a family has by stretching the income through astute shopping and by the services she provides for the family. By wise and prudent management, a housewife may so reduce the cost of maintaining a household that her contribution to the family's coffers may be greater than it would be if she took salaried employment outside the home. While many, if not most, modern women find more emotional satisfaction from salaried employment than from being a housewife, there are many women who find great pleasure in being homemakers, and whose husbands enjoy and appreciate their homemaking skills. These women should not be made to feel guilty for *not* working outside the home any more than other women should be made to feel guilty for preferring careers over marriage, or for combining marriage with a career.

Most young couples find that their marital adjustment in money matters is facilitated if they have some sort of budget for spending. A budget is not primarily a plan to save money, but a plan for the distribution of income so that a couple may obtain more of the things that they need and want. There is no ideal budget that will fit the needs of every couple, just as there is no ideal pattern of decision-making in money matters. In some instances, the husband is more temperamentally suited to paying the bills, and in other cases, the wife is. The important thing is for the person who writes the checks to refuse to let this position cause him or her to take advantage of the other and for the other partner to have at least moderate trust and confidence in the bill-paying spouse.

The partner who is given the responsibility for handling the money should certainly keep the other well informed as to the current state of their financial affairs, and no major decisions regarding the distribution of their income should be made without the knowledge and agreement of the spouse. And the spouse who does not have the actual task of managing the money should assume the

responsibility of being fully aware of the family's financial situation and tailor spending accordingly. A women who grapples each month with the problem of stretching the income to cover all the family's necessary expenses will bitterly resent a husband who blithely announces that he has just bought a new set of golf clubs, or that he has decided to buy several hundred dollars' worth of darkroom equipment and take up photography as a hobby. Similarly, a husband who has charge of the family's finances will feel used if his wife never concerns herself with the bank balance of the family's indebtedness and spends an excessive amount of money on clothing for herself. Having a budget helps to circumvent these abuses and also allows the husband to have his golf clubs and the wife her new clothes, if the income permits.

A tentative estimate of the family's income and expenditures for a period of time, a **budget** is a guide to the intelligent use of money. It is perhaps most valuable in the early years of marriage when the income is usually lowest. When both partners in a marriage understand how much money is available and how it must be spent, neither is likely to resent having to forgo possessions or activities that are beyond their income.

Some couples feel more secure with a very detailed budgeting and bookkeeping system in which every penny spent is accounted for. Others find such a comprehensive system too rigid and time-consuming, and prefer a very loose spending plan whereby necessities are planned for, then savings, and the remainder is spent without any kind of recordkeeping at all. If one partner is the type who is uncomfortable without a detailed spending record, and the other is driven to distraction by having to record every penny spent, a dual system whereby major expenditures are planned and recorded but separate systems for husband and wife are used for individual spending is probably the best solution. Thus, the compulsive partner can carefully itemize his every expense, and the more relaxed spouse can lump a lot of spending under "miscellaneous." If each can view the other's system as valid, such a dual system can be workable and achieve the same result as a single system. Whatever system of budgeting money is used, it should not be a source of friction in the marriage. If it becomes so, another system that is more satisfactory to both should be found.

While every couple must find their own system of budgeting and recordkeeping, a general outline for distributing the family income is as follows:

1. List all income that can be depended on each month.
2. List all fixed expenses for each month, such as rent, utilities,

installment payments, insurance, investments, magazine and newspaper subscriptions, and pledges made to a church or other organizations.
3. List all fixed expenses that are not due each month, such as car licenses, state and federal taxes, and tuition. Calculate the amount of money that must be set aside each month in order to meet these expenses when they are due.
4. Subtract the monthly expenses from the monthly income, and set aside a portion of the remainder for unexpected expenses.
5. Estimate the amount needed for variable expenses such as clothing, food, entertainment, gasoline and car upkeep, gifts, and household maintenance. These estimates will vary with experience and circumstances.

This spending plan will enable a couple to distribute their income equally over the year so that it is relatively stable at all times. Christmas shopping and income tax time will be planned for and will not impose the financial strain that so many families experience.

The time to begin thinking about a budget is *before* marriage, so that a couple can realistically plan their expenditures after marriage. For example, Barbara may have a take-home salary of $550 a month, while Richard's salary may be $800 a month. When they marry, their combined salaries are $1350 a month, and they may each have unrealistic expectations of how much more they can afford with their combined salaries. Both may have been sharing an apartment with another person, for example, with each paying approximately $150 a month for rent. When they marry, they may rent an apartment for $300 a month, leaving them with $1050 a month. With that much money to play around with, they may throw caution to the winds and buy several rooms of furniture, ending up with payments of $300 a month, and reducing their remaining money to $750. Richard's car payment of $200 further reduces it to $550, and since they have moved into a new, modern apartment quite a distance from Barbara's job, they need to buy a second car for her. The payments of $140 a month eat into their remainder, leaving them with $410. Food will cost them about $75 a week, including the meals they eat out, so that their remaining income is only $110. Without any money set aside for savings, they have only $110 to pay for clothing, medical and dental expenses, gasoline, car upkeep, health insurance, automobile and apartment renter's insurance, and other necessary expenses. No money is available for vacations, for emergencies, or for entertainment. Convinced that $1350 a month is enough to cover their every need, they may foolishly borrow money to pay the expenses not covered by their salaries, in the optimistic belief that their finances simply need to be "smoothed out" by a loan. The loan payments simply add to their money drain, and they will probably find themselves in serious financial trouble. If they have a child, their financial troubles will be multiplied, whether or not Barbara quits her job. There will be medical bills, the cost of nursery furniture and baby clothing, babysitting expenses, and the added cost of the baby's formula and baby food.

Had this couple made a budget before they married, they could have avoided much stress and unhappiness in their marriage. The early years of marriage should be years of building up a nest egg, and not of going into debt. Rather than buying furniture and paying interest on the furniture loan, they would be better advised to refinish, refurbish, and re-cover furniture they find at garage sales or in their families' attics. The money saved should be set aside for a future home or for emergencies. Before a couple decide to borrow money to buy something they want, they should be sure that they can make payments on the purchased items without undue strain and that their savings account affords a comfortable cushion for emergencies. The kernel of this approach to finances is, "Don't borrow money unless absolutely necessary," and "Be highly cautious in making time payment purchases."

Many couples find a spending plan that does not have some reward as its goal a relatively meaningless exercise in arithmetic. For them, there must be an ultimate plan that is important to them before they can give any spending plan their cooperation. They may have a long-range goal of quitting their jobs for a year and sailing in the Caribbean. Or they may be determined to spend a month in Europe biking across the countryside. They may be spurred by a vision of owning their own ski lodge in the mountains, or of having a first-rate gourmet restaurant that they operate themselves. A comfortable and secure life after retirement may be the goal, or establishing scholarships for needy students, or contributing to an important cause.

Whatever their goal, these couples will save as much money as possible by economizing on housing, transportation, food, clothing, and entertainment. For them, a compact automobile will be the choice over a larger, more expensive car, and their home and its furnishings will be selected with an eye to comfort and attractiveness rather than to status considerations.

The in-laws. Almost every comedian has a supply of mother-in-law jokes, and they seldom fail to bring loud guffaws from people who have experienced some conflict with their in-laws. In some cases, the friction between a married individual and the parents of the spouse is due to the married person's feelings of inadequacy and insecurity. Because they expect their in-laws to criticize and find them lacking in some respects, they react defensively to every action and word. If financial aid is offered, they bristle and angrily refuse it; if no financial aid is offered, it is interpreted as rejection and lack of acceptance. In other cases, parents may try to continue to play a parent role and advise and direct a married child who rejects this parent role. Such a parent may then feel no longer needed and will react by directing hostility toward the child's spouse (Bell, 1971a).

In some instances, the parents may have exaggerated ideas of their children's value and believe that they have married "beneath them" (Waller & Hill, 1951). Furthermore, married children who find it difficult to stop turning to parents for help create marital difficulties because their spouses may interpret such dependence

"It's your mother."

on parents as a lack of marital loyalty. If the dependent spouse is the husband, his wife may interpret his dependency on his parents as an indication of his inadequacy and conclude that he is less than a "man."

Trouble also may arise when each partner compares the spouse with the same-sex parent, who has much more experience in fulfilling his or her marital role. A man who negatively compares his bride's cooking to his mother's, for example, may be overlooking the fact that his mother has had more years of cooking experience than his wife has been alive. If he were able to compare his mother's abilities with his wife's when the two were equal in experience, his feelings about their relative merits might be vastly different. Furthermore, since each spouse has been shaped and influenced by a different family of origin, each will be convinced that his way constitutes the "right" way, and there will have to be some adjustments made in the thinking of both rather than each ridiculing the parents of the other for being so "wrong." This is especially true in matters that pertain to family traditions. A southern woman for whom Thanksgiving means a family dinner of turkey and cornbread dressing, for example, may be shocked and repulsed to discover that Thanksgiving to her spouse's family means a dinner of baked eel. Unless each is aware of the fact that tradition depends on one's own experience, a family's traditions can become converted into a springboard for a lifetime of insults and recriminations.

Although in-law problems are common (Burgess & Wallin, 1953; Landis & Landis, 1973; Stryker, 1955), contradictory complaints have been found. One study, for instance, found the most common complaint to be that in-laws were meddlesome and dominating, but the second most common complaint was that the in-laws were distant, indifferent, thoughtless, and unappreciative (Duvall, 1954). It would appear that many couples perceive their parents-in-law as either too close or too distant.

Because women are more likely to have similar roles than men are, more in-law problems are between a wife and her mother-in-law or sister-in-law than between a man and his father-in-law or brother-in-law (Baber, 1953; Bell, 1971a; Komarovsky, 1962; Landis & Landis, 1973; Shlein, 1965). Conflict with a mother-in-law is more frequent for both husbands and wives (Landis & Landis, 1973; Komarovsky, 1962), with half of women in general reporting mother-in-law or sister-in-law problems (Landis & Landis, 1973), although college-educated wives appear to have less conflict with their mothers-in-law (Bell, 1971a).

A young wife is caught between her own mother's fears of rejection and her mother-in-law's fears of criticism. If she adopts her own mother's method of cooking or decorating or entertaining, her mother-in-law may feel that her method has been criticized. If she adopts her mother-in-law's method, her own mother might feel that *she* is being criticized and rejected. The bride's problem is compounded by the fact that both her mother and mother-in-law—both mature, experienced women—are eager to teach her how to fill her new role. Diplomacy, tact, and a sense of humor are essential in avoiding friction in such a situation.

Because of the difference in their worlds, mothers-in-law are less likely to be critical of their sons-in-law or to try to teach them how to fulfill their roles (Baber, 1953). Nevertheless, 42 percent of husbands have reported their mothers-in-law to be a main source of friction in their marriages (Landis & Landis, 1973). Such conflict between a man and his mother-in-law may arise when a mother continues to try to control her married daughter, or when a mother-in-law is dissatisfied with her own husband and tries to mold her son-in-law into her idealized image of the husband she has never had. Sometimes, too, a mother may try to mold her daughter into the same wife-role that she herself has lived, forgetting that she and her daughter have different husbands (Bell, 1971a).

Conflict between a woman and her father-in-law is much less frequent, and only 11 percent of marriages have reported such friction (Landis & Landis, 1973). In many instances, the relationship between a father-in-law and daughter-in-law may be slightly flirtatious, and ego-satisfying to both (Bell, 1971a).

Similarly, there is less friction between a son-in-law and father-in-law, so long as the father-in-law accepts his son-in-law's ability to earn a living (Bell, 1971a). Jealousy between a father-in-law and son-in-law is negligible if present at all (Baber, 1953), and conflict between these two has been found in only 15 percent of marriages (Landis & Landis, 1973). Although a father-in-law and son-in-law have the same primary role responsibilities, the way in which they fulfill them is not subject to detailed and public comparison as a woman's role is, and a father-in-law is less apt to try to influence his son-in-law's role as a husband, as long as he is adequate in his occupational role (Bell, 1971a).

With the coming of children, the mother-in-law becomes a grandmother, and a new area of conflict may arise, as both grandmothers may consider themselves the best authority on the rearing of children. In some instances, the grandchild becomes a puppet through whom the mother and grandmother play out their hostilities toward one another. In other instances, the grandchild may provide a positive influence, providing a common focus of emotional and social involvement for both parents and grandparents (Bell, 1971a).

Even though in-law friction is common, our society is generally more accepting than some other cultures are. In more than half the world's cultures, in fact, a man and his mother-in-law are expected to avoid each other (Bell, 1971a). Perhaps many of the in-law problems in our society could be avoided or lessened if every married couple would remember that someday they may be mothers-in-law and fathers-in-law themselves. In-law friction can also be avoided if couples wait until they are emotionally, financially, and educationally ready for marriage and need not depend on their parents for aid—which carries with it the right to give advice and direction.

As is true in almost every other area of marriage, the older a couple are when they marry, the less difficulty they have with in-law problems. Those couples who marry under the age of 20 have more in-law conflict than those who wait until after the age of 24 to marry (Landis, 1946; Landis & Landis, 1973).

In-law conflict is also much more likely to arise if the young couple live with either set of parents, especially if they live with the groom's parents (Burgess & Wallin, 1953; Locke, 1951). The fact that a great deal of in-law disharmony is feminine in nature, and that it is intensified when the mother-in-law and daughter-in-law live in the same house, seems to be a truth that has long been recognized. For example, it is written in the Talmud, "Can a goat live in the same barn as a tiger? In the same fashion, a daughter-in-law cannot live with her mother-in-law under the same roof." The following factors have been found to be characteristic of young couples who get along well with parents and parents-in-law: There has been parental approval of the marriage; the first meeting of the future mate's parents has been under friendly circumstances; the young married couple live separately from either set of parents; the marriages of the parents are happy; there are no religious differences with the parents; there has been a traditional courtship and marriage; and the mates are similar in cultural background (Marcus, 1951; Sussman, 1954). These points lend support to the idea that one marries a family as well as a spouse.

All too frequently, married couples create in-law problems because of problems within the marriage. A husband may tease a wife in a hurting manner in front of her parents, for example, thereby showing disrespect for her and for her parents. His actual hostility may be directed at his wife's sexual coldness, but he may be unable to discuss it with her directly because of his own sexual inhibitions. By a show of disrespect in front of her own parents, he is able to hurt her as she hurts him, and at the same time punish her parents for not preparing her more adequately for her role as a sex partner. Many people bring up areas of stress *only* when they are in front of others. In this way, they can express their hostility at a time when their mates will be reluctant to fight back because of the embarrassment they would feel at having an argument in front of others.

In a similar manner, a man may control all his hostility toward his wife until she is with his family and then make disparaging remarks about her cooking or her childrearing techniques, comparing them unfavorably with his own mother's methods. By thus aligning his loyalty with his mother against his wife, he creates a situation of conflict between the two of them, and also manages to hurt his wife in the process. If he is sufficiently passive-aggressive, he may also derive pleasure from the fact that his wife may hurt his mother, toward whom he may also have some hostility.

The happier the marriage, the fewer the in-law problems (Landis & Landis, 1973). The most successful adjustments in the area of in-law relationships are those in which there is willing compromise on both sides in the interest of harmony, and when both the husband and wife actively like and make friends with their in-laws.

Since people have more comfortable lives now and receive better medical care throughout their lives, young couples and their parents are more likely to be peers in a social and psychological sense than they were in the past. Their lifestyles may be more similar than dissimilar, and consequently, there may be a decrease in in-law conflict. Furthermore, young couples are less likely to remain in the immediate vicinity of their parents after marriage, and they may have to travel long distances to visit one another, with a result of a lessening of strain between them.

Leisure time in marriage. The manner in which a couple spend their leisure time is an area that, perhaps surprisingly, causes many problems. When a couple marries, their friendship patterns change to some extent; while they are generally free to keep same-sex friends, they are discouraged from spending "too much" time with them, and friends of the opposite sex are usually given up. New friendships are established from contacts that each partner makes in his or her own sphere of activity—from the neighborhood, from the work environment, as well as from church, clubs, and other organizations. Conflicts sometimes exist between partners about whom they will associate with, particularly if their cultural and leisure tastes differ. Couples without children are more likely to continue, much as they did when they were single, to choose activities based upon their own personal needs and satisfactions. The

greatest change in leisure choices of a couple comes with the arrival
of children. Parenthood brings about an emphasis on family oriented activities as opposed to those activities available to couples
without children.

Generally, dissatisfaction in the use of leisure time arises when
the time spent is conducive neither to personal growth nor to the
growth of the marriage and when one or both partners believe in
the theme, "My time is your time." One's leisure time becomes duty
or obligation time if it is always spent doing something the other

wants to do. Similarly, the idea that one's leisure time is useless unless one's spouse also has leisure time at the same hour destroys the enjoyment of time spent by oneself. Certainly, if both partners are free at the same time and both are inclined to the same activity, they should enjoy it together. But if the husband feels like baking bread and the wife feels like going skeetshooting, there is no reason why she should help him knead his dough or why he should help her load her shotgun. Each can enjoy his or her own pastime, and perhaps they could eat the bread together afterwards.

Similarly, there is no reason for a woman to feel herself a "football widow" when the TV programming is saturated with college football on Saturday, professional football for six hours on Sunday, and professional football again on Monday night. Many women feel that the only way they can be a part of their husband's life is to also become an ardent football fan. If a wife actually enjoys football, joining her husband in front of the TV set is fine, but if she is really faking her enthusiasm, she would be happier if she found an activity that she did enjoy to occupy her time while her husband is engrossed in football.

Vacations have become areas of dissent for many couples. The moments of solitude and privacy that people enjoy during normal times are often missing during a vacation. Furthermore, the tendency to see as much as possible in the time allowed causes people to set out on whirlwind vacations that are more enjoyable in retrospect than they are at the time. The person who has just returned from such a vacation may respond to the question, "Where did you go?" with a weary, "I don't know, the film hasn't been developed yet."

In addition to the fatigue and lack of emotional safety-valves during a typical vacation is the fact that the partners may not agree on the places they wish to visit. Furthermore, sleeping in strange beds, eating unfamiliar food, encountering the discomfort of high altitudes, insects, and other irritants, as well as worrying about how to pay for all this discomfort, frequently cause a couple to come home snarling at each other. Advanced planning and a slower pace probably would eliminate a lot of the frustration experienced on many vacations, but the greatest problem is probably the feeling of resentment that either may have because of disappointment in the vacation spot chosen. She may despise camping trips and endure them because her husband loves them; he may be disappointed because she never shows enthusiasm for his interest. Better that he go on weekend camping trips with a friend and save vacation time for something they both enjoy. Or, better that he spend his vacation camping and she spend hers someplace else and the two of them go on weekend trips together. A vacation should be a time of physical and emotional renewal for both, and if it is not, some adjustments are in order.

Now that we are experiencing the decline in travel occasioned by the reduced ability to afford the high cost of petroleum, couples who have relied on trips away from home to add spark and zest to their marriages will have to alter their pattern of living. Rather than driving several hundred miles and arriving tired and irritable at a motel, they may instead drive across town and check into a motel for the weekend, and enjoy the luxury of being waited on and pampered, without being exhausted from a long drive. Rather than flying off for the weekend, they may rediscover the fun of taking the family to the park for a picnic. While the energy crunch may cause some families to intensify their negative attitudes toward each other, it may well cause other families to rediscover simpler pleasures and to enjoy each other more. In the vast majority of cases those couples and families who are willing to work toward improving family relationships and family unity work about as consistently and diligently under one set of circumstances as they will under another.

THE MIDDLE YEARS

The stage of marriage in which the children leave home and the husband and wife are left alone together exerts different pressures on each. For the husband, his career is often at its peak, and he is deeply involved in it and does not require his wife's assistance as he might have done at the beginning of his career. He therefore derives his utmost role satisfaction from his work, unless he is dissatisfied with his position and his future expectations and sees himself as an occupational failure.

For the wife, a new role is demanded because an important function has been lost. She may take on new roles by finding other interests, such as volunteer work, but if she has planned to recapture the romance of her early marriage, she will probably be disappointed and frustrated. At a time in her life when her own sex drive is at its peak, and when she has thrown off most of her sexual inhibitions, her husband's sex drive is waning. Furthermore, he is likely to be experiencing some terror of growing old and losing his virility, and his wife is a reminder to him of his own age. A woman tends to evaluate her aging process by the number of wrinkles she sees when she looks in the mirror. A man, on the other hand, is

The Middle Years **313**

likely to judge his aging process by the number of wrinkles on the face of the woman with him. Looking at his wife across the breakfast table may make him feel old and depressed, while looking at the unlined face of a young woman may make him feel young. For this reason, a middle-aged man may seek to bolster his sagging ego by having affairs with younger women. And a middle-aged woman may seek the sexual satisfaction she is not receiving from her husband by taking younger lovers whose sex drive matches her own. Unless the two partners can understand the motivation behind their own and their spouse's compulsive behavior, they may conclude that their marriage is a farce and either end it or remain married in name only, without any worthwhile or meaningful personal interaction.

For most couples, there are at least fifteen years of marriage after their last child leaves home (Mead & Kaplan, 1965), in contrast to the 1890s when the average woman was a widow when her last child left home (Deutscher, 1964). Most couples either adjust to these post-parental years with increased happiness or at least stay together and decide that marriage is preferable to divorce (Hunt, 1962).

THE RETIREMENT YEARS

The number of older people in the United States is large and continues to grow rapidly. The proportion of the population 60 years of age and over has more than doubled from 1900 to 1975. Since 1900 there has been a gain of twenty years in life expectancy, bringing it to 71.9 for males and 75.9 for females (Siegel, 1978). Therefore, the period of retirement and the need to plan for it has taken on a greater significance as a greater proportion of the population grows older each year. In 1976 there was a total of 22,934,000 retired persons who were 65 years and over. By the year 2000, it is predicted that there will be almost 32,000,000 retired persons 65 years of age and over (Statistical Abstract, 1977).

A man's retirement is a relatively new phenomenon in our society (Donahue, Orbach, & Pollak, 1960). Prior to recent times, when a man's working life was spent in a salaried position or in a profession, he remained an integral part of his work community as he aged. As his work load was increasingly taken over by younger men in the family, the older man remained an important source of direction and advice. Retirement in present times, however, can be more sudden and less gradual.

For a man who has derived his sense of identity and self-worth through his occupational status, retirement can be a traumatic event and the retirement years can seem empty and meaningless. In fact, if a man sees retirement as the end of his productivity and his value as a person, retirement may actually hasten his death. There are many retired men who simply sit and await their deaths, unable to find any reason to live without their known occupation to give meaning to life. Men who have been in this position, and then found a new interest or a new goal in life have found that their vigor and will to live returned, and thereby added years to their productive lives.

If the married couple have failed to maintain closeness and an affectionate relationship, retirement can create much discord and unhappiness in a marriage. The wife may feel that her husband is an unwelcome intruder into her world, and may dread the extra work and lower income of retirement (Donahue, Orbach, & Pollak, 1960). She also may have adjusted to the "retirements" in her own life—leaving a job for childrearing and losing her mother role when her children left home—and have little sympathy for her husband's sense of loss of purpose.

In marriages in which the lines of communication have been kept open and in which the couple have remained friends, retirement more frequently than not adds to their enjoyment of life. There may be a more egalitarian sharing of household chores and responsibilities. Travel and hobbies that were too time-consuming before now become possible, and couples who successfully adjust to retirement derive satisfaction from their interests and friends. Retirement also allows more time for relaxed sexual activity. Retired couples may find that their sexual interest and vigor are greater than they were during their earlier years together when business and children demanded most of their time and energy.

Probably the single most important factor that determines a couple's enjoyment of their retirement years is financial security, and the wise couple has planned for that eventuality. Overall, the income level for families with heads 65 years of age and over is low in comparison with other families, averaging only $7298 against a total median for all families of $12,836. (Siegel, 1978). For many working people, the company pension plan offers hope of a comfortable old age, but the fact is that only a minority of employees stay on the job long enough to qualify for a company pension plan. Most companies require an employee to be on the payroll for ten years and to have reached the age of 40 to qualify for benefits. Furthermore, under the present law, an employer can stop contributing to a pension plan for any reason. Unless there are adequate resources or insurance to pay the pension fund, the worker loses.

The most satisfactory pension plans allow employees to begin earning pension credits after only minimum service at the company and credit them for the time worked before they become eligible for the pension plan. The better pension plans also compute pensions by a formula that uses the employee's highest-income years, and are administered by trustees who are not under the control of the company or union. Few pension plans have all these features, and employees would do well to investigate the pension plans of their company when planning for their retirement.

An alternative offered by many companies is a profit-sharing plan that is by definition fully funded. Under a profit-sharing plan, there is no danger of a worker's being short-changed if the plan is terminated. However, workers who leave the company take their shares with them, usually spending them rather than investing them for their retirement.

About half the labor force lacks pension coverage, and of the half that is covered, only about 10 percent keep their jobs long enough to acquire pension rights. In 1976, there was a total of 7,303,000 persons receiving full social security benefits with an average monthly income of $225.

Most pension experts agree that reform is needed in pension plans, but there is little agreement on what direction reform should take. Some say the current system puts the burden of providing adequate retirement on the Social Security system. They reason that most workers receive pension credits for only a fraction of their total work years because of high employee turnover. Consequently, most workers receive pensions inadequate to meet their retirement needs. Congress is therefore constantly pressured to make the Social Security system the mainstay of retirement incomes. Proposed legislation would strengthen safeguards against pension-fund abuse and also lower vesting requirements in some industries, but none of the legislative proposals would extend coverage to workers now left out of the system entirely—principally those in establishments that are non-union or those who are agricultural workers. Furthermore, engineers and other workers who typically change jobs at less than five-year intervals are not provided assistance under these plans (Arnold, 1973).

The United States Senate has passed a pension reform bill that contains many corrections of the present inadequacies of company pensions. An employee would begin to build up a right to share in the benefits of the company's pension plan (a right called **vesting**) after having been with the company five years, and each year from the worker's sixth to tenth years, the vesting share would rise 5 percent, so that at the end of ten years, the employee would be entitled to half of the maximum retirement benefits. Every year from the eleventh to fifteenth, the share would rise 10 percent, so that after fifteen years 100 percent would be vested in the pension fund for the worker's full benefit. If the worker died at any time, the survivor would be entitled to 50 percent of the benefits owed the worker at the time of his or her death. Under the plans of the current Senate bill, a worker could transfer benefits from one company to another when he or she changed jobs, if both the old and new employers agreed to the switch. Safeguards against mismanagement of the pension funds are also written into the plan, and periodic public disclosure of fund financial activities is required. The new plan allows persons who are self-employed to deduct an amount equal to 15 percent of their earned income, up to $7,500 a year, for contributions to their own pension plans (Hess, 1973).

As of July 31, 1971, all pension-fund administrators are required by law to furnish upon request a written explanation of the pension plan. All employees should become acquainted with the details of their pension plans so that they can make plans for their retirement.

Couples who wish to live in retirement at the same standard they enjoyed during their working years will need approximately 70 percent of their present take-home pay after retirement. In planning for retirement, financial authorities advise as a couple's first objective a solid savings account; then stocks, bonds, and other investments may be considered. The rate of inflation, however, decreasing the value of the dollar, is frequently greater than the interest received on savings accounts. Thus, at 6 percent interest, a savings account may actually lose money for the depositor. The same is true in the case of variable stocks and bonds. Owning a home is generally a sound investment, especially since one may now take advantage of the reduction in the capital-gains tax. In planning for retirement, inflation should be taken into account, but at the same time consideration must be given to the fact that it may cost as much as 30 percent less to live in retirement. According to the Bureau of Labor Statistics, the average retired couple spends annually 26 percent of their income for food, 35 percent for housing, 9 percent for transportation, 8 percent for medical care, 6 percent for gifts and contributions, and 6 percent for other expenses such as recreation, books, etc. (Ripley, 1973).

CONCLUSION

As can be seen, there are different problems at different stages of marital life, and each couple must adjust to these general problems as well as to the specific problems arising from the unique combination of personalities in every marriage.

There has never been a marriage without some problems, and half of all marriages encounter serious problems. If the problems are severe, many will end the marriage; but others solve the problems, live with them, or simply ignore them. One Gallup poll found that 10 percent of the married women interviewed had seriously considered divorce at some time (Gallup, 1962), and 14 percent of married college-educated women have been found to have considered divorce (Bell, 1971a).

The price of maladjusted marriages is not only a lack of emotional satisfaction to the marital partners, but also a lowered state of physical health and morale. The state of a couple's marital adjustment both influences and is influenced by their general well-being, and those with the most serious health problems are likely to have the most unsatisfactory marriages (Renne, 1970).

The next chapter will explore some of the ways couples deal with the conflicts that arise from the need to adjust in marriage.

CHAPTER 11

DEALING
WITH CONFLICT
CREATIVELY

The test of man or woman's breeding is how they behave in a quarrel.
GEORGE BERNARD SHAW

There is a magnificent scene in the film *The Lion in Winter* in which Eleanor of Aquitaine, Queen of Henry II of England, imprisoned after joining her sons Richard I and John when they revolted and attempted to murder their father, raises her head from the floor where her husband has knocked her, and, with a philosophical shrug, says, "Well, what family doesn't have its ups and downs?"

The fact that marital conflict is longstanding and universal has been projected by poets and playwrights, historians, and novelists. A prime example is the nearly constant marital dog-fight portrayed in *Who's Afraid of Virginia Woolf?* The marriages of such diverse personages as Socrates, Abraham Lincoln, F. Scott Fitzgerald, and Robert Frost are known to have been stormy and marked by discord and strife. And there are few married people who would dispute the statement that conflict exists to one degree or another in every marriage. Indeed, it is not the existence of conflict in a marriage that determines its success or failure, but how the conflict is resolved or managed by the marital partners.

Just as no one method of marital adjustment best suits every couple, so there is no one method of conflict-management that brings the most satisfaction to every couple. Some couples prefer to drain off their anger and frustration at each other by first engaging in some physical activity such as golf or tennis or floor-waxing, and then sitting down together and calmly discussing their point of disagreement. Other couples prefer to have grand wall-banging, door-slamming shouting matches that end in dramatic reconciliation and lovemaking. There are also tactics such as nonverbal signals that say "Don't talk to me now, I have to cool off first," which the spouse recognizes and respects.

Whatever form their conflict-management takes, those whose marriages are satisfying arrive at some method by which they face and deal with their differences. In contrast, those whose marriages end in divorce either never face conflict realistically or fail to arrive at a successful method of coping with it (Scanzoni, 1968).

THE NECESSITY OF CONFLICT

Perhaps the only thing that can be said with certainty about marital conflict is that it cannot be ignored—at least not indefinitely. A couple may attempt to evade the unpleasant tension and anxiety created by marital conflict by suppression or repression. Through **suppression**, conflict is consciously pushed to the back of their minds, and they deliberately decide to avoid dealing with it. They may **repress** conflict by unconscious blocking and denial so that they are never consciously aware of it. If repressed, conflict will be disguised in various compulsions, obsessions, and anxieties, or will result in depression or physical complaints. Conflict that is repressed or suppressed will therefore be expressed in *some* way in the marital relationship, and to attempt to avoid it is not only futile, but dishonest (Crosby, 1973), and more often than not adds to the friction in an already troubled marriage.

Furthermore, the children of a married pair who repress or suppress marital conflict will be denied models of creative management of conflict. They may go into their own marriages with memories of parents who "never spoke a cross word to one another." Trying to emulate their parents, they will suppress their own conflict, and compare their parents' seemingly ideal marriage to their own imperfect marriage and erroneously conclude that their own marriage is extraordinarily deficient.

Just as marital conflict cannot be ignored, neither can it be abolished, except by separation or divorce (or death) (Sprey, 1972). Instead, marital conflict is a natural part of the relationship between a married couple and is in itself neither good nor bad. Like jealousy, conflict can either be a force that is detrimental or growth-producing, depending on the manner in which it is handled. Also like jealousy, conflict is a part of the relationship between a man and a woman that frequently looms as a threat in and of itself, and is too often avoided as if it were an evil force that could rip asunder the loving relationship of a couple. The fact is, however, that married partners who deny their negative feelings will eventually find it impossible to express their positive feelings also, and their marriage will degenerate into a gray state of apathy. The alternative to a marriage with conflict, therefore, is one in which there is no vitality, no excitement, no interest, and, eventually, no love.

This is not to say that a successful marriage is one that is characterized by discord and strife. On the contrary, continual tension and warfare can lead not only to marital dissatisfaction, but to such physical reactions as ulcers, headaches, and the nervous tics of children (Blood, 1960).

A vital marriage has neither too little nor too much quarreling. If there is too much quarreling and hostility, the intimacy between the couple is destroyed. If there is too little, then the partners are being phony and insincere in their efforts to be all-loving and always-nice to one another, and there is no chance for their relationship to be one that is genuine and growth-producing. A genuine relationship between a man and a woman necessarily includes anger and resentment at the human shortcomings of each. Not only does suppression of these negative reactions fail to provide the partners an opportunity to look at their own shortcomings and to try to change them, but it leads to indifference toward one another.

There is seldom surprise on the part of relatives, friends, and neighbors when a marriage that has been marked by physical violence ends in divorce, but there is shock and disbelief when the marriage of the always-amiable couple ends—frequently after many years together. A couple may live together for two decades or more in seeming harmony, showing perfect politeness and courtesy to one another, and then divorce when their children are grown. To their friends' shocked, "You seemed like a perfect couple!" they may agree with, "We never had an argument, never exchanged cross words." If they are able to articulate their feelings, they may say, "We bored each other to death," or simply, "We had no real feeling for each other." In such marriages, sex is almost always infrequent or nonexistent. It is not uncommon, in fact, for people seeking marriage counseling to present a picture of the utmost compatibility in every area, but to report that they have very little sex. These people have suppressed all the natural disagreements and tensions of an intimate relationship in order to have peace, quiet, and security. They buy peace, quiet, and security, however, at the expense of fun in sex, and sex therefore becomes something to be avoided—at least with each other (Charny, 1971).

In every relationship there is both love and hate, and sometimes the distance between them is very narrow. Both too much and too little quarreling represent a failure to create a healthy fusion of this love and hate (Charny, 1971). Couples who manage to express both feelings have a healthy tension that makes them vital, attractive people, in contrast to the apathetic, grim couples who deny passion in any form, be it anger or sexual desire. Couples who freely express their feelings seem to have a gusto and enjoyment of all aspects of life that is lacking in the lives of their more cautious and careful counterparts.

Conflict itself, therefore, is not detrimental to a marriage and is, in fact, a necessary and healthy aspect of a vital relationship. It is the manner in which conflict is managed that determines whether it adds to the growth and depth of a relationship or whether it eventually leads to the divorce court or to a lifetime of apathetic indifference together (Sprey, 1972).

TYPES OF QUARRELS

There are two types of marital quarrels—one destructive and the other productive—and the type that characterizes a couple's interaction will determine the effect of marital conflict on the individuals in the marriage and on the marriage itself. **Destructive quarreling** concentrates on the egos of the combatants and is belittling and punishing and alienating. **Productive quarreling**, on the other hand, is directed at the issues on which the couple differ and avoids hitting the sensitive spots of each individual (Duvall & Hill, 1972).

"You good-for-nothing . . ."

Barbara and John came for counseling because of John's secondary impotency. Although he had both morning erections and erections when he masturbated, he was unable to achieve or maintain an erection when he and Barbara wanted to have sexual intercourse. Barbara was a very angry young woman who had been deprived of love and acceptance by her parents and who now demanded it from her husband. She was quick to believe that it was being deliberately withheld from her because she equated sexual intercourse with love, and her husband's impotency was interpreted as intentional and deliberate rejection. Whenever a session of kissing and sexual caressing failed to culminate in sexual intercourse, she cruelly berated him with taunts about his "flabby penis," frequently extending her hostility for several days.

John had grown up in a home with a belligerent, hostile mother and a weak, passive father, and the pattern of male submission and female cruelty seemed natural to him. He also unconsciously enjoyed the fact that he could withhold from Barbara the one display of love that was most important to her, thus getting back at her for her demanding attitude, and if Barbara had not insisted, he probably would not have sought help for his impotency. Therapy for this couple, in addition to sensate-focus techniques discussed in Chapter 9, consisted of helping the two to arrive at a more healthy management of their anger and resentment.

Barbara learned to express her natural frustration at John's impotency in more productive ways by telling him how she felt because of his impotency and not by attacking him as if it were a deliberate rejection of her. By examining her own feelings, clarifying them, and identifying them, she was able to see that she was afraid of being abandoned. She was able to express these feelings to John, and her admission of her dependency on him made her seem less formidable and less threatening to him. John, on the other hand, was encouraged to express his natural feelings of resentment and hostility toward Barbara's cruel taunts, and their relationship moved toward a more balanced, healthy state of conflict-management, with the firmness of John's penis during sex play serving as a barometer of their marital equilibrium. When Barbara treated the impotency as a marital problem and not as John's rejection of her, she was able to refrain from making sarcastic, belittling remarks to him. When John was able to respond appropriately to Barbara's rational approach to the problem, as well as to her lapses into sarcastic hostility, he was able to allow his body to respond in a natural manner to his sexual feelings.

QUARRELING CUES

Couples who neither fear marital conflict nor use it as a means of hurting one another learn to interpret cues that each sends out when there are tensions and resentments that need to be ventilated. A woman might become petulant and nag her husband or her children about trivial things that she ordinarily would overlook. She may become exceptionally tidy, bustling about straightening magazines and emptying ashtrays, while she frowns at her husband's beer can, his bare feet, and his unshaven face as he watches football on TV. The experienced husband can sense the storm warnings and knows that a quarrel is coming that probably will boil down to "I'm bored and want to do something exciting, and I resent your

obvious enjoyment of something I don't enjoy." If he also has some axes to grind, he may simply gird himself for battle, and the two can each vent their spleen in a tension-reducing explosion. If he believes that his wife is justified in feeling cooped up and hostile, he may circumvent a quarrel by extending an invitation to dinner or to a movie later in the evening. If her frustration is solely due to boredom, she will recognize his maneuver for what it is, and gratefully accept it. If there are other smoldering resentments, however, she may insist on bringing the quarrel to a climax and clearing the air before accepting an invitation.

If it is the husband who is spoiling for a fight, he is likely to be overcritical, grouchy, and complaining, and his wife will tailor her responses according to her own feelings and her estimation of the basis for his feelings. If she believes his hostility is due to sexual deprivation, for example, she may rightly expect their quarrel to end in sexual intercourse, and they may both find their sexual pleasure enhanced by the prior release of pent-up anger (Ehrenwald, 1971).

There are also times when a spouse may recognize that the partner's quarreling cues are actually displaced responses to pregnancy, menstrual tension, hunger, fatigue, or illness. The partner then may rightly decide to hear the mate out and offer assurance and sympathy rather than countercomplaints (Duvall & Hill, 1972). Tact is imperative in these situations. A husband who patronizingly says, "Oh, I remember! It's time for your period—*that's* why you're so bitchy!" will regret it. And the wife who hovers over a tired and hungry man with erotic murmurs is apt to get a less than polite response.

RULES AND RESPONSIBILITIES

There are thus aggressor responsibilities—to recognize in oneself feelings of uneasiness, frustration, and discomfort, and to be willing to do something about it—and aggressee responsibilities—to assess the situation and either circumvent a quarrel through appeasement gestures when they are appropriate, or to meet the aggressor in a direct confrontation. For a partner to deny his or her responsibilities by walking out and then returning as if nothing had happened not only is damaging to the person and to the relationship, but also denies the partner the right to express real feelings. Couples who habitually postpone or stifle their resentment lose the opportunity to allow their relationship and their affection to grow and mature into a more intimate closeness.

"Honey — I came back."

CHRISTIANSON

If a quarrel does become full-blown, there are rules that each partner must observe if the quarrel is to be a productive and beneficial one (Duvall & Hill, 1972). For example, both partners should spell out what is bothering them, specifying the things they do not like and the changes they want made in the relationship. The age-old "What's wrong?" "Nothing!" or "If you don't know, I'm not going to tell you!" gambit is unfair, as neither partner can be expected to read the other's mind. It is also ridiculous and untrue to charge, "If you really loved me, you'd know what is wrong!"

In presenting their grievances, the partners should stick to the point and avoid side issues. If the husband is angry at his wife for being extravagant, he should confine his complaints to the amount of money she spends, and not drag in her mother's spending habits or the length of her brother's hair.

Once a quarrel has been started, each partner should stay with it until it is thrashed out to the satisfaction of both. If one partner withdraws into hurt silence, the other partner is placed in the unfair position of doing a monologue, and resolution and reconciliation are impossible.

Furthermore, couples must be scrupulously fair and confine their attacks to the problem and not each other. Underlying the most rip-roaring argument should be a partner's confidence in the love and acceptance of the other. By avoiding areas of particular vulnerability, partners signal to each other their continued love, and allow each other the freedom to freely express all anger without fear of losing the mate. To say to a husband, "What's the big idea of spending the entire evening looking down Marilyn Jones' cleavage?" may start a good tension-releasing quarrel, but to say, "If Marilyn Jones knew you only lasted a minute and a half, she wouldn't have been so excited when you flirted with her," is a devastating blow that is unfair and destructive, as it conveys a lack of love and acceptance.

Just as experienced partners give each other cues when they want to quarrel, they should also give cues to each other when their tensions lessen and they are ready to make up. The one who first signals readiness for a reconciliation has the responsibility of recognizing his or her own easing of tension. To move toward an end to the quarrel when there are still festering resentments is not conducive to productive quarreling and is not fair to the partner who takes the spouse at face value and believes his or her anger is over.

Reconciliation begins when one or both partners recognize the other's point of view, and a move is made to find the causes and possible solutions to the problem. Before there can be a genuine conclusion, both partners must be relieved of their tensions, resentments, fears, and anxieties. The conclusion may be to seek marriage counseling, or it may be to think more about the problem before making a final decision, but it is important that both feel that they have said all they need to say and that neither is left with a feeling of lingering tension.

The technique of role-taking is often helpful in marital conflict-management. In **role-taking**, a couple agree to limit their discussion to the problem at hand, and to avoid mentioning other problems. The wife first states her grievances completely, while the husband listens *without interruption or comment*. When the wife has fully stated her complaints, the husband then restates them to the wife's satisfaction, using the wife's point of view.

When the wife feels that her grievances have been satisfactorily stated by her husband, then she listens without interruption while he states his grievances. Using his point of view, she restates his complaints to his satisfaction. Both then examine the problem to see if there are points on which they both agree. They can then identify the particular points on which they disagree, and try to resolve them by some sort of compromise. In most cases, the fact that each has arrived at an understanding of the other's point of view allows them to see many points of agreement, and if they are unable to arrive at a compromise on their points of disagreement, each at least respects the other's right to his or her feelings (Saxton, 1968).

Quarrels that progress and end in this manner are strengthening forces in a relationship and should not be feared. Many such quarrels, in fact, reveal to the partners just how deeply they are committed to their relationship. When they have honestly expressed their grievances and aired their complaints, they may say to one another, "If we can survive this, we can survive anything!"

CAUSES OF CONFLICT

The underlying causes of most destructive marital conflict are false assumptions that couples all too frequently hold when they enter marriage. The most prevalent of these is the premise that one who loves you will never betray you or be disloyal to you or knowingly hurt you.

Hate and disappointment. In spite of the fact that everyone marries a human being who is bound to be fallible, every newlywed nevertheless is sure that *his* or *her* spouse will not be disappointing, or fail to live up to hopes and expectations. Inevitably, since human beings are human beings, a trust is broken, there is disloyalty, selfishness, or cowardice, and one or both partners are disappointed and disillusioned. With moral indignation to bolster the hurt, the injured one has a choice: To flay the guilty one with accusations and recriminations and win a moral victory; to swallow hurt and disappointment and pretend it never happened; to rationally discuss with the mate the breach in the relationship; or to plant one's feet firmly on the ground and express outrage and refuse to allow the situation to continue.

Regardless of the path chosen, the injured mate will have a new emotion in his or her repertoire of marital feelings, and it may well be one that causes anguish and despair, because it is the feeling of hate. Many people believe that hatred is the opposite of love, and they therefore deny any feelings of hatred for their spouses because they believe that hatred has no place in a successful marriage. The truth, however, is that instead of being polar opposites, as most people believe, hate and love are actually natural companions (May, 1969), and it is *indifference* that is the polar opposite of love.

To enter marriage with the unrealistic expectation of never being disappointed makes a couple particularly vulnerable to shock and horror at the hatred that follows disappointment. When the person on whom one bases all hopes and dreams proves to be less than perfect, it is disappointment that leads to the feeling of betrayal and the emotion of hatred. By denying disappointment, couples shut out their awareness of the true cause of their pain (Krich, 1970) and instead take on a moral stance that says, "You *should* not do that" or "That's *wrong* of you to do." But it is not the morality of another's actions that causes us pain, rather, our own disappointment when we discover that one whom we love has shortcomings and human failings. The more we are unable to accept our own weaknesses and inadequacies, the more likely we are to be disappointed when we discover them in a loved one, and the more likely we are to be self-righteously indignant when we are disappointed. The mature, realistic person knows that disappointment is inevitable in a relationship and is able to deal with it in a straightforward manner, without taking on the additional pain of feeling morally injured. To be sure, disappointment in a loved one is painful and it arouses feelings of hatred and rage, but disappointment need not be devastating (Crosby, 1973).

Many a husband and wife who experience a feeling of hatred toward their spouse have concluded that hate has destroyed the love they once held for their mate and have abandoned the relationship. And there are instances when the human frailties of one or both cause irreparable breaches, and when the betrayal of trust is too flagrant ever to be accepted. Reconciliation then may be impossible because of the hatred and bitterness in the relationship. But in most marital conflict, the entrance of hatred into the loving relationship can be an element that promotes individual growth and increased awareness. The fact that we can feel hatred toward someone whom we also love must be accepted if individuals are to achieve a genuinely honest relationship.

It may be this hate, this other side of the coin of love, that makes the relationship vital and meaningful. Any trait that is unchecked by its opposite can be carried to the extreme and may develop into a virtue-turned-vice. Almost every vice, in fact, can be looked upon as a virtue carried to the extreme, without the balancing effect of the opposing trait. A generous man, for example, must have a counterbalancing element of selfishness, or his family will suffer deprivation because of his irresponsible, excessive generosity to others. The habitual liar may be one who always wants others to feel at ease, and the promiscuous person may carry acceptance of others to an extreme, without using discretion or discrimination. A person who is unfailingly all-accepting and all-forgiving usually depends on those close to him to act out or verbalize his own frustrations and hostilities. His spouse and children may hold his placid disposition in awe, but they will also usually secretly wish that he had a little more spirit and will probably resent the fact that they have to fight his battles for him.

While our Judeo-Christian tradition has emphasized the virtue of loving, we have failed to place hating in its proper counterbalancing context. We all have dual natures, one loving and the other hating. Unless we achieve a healthy balance between them, we will have relationships that are insipidly dull or cloyingly sweet or that are hopelessly filled with mistrust and suspicion. To overlook another's faithlessness or disloyalty—however human—is to reduce oneself and one's marriage to a meaningless marshmallow-smooth nothingness, but to continually watch for evidence of betrayal is to live in a continual hell. How much better to have a vital, alive relationship in which the capacity for both love and hate is acknowledged by both, and in which there is a healthy tension between the two emotions.

The problem of dealing with and expressing the hatred in a relationship without destroying the relationship itself is, of course, a central one. Many couples who admit their hateful feelings to themselves are so horrified at their feelings that they retreat into themselves in a sudden attack of guilt. To discover a murderous rage toward a loved mate is disconcerting, but it is normal and perhaps a measure of one's love, since indifference would characterize one's reaction to the misdeeds of a partner who was not loved.

It is important that married couples remember that it is their actions that may be harmful to the other, and that their fantasies will do no harm. An angry wife who relishes the mental image of her unfaithful husband's agony as she slowly tweezes out each of his pubic hairs, one by one, does her husband no harm and allows herself a great deal of psychic release by her fantasy. By adding a sense of humor to their hateful and hurt feelings, couples will find that they regain a sense of perspective. If an individual can chuckle at the revenge fantasized for the mate, disappointment is lessened, and the person will feel more in control of his or her own reactions and less a victim of circumstances. Since it is only fantasy, the more bizarre the revenge, the more satisfying it may be, even if it is of bloody mayhem. The important point to remember is that fantasies are not real and therefore not harmful (Charny, 1972).

Frames of reference. The second false assumption that contributes to faulty conflict-management is the belief that those whom we love naturally have the same frame of reference that we have, and that every situation appears the same to one's spouse as it appears to oneself. The truth is, of course, that we each perceive the world and the events in it in a unique way, and it is possible for two people to experience the same event and yet perceive it in different ways—a fact that is well known to courtroom attorneys and to marriage counselors.

One's frame of reference is based largely on the values, assumptions, and expectations that a person develops during his first few years of life (Saxton, 1968), and it is impossible to find another person with a frame of reference identical to one's own. If there are wide differences in the frames of reference of a married pair, each will find it extremely difficult, if not impossible, to understand the other's point of view. If the disparity in perception exists in the majority of their interactions, cooperation between them may be impossible and the marriage may never be satisfying to either.

''**That's** not what I meant''

When Carol, a divorcée, married Jeff, she was delighted that her two young sons would have a father to share the discipline with her. She and Jeff had discussed their feelings about children's conduct, and they both agreed that they should insist on certain standards of behavior and that the boys should be "corrected" if they failed to observe the rules. There came a time when the boys were particularly unruly, and Carol asked Jeff to "correct" them. He complied by whipping them with a thick leather belt. "Correcting" to Carol had meant nonphysical punishment, but to Jeff it implied a sound thrashing. Each had arrived at his or her interpretation of the word through the particular frame of reference that each had. Conflict that centered around the discipline of the children therefore arose because of the differing points of view toward appropriate punishment.

When two people attempt to live together in the intimate state of marriage without the ability to understand the other's point of view, each is unable to predict how the other will react in any given situation. Since much of the feeling of stability in a relationship comes from the predictability of the other's actions and responses, unpredictability causes confusion and a feeling of apprehension. This is not to say that occasional novel behavior that does not deviate radically or cause too severe a jolt is harmful to a marriage. In fact,

"Of <u>course</u> I'm not being logical. I'm not <u>trying</u> to be logical."

such unpredictability may add interest and excitement to the marriage and be rewarding and beneficial. A marriage that cannot tolerate any unpredictability on the part of the partners is one that has no tolerance for ambiguity. Every move the other makes has to be accounted for and explained satisfactorily, and any deviation from routine behavior causes uncertainty and confusion. The more tolerance a couple have for ambiguity in life, the less distress they will feel when they are unable to always predict each other's behavior, and the more pleasure they will find in occasional whimsy. It is when people become rigid in their expectations and totally unable to accept any unpredictability from their spouses that instability in the relationship occurs.

It is most damaging to a marriage if unpredictable responses are always negative rather than positive. Thus, when one partner tries to create a particular atmosphere or attempts to effect a particular response in a mate, he or she may meet with totally different responses than had been expected or hoped for. A man who wants to create a romantic, loving atmosphere, for example, may bring his wife a dozen roses and a sexy nightgown as a surprise gift. If her childhood observations and experiences have taught her that men bring women presents when they are guilty of some misconduct, she may respond with suspicion and icy withdrawal—the exact opposite of the response he expected. Consistent negative feedback in a marital relationship will result in both partners feeling tense, awkward, defensive, and even disoriented (Saxton, 1977). In the intimacy of marriage, marital partners at times drop their customary defenses, and are therefore especially vulnerable to attack, real or fancied. The spouse who consistently receives negative responses feels betrayed and self-image suffers, sometimes permanently.

It is the damaged self-image that is the most devastating casualty in a marriage in which there are divergent frames of reference. A wife who sees herself as an intelligent, aware person may bring politics into the dinner table conversation with her husband, perhaps giving him the results of some research into a particular political candidate's voting record. If her husband's frame of reference sets women solely in the kitchen and nursery, he may view her conversation as unfeminine, aggressive, and ludicrous, and his response may be rude or patronizingly deferential. In order to defend her self-image, the wife must either accept the devaluation, with a resulting loss of interest in the marital relationship, or she must make an effort to change her behavior to become more in line with her husband's expectations. More often that not, the person whose self-esteem has been attacked will reduce the estimation of the other's significance and thereby reduce his or her own vulnerability (Saxton, 1977).

On the other hand, when persons receive positive feedback that is congruent with hopes and expectations, their self-image is reinforced and they feel confident, secure, and self-assured. The self-assurance they feel in their marriage generalizes to all other spheres of their life so that they have a permeating sense of well-being (Saxton, 1977).

Togetherness. The third false assumption that leads to destructive marital conflict is that two people who marry should spend the majority of their time together, and that neither should plan activities that do not include the other. As has been emphasized time and time again in this book, too much togetherness ultimately becomes restrictive for one or both partners, and too little individuality and too few personal interests and friends spell an end to growth and excitement in life. When one partner depends on the other to plan his or her social life, or when one of the spouses decides to plan the recreational outlets of the other, conflict is certain to boil under the surface, and its eruption may be devastating to both partners.

When a couple enters marriage in the spirit of joining together in their individual quests for fullness of experience and individual growth, each expects the other to have individual interests and to pursue ideas, activities, and relationships of his or her own. Thus each has individual experiences and at the same time can share the experiences and growth of the partner, so that the growth and experiences of each are expanded by the sharing with the other.

Internal conflicts. The fourth false assumption underlying much marital conflict is that all marital conflict comes about when one partner wants or needs one thing and the other wants or needs something else. To be sure, this is one cause of conflict, and it can be met by allowing one partner to take an authoritarian stand and make arbitrary decisions, or by one partner's accepting the needs of the other and forgoing personal needs, or by each in turn sacrificing personal needs for the fulfillment of the needs of the other. The most growth-producing form of conflict-resolution arising from conflicting needs between the partners is a democratic form of problem-solving in which both partners discuss the problem together and agree upon a solution that is satisfying to both (Saxton, 1968).

Much marital conflict, however, arises not from the conflicting needs of the partners, but from internal conflict within one or both partners when there are two opposing needs within the one individual. When people are torn by drives, instincts, and values pulling against each other, they are unable to deal with opposing needs between themselves and their mates in a creative, autonomous, spontaneous manner (Crosby, 1973). A woman, for example, may need to be both independent and cherished and cared for by another, so that at times she is crisply efficient and aggressive, and at other times yielding and receptive. Her husband may be perfectly capable of recognizing and responding to her conflicting needs, and he may find her more exciting and interesting because of her complexity. But she may have difficulty accepting the opposing traits in herself, and her inability to move comfortably from one role to the other may cause her to be defensive and contradictory in her relations with her husband, leading to marital conflict. In these cases, the real nature of the conflict must be explored by both partners, and the one experiencing the inner conflicts should assess the feelings and arrive at an understanding of the basis for them.

Much of all social interaction consists of patterned behavior that has a predictable outcome and that conceals some personal motive. These recurring modes of interpersonal transactions are termed **games** by Berne, and were succinctly described in his provocative book, *Games People Play* (1964). According to Berne, these games are necessary and desirable, as long as they are not destructive, for they allow people to receive responses that they need from other people. When a game is destructive, however, its function is to al-

low an escape from reality (or at least a certain escape from reality occurs), and the result is usually unhappiness and a feeling of deprivation.

Marital games are among the most destructive and perpetual of all. The most frequently played marital game Berne titles "If It Weren't for You." An example of the "If It Weren't for You" game is the loquacious and demanding woman who marries a quiet and retiring man. Her continual chattering and excessive demands drive him away, and he spends as much time as possible at the office, never taking his wife out and never being at home so that she can invite guests in. His wife continually complains about the absence of a social life, saying, "If it weren't for you, I would have friends," while he complains about his wife's nagging, saying, "If it weren't for you, I would stay home more." A contract was drawn by them and a marriage counselor whereby she agreed to cease making negative statements and to be consistently agreeable and nondemanding. He agreed to stay home with his family more and to join his wife in social activities. After each could no longer play the "If It Weren't for You" game, the wife's terrible fear of social situations emerged. She had always felt socially inept and had unconsciously chosen a nonsocial man who would protect her from having social encounters. When he no longer had his wife's caustic tongue to use as an excuse, the husband was forced to admit that he had a deep fear of a close relationship with another person, and that he found more emotional satisfaction in his work than he did in an intimate relationship. He had married a woman who could drive him away with her negative attitude, thus enabling him to do what he wanted to do in the first place.

Conflict-avoidance games—rationalizing an inner conflict by looking for plausible reasons behind one's behavior, rather than facing the primary reason or projecting one's own traits onto a mate in order to avoid looking at them in oneself, or transferring one's feelings about an earlier significant person (particularly a parent) to a spouse—only lead to more conflict within the individual and between the partners (Crosby, 1973). Self-actualizing couples will refuse to rationalize or to play destructive games. Instead they accept themselves without illusions or delusions. They can see their own strengths and weaknesses and can identify their own conflicts and hangups, and thus free themselves to deal creatively with the conflict within the marriage (Crosby, 1973). When both partners work together to resolve the problem arising from the internal conflict of one, the relationship is strengthened and the partners are free to move closer together (Saxton, 1968).

Win or lose. Making conflict a win or lose situation makes it very costly because there must always be a loser. Thinking about the *purpose* of a conflict helps to deal with it creatively (Schulz & Rodgers, 1975). For example, resolving a conflict about which movie to see on the basis of who wins the right to make such choices would be better resolved by considering a number of movies that would be mutually enjoyable and satisfying. Keeping the purpose in mind—an enjoyable night out—helps both partners to resolve this conflict satisfactorily.

LEARNING CONFLICT-MANAGEMENT

Since marital conflict is patently inevitable, and since frustration necessarily exists in every loving relationship, married couples who desire a satisfying, rich, joyful life together must resolve the problem of how to deal with their conflict, and the manner in which they manage conflict may be the pivotal factor in their marriage.

Partners may confront each other in very overt, direct ways, or use more subtle means, as in withholding something that the other wants. The latter is one of the most damaging to a relationship because there is not an acknowledgment of the conflict and, therefore, it cannot be settled. Instead, the partner usually "senses" something is wrong, makes a counterattack that is equally withholding, and the conflict persists to erode intimacy.

For many people, effective conflict-management must be learned in a conscious, deliberate manner, since they did not receive adequate training in conflict-management in their observation of their parents, either because the parents concealed all their conflict from their children or because their own conflict-management was faulty and ineffective. Similarly, peer groups seldom provide good experience in conflict-management, because the emotional trauma associated with peer conflict makes productive learning impossible and individuals instead learn to avoid conflict (Boulding, 1966). Productive, growth-producing conflict-management must often be learned in adulthood—either by reading and discussion with one's mate or by professional training in the productive management of conflict.

Fight-training. Dr. George R. Bach, co-author of *The Intimate Enemy* (1969), has instituted fight-training sessions for the couples he counsels and has found that 85 percent of them lived much more satisfying lives after receiving the training. The rate of reconcilia-

tion among the couples with problems also increased sharply after fight-training was introduced.

Fight-trainees are taught to display their "belt lines" openly and fairly and to guard against below-the-belt blows. However, some marital partners have such unrealistically high belt lines that no blows can be absorbed and no healthy aggressive approaches can be made by their partners. Still others may set their belt lines so low that needless injury is masochistically invited. Trainees are encouraged to set their own boundaries by shouting "Foul!" when their supervulnerable spots are hit during an argument. Combatants are also encouraged to do their fighting when they are in a rational frame of mind and to make an appointment for their fights. They are furthermore trained to listen during a fight and to gain as much information as possible from their partners by pausing frequently and asking, "What are you trying to tell me? What do you mean by that?" or by being sure that the other understands how a particular remark was interpreted by saying, "Let me tell you how I heard that." Marital fighters are also trained in the art of ending a fight and in signaling an "emergency brake" that will be honored by both parties when the heat of battle has reached a point that is intolerable. Expressions such as "Please stop!" or "Cool it!" can either signal a temporary halt or can bring a fight to an end. Experienced fighters learn that faking an emergency brake when their emotions are not really bruised beyond continuing will result in more trouble than they had to begin with.

Successful reconciliations are programmed by instructing fight-trainees in the art of making up without sniveling, pouting, looking hang-dog or maudlin, or stepping out of character to perform phony charitable acts. Dr. Bach offers 17 exercises as a general guide for people who wish to learn constructive and elegant fighting styles. In condensed form, they are:

Exercise No. 1. In an inner dialogue, one partner asks questions about his or her feelings at the moment: Am I really angry, or am I only annoyed? How far can I be pushed before I become really hostile?

Exercise No. 2. If the answers to the first inner dialogue have convinced a partner that there is really reason to fight, a second inner dialogue is held: Should I really fight about this? How afraid am I of this fight? Am I ready to be honest as well as tactful in this encounter? Am I ready to fight about the real issue and not about a trivial matter that camouflages another deeper grievance?

Exercise No. 3. The aggressor lets the partner know that a fight is wanted and pins down a time and place for it. In stating the issue, the aggressor makes sure that the anger is not misinterpreted as being greater or less than it is.

Exercise No. 4. Both partners review the rules of fair fighting. Physical violence is outlawed. Belt lines are respected. Each will give information to the other. Each must be as ready to listen as to talk. Each must provide feedback to the other so that there is no chance of misunderstanding the other's meaning. Both must confine themselves to immediate issues and not to the past. If necessary, they may fight before an audience or in front of a referee.

Exercise No. 5. Partners discuss the previous four exercises before going on to the substance of the argument.

Exercise No. 6. All explosive temper outbursts and insults must be dispensed with before the issue is stated, and both should be certain they transmit exactly how they feel about the emergence of the matter.

Exercise No. 7. The nonaggressor states what he or she thinks the other's grievance is, and the aggressor verifies or corrects the interpretation of the problem.

Exercise No. 8. The nonaggressor may respond to the aggressor's demand and launch a counteroffensive if he or she wishes.

Exercise No. 9. Both partners may correct any false or irrelevant echoes of the previous exercise.

Exercise No. 10. Intermission. For an hour or a week, or more, depending on agreement, each partner repeats the first and second exercises and meditates about ways to advance his or her own cause.

Exercise No. 11. Exercises No. 6 through No. 10 may be repeated as often as mutually acceptable.

Exercise No. 12. Mutual disengagement. Each partner articulates the changes that have taken place and what each has agreed to do to implement the changes.

Exercise No. 13. A fourth inner dialogue: What have I learned from this fight? How badly was I hurt? How was my partner hurt? How valuable was this fight? How useful was it in providing new information about myself, my partner, and the issue? How do I feel about the new position we created?

Exercise No. 14. Making up and resuming peaceful relations.

Exercise No. 15. Evaluating the fight.

Exercise No. 16. Establishing penalties and changes that partners agree upon after judging their fight.

Exercise No. 17. Preparing for the next fight over leftover tensions and unresolved issues from the last fight, using agreed-upon modified strategies, taboos, and freedoms.

An interesting study was conducted by Epstein and Santa-Barbara (1975) in which conflict behavior in clinical couples was examined. The intent was to observe how husbands and wives perceive each other in a conflict situation in terms of cooperation and exploitation, and how these perceptions affected behavior toward another. Using as a criterion their scores over a number of trials on games in which the couples could cooperate or compete, the investigators grouped 180 couples into four types, according to how they resolved the conflicts: Those who typically reached stable, cooperative outcomes were called *"Doves."* Those who reached stable outcomes with high mutual conflict were called *"Hawks."* When one spouse tended to gain at the other's expense, the couple was classified *"Dominant-Submissive."* Those who did not reach any type of stable outcome were called *"Mugwumps."*

Epstein and Santa-Barbara found that all groups expected more cooperation than defection from their partners, but perception of the other's cooperation was paired with *actual* cooperation only by the Dove group. The Doves were better at predicting their spouses' actions than were the other groups, but this accuracy was less important in reaching a stable outcome than was general cooperativeness. In the other groups, the prediction of a high level of cooperation reflected more wishful thinking than actual cooperation.

The Doves expressed more cooperating intentions than the other groups and responded accordingly. By contrast, the Hawks were more likely to be exploitative when they expected their spouse to cooperate. Overall, the Hawks expressed more exploitative intentions than the Doves, although in the beginning of the game the Doves did express as many exploitative intentions as the Hawks. The difference came when the Dove couples, after expressing individualistic intentions, were able to abandon them in favor of a mutually beneficial outcome. Doves were therefore more flexible in their relationships than the other groups. The Epstein and Santa-Barbara study thus indicates that if a marital relationship is basically strong, there will be an underlying agreement between the partners that conflict will persist only up to a certain point; after that, the mutual goal of preservation of the relationship will take precedence over the temporary conflict.

Learning to deal with conflict in a creative manner is essentially a matter of learning to cooperate within a framework of continuing differences and fundamental disagreements (Horowitz, 1967). Rather than striving for adjustment, accommodation, or consensus, therefore, cooperation must be the keystone of a couple's conflict-management. A set of shared, mutually understood procedural rules is needed for cooperative conflict-management, and adherence to a set of shared rules appears to be more important than similarity of attitudes or shared values. It is possible, in fact, for harmony to exist in a marriage in which there are great differences in beliefs or values. Unhappiness in marriage likely arises more from a couple's inability to live and deal with their differences than from the differences themselves (Sprey, 1972).

Transactional analysis. For many couples, the framework of transactional analysis, mentioned in Chapter 1, provides a good starting point for self-training in creative conflict-management. Using the premise that every person is composed of the Child (the inferior being who feels "You're OK, I'm not OK"), the Parent (the critical judge who believes "I'm OK, you're not OK"), and the Adult (the realistic person who feels "I'm OK, you're OK") as outlined by Harris in *I'm OK, You're OK* (1967), a couple can learn to understand and discuss their own conflict in terms that have identical interpretations for the two of them—thus bringing them closer to understanding one another's point of view. By using the terms Parent, Child, and Adult, the partners can see that it is often the Parent or Child who takes command in marital conflict, and that conflict-resolution is impossible unless the Adults of both are communicating (Crosby, 1973).

In a self-actualizing marital relationship, each partner strives for the atmosphere of Adults who take an "I'm OK, you're OK" position in their conflict-management. In this manner, each partner works with the present reality of the situation, always aware of the needs and demands of the Child and Parent in the self and the partner. With self-awareness and honesty, partners can recognize in themselves their own games by which the Child or Parent tries to get continual reassurance of the affection of the other or expresses judgmental criticism as a means of gaining moral one-upmanship over the other.

By learning the principles and language of transactional analysis, a married pair can increase the probability of working within the same frame of reference, while at the same time increasing their self-awareness and their sensitivity to the demands and responses of one another. By releasing themselves from the bondage of their "Not OK" Child and their punitive Parent, a married couple can become free to be themselves. Only when persons are free to be themselves can they relate to others as the people they actually are and not as symbols of someone else—usually a parent—from the past. The principles underlying transactional analysis can be self-taught by reading books such as *I'm OK, You're OK* or Eric Berne's *Games People Play* (1964). Readers may not choose to adopt such

expressions as "You hooked my Child" when they discuss their problems, but they will be made aware of some of the reasons behind their own and their mate's actions, and their ability to communicate will therefore be enhanced.

CONCLUSION

It should be pointed out that communication does not guarantee a successful marriage and that even Adult-Adult communication may not be able to resolve all marital conflict in a satisfying manner. There are some instances in which divorce is the only route by which a couple can achieve individual growth, in spite of honest efforts at compromise and mutual understanding. Not all conflict can be satisfyingly resolved, and a mark of maturity is the ability to accept the fact that there are some areas of disagreement and disappointment in one's marriage that are unresolvable. If the areas of disagreement far outnumber the areas of agreement, or if their importance to one or both is critical, a dissolution of the marriage may be the only rational decision. The belief that all marital conflict can be resolved through honest effort and open communication is unrealistic and leads to feelings of guilt and inadequacy on the part of marital partners who find themselves unable to happily solve all their problems.

CHAPTER 12

BECOMING PARENTS

He was not brought by the stork: He was delivered by a man from the Audubon Society personally.   FRED ALLEN

Imagine, if you can, what would happen in the United States if all the children suddenly followed some Pied Piper to a children's paradise, leaving empty schools, idle pediatricians, vacant toy stores, and millions of unemployed Americans. The number of industries and businesses that exist because of the children in our society is endless—manufacturers of nursery furniture, children's clothing, baby bottles, baby food, and toys, to name a few—and there are many other businesses, such as the dairy industry and sports equipment manufacturers, that largely depend on children as consumers. The promotion of parenthood is, therefore, one of the mainstays of the advertising media in America. A large percentage of TV and radio commercials, and of newspaper, magazine, and billboard advertising carries the subliminal message that parenthood is fun, beautiful, noble, and above all, healthy and normal. Hamburger chains picture happy, loving parents eating french fries with their cute, bright, grateful children. Detergent manufacturers show happy, tireless mothers gently brushing the rosy cheeks of their adorable babies with freshly laundered, fuzzy blankets, while the baby gurgles in delight and rocks on his round, freshly diapered bottom. At Christmas time, the slick fashion magazines carry jewel-toned portraits of beautiful socialites and their charming children. ("This year Mrs. Svelte's daughters wear green velvet, last year it was red.") Easter would simply be a religious event, with no commercial value, if it were not for the practice of outfitting children with new clothes, Easter baskets, chickens, bunnies, and various other costly gifts. And Mother's Day and Father's Day are celebrations that provide profit for the retailers as well as topics for Sunday sermons.

THE PROMOTION OF PARENTHOOD

While we no longer look with wholehearted approval and envy at families such as that in Frank Bunker Gilbreth's *Cheaper by the Dozen,* many people do regard parenthood as one of the natural and inevitable components of marriage, and pronatalism is woven into the fabric of the American dream.

Children have traditionally been viewed as the fulfillment of a marriage, if not the primary reason for marriage. It was taken for granted that a couple married, produced children, and later enjoyed their grandchildren. In the extended families of the past this was true, but all the adult members helped care for the children, and the responsibility for their care, education, and socialization was not solely that of their parents. It was probably for this reason that in the extended family postpartum depression was seldom found, since a woman was not forced to immediately shoulder the responsibility of an infant at a time when his need for mothering was greater than her need to nurture (Rossi, 1971).

There were also other reasons for having children that were bound up with a family's survival.

Up until the fairly recent past, the agrarian economy and the high mortality rate demanded large families. The more strong hands a farm family had to help with the crops, the more secure they were, and the greater was the probability that the land would stay intact and within the family. There was also a need to populate the country in order to insure its expansion and defense. Every nation, from the ancient Hebrews to present-day China, has recognized the need for a backlog of young men and women to replace those lost to war or disease. A constant replacement of old and young adults, of course, requires a stable birth rate. And, if the population needs to be increased in order to build up a country's defense system, then the birth rate must be accelerated. The large families of yesteryear, therefore, not only aided the individual families in their own survival needs, but added to the strength of the country's defense and economy.

Added to these reasons for the traditional promotion of children was the fact that procreation made sex seem cleaner and more permissible. Since women have been viewed through the ages as the evil agents who tempt men into carnal pleasures, childbirth has also served the purpose of punishing women for their role in sexual intercourse. "Woman will be saved through bearing children," wrote St. Paul to Timothy (I Timothy 2:14-15), and generations of women have continued to feel that childbirth and motherhood absolved them of the "sin" of sexual intercourse. (Men may believe that the cost of the child—estimated conservatively $45,000, not including college—is sufficient punishment for their own sexual "sin.") By convincing themselves that childbirth sanctified or purified sex, women may very well have been trying to turn a sow's ear into a silk purse, because they were stuck with childbirth and motherhood in any case, since there were no really effective contraceptives. It is doubtful that women of the past looked forward to childbirth, especially since childbirth was usually a painful, exhausting experience unmodified by painkillers, anesthetics, or any techniques for reducing the discomfort of giving birth. And it is also doubtful that all women of the past enjoyed motherhood, any more than all women of the present enjoy it. Nevertheless, most women held childbirth and motherhood in high regard, at least publicly, and considered themselves inferior beings if they were unable to conceive, deliver, suckle, and rear a child. Women not only allowed males to view childbirth and motherhood as a glorious ideal that negated the sinfulness and nastiness of sex, but even convinced themselves that they could justify their own sexuality only through the pain of childbirth and the drudgery of motherhood. Thus, converting a potentially odious inevitability into a holy estate was an even greater example of psychological sleight of hand than was Tom Sawyer's white-washing job.

THE "MATERNAL INSTINCT"

After the diaphragm was introduced as a contraceptive in the 1880s (Rollin, 1971), the sanctification of motherhood was somewhat replaced by the advancement of the belief that women had an inborn, biological maternal instinct that drove them to *desire* motherhood. A woman who did not profess a wish for children was therefore denying her biological destiny and causing unhappiness and frustration for herself. Freud, whose understanding of women was biased by his own Victorian environment, went so far as to advance the theory that a woman strove to have a child as a substitute for a penis (Rollin, 1971). (Freudians and Neo-Freudians always seem to overlook the fact that little boys are as disappointed at not having

"If parenthood was good enough for my parents,
it's good enough for me."

a uterus and the ability to "make babies" as little girls are at not being able to urinate standing up.)

In today's world, none of these traditional reasons for having children is valid or relevant. Rather than needing to expand our population, we stand in critical need of halting its growth. Our urban, mechanized society does not benefit from extra workers, and there are inexpensive, safe, effective contraceptives available to all. Furthermore, there are few people today who believe that marital sex is a sin or that women are, or need to be punished for being, evil temptresses. Sadly, however, the myth of woman's biological instinct for motherhood still exists, although it is largely promoted today by men and women who *need* to believe in it. Some, like George Gilder (1973), see marriage and motherhood as the root of all human sexuality and as the only force that socializes the human male and prevents his becoming violent, exploitative, and totally hedonistic. According to Gilder, if women are accorded full equal-

The "Maternal Instinct" **349**

ity with men, given equal pay for equal work, and allowed to freely choose whether or not to have children, then men will have no reason to be civilized and no way to assert their own masculinity. Procreation to Gilder, then, is not only a woman's biological destiny, but her *duty* to men, society, and civilization. Presumably, the only thing that prevents males in our society from asserting their manliness by swinging through the treetops and clubbing women over the head and raping them is the function of childbearing and motherhood on the part of women.

The idea that there is a biological drive on the part of women to have babies is, of course, sheer nonsense. Women are biologically *equipped* to conceive, bear, and suckle infants, just as men are biologically equipped to impregnate women. But the **desire** for children is a matter of cultural training and of individual personality characteristics and not a biological drive.

The "maternal instinct" has been shown to be nonexistent even among animals. In one study (Harlow et al., 1966) female monkeys who were raised with varying degrees of social deprivation—no mothering at all, a cloth surrogate mother, or peer association only—had inadequate adult mating responses, and half of those who were inseminated had to be bred through the use of restraining racks that positioned them for copulation. The other half of the inseminated monkeys voluntarily copulated, but only after a period of several years and many mating sessions. When the monkeys delivered offspring, they frequently refused to nurse them and sometimes badly mauled them. Most of the monkeys deprived of peer contact were totally inadequate and abusive as mothers, but the majority of those raised with peers from the age of one year were adequate mothers. A few of the monkeys delivered subsequent offspring, and all—even some who had been very abusive with their first-born—were surprisingly adequate with their second-born, although their social behavior was infantile. This study clearly shows that in these monkeys both mating behavior and maternal behavior had to be *learned*.

Furthermore, the idea that nurturance and tenderness are a woman's natural reactions to an infant is a culturally learned stereotype. When Margaret Mead gave the children of New Guinea dolls to play with, the girls ignored them, but the boys rocked them and crooned lullabies to them in a very maternal way (Mead, 1930). In today's changing world, young men are able to exhibit their maternal feelings toward their offspring, and society is beginning to recognize the fact that "mothering" can be done by a man as well as by a woman.

PRESENT TRENDS

For the first time in history, men and women have a choice about becoming parents. The oral contraceptives on today's market are virtually 100 percent effective, and medical science is improving the intrauterine devices as well as other contraceptive means. Should a contraceptive device fail, abortion is safe, legal, and readily obtainable for the first time in the history of the United States. Since childbirth is a matter of choice, rather than a matter of inevitability, couples no longer need to find silver linings in their clouds by convincing themselves that children are necessary for the stability of a marriage or for the fulfillment of a woman's biological needs.

The trend today is toward having fewer children. Women are waiting longer to marry than they did previously—the median age for brides in 1977 was 21.6 and 24.0 for men. This reflects one full year change since the 1960s. (U.S. Bureau of the Census, 1977, No. 307).

Furthermore, there is a growing trend among young couples to remain childless. The actual percentage of childless married women 20 to 24 years old has risen from 24.2 in 1960 to 41.7 in 1976 (Statistical Abstract, 1977). Similarly, the number of couples who plan to have only one child has grown in the past decade—from 6 percent in 1967 to nearly 12 percent in 1976 (Statistical Abstract, 1977). The number of women who planned on only one or no children increased more than 80 percent in the early seventies. Furthermore, according to a December 1977 Census Bureau report, the number of children that young women want has dropped from an average of 3.77 per family in 1957 and 3.1 in 1967 to an average of 2.1 in 1977 (U.S. Bureau of the Census, 1977, No. 316).

There was a sharp decline between 1960 and 1975 in the birth rate, but current figures indicate a stabilization in the birth expectations of young women (U.S. Bureau of the Census, 1977, No. 316).

If the average number of children in a family stayed at 3.5 for the next 40 years, we would face the crisis of a country burgeoning with something like 500 million people, or more than double our present population of 220 million. On the other hand, if every family held their offspring to no more than 2.1, the present population would remain stable; and if the present trend continues, we may realize either a stable or a declining birth rate. In contrast to the first nine months of 1971, when babies were born at the rate of 2.39 for each family, there were only 2.08 babies per family born in the first nine months of 1972, an all-time low that is even below the "replacement" rate of 2.1 (Commission on Population Growth, 1972).

FANTASY VERSUS REALITY

Parenthood is so romanticized in our child-oriented society that the disparity between the fantasies of having a child and the actual experience of having a child often, if not always, causes a severe jolt to the emotional equilibrium of the parents and to the marital relationship itself. In a study of conjugal violence (Gelles, 1975), it was found that in a small percentage of families incidents of violence occurred while the wife was pregnant. Factors such as sexual frustration and the stress of the pregnancy contributed to the eruption of violence. In a larger percentage of cases, crisis occurs with the birth of the child. One study of urban, middle-class parents whose children were under the age of five years (LeMasters, 1957) found that 83 percent of the couples had experienced a "severe" or "extensive" crisis at the birth of their first child. (Significantly, *all* mothers with professional training and extensive professional work experience suffered extensive or severe crisis.) The majority of these couples had wanted the child, had satisfactory marriages, and were free of maladjustment or neuroses. The consensus among the couples in the crisis group was that they had been inadequately prepared for parenthood. As one mother in the group stated, "We knew where babies came from, but we didn't know *what they were like.*" The findings of a later study (Dyer, 1963) support the idea that the introduction of the first child into a middle-class marital system constitutes a crisis situation. Another study (Hobbs, 1965) found no first-time parents in the broader sample studied who had experienced a severe or extensive crisis event at their baby's birth, even among the middle-class subjects. This later study, however, sampled parents whose children were less than 18 weeks old, as opposed to the older first children of the other studies, raising the possibility that parents may need to deny the extent of their crisis reaction to the birth of a child when the crisis is still in an acute stage, or that the negative aspects of first-time parenthood may seem more critical when viewed in retrospect, colored by a few years of economic adjustment, lessened social activity, and general disenchantment with parenthood. At any rate, the findings of crisis resulting from the introduction of a new, third party into a two-party system is consistent with studies concerning small groups (von Wiese, 1932; Wilson & Ryland, 1949) that have reported the

two-person group to be the most satisfactory of human relationships and the three-person group to be the most volatile. When a baby causes a reorganization of a group system from a pair to a triangle, there is almost inevitably a situation in which two of the three constitute a pair, while the third is an isolate. Either husband or wife may resentfully feel semi-isolated by the other's attachment to the baby, or the parents may maintain their former pair relationship while making the baby the semi-isolate and earning for themselves the judgment from relatives and friends of being poor parents. The birth of a first child also forces the married pair to take the final step toward adult responsibilities, a step that is regarded by some as the final transition to maturity in our culture (Havighurst, 1953). Such an irrevocable move is, in itself, enough to cause some anxiety on the part of many people.

Couples who opt for no children may have happier marriages than those who have children. According to studies conducted by Dr. Harold Feldman of Cornell University, couples who have children have a significantly lower level of marital satisfaction than those without children (Rollin, 1971). Furthermore, if a couple has only one child, they will be happier than if they have two children, and if they have two children, they will be happier than if they have three. If they continue to have children, in fact, the father is more likely to desert the family, and the mother is more likely to become mentally ill (Nye et al., 1972). Large families create more stress for fathers than they do for mothers, probably because after the fourth child a woman sees her children as her life's work since she usually cannot find time for anything else. Unlike the women with only one or two children who can find other rewarding roles, and unlike the women with large families who have dedicated themselves wholly to their children, the women with three or four children can do neither, and they are therefore more dissatisfied. In some cases, of course, large families are happier than medium-sized families, but they are never happier than small families. Small families have consistently been found to be superior in satisfaction for the married couple and their children. The married couple enjoy each other more if their family is small, and they also enjoy their role as parents more (Nye et al., 1972).

Of particular importance is the degree to which couples control the number and spacing of children according to their desires. Marital adjustment has been found to be critically affected by the ability of a couple to control the number of children they have and to have only the number they wish (Christensen, 1968; Reed, 1947). Married couples must either use effective birth-control methods or adjust their attitudes about the number of children they actually want. Thus, marital adjustment in relation to the number and spacing of children seems to be largely a matter of adopting the philosophy, "If you can't have the one you want, then want the ones you have." The fact that couples are usually unable to adjust their attitudes about the number of children they want is evidenced by the findings in the mid-1960s (Ryder & Westoff, 1969) that about a fourth of American couples with wives under the age of 45 already had more children than they had wanted. About half of the black couples sampled had more than they wanted. It has been estimated that about half of the population growth in the United States in the early 1960s was due to unwanted births, but the proportion of unwanted births has undoubtedly declined in the past decade because of improved contraceptive methods. Couples also seem to be unable to satisfactorily control the timing of pregnancies. In fact, 64 percent of whites and 82 percent of blacks reported that some of their children were born before they were wanted (Ryder & Westoff, 1969).

The cultural pressures exerted on women to enjoy motherhood cause many women to displace their dissatisfaction with motherhood to dissatisfaction with the homemaker role. It is more socially acceptable for a woman to say that she hates the job of cleaning and cooking than it is for her to say that she hates diapering and breastfeeding. Also, many women who dislike their children and resent having them displace their resentment onto their husbands and find fault, nag, criticize, and humiliate their husbands rather than their children. The price paid for unwanted children is high in terms of unhappy marriages and unhappy individuals, not to mention unhappy children, who pay the highest price of all.

There is more likelihood of having an unwanted child when there are several children in the family than there is in a small family, and there is less probability of parental enjoyment as the number of children increases (Rossi, 1971). In many cases, as the parent finds less and less satisfaction from the parent role, less attention is paid to the last child's demands and less verbal stimulation is given to the child. Last children, therefore, are more likely to cultivate winning, pleasing manners and to be charming and sociable as adults in a continuous effort to win the love and approval they were denied as children (Rossi, 1971).

ALTERNATIVES FOR PARENTHOOD

For couples who do want children, and who have healthy, sound reasons for wanting them, as well as the ability to provide them with financial, emotional, and physical support, there is the option of either adoption or the traditional do-it-yourself method. Some couples may choose to adopt a child because of their concern about overpopulating the world. Adoptive parents will find that contraceptives, including abortion, have reduced the number of babies in this country available for adoption, as well as relaxed some of the stringent adoption rules. Many overpopulated countries, however, have children available for adoption. More and more people are discovering that they can love and enjoy a child whose ethnic heritage is different from their own, just as many are enjoying sharing their love and lives with a child who became a family member when he was past the age of infancy and therefore not as "adoptable" as younger children.

Some couples who wish to have their own biological children may be unable to do so because of the sterility of either husband or wife. There are various disorders that may cause sterility in men or women. Among males—who are responsible for childlessness in about 30 percent of cases (Amelar, 1966; Clark, 1959)—sterility results from a variety of causes. When the man's sperm count is considered to be too low for conception, semen from many ejaculations may be collected and frozen for a period of months. After thawing, the semen is concentrated by centrifugation, which causes a much greater sperm concentration than usual. During the woman's period of ovulation, a certain quantity of seminal fluid is placed directly into the uterus on several successive days (Kleegman et al., 1970).

Sometimes a man's fertility is adversely affected by either too much or too little sexual activity (Charny, 1963; Masters & Johnson, 1967). On the average, the optimal time interval between ejaculations is about 48 hours for maximum fertility.

Among women, sterility may be due to congenital anatomical defects such as imperfect fallopian tubes or uterus. Sometimes a woman completely lacks one or all of these organs, as well as a vagina. Sometimes, too, reproductive organs become infected through venereal disease or other causes, leading to the closing of the fallopian tubes. Douching with water under pressure, for example, can force harmful bacteria into the fallopian tubes with a resulting infection and scar tissue that permanently close the tubes. There may also be improper development of ova or, in rare cases, an inability of the ovarian covering to rupture and allow the release of the ova.

Hormones also play a part in female sterility. Recent Japanese experiments have discovered that intramuscular injections of prolactin—the lactogenic hormone—for several days prior to a menstrual period somehow reverses sterility in many women. Scientists are unsure of how or why prolactin affects female sterility; they only know that it sometimes does.

In some cases, a woman develops antibodies that are antagonistic to all sperm, or to the sperm of her husband in particular (Masters & Johnson, 1960, 1961, 1966). When antibodies are present, couples are advised to keep the antibodies and sperm separated for a period of 6 to 12 months by using a condom during sexual intercourse. During that time the antibodies hopefully disappear, and pregnancy then becomes possible until they appear again (Thosteson, 1973).

In cases of antibodies that are antagonistic to the husband's sperm, or in cases when it is the husband who is sterile, **artificial insemination** of the wife can enable them to have a child through pregnancy. Through artificial insemination (AI), the sperm of the husband (AIH) or of a donor (AID) are inserted into the uterus of the wife at the time of the month when conception is most likely to occur. Pregnancy results in 80 percent of the cases when sperm belonging to someone other than the husband are used, but in only 5 percent of the cases when the husband's sperm are used. (In cases of antagonistic antibodies, of course, donor sperm would have to be used.)

Artificial insemination is increasing in popularity in the United

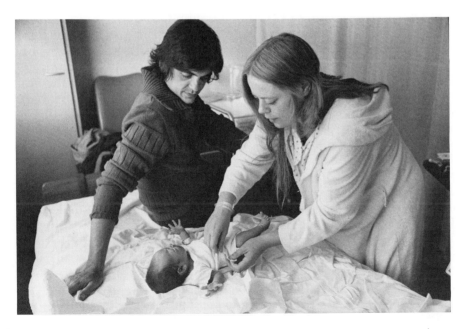

States. In 1955, there were an estimated 50,000 cases of AI, in 1958 there were 100,000 and in 1970 there were 200,000 (Lehfeldt, 1961; Smith, 1970). Although the Roman Catholic Church is opposed to artificial insemination from either a husband or nonhusband donor, **assisted insemination** is allowed. In this method, an instrument is used to push the husband's sperm into the cervix after it has been deposited in the vagina during marital intercourse.

In cases of female sterility, or in cases in which a woman is capable of conceiving a child but incapable, for one reason or another, of carrying it to term, adoption is still the most feasible answer for a couple wanting a child, although laboratory tests in England and the U.S. indicate that a human egg can be fertilized outside the body of the woman producing it and then be implanted in the uterus of a host mother. Perhaps in the future it will be commonplace for a woman who is unable to conceive a child in the usual way to be able to experience pregnancy and motherhood if she so desires.

For fertile couples who would like to give nature an assist in the reproductive process, there are certain coital positions that facilitate the union of sperm and egg. The face-to-face, man-above position is excellent for impregnation, especially if the woman keeps her knees raised after the ejaculation so that the sperm are aided in entering the uterus (Ellis, 1960; Greenblat, 1962). Also recommended as a favorable position for conception is the knee-chest rear-entry position. In this position, semen remains in the vagina for a longer time, and it is closer to the uterus than in any other coital position (Eichenlaub, 1961; Greenblat, 1962).

If a couple has an eccentric, wealthy Aunt Elizabeth whose will named as sole heir the first child named Elizabeth, they might be interested in the theory of Dr. Landrum B. Shettles of Columbia University. According to Dr. Shettles (1972), the sex of a child can be predetermined by taking note of the fact that the X (female) sperm has a large, oval-shaped body and short tail, while the Y (male) sperm has a small, round-headed body and long tail and weighs about 4 percent less than the X sperm does. Presumably, the lighter, smaller-headed, longer-tailed Y sperm move at a faster rate than X sperm do, and the larger-headed, heavier X sperm are stronger and live longer than Y sperm. In order to predetermine the sex of a child, it is necessary to control which sperm—male-producing or female-producing—will reach the egg first. According to Dr. Shettles, such control is possible. If a boy is wished, Shettles recommends that the wife douche before intercourse with a mixture of two tablespoons of baking soda in a quart of water. He further suggests deep penetration during intercourse, an orgasm on the part of the wife, and that the couple postpone intercourse until just *after* the time of the wife's ovulation. The rationale behind these suggestions is that the alkalinity of the douche and of the woman's secretions during orgasm neutralizes the acid condition of the vagina and lessens the threat to the weaker, male-producing sperm. More male sperm are produced during a period of abstinence, and timing intercourse to follow ovulation allows the fast-moving Y sperm to reach the waiting egg first. Furthermore, deep penetration puts the sperm farther into the vagina, thus shortening the hazardous vaginal journey.

To increase the chances of having a girl, a douche of two tablespoons of vinegar to a quart of water is recommended before intercourse. Shallow penetration at the time of ejaculation, an absence of orgasmic response on the part of the woman, and regular intercourse up to two or three days before ovulation and then ceasing help to insure that the weaker male sperm will die off before the egg arrives in the fallopian tube to be fertilized (Shettles, 1972). While this method would seem to offer promise of determining a child's sex, it should be emphasized that many scientists do not accept Shettles' theory, leaving adoption as the only *sure* way to get a preferred-sex child.

CONCEPTION

As soon as an ovum is penetrated by one of the millions of sperm moving toward it, a protective shield forms around the egg that prevents other sperm from penetrating it. Fertilization—the joining of the gene-carrying portions of the nuclei of the sperm and ovum—results in the full component of 46 chromosomes common to all human cells.

From the moment of fertilization to the second week, the conceptus is called a **zygote**. Through mitotic cell division, the zygote forms a spherical cell mass and moves through the fallopian tube to the uterus. Three internal layers are formed within the cell mass: the **ectoderm**, the **endoderm**, and the **mesoderm**; these three layers make up the **embryonic disc**, from which the embryo develops.

The conceptus is referred to as an **embryo** from the second to the eighth week. During this time it becomes implanted in the uterine wall, and the ectoderm, endoderm, and mesoderm become differentiated. From the ectoderm eventually come the nervous system, sense organs, mouth cavity, and skin; from the endoderm come the digestive and respiratory systems; and from the mesoderm come the muscular, skeletal, circulatory, excretory, and sexual systems.

The **amnion**, a thin, transparent, tough membrane, forms around

Conception **359**

the developing embryo, and the cavity fills with **amniotic fluid** in which the embryo is suspended by its **umbilical cord**. By floating in a liquid environment, the embryo is protected from jolts and injuries and can also move about and change positions. This membrane and fluid form the "bag of waters" whose rupture in the last stages of pregnancy signals impending childbirth.

Through diffusion and absorption within the **placenta**—the special organ for interchange between the mother and embryo—the embryo absorbs food and oxygen and eliminates carbon dioxide and other metabolic waste products. Both maternal and fetal blood circulate within the placenta, but they never intermingle. The cellular barrier between the two systems prevents the passage of most bacteria and other disease germs, but some antibiotics and certain viruses and disease germs are capable of crossing the barrier.

From the eighth week to birth, the conceptus is called a **fetus**. By this time all rudimentary systems of the body have appeared and they continue to grow and become elaborated during the fetal stage

1 (*left*) When an egg enters the fallopian tube, follicle cells (zona radiata) adhere to its surface.

Nucleus

Acrosome

2 (*above*) Sperm.

3 (*left*) Enzymes released by the acrosome at the time of fertilization cause the egg surface membrane to permit entry of the sperm.

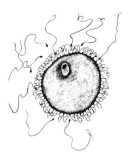

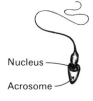

4 (*right*) When the sperm first penetrates the egg, a fertilization cone surrounds the sperm nucleus, preventing the sperm tail from entering the egg.

5 (*right*) The gene-carrying portion of the female nucleus and the male nucleus join and then re-form into two bodies as the first cell division occurs. The fertilized egg now contains the full component of 46 chromosomes common to all human cells. Fertilization is now complete.

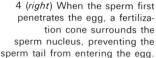

of development. At the eighth week, the fetus is almost 1 inch long and weighs about 1/30 of an ounce. At birth, the average infant is 20 inches long and weighs 7 pounds.

BIRTH

The birth of a child can be expected somewhere around 280 days from the date of the beginning of the mother's last menstrual period. Brunettes tend to deliver their babies slightly sooner than blondes, and athletic women about 20 days sooner than sedentary women. Infant girls are usually born a week or so sooner than boys.

One often hears the myth that a seven-month fetus is stronger than an eight-month fetus. This myth has its origins in the fact that many single women became pregnant, and it takes them about two months to arrange for a wedding. Thus, a strong infant born seven months after a wedding is very probably in reality a nine-month fetus. An eight-month fetus, on the other hand, usually *is* an eight-month fetus, and therefore weaker than a nine-month fetus. The closer to term a baby is delivered, the better are its chances of survival.

In almost all instances, babies are born head-first in a **longitudinal position**. The flexibility of an infant's skull allows for easier birth, but the facial features may be bruised and swollen and the head may be irregularly molded during the birth process. Within a few days, however, the skull reverts to its normal shape, and the facial features also become regular in appearance.

When the baby is born buttocks-first in a **breech position**, as happens in about 4 percent of longitudinal births, the infant's buttocks and genital area will be temporarily swollen and discolored.

Sometimes—once in every 200 births—a fetus lies crosswise in the uterus in the **transverse position** and has to be turned before birth or delivered by caesarean section.

Childbirth itself (**parturition**) consists of three stages. Contractions of the uterus, lasting about 30 seconds each, begin occurring about every 15 to 20 minutes during the first stage. As time progresses, the contractions become more frequent, more intense, and last for longer periods of time. Toward the end of labor, the contractions last a minute or more and occur every 3 to 4 minutes. The cervix dilates during the first stage of labor from an opening 1/8 inch wide to one about 4 inches wide. The amniotic sac ruptures and the amniotic fluid flows through the vagina during this stage, and the mucous plug, flecked with bright blood, that has served to keep the uterine environment germ-free is expelled.

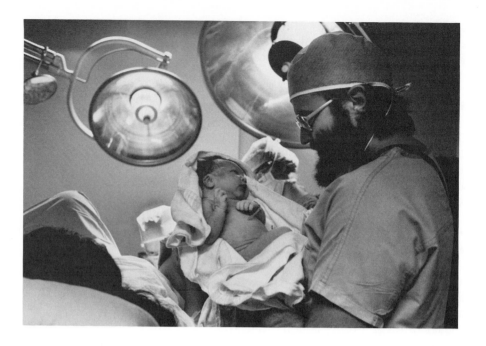

The second stage of childbirth begins when the cervix is fully dilated and continues until the birth of the fetus. The birth of the placenta—occurring about 15 minutes after birth of the baby—marks the third stage of parturition.

Immediately after the expulsion of the placenta, the mother's pituitary gland begins to produce **prolactin**, the lactogenic hormone that induces lactation. True milk is not produced in the mother's breasts for two or three days, but **colostrum**, a high-protein fluid, is present immediately after birth. This substance is believed to provide immunity to many infectious diseases during the early months of an infant's life. As the infant suckles the mother's breast, the sucking prompts uterine contractions that help return the enlarged uterus to its normal size.

Although not generally considered a sexual act, childbirth and lactation are as much a part of a woman's sexuality as coition is. Indeed, there is a great deal of similarity in the physiological reactions of a woman experiencing sexual excitement and orgasm and that of a woman experiencing undrugged childbirth such as the "natural" childbirth method advocated by Dr. Grantly Dick-Read, among others. There are also physiological similarities between a woman's responses during sexual intercourse and during breastfeeding. Another connection between orgasm and breastfeeding is the phenomenon of milk leakage from the breasts during and immediately after orgasm in some women. And women who breast-feed their babies have been found to be more responsive and tolerant in other sexual areas than women who do not breastfeed (Newton, 1971).

Women who breastfeed their babies will usually have a delayed onset of menstruation following delivery, but ovulation can occur before the first menstrual flow. This set of circumstances accounts for the fact that an average of one woman in 20 becomes pregnant again without having menstruated after childbirth.

MULTIPLE BIRTHS

Multiple births occur about once in 80 to 85 births. Twins are born once in about 80 births, triplets once in 80 × 80 births (6400), quadruplets once in 80 × 80 × 80 births (512,000), and so forth. Fraternal twins occur when two ova are fertilized, and identical twins occur when one ovum is fertilized, divides, and then separates. Two ova are usually involved in the development of triplets, with one of

"Where do babies come from? Daddy doesn't know."

the two fertilized ova dividing and producing identical twins, but three different eggs may also be fertilized and produce triplets. Two fertilized ova, each of which splits to produce two sets of identical twins, are usually involved in the birth of quadruplets.

NAMING THE BABY

Most parents-to-be spend many hours considering possible names for their future offspring. Just when they think they have settled on a name that is perfect, one of their mothers or a neighbor will say scornfully, "I used to have a dog with that name," and they go back to their list of names. Steering a path between the too-cute names on the one hand and the too-somber names on the other, while being careful not to favor one side of the family over the other, is a difficult task, but an important one. Studies by Georgia State University psychologist John McDavid and his associate Herbert Harari (1966, 1973) indicate that one's self-concept may be greatly influenced by his or her name. Names such as Elmer, Otto, Hubert, Percy, Gladys, Gertrude, and Rhonda are stereotyped as belonging to persons who are dull and unattractive, and children with those names are likely to react to taunts from other children by becoming belligerent, aggressive, and antagonistic. Children with popular names such as David, Susan, Sally, Elizabeth, Michael, and Stephen are more likely to be popular children and to make better grades in school. Certainly there are exceptions to this finding, notably such luminaries as Hubert Humphrey, Rhonda Fleming, and Gertrude Stein, but the fact remains that a child should not be saddled with a name that will cause embarrassment or confusion, even if the name belonged to one's famous great-grandfather or grandmother.

WORKING MOTHERS

Since nearly half of all married women in their early 20s and more than 40 percent of those in their late 20s are employed (Is the American family in danger?, 1973), the question of whether or not a mother should work is increasingly important in American families. Certainly the trend toward working mothers will have an effect on the character of the family. Women who feel a strong desire to work, or who have an economic need to work—and most young married women have both desire and need—often have to choose between very expensive and hard-to-find private childcare or less expensive but often inadequate daycare centers. There is therefore a demand among women for government-operated daycare centers for children of working mothers. Former President Nixon vetoed a childcare development bill in 1972, calling it fiscally irresponsible and administratively unworkable. Women will undoubtedly continue to push for these centers, however, and they will probably become a reality in the near future.

When the state takes over a function that has traditionally been that of the family—the care and socialization of children—serious questions arise. Will such centers result in a loss of our much-prized individuality in the necessary increase in group cooperation? Critics of state-operated daycare centers warn of the "mind control" that the state may acquire over the young. Proponents insist that the family will retain the strength it has always had and that values and ethics will continue to be taught and maintained within the family. Proponents of daycare centers point to the kibbutzim of Israel as evidence of the very positive influence group socialization can and does have on the young (Perutz, 1972).

In an exploratory study involving more than 100 families in which both parents were in the home and had children between the ages of 3 and 5½ in daycare centers (Winett et al., 1974), no mental or social differences were found between the daycare children and children who stayed at home with their mothers. These families were primarily white, middle-income families, and the daycare centers they attended represented many different types, some better and some worse than average.

The authors of the study concluded that "children are not harmed by daycare and babysitting arrangements and that the family structure seems flexible enough to both accommodate and allow for these arrangements." Couples who had children in daycare centers were found to have a more egalitarian sharing of childcare and household chores than did couples whose children stayed at home with their mothers. A side effect of working mothers and daycare centers, then, will apparently be closer involvement of the father in the care and socialization of the child. Interestingly, opponents of government-subsidized daycare centers who darkly predict a breakdown of the American family if women are aided in their desire to work outside the home ignore the fact that our government subsidized daycare centers three decades ago. During World War II, when women were needed to help in the war effort, the government willingly subsidized daycare centers for the children of working mothers. Little concern, or none at all, was expressed at that time over the effect on children of being placed in a daycare center.

The majority of studies have found no significant differences in the emotional adjustment of the children of working mothers. This finding has been consistent with both young children (Hand, 1957; Nye et al., 1963; Siegel et al., 1959) and with adolescents (Burchinal, 1963; Nye, 1963; Peterson, 1961). There does, however, seem to be a relationship between the motivation of the working mother and her attitude toward her employment and the emotional adjustment of the children. Mothers who enjoyed their jobs were found in one study to have children who were nonaggressive, while mothers who disliked their jobs tended to have aggressive, hostile children (Hoffman, 1963). Other studies (Gold, 1961; Nye, 1958) have reported a difference in the effect of working mothers on boys and girls, particularly in middle-class families. These studies have concluded that there is more delinquency in the sons of middle-class working mothers, but not in the sons of lower-class working mothers. This may be the effect of the mother's attitude toward the father in the household when his income is inadequate and she is forced to work (Douvan, 1963). Girls of working mothers tend to admire their mothers more and to have more clearly formed self-concepts and less traditionally feminine personalities (Nye & Hoffman, 1963).

Working mothers themselves report greater satisfaction from their jobs than their nonemployed sisters do with housework, and they also find more pleasure in their children (Hoffman, 1963). Furthermore, they suffer fewer physical symptoms of distress and, in general, are more satisfied with their lives and with their state of health than are nonemployed women (Feld, 1963).

An interesting recent federal guideline formulated by the Equal Employment Opportunity Commission insists that company childbearing leaves of absence must be the same for both sexes. Not only is it illegal for a company to fire a woman because she is pregnant, but also they must grant both her *and her husband* maternity and paternity leaves. Viewed as a leave to bring up Baby rather than a leave for childbirth, these rules have been adopted by very few employers. If they are adopted on a large scale, large sums of money will be expended in lost employee time, but at the present time they are part of the equal employment opportunities for men and women. If they are implemented, it will be interesting to view their effect on the structure and character of the family.

NO TRAINING FOR PARENTS

Mary, Joan, and Elise are high school chums. Mary plans on becoming a nurse, so she and her parents are planning on approxi-

mately four years of college and nursing school before she can get
a degree in nursing and begin her career. Joan wants to be a lawyer,
and she knows that she has at least seven years of college training
ahead of her. Like Mary, Joan is willing to put in the years of study
in order to prepare for her chosen life work.

Elise plans on marriage and motherhood, so she does not plan on
training of any kind. She has babysat for neighbors and taken a
home economics course, and she is sure that she can be a good
mother. And her mother and her grandmother are sure that she can
be a good mother. After all, they and society reason that girls have
common sense and an inborn maternal instinct that guarantees
that they will know how to give a helpless infant the nurture and
care he needs, a toddler the protected independence he needs, the
school child the acceptance and responsibility he needs, and the
adolescent the dignity and guidance he needs.

Probably the most important job in the world—that of producing,
nurturing, educating, and socializing the next generation—is put
in the hands of men and women with no training, no qualifications,
and no necessary aptitude for the job. Women are falsely assumed
to have some mysterious biological trait that fits them for motherhood. Men are equally falsely assumed to be unimportant except
for their fertilizing function anyway, so no training in parenthood
is considered necessary for them, either. Society expects people to

have many years of formal education to be physicians, lawyers, psychologists, or engineers, and to serve an apprenticeship to be plumbers, electricians, or bricklayers, but a couple become parents when the woman delivers a baby.

CHILD ABUSE

Obviously, there are many parents who are ill-equipped for the role. In the United States alone, there are 50,000 reported cases of child abuse each year. These are cases that involve severe injuries such as fractures of the skull and long bones and subdural hematomas, or less severe injuries such as bruises, burns, and minor fractures (Steele & Pollock, 1971). These are injuries that become apparent through medical examination. Countless other children are abused in less cruel ways, and their bodies bear no bruises to attest to their mistreatment. A child can be rapped sharply on the head with the knuckles, for example, and have no telltale bruise or swelling. He can also be deprived of food, drink, or other bodily needs on a regular basis without showing visible signs of malnourishment or of chronic discomfort. Examples of child abuse are so widespread, in fact, that we tend to have become inured to it. Harried shoppers may watch in mild disapproval as a mother viciously jerks a dawdling toddler's arm, or as a tired infant is spanked for crying, but the mother is likely to be thought of as stupid rather than as a child abuser. And if the abusing mother were confronted by an indignant observer, she would probably self-righteously claim her right to "discipline" her child in her own way, and the other onlookers would doubtless agree, even though they might disapprove of her methods.

Both these examples constitute child abuse, however, and can be found among people of all socioeconomic and educational strata. Child abuse is typically punishment that is too harsh and that is administered when the child is too young to comprehend what the parents expect or to behave according to the parents' unrealistic expectations (Steele & Pollock, 1971).

Research into the personalities and histories of battering parents has shown that they are people who have not found the love and acceptance they need, and they look to their babies and young children to provide it. When the infant or child instead proves to be demanding and imperfect, the parent lashes out in self-righteous fury. Significantly, the parents who have abused their children frequently express the attitude that the child *deserved* being hit, burned, shaken, choked, or otherwise hurt, and their emotion is best described as self-righteous indignation. Abusive parents usually were themselves abused as children, and they are usually quick to state their intention to rear polite, conscientious, law-abiding children who obey the rules of society.

Abused children are not ignored children. Instead, they usually have a mother who hovers over them, critically watching their every move. The typical parental pattern is one of impossible demands, constant criticism, and total disregard for the child's needs and rights. There is never a feeling on the part of either the child or the parent of having been cared for or cared about from the beginning of life (Steele & Pollock, 1971). Nurturance is thus replaced with demands, and acceptance is replaced with criticism and punishment. Merely to say that a child needs attention, then, is to overlook the fact that attention can be either negative or positive, excessive or satisfying.

While there are far too many parents who physically abuse their children, there are even more who psychically abuse them. A child may be ridiculed, humiliated, and derogated without bearing visible scars, but the emotional scars are deep and usually permanent. Parents who are unhappy, frustrated, and angry may vent hostility on their children rather than on another adult. Obviously, the premise that rearing a child is a job that anybody can do well is false. There are some childcare experts like Dr. Lee Salk, author of *What Every Child Would Like His Parents To Know* (1972), who maintain that being a parent is such a difficult job that there should be a national parent-education program. However, in a society that likes to believe that sex, motherhood, and football are natural proclivities of the human race, it is doubtful that funding would ever be forthcoming from any governmental or private agency for training men and women to be good parents.

One of the saddest, but most understandable, situations encountered in family counseling is that husbands behave toward their wives as their fathers behaved toward their mothers, wives behave toward their husbands as their mothers behaved toward their fathers, and each parent behaves toward the children as their own parents behaved toward them. Parents who knew ridicule and harsh criticism as children will use ridicule and harsh criticism in dealing with their own children, and parents who were physically abused as children will be physically abusive toward their children. In almost all cases, the individuals concerned are completely unaware that they are mimicking their own parents, and they may in fact relate with great bitterness behavior that they observed in their own parents, all the while oblivious to the fact that they display exactly the same behavior. If the similarity of childhood experience and adult behavior is pointed out to them, or if they become aware of it themselves through new insight, they typically are disgusted and revolted, stating that they always swore to themselves that they would never do to their wife, husband, or child the things they deplored in their parents. Nevertheless, they learned marital and parental behavior from their own parents, and these are the models they have followed.

REASONS FOR WANTING CHILDREN

A couple who contemplates producing or adopting a baby should examine their own reasons for wanting a child and then objectively appraise their own capacities for parenthood. A man who wants an heir to carry on the family name, for example, is more concerned with the name than the game and would do better to buy a racehorse and give it the family name. It would be cheaper than raising a child, and there is a bigger chance of having a winner.

Similarly, a man who believes that keeping his wife pregnant is proof to the world that he is sexually virile can surely find some less damaging way to assert his potency. Men who feel insecure about their own manliness unless they have visible proof of their virility are victims of the *macho* myth, whereby a man who is a *man* is a figure of swaggering strength and bravery. From this viewpoint he is, of course, superior to women, and he proves his superiority by aggressive sexual conquests. There are fewer men today who subscribe to this stereotypic image of manliness, and even fewer women. The ability to sire a child, furthermore, is no proof of sexual competency. It is merely proof that sperm production was adequate on at least one occasion. Men who feel that insemination is tantamount to a sexual seal of approval should remember that the rabbit is one of the most prolific animals and also one of the most innocuous.

There are other reasons why men may feel a need to produce children even though they are not adequately prepared to be fathers. They may have a strong need to maintain the masculine monopoly on importance in the world, or they may have a "King Kong Complex," or they may need children to show the world how prosperous they are (Silverman & Silverman, 1971).

The man who feels his masculine superiority threatened by female independence may try to keep his wife pregnant in order to handicap her. As long as she is confined to the home by pregnancy and childcare, he reigns supreme as the family provider. Furthermore, such a man reasons that his wife is not likely to be around

other men, or to be attractive to those men with whom she does come in contact, so the insecure male finds relief from his anxiety about his wife's being unfaithful to him by keeping her body swollen with pregnancy and by keeping her too busy with childcare duties to have time for sexual affairs. If such a man's wife were to work, her income would make his seem less important, and he would continually fear that she would find other men more desirable than he. For the man whose masculinity has to be fed by his wife's inferiority, children are simply by-products of his selfish efforts to keep her from developing as a person. The children themselves are unimportant. The important thing to this man is for his wife to be a baby-producing machine.

Men who have a "King Kong Complex" have a similar selfish need to create a system around themselves in which they are the rulers and masters. Probably feeling subordinate in every other area of their lives, they can demand respect and obedience from their children because the children are physically smaller and weaker. An inadequate man, in an occupation of small stature, therefore, may meekly accept insults or disregard all day, but when he comes home he may be a tyrant who demands that his wife and children give instant obedience to his every command or suffer beatings or tongue-lashings. Since men with a King Kong approach can only intimidate small children and frail women, they have to keep their wives pregnant as often as possible. Frequent pregnancies not only make their wives dependent on them, and therefore fearful of displeasing them, but provide a steady supply of inferior beings to intimidate. As the older children escape their tyrannical father's clutches, new infants take their place. Again, this is an example of a man's selfish determination to feel strong and important at the expense of several human beings.

The man who has children in order to signify his financial success is equally selfish and self-centered. For this man, having children announces to the world that he is through with his years as a student, through with his years as a struggling young apprentice in his profession or occupation, and that he has now arrived as a man of substance and financial responsibility. When his child is born, he may jokingly announce to his business colleagues that he has "a new tax deduction," with the implication that he is in a tax bracket that is aided by numerous expenses that can be written off as tax deductions. As his children grow, he will make frequent references to the cost of their orthodonture, their dancing lessons, their summer camps, and the future cost of their college education. What he is really saying, of course, is "See how well-to-do I am? I can afford to provide my several children with the very best. Only a prosperous man could afford so many children who get so much." While these children live in more comfortable homes than the children of the *macho* or King Kong fathers usually do, they have nonetheless been brought into the world as advertising for their father's success, and not as human beings to be cherished and respected for themselves. It may be for this reason that so many children of affluent fathers turn against the trappings of prosperity and deny their fathers the opportunity to complain-brag about the cost of their clothing or education. The school dropout, living in ghettolike conditions with a group of peers, wearing ragged jeans and sporting the pallid complexion of one who sleeps all day and plays all night, offers his frustrated parent nothing to complain-brag about. Instead, his father may pretend to have pressing business elsewhere when the subject of children comes up—a fact that his child may well be aware of and that may give him a sense of gleeful revenge. A parent who wails to his rebellious child, "How can you do this to me after all I've done for you?" denies that all he has done for his child has really been done for himself, but the child may unconsciously recognize that he has been a medium through which his father sought recognition. Children may be misled by parents' rationalizations and excuses, but they are seldom fooled on the unconscious level.

Women probably have even more selfish reasons for having babies than men do. Since women have traditionally been regarded as intellectual inferiors who were fit only to concern themselves with housework and children, they have been unable to find the same kind of recognition that men have found. While the pages of history do occasionally name women, such as Madame Curie and Florence Nightingale, who have achieved a goal in a professional field, they are remarkable for their achievements as well as for the fact that they are women. The average woman traditionally has not aspired for personal recognition, but has achieved her feeling of esteem through the accomplishments of her husband and sons. A woman who realizes that her husband will "never amount to anything" may therefore unconsciously decide to achieve recognition through her children and *their* achievements. If a vicariously achieving mother does not soon volunteer information about her child—"he's in an advanced reading class," "she's president of her class," "he plays football," "she's a doctor," "he's general sales manager of his company"—the reason often is that he is in jail (if a boy) or pregnant and unmarried (if a girl). Only the healthy woman who achieves in her own right is so busy with a full life of her own that she feels no need to boast about her children's lives.

Some women are driven to motherhood by a strong need to vicariously relive their own childhood and make it happier and more stable (Flapan, 1969). By giving their own children the loving, generous mothering that they never received from their own mothers, they may try to make up to themselves all that they missed as children. Although these mothers are indeed superior to their own mothers in providing loving care and attention to their children, they are never satisfied with their mothering capacities unless they measure up to their ideal of perfection—an impossibility for anyone. Furthermore, they are never able to achieve a mature enjoyment of their children, because they are partially reliving their own childhood through their children and comparing their own performance with that of their mothers. They fragment themselves into three persons: the mother-that-should-have-been, the child-that-used-to-be, and the mother-that-is, and their role satisfaction is therefore diluted and distorted. Like all selfish motives for having children, this one fails to bring the joy that the mother hoped for, because she will continually find fault with her own maternal perfection, and it will fail to provide the children with a healthy view of mother-child relationships.

A related example of misguided maternalism is the woman who feels a need to justify her own childhood misery by creating a better environment for her own children than she had. She may rationalize that her own unhappy childhood was training in what *not* to do as a mother. In this way, her childhood suffering is ennobled with purpose and meaning, and being a good mother becomes a compelling goal (Silverman & Silverman, 1971). Although her idea of the meaning of life would be shattered if her goal were denied her, it would be far better for her to find inner serenity through therapeutic measures than to try to find it by a lifetime of "undoing" the sins of her parents. Children deserve to be brought into the world as the individuals they are, and not as symbols of the child that the mother once was or wanted to be.

Women also frequently decide to have a baby because they feel immature and childish, and they need something to make themselves feel grown up. They reason that having the responsibility of a baby will prove their maturity, and they enjoy having the ability and the right to be in authority over someone else, even if the someone else is a helpless infant (Silverman & Silverman, 1971). A woman who feels immature simply because she is childless, of course, *is* immature, and needs to become an adult in actuality before she takes on the job of being a mother. By forcing their children to help them grow up, such women remain childish, immature, and selfish. They may find that their children grow up before they do, and they may resent the fact that the children did not passively remain helpless long enough for them to acquire a feeling of competence.

An immature woman may also want to have a baby in order to assert her own femininity. The more uncertain she is about her adequacy as a female, the more children she may need to have in order to prove to herself and to the world that she can do those things that women are "supposed" to do. For her, saying "I am a mother" is the same as saying "I am a sexually competent woman with no conflicts about my own femininity or sexuality." The ability to conceive and bear a child, however, is no proof that a woman is sexually adequate, since it is possible for her to be impregnated while she is totally unconscious. Pregnancy simply means that viable sperm reached a mature ovum and combined to form a conceptus. An adoptive mother of one may be more sexually adequate than a woman who has borne ten children.

Boredom drives many women to pregnancy, but a woman who wants to have a baby because she is sick and tired of her low-paying, boring job should take stock of the situation and face it honestly. If she is not equipped for any job other than the insignificant one she has, she probably isn't equipped for motherhood, either. Before she takes on the job of being a mother, she should consider improving her own skills and abilities. They will lead not only to a better job, but to a more adequate person, whether or not she later decides to have a baby.

The working woman who believes that the grass is greener in Peanut-Butter Land should remind herself that motherhood is the one occupation that gives no leaves of absence, vacations, sick leave, or bonuses. It is also a 24-hour-a-day job, with no time off, and if she decides to quit, there is nobody to give notice to. If a woman yearns to be out of the rat race of working 9 to 5, and is considering motherhood as an easy exit, she should consider something more within her abilities, like malingering.

Couples often decide to have a baby in order to save a floundering marriage. Rather than drawing a couple together, the added physical and financial strain of a baby is likely to drive them farther apart. The baby is then blamed—if not consciously, then unconsciously—for not fulfilling its function and is rejected by one or both parents. Furthermore, a woman who hopes to keep her husband by becoming the mother of his children may find that the marriage-knot is kept securely tied when children are produced under these circumstances, but she will probably not keep her husband emotionally and spiritually. Sooner or later, this type of pressured man may look for love and fun outside the marriage. Or, as is also true in many of these cases, the wife may discover to her dismay that her husband is the victim of the Madonna concept, whereby women have sex, but not *mothers*. A man who has this concept may find that he is impotent with his wife after she becomes a mother, and may look elsewhere for sexual pleasure. Revered as a mother but rejected as a sex partner, his wife may find cold comfort in her children's love and may instead resent them for keeping her bound to hearth and home when she could be looking for a man who would appreciate her as a woman.

Similarly, a person who has never known love may want a child because he or she believes that a child will be loving and accepting. For too many women, having a baby means instant identity. A woman who has never known the feeling of a strong self-identity may leap into pregnancy because being somebody's mother is better than being nothing. Furthermore, pregnancy wins for many women attention and pampering that they never before received, and gratifies their infantile need for affection and attention (Lerner et al., 1967). For the first time in their lives, someone—the obstetrician—is vitally interested in them and in their condition. These women may use pregnancy as an excuse to indulge themselves by overeating, oversleeping, and by focusing all their attention on their own bodily sensations. After the baby's birth, they still may derive some vicarious feelings of importance from the interest their pediatrician has in their baby. These two professionals—obstetrician and pediatrician—are more important to many women than their own husbands are. Sadly, such women may soon be jealous of the attention their babies get, and they may quickly become pregnant again in order to regain their position in the limelight.

Other unhealthy reasons for becoming a mother include the need to negate feelings of depersonalization, the attempt to "belong," the wish to provide parents with grandchildren, and the fear of going against religious dictates. The woman whose feeling of self is marginal may experience greater feelings of existence during pregnancy because of her distended abdomen, her swollen breasts, and the fluttering of life that she feels inside her womb. With the birth of the infant, her feelings of depersonalization may return, and she may become pregnant again and again in order to experience the good feeling of being alive and of existing. Unfortunately, her preoccupation with her own bodily sensations and her tenuous contact with reality make her a very inadequate mother, and her children are ignored or discarded like unimportant trifles once they are born.

The price of "belonging" to a suburban set of young couples may be having children, talking about pediatricians and potty-training, and living in a "good" neighborhood for children, but couples who have children merely in order to belong to a certain social set are using children as social entrees, rather than seeing them as individuals to be loved and cared for.

And the couple who have a child in order to please their parents by making them grandparents are committing a doubly selfish act. They are using children to buy parental approval for themselves, and they are acting out the selfish wishes of their own parents, who are more concerned with having the fun of being grandparents—who can spoil their grandchildren on weekends and escape the responsibility of their daily care—than they are with the rights of their married children to live their lives to suit themselves.

The couple who feel compelled to obey the dictates of their religion, even if they dislike children, are placed in a singularly dishonest category. They can smugly bask in the fact that they are obedient Roman Catholics or Orthodox Jews, for example, even though they may strongly resent the demands placed upon them by their children. If Roman Catholic, they have been taught that sexual intercourse is a sin if for pleasure only and does not allow for the conceiving of children. If Orthodox Jew, their teaching has been that a woman's main function in life is to bear children, her ultimate goal to have a male child. Resolving the issue of religious obligation versus the rights of individuals is a question that de-

mands honest self-examination, and it is an issue that cannot be dismissed lightly. It is, however, an issue that must be squarely faced by every member of a religious body that places procreation in a supreme position.

There are many other invalid reasons why a couple may decide to have a baby. They may already have two or three boys, for example, and would like to "try for a girl." Or a woman may feel old and useless once her youngest is in school, and she may reason that a baby will make her feel young and needed again. Or there may be pressure from parents and friends to have a baby. No sooner does a young couple shake the rice from their pockets than their friends begin asking *when*, not *if*, they are going to start a family. Couples are frequently made to feel deviant and un-American if they admit to not wanting children, and some succumb to the pressure and have a child just to please their friends, or to provide their parents with a desired grandchild.

CONCLUSION

In too many instances, the decision to have a baby is based on expectations of what the child will provide the parents. When this is the case, there surely will be disappointment and regret, because a baby is primarily made up of *needs*, and it is his needs that must be gratified by the parent, and not the other way around. Furthermore, there is no guarantee of eventual return or reward for providing the needs of a child. Parenthood is a *giving*, guiding, full-time responsibility that lasts forever. Once a parent, always a parent. You cannot divorce a child, and you do not cease to be a parent even when your child becomes a parent. A child does not necessarily grow up to love, honor, and care for his parents in their old age. He does not necessarily grow up to fulfill all the unrealized dreams and ambitions of his parents. He does not, in fact, necessarily grow up to be a person who likes or is liked by his parents.

So who should have children? And why? Only those who are satisfied with themselves and with their spouses. Only those who have arrived at a point of self-knowledge and self-confidence so that they do not look to others to provide them with a feeling of identity and self-worth. And, most important, only those who find delight in watching a child discover the world and who believe that a parent's responsibility is to provide an atmosphere that is secure and accepting. For these people, parenthood is likely to enrich their lives and their marriages. Furthermore, the children of such actualized people are likely to be good parents themselves, and to have children who are emotionally stable and free from the destructive aggression, greed, suspicion, and lust for power. If *every* family could be self-actualized, if every child were a wanted child, and if every parent were a good parent, it is not too far-fetched to believe that the nations of the world could live in peace with one another, and that all people could freely enjoy life rather than hoping to endure it.

CHAPTER 13

SPECIAL FAMILIES

To follow foolish precedents, and wink with both our eyes, is easier than to think.   WILLIAM COWPER

379

Consider the families in a block of homes in a typical American neighborhood in suburbia: On the corner, in a split-level ranch-style house, live the Smith family. Mr. Smith is a computer analyst and his wife teaches school. They have two children. The Smiths are white. Next door to them live the Morgans and their baby son. Mrs. Morgan stays home with the baby while Mr. Morgan works as an electrical engineer. They are also white. The families in the next five houses are all similar to the Smiths and the Morgans; they all have children and they are all white. Then there is the Kim Soo family. She is a Caucasian housewife from Arkansas, while he is an accountant from Korea. They have two delightful children with blonde hair and almond eyes. Next door to the Kim Soos are the Kwants from Holland. Their front door is decorated with a pair of wooden shoes, and they occasionally entertain their neighbors with an Indonesian dish. Across the street are the Thompsons and their six children (they are Catholic), and next door to them are the Freidmans. Mr. Freidman was raised an Orthodox Jew, but when he married Mrs. Freidman, he joined her Baptist church. The Freidman children have never met their Grandmother and Grandfather Freidman, because these grandparents declared their son dead when he married a Gentile and they have had no contact with him since his marriage. There are no black families living in this neighborhood, but there is one several blocks away. There is one divorcée and her children in the neighborhood, she works such long hours that nobody ever sees her, and her children are in a daycare center, so the neighborhood children rarely see them, either. There is a middle-aged woman living in the middle of the block whose husband lives in another state. The rest of the neighbors make jokes about her because she has told them that she is sexually deprived and that she needs a man. Sometimes when the neighbors come home late at night, they see her sitting on her front porch, and they nudge each other and laugh because they remember her outspoken statements about needing sex. The men laugh and say that they can understand why her husband lives away from her, and the wives shun her as much as possible. Everyone agrees that her two teenage sons are "odd."

The people in this neighborhood are decent, law-abiding citizens. They pay their taxes, they attend church, they go to PTA meetings, and they support the Little League, the Girl Scouts, and the YMCA. They do not consider themselves prejudiced or bigoted, and they subscribe to at least one intellectual publication and attend avant-garde plays at the local theater.

Into this peaceful atmosphere comes a threatening situation: One of the neighbors moves, and a black man and a white woman are seen entering the house with a real estate agent. Like wildfire, the rumor spreads that a racially mixed couple are buying the house and moving into the neighborhood with their children. The reactions range from shocked disbelief to outraged indignation and threatening telephone calls to the real estate company handling the sale of the house. Several families wildly announce that they will sell their homes before they will live in a "deteriorating neighborhood." The children hear their parents discuss the rumor and talk among themselves about the "black and white children" who will be moving into the vacant house. Some of the children envision children who are black on one half of their bodies and white on the other half; some become fearful because their parents sound so frightened; others await the newcomers with excited curiosity. A petition is circulated, but before anybody decides what to do with it, a family moves into the house, and all breathe a sigh of relief when they turn out to be white.

The husband is an Austrian Jew and speaks with a thick Viennese accent, and the wife is from Germany, but they are still both white, and therefore acceptable. One of the neighbors, with high good humor, jokingly remarks to another neighbor that the block is becoming a small United Nations, with Koreans, Dutchmen, Austrians, and Germans. The former Jew delivers mail that was mistakenly put in his box to the new neighbors, is invited in and served bagels, and comes away smiling with nostalgia. A crisis has been averted. The neighborhood has been preserved.

This same neighborhood is reproduced many times over throughout the United States, with variations on the predominant race represented. The typical family consists of a married pair—usually of the same race, nationality, and religion—and their children. They represent society—that nebulous "they" that determines what is and what is not acceptable. And society does not readily accept anything that is different. Thus the Jew-turned-Baptist is more acceptable than the Korean married to a white woman from Arkansas, and the European family is more acceptable than the divorcée and her children. And the lonely woman who has been deserted by her husband is acceptable to no one.

SOCIAL REJECTION

Why is it that society demands that all its members go in matching pairs, two by two, like the animals of Noah's ark? Is it really because society is concerned with the stability and the predictability of the American family, or is it because of prejudice, bigotry, and ignorance? More than likely, it is due to a combination of the two. Certainly, a society in which all the members were exactly alike would be more ordered and easily controlled. Every member would have the same cultural background, the same traditions and values, and the same customs. Everyone would think alike, behave alike, and respond to each other in a like manner. Such a society can be organized in a colony of white mice, or in a flock of pigeons, but not in a society of modern human beings.

With our mobile society, where men and women of differing backgrounds work side by side, it is inevitable that there will be pairings of dissimilar people. Sometimes the contrast is not visibly apparent, as in the union of a Southern Baptist and a Roman Catholic, and sometimes it is very visible but not particularly threatening, as in the marriage of a Chinese-American and a Caucasian. It is when the difference is very visible, and very much in contrast, as in the marriage of a white and a black, that society is displeased. The white and the black may both be from the same state and city, may both have attended the same university, hold the same degrees, work in the same profession, and belong to the same church, but there is a difference in the pigmentation of their skins, and society therefore says that they are offensive to the orderly structure of the American family. Exactly where this confused bit of thinking originated is not known.

By the same token, if a family is headed by a divorced or separated man or woman, society is sometimes quick to reject and to be suspicious of their influence on the "normal" families and their children. Members of a broken home are frequently shunned by society as if the divisiveness in the former marriage were contagious. In many cases, even agencies that deal with the traumas and despair associated with a troubled marriage add to the guilt of the married partners by taking a condemnatory attitude toward divorce. In a pamphlet distributed to persons contemplating divorce in Sonoma County, California, for example, the official stance of the Conciliation Court is that ". . . every divorce statistic means two people have failed in life's most noble and important relationship—failed themselves, failed their children, failed their Creator, and failed society" (quoted in Krantzler, 1974, p. 39).

Divorce is becoming increasingly common in our society. One of the most obvious changes in lifestyle between the 1960s and the 1970s was a doubling of the divorce rate (Pocket Data Book, USA, 1976). Whereas the number of couples divorcing each year was

400,000 a decade ago, there are now over 750,000 such couples annually, and a surprising number of them have been married many years. Obviously, divorce is a fact of American life and must be accepted as such.

The reasons for such social rejection of the "deviant" family are varied. In some cases, it stems from the viewer's envy and unfulfilled love needs. When the average person meets a racially mixed couple, for example, he may believe that their love and devotion to one another must be unusually strong for them to go against the standards of a racially prejudiced society. The idea of a love that flaunts convention, that would give up a crown for a loved one, that would jeopardize a career for a loved one, is romantically appealing. Since most marriages are more prosaic and less romantically exciting, the racially mixed marriage may be envied by the person whose marriage is safe but dull. By denouncing a racially mixed pair, the envious person can deny his own envy and boredom, while at the same time gaining some vicarious pleasure from thinking about the marriage that he imagines to be more exciting, glamorous, and love-filled than his own.

Similarly, a woman who has never married but has children incites the wrath of both men and women because she stirs their feelings of envy and of guilt. A woman who has had premarital sex may project her own guilt feelings onto the unmarried mother and punish her for the same behavior that she feels guilt for in herself. She may also, if her own marriage is unhappy, envy the unmarried woman's strength to go against convention and rear her children alone, and her envy may cause her to express self-righteous wrath toward the woman and her children.

Men may scorn the unwed mother because she nudges their guilty conscience. Many men who have premarital, extramarital, or postmarital sexaul relations selfishly leave contraception to the woman to worry about, and if the sexual encounter is a brief one with a woman they never see again, the sight of an unwed mother may make them guiltily wonder if there might be, somewhere, a child of their own being raised by an unwed mother. To assuage their own guilt feelings, they reject the unmarried mother and her children, who remind them of their own irresponsible sexual encounters.

After black-white couples and unmarried mothers, the divorcée and her children probably receive the most public disapproval. The divorced woman feels the sting of public scorn expressed in many subtle ways. To many, a woman who is divorced is a reject, a woman who was not valued by her husband, or otherwise he would not have let her go. To others, a divorcée is seen as a sexually promiscuous, ruthless predator who is constantly scanning the horizon for every other woman's husband. Single men may fear that she has hidden qualities that caused the breakup of her marriage, and avoid any emotional entanglements with her, while married women may fear that she is so sexually uninhibited that all men will desire her, and thus avoid her in order to "protect" their own marriages. Few see the divorcée as a hard-working woman of good character and conduct, despite the fact that divorce is so common that there is almost no one without a friend or relative who is divorced.

Religiously mixed couples are next in society's disfavor, while widows, couples of different nationalities, age, or intelligence receive the least amount of social disapproval and rejection. The amount of disapproval that a religiously mixed couple receives depends on the religion of the person judging them. A Presbyterian, for example, may merely make note of the fact that his neighbors are religiously mixed if they are Catholic and Jewish, but may be more interested and disapproving if they are Presbyterian and Jewish. Similarly, if a person meets a religiously mixed couple whose religions are Shinto and Buddhism, he will probably see their religions as a part of their national origins, and be unmoved. If the Shintoist is married to a Methodist, however, the same person may be vaguely uncomfortable and disapproving, without being able to say why. To the bodies of organized religion, religiously mixed marriages are strongly objectionable, because they may cause a weakening of religious faith and because they may result in a depletion of the number of people aligning themselves with a particular religion. The disapproval of the average person, however, is usually simply a rejection of any form of behavior or lifestyle that is contrary to one that he can imagine for himself.

In the case of the widow and her children, society tends to shun and ignore anything that reminds them of the inevitability of death. Although widows are accorded more sympathy than divorcées are, their problems are similar. In a society of couples, the widow is a social fifth wheel, feared by some and ignored by many others.

Any person who contemplates marriage to a member of another race, religion, or nationality; any unmarried woman who contemplates keeping her unborn child and raising it alone; any married couple who contemplate divorce or separation; and any married couple who plan to live together until death separates them should look squarely at the lives they can expect to lead if or when they enter into a racially or religiously mixed marriage, raise a child alone, get a divorce, or face widowhood.

THE UNMARRIED MOTHER

From 1960 to 1975 there was a rise in live births to unmarried women from 5 percent to 13 percent of all live births (Pocket Data Book, USA, 1976). In the case of the unmarried woman who keeps an illegitimate child, her future is dismally predictable. If she is a teenager, and amost 41 percent of the unmarried mothers were under 19 in 1975, she will probably have to quit school and take a job to support herself and her child. Since her education is limited, her earning power will be meager, and she will face financial hardship, even if she lives with her family (Campbell & Cooking, 1967). If she is older, with a secure job or profession, she will still be faced with the medical bills and childcare costs, as well as with the problem of adjusting to the public disapproval she will meet. In some cases, her job would be jeopardized if the illegitimacy of her child were known, and she may have to fabricate stories about a secret marriage or the death of a nonexistent spouse to explain her solitary state. If she moves to another town and calls herself a divorcée or widow, there is still the chance of meeting someone from her hometown who knows the truth. She also may have the problem of explaining to prospective employers the fact that her "married" name is the same as her maiden name on school records and references.

In making friends, the unmarried mother will have to guard against revealing her secret; however if she meets a man she wants to marry, she will have to tell him the truth or forever fear that he will discover it. When her child is old enough to ask about his father, she will have to concoct a story that will satisfy his curiosity and at the same time be above suspicion to others. If she elects to tell the child the truth, she will have to deal with his reaction and possible hurt. To be sure, there are some unmarried women who raise their children alone, and do so with honesty, courage, and success. But unless an unwed mother is a famous actress or some other luminary, living in an environment where illegitimacy is less stigmatized, the life of the unwed mother is usually fraught with tension brought on by deception, fear, and loneliness.

OTHER SINGLE-PARENT FAMILIES

If a woman is raising a family alone because she is divorced or widowed, her situation is better than that of the never-married woman, but it is nevertheless frequently characterized by too little money, too little time, and too little social contact. During the seven years after 1970, the largest proportional increase among single-parent families was for divorced persons maintaining families, their numbers have doubled in that span (U.S. Bureau of the Census, 1977). Today, five out of six heads of households are women, raising the total from five and one-half million in 1970 to seven and one-half million in 1976. Probably the single most pressing problem for the mother-headed family is poverty. Most women are not paid salaries that are adequate to cover the needs of a family, and many divorced fathers fail to contribute to their children's support because they have remarried and taken on the expense of a second family. At any one time, in fact, at least 40 percent of divorced fathers are delinquent in their child-support payments (LeMasters, 1973).

A widow is often little or no more financially secure than her divorced sister. A life insurance survey found that two-thirds of the insured husbands of widows had left total assets of less than $10,000, and 44 percent had left their families less than $5,000. In 1960, approximately 900,000 of the 11 million widowed people in the United States had dependent children (Berardo, 1973), and the Vietnam casualties undoubtedly added to that number. There are more than 2 million children in the United States whose fathers are dead, representing 71 percent of the approximately 3.4 million orphaned children. Less than 3 percent have lost both parents, and 27 percent have lost their mothers (Berardo, 1973), so the burden of raising children who have lost one parent is usually that of the mother.

When the family is headed solely by the father, as almost 0.5 million families are (Gaylin, 1977), there is a greater likelihood of financial security because of the male's higher earning power. A father is more likely to have domestic help and therefore to be less physically and emotionally exhausted from the sheer effort of doing all the housework, laundry, cooking, and marketing, while at the same time earning the money to pay the rent and provide other necessities and meeting all the emotional demands of the children. A man may experience a greater feeling of role change than a woman, however, when he takes on the mother role as well as the father role. A woman may continue to do much the same thing after being divorced or widowed that she did before. If she was employed before, she will be accustomed to juggling two jobs, and the change for her will be primarily in the reduced income and lessened social status of a single-parent woman. A man, on the other hand, is usually not accustomed to being the sole person responsible for the home while also working outside the home. Even if he can afford household help and after-school care for his children, a father who is raising his children alone may experience a more profound sense of change than a divorced or widowed woman feels. It may be for this reason that fathers more frequently remarry than do mothers, although 80 to 90 percent of divorced or widowed mothers do remarry (LeMasters, 1973).

DIVORCE

The divorced woman with a family not only frequently has financial problems and the responsibility of providing her children with adequate care while she works, but also probably has emotional adjustments to make, a new social life to build, and the added burden of helping her children adjust to their new life.

When a childless couple divorce, the divorce decree ends their marriage and, often, any future involvement with each other. With elation, with bitterness, or with regret, the childless couple leave the courthouse with only their memories to form a link between them. But for the couple with children, divorce ends the marriage, but not the involvement with one another. Rather than being a final act, the divorce is simply a factor to which the family must adjust and adapt, and it represents a process that may take many years to complete (Westman & Cline, 1973). It begins with the disillusionment that a couple experience when their marriage fails to make them happy, and it ends only when one of the divorced pair dies. So long as there are children, there will be a link between the formerly married pair that neither remarriage nor absence will dissolve.

Whether or not children are involved, divorce is a process not unlike the experience of widowhood. Rather than losing a loved one to death, the divorced person has suffered the death of a relationship, and there is a necessary period of grief and mourning that must be experienced before the divorced person can go on with a life free of the ambivalent feelings of love and hate, and resentment and dependency that so often characterize the emotions of the newly divorced. Similarly, a divorced person can expect to experience an "anniversary grief reaction" around the time of the separation or other dates of special significance, just as one might whose spouse is deceased. While there are great individual variations, most divorced people reach the peak of their mourning about six months after their divorce, and then soon gain a feeling of having survived, with most, if not all, of the psychic wounds healed. This period of mourning is essential if the divorced are to feel themselves finally independent and single. Some, who have accepted the death of their marriage before the divorce, experience a mourning period of shorter duration, but all who divorce experience grief and mourning to some extent (Krantzler, 1974).

The mourning period has ended when a divorced person no longer feels a 24-hour obsession with resentment and bitterness and only feels an occasional flash of anger. Also, there is a loss of feelings of shame, and the person begins to see old friends again and to make new ones. More time is spent trying to find solutions to problems, and less time is spent complaining about them. The divorced person begins to enjoy personal interests and to appreciate other men and women as *people*, rather than as stereotypes into which all males and females are lumped. A divorced person has finally come to grips with the divorce when there is realization that divorce is the only possible solution to a self-destructive marriage, that it is not a punishment for failure, and that there are other normal, worthwhile people in the world who have had the courage to end a hopelessly unhappy marriage (Krantzler, 1974).

In the early years after a divorce, there are legal issues concerning custody, child-support, and visitation, as well as emotional issues involving the children's adjustment and emotional equilibrium. Old conflicts remain and new ones may be introduced. If a couple has had bitter quarrels over the management of the children, for example, they will probably continue to do so. If there has been a pattern of passive-aggressive hostility in their marriage, that pattern will undoubtedly continue after the divorce, and unfortunately both parents may express their hostility through the children. Quite often, a divorced couple continue to fight and hurt one another in an unconscious desire to keep their old relationship alive. Involvement with one another—however unpleasant—keeps them still a part of each other's lives, and they may have endless legal and personal battles as a way of keeping their relationship from completely dying (Williams, 1974).

Impact on children. Most divorces occur after seven to ten years of marriage, when the children are between the ages of three and seven years, the age at which the impact of divorce is the greatest (Westman & Cline, 1973). The reaction of children to divorce varies, but almost all experience confusion, fear, guilt, and anxiety.

Whereas each parent has only one new life to adjust to, the child of divorced parents has two new lives to try to integrate, and the attempts to do so are often clumsy and misinterpreted by the parents (Williams, 1974). Some children become behavior problems or develop psychosomatic illnesses, because they secretly hope that their parents will be reconciled in their joint parental concern.

Divorce **389**

Other children may fan the fires of parental conflict in an attempt to keep the parents together. A daughter visiting her father on the weekend, for example, may exaggerate the punishment she receives from her mother for minor infractions of rules, and hint that her mother is away from home more often than she should be. When she goes home, she may complain to her mother that her father ignored her and failed to feed her properly, intimating that her father spent most of the weekend in a drunken stupor. Both parents may then react with rage at each other, while the child feels some false security in the feeling that her parents are still "together" in the only way she has ever known them—as antagonists.

Most children whose parents divorce believe that the divorce is largely due to their own misbehavior and "badness," and they therefore feel a considerable amount of guilt. Since their parents may have argued about the children, they conclude that they are the cause of their parents' unhappiness. They also feel that the departing parent is rejecting them and abandoning them, and there may be the fear that the remaining parent will similarly abandon them. To protect himself against abandonment, a child may become his mother's shadow, clinging tenaciously to her whenever he is with her, and crying hysterically when she leaves. Older children with fears of abandonment may become rigidly "good," conforming exactly to their parent's wishes and never expressing any spontaneous

or real feelings of their own. They may feel a strong sense of protection toward their divorced mothers and wish that they were strong enough and old enough to take care of them. Their knowledge of their own smallness and weakness causes them further anxiety and feelings of guilt, and they may strive for a maturity beyond their years in an effort to compensate. These children may try to take on the responsibility of the absent parent, helping the mother with all decisions and with the care of younger children in the family. In trying to become an adult, they miss the necessary play of childhood.

At least one child out of every six lives with the anticipation of the parents' divorce, the actual experience of their divorce, or the aftermath following the divorce (Westman & Cline, 1973). Children of divorce experience the confusion of an unhappy marriage; they are denied parents who have affection and respect for one another; they must face the changes that take place when the parents part; they must live with their own feelings of guilt and anxiety; and they have parents who are so preoccupied with their own unhappiness and fears that they cannot fill their roles as parents as well as they could if they could share their responsibilities in a strife-free atmosphere. Few children of divorced parents escape the ordeal without scars.

Children of divorced parents will probably have to adjust to a new stepfather and stepmother, stepsiblings, half-siblings, and possibly future divorces. They may be torn by feelings of disloyalty to the parents if they like the stepparents, and they may never stop hoping that the parents will be reunited. Children with new stepparents may shock and anger their parents when they make clumsy efforts at creating a cohesiveness among all the parents and stepparents.

"You'd make a good maid"

An example of this was Kevin, the child of a beautiful but irresponsible woman, whose father married Rhonda, a warm, affectionate woman who enjoyed cooking, sewing, and other domestic arts. Kevin hurt his stepmother deeply and angered his father when he smiled warmly at Rhonda, as she handed him a slice of hot gingerbread, and said! "You'd make a good maid for my mother." There was no derogation intended in Kevin's remark. Rather, it was an attempt on his part to unite his mother and his stepmother, with each woman remaining herself. An adult might have instead voiced the wish that the mother could have some of Rhonda's qualities, but a child is more likely to accept people for what they are and to wish that they would all like one another and live together in harmony.

The impact on children of a divorce seems grim indeed, but much of the trauma stems from confusion on the part of parents and children rather than from the events surrounding the divorce itself (Steinzor, 1969). Frequently, parents are themselves unsure of the real reasons for their divorce, and they are therefore unable to give their children a definite reason. They also often seek to assuage their own guilt feelings by manipulating their children so that they are placed in a position of having a voice in the decision to divorce.

The failure of parents to clarify their reasons for divorce and their cowardice in not assuming full responsibility for their own marriage and divorce create extreme confusion for the children and set the stage for prolonged family tension. Family counseling can enable the parents to identify their real sources of conflict, and if the problems cannot be solved, the couple will at least be spared the painful and humiliating experience of a divorce that is based on reasons that are mysterious to one or both.

When the parents are realistic and knowledgeable about their reasons for getting a divorce, they can and should share this information with their children and help them to accept it and adjust to it. Couples who are honest with themselves will not give as a reason for a divorce the hostile accusation, "Mommy has a new Daddy picked out for you," or "Daddy doesn't love us anymore." Instead, they will offer more basic and candid reasons, such as, "We have changed a lot since we married. We don't enjoy the same things any more, and we don't enjoy each other any more." It is important for parents to stress that the reasons for the divorce are strictly matters between the parents, and that the children had—and should have—no influence in the decision to divorce. It is also important for the parents to stress to the children that the divorce is for the purpose of making everyone in the family happier and that both parents will continue to be *parents*, even though they will no longer be husband and wife. Children should be thoroughly prepared for changes in their lives, such as moving, new homes, and new schools, and the parents should not expect the transition period to be an easy one for the children.

Contact between the parents is important following a divorce, and the contact is most beneficial to the children if it is direct, and not through middlemen such as attorneys or relatives. For two people who once cared enough for each other to marry and conceive children to avoid directly discussing those children's welfare is ridiculous and tragic.

The absent parent—usually the father—is in the uncomfortable position of being both responsible for his children and apart from them. The parent leaving the home directly suffers the trauma of separation from the children. One study (Hetherington, Cox & Cox, 1977) found that most fathers saw their children less and less as time passed with the result that they developed a strong concern over the sense of loss this gave them. For many fathers, the strain is too great, and the children become less important than their new families. Most men are initially sincere in their intention to make child-support payments, but they often become convinced that their children are not directly receiving benefits from their child-support checks, and they resentfully conclude that they are paying for their ex-wives' clothing, furniture, and automobile. They may rationalize that they have no moral obligation to support their children as long as their ex-wives are able to do it alone, and they may begin to look for legal ways to avoid making their payments. Or they may simply stop their child-support payments illegally. Unfortunately, the law is lax where child-support delinquency is concerned, and the onus is usually on the mother to see that the father makes the payments. The rationale behind the laxity of enforcement of child-support laws is that the man who is jailed for nonpayment cannot earn money and, therefore, it is futile to try to enforce the law. There is also the belief that a man will simply quit his job if the state plans to claim his salary to pay delinquent child support.

The fact that the support of children is often considered to be the sole responsibility of the parent who has them leads to bitterness on the part of the parent with custody, while the delinquent parent has to rationalize his actions by convincing himself that the custodial parent squanders or confiscates any support money sent. The real losers are the children, who grow up believing that their absent parent did not care enough about them to contribute to their support. Frequently, there is also a tit-for-tat withholding of visitation privileges when the father is delinquent in child support, so that the children and the father are denied the pleasure of seeing each other.

Fathers who see their children only one time a week or month or year also have the problem of walking a line between overindulgence and seeming indifference. Since the father usually has more money to spend on expensive gifts for his children, the children may come to view a trip to visit him as another Christmas, and home and mother may seem pale by comparison. The father's gift-giving may then become a source of conflict between the parents, with the mother accusing the father of buying the children's love and the father accusing the mother of begrudging the children any fun.

On the other hand, if the father does not make the children's visits especially rewarding in terms of gifts and excursions, the children are likely to feel that a visit to the father is less fun than staying home and playing with their friends. The solution would seem to be for the father to keep expensive gifts to a minimum and to rely instead on excursions and outings to make the children's visits to him exciting. (And the children's mother should refrain from making joy-killing comments about how long the father's stamina would last if the children lived with him, and instead appreciate the fact that the children associate their father with pleasure.)

Rebuilding a social life. Divorce can be a blow to both parents' feelings of confidence, sexually and in social situations. Rebuilding a social life is frequently difficult for both the divorced father and mother. One study (Hetherington, Cox & Cox, 1977) found that the divorced mother most often felt helpless and physically unattractive. The divorced fathers, on the other hand, complained of not knowing who they were and of having no structure or home in their lives. These doubts tended to erode their sense of self-esteem, causing them to feel they did not handle themselves well around others. In order to counteract these feelings, the men in the study tended to become more socially active and involved in self-improvement during the first year of separation.

It is perhaps easier for the divorced father to meet new people, since he is usually more mobile than the divorced mother and has more opportunities. A mother usually must choose her home with regard to the children's schools and friends; this can mean remaining in the family's home in the suburbs, or moving to a family-centered apartment complex. In either setting, the social life is primarily couple-centered, and the lone woman may find herself banding with other lonely women rather than being a part of a larger social scene.

The belief that children should be raised by their mothers, and that there is some inadequacy in the male's character and intellectual capacities that renders him incapable of caring for young children has led to a common and unfair situation. The mother gets the children, a low-paying job, inadequate and usually delinquent child-support payments, and relief from her role as mother every other weekend when the children go to their father's apartment and swim in his pool while he watches TV. If the father remarries, the children may be watched over by his new wife while he plays golf with his friends. A man's responsibility in having produced a child is heavily weighted in terms of his child-support payments, and these are usually far less than an equal share of the actual cost of housing, food, clothing, medical and dental care, and educational and entertainment expenses for the child. A judge who ordered a divorced father to baby-sit two nights a week with his children, or

who required that the father have an equal responsibility in making decisions about the children would make international headlines, and millions of divorced mothers (and possibly their children as well) would no doubt be thankful.

The younger divorcée may find it relatively easy to resume the social life of a single woman. If she has children, the primary difference in her social life after divorce and before marriage would be in the presence of and responsibility for the children. She can no longer go out on the spur of the moment—she will have to arrange for a baby-sitter ahead of time. And friends may not drop by unannounced as they might have done before her marriage, because they know how busy she is with the children.

For some older divorcées, building a balanced social life may be difficult, because they cannot so naturally frequent the singles' bars and nightclubs where they might meet new people. The older divorcée, therefore, may be dependent on friends, relatives, and co-workers to introduce her to new people and to launch her in a new social life. However, many older divorcées have *less* difficulty establishing a new social life than younger divorcées. Free of the impediments of very young children and sexual inhibitions, they are frequently desirable to both younger and older men, and may have a more exciting whirl of dating than they had when they were young and single.

Sexual frustration is almost always a part of the divorced person's adjustment problems. Even if their marriage and sex life were unsatisfactory, there was usually some sexual contact between the married couple, and the total curtailment of sex usually causes a great deal of sexual frustration for both. In addition, both husband and wife are usually suffering from feelings of sexual undesirability and a need to prove to themselves that they are sexually desirable. Many divorced men and women go through a period of meaningless sexual encounters to convince themselves that they are still sexually attractive to others. (It is probably for this reason that a woman's married friends look at her with less than a trusting eye right after her divorce, particularly if they know that their husbands are inclined to take advantage of any sexual opportunity.)

A woman's first date after a divorce may be an emotionally traumatic experience, particularly if she was married for many years and still has small children. She will have forgotten how to behave on a date, and she may make social blunders, like putting out her hand to keep her date from falling forward when the brakes in the car are applied. With experience, she will adjust to the new dating situation, but her children may not so easily adjust.

To a small child, mothers and fathers go together, and when one is no longer there, the logical course of action is to find a new one. Chidren may therefore greet each new date with the query, "Are you going to be my new daddy?" If they particularly like a man, they may embarrass their mother by dragging her from the room and loudly exclaiming, "I like him! Why don't we marry him?" A mother who can keep her sense of humor, while expertly blocking the doorway, will soon learn how to manage the situation and keep her dates from bolting.

Credit discrimination. The 70s saw the passage of laws on the state and federal level that guarantee women equal rights and protection in many areas. But this does not mean that problems may not be encountered in securing these rights. Discrimination in granting credit based on sex or marital status is no longer legal. Thus, women cannot be denied charge cards, bank loans, or personal credit for reasons other than personal income or credit history. This law may be circumvented by a loan institution that chooses to do so, because the law does not require a reason to be given for the denial of credit to an individual. A divorced women being denied credit because of her divorced status would be unable to ascertain accurately the reason for her refusal. Lawsuits are the only recourse at this point, and are expected to arise. These anticipated lawsuits will serve to clarify the new law.

DEATH OF SPOUSE

There are 69 males for every 100 females age 65 and over because of the higher mortality rates for men and higher remarriage rates among widowers. The older woman is much more likely to be widowed, not to be married, and to live alone (Siegel, 1978).

After the death of a spouse, there is normally a period of grief and mourning, during which time certain behaviors are characteristic, including shock, denial, tears, restlessness, sleeplessness, somatic complaints, withdrawal from others, irritability, and anger. Grief and mourning become pathological when (1) the person continues to deny the death and remains preoccupied with the lost loved one; (2) when reproach and guilt are excessive; or (3) when grief is expressed through projective identification, that is, grief is denied in oneself and attributed to someone else (Maddison & Raphael, 1976). Some degree of identification with the deceased is normal and constructive in adapting to the changed life circumstances. However, some forms of identification, such as symptomatic identification when the bereaved person develops symptoms of the deceased person's last illness, are considered maladaptive.

Currently, women who become widowed at a more advanced age still outlive their husbands by about 16 years (Siegel, 1978). There is not a great deal of difference between the divorcée's and widow's adjustment problems in the areas of social isolation and discrimination.

During the first year following her husband's death, the typical widow goes through three phases—impact, recoil, and recovery (Silverman, 1974). The **impact phase** immediately follows the husband's death and is characterized by numb, automatic behavior that is in keeping with the widow's usual character. A woman who is strong, poised, and efficient will remain so during the days immediately following her husband's death, because the reality of the death has not fully penetrated. A woman of this personality makeup will greet friends at the funeral, be concerned about their comfort, handle the funeral arrangements efficiently, graciously accept and acknowledge tributes and expressions of sympathy, and be a tower of strength for her children.

This period ends when the reality of death strikes, and the **recoil phase** sets in. During the recoil phase, the widow may experience intense anger at her husband for leaving her, at God for allowing his death, and at the world for continuing its business in the face of her despair. She also usually feels guilt at not having been able to prevent his death, and fear and anxiety at being alone. Many women have some hallucinatory moments during which they hear their husbands' voices or momentarily believe they see them.

During this period, a woman's friends may begin to express less sympathy and to be embarrassed or annoyed at her continued depression, because it reminds them of their own eventual death and of the probability of becoming widowed themselves. Husbands of friends, either out of genuine affection and a wish to console or out of an exploitative motive, may make sexual overtures and further confuse and embitter the widow, who increasingly feels that she no longer belongs with her old married friends. To keep her husband's memory alive, she may bore and embarrass her acquaintances and children with her reminiscences of her husband's life and of the details of his death.

When the recoil period ends, the widow will begin to let go of the painful memories and to look around her for new friends and a new life. It is during the **recovery period** that she discovers the same social, financial, and occupational discrmination that besets divorcées and separated women. The average age of the widowed woman is 56, and she finds that she is desired by few industries, banks, restaurants, churches, neighborhoods, or men. She has social, intellectual, and sexual needs, but she frequently lives in a social, intellectual, and sexual vacuum. She is fortunate if there is a counseling service for widows in her community or a volunteer group of widows who help each other. To be completely adjusted to the state of widowhood, a woman must come to view herself as an entity apart from her husband, able to live in a world without him and able to form new, satisfying relationships.

Since there are 10 million American widows, and one of every 20 persons is either a widow or a widower, the needs of the widowed should be given much more attention than they are. Society should be able to allow the widow to experience a period of grief without reacting with fear and embarrassment.

CHILDREN IN SINGLE-PARENT FAMILIES

Whether the head of a single-parent family is divorced or widowed, separated or never married, man or woman, the question that plagues parents, as well as society, is whether children grow up to be maladjusted because of the lack of two parents in the home. The age-old stereotype has been that children from broken homes are social misfits, school dropouts, delinquents, and generally unsavory characters. But are they?

Most studies of the effect on children of one-parent homes have focused on the development of boys who were without fathers (Biller, 1970; Greenstein, 1966; Hetherington, 1969; Santrock, 1970). The picture that emerges from the studies seems to be that the earlier a boy and his father are separated, the more affected the boy will be in his early years, but that the effect decreases as the boy grows older. Preschool-age boys whose fathers are gone have been found to be less aggressive, more dependent, and to have more feminine patterns of interest than boys of the same age whose families are intact. As the boy grows older, however, he is influenced by pressures outside the home resulting in his adopting masculine patterns of behavior. His behavior in time becomes culturally appropriate, even if he still has a feminine orientation. In some cases, a boy may develop extremely masculine behavior in order to compensate for his insecure masculine identity, and engage in aggressive, asocial behavior. If the boy is older than six years of age when his father leaves home, there do not seem to be any significant differences between his development and that of boys who are brought up in intact homes (Hetherington, 1973).

In one of the few studies of a group of girls who grew up without fathers, Hetherington (1973) found that few effects were noted in the preadolescent years, but that there were significant effects that showed up during adolescence. These girls had no difficulty in establishing feminine identities, since their same-sex parents were in the home to serve as role models, but there was a failure to establish appropriate behavioral patterns in interacting with men.

Girls whose parents were divorced were found to be inappropriately assertive, seductive, and sometimes sexually promiscuous, while girls whose fathers had died were found to be excessively shy and uncomfortable around men. A greater difference was noted between girls who had grown up without fathers and girls whose families were intact if the girl had been separated from her father before she was five years old. The difference in the girls' reaction to men is probably due to a difference in the way they remember their fathers. Girls whose parents are divorced may remember their fathers with resentment that is colored by their mothers' opinions. They may view their mothers' lives as unsatisfying and conclude that

happiness is not possible without a man. Having had no opportunity to learn appropriate ways of relating to males, however, and having ambivalent and apprehensive feelings about men because of their negative memories of their fathers, they may pursue men in highly inept and inappropriate ways. In spite of their feelings of anxiety around men, they are more likely to begin early dating and to engage in sexual intercourse at an early age. Girls whose parents are not divorced but are in continual conflict may also find their relationships with men affected. According to one study (Uddenberg, 1976), these girls often take on the parent's negative pattern of relating and may particularly identify with a mother's ambivalence toward her husband and transfer this attitude toward their male partners and toward men in general.

Girls whose fathers are dead are more likely to have fond memories of them, which also are colored by their mothers' memories and by the emotional support and social approval that has been accorded their widowed mothers. These girls may romanticize their fathers' memories to the extent that every other male is inferior in comparison, or they may generalize their exaggerated memories of their fathers' good qualities to the extent that all males are viewed as superior beings to be treated with deference and apprehension (Hetherington, 1973).

While these studies would indicate that one-parent homes are indeed a factor in maladjustment, there are other studies that indicate the children in single-parent homes are better adjusted than are children in unhappy, unbroken homes (Nye, 1957; Perry & Pfuhl, 1963). According to one study, the amount of conflict that existed between the husband and wife before the divorce played a part in the adjustment of the children (Hetherington, Cox & Cox, 1977). Divorce tended to improve the father-child relationship where there had been a high degree of conflict between the parents. The children were better adjusted and an improvement was found in the mother-child relationship when little conflict had existed between the parents. Essentially, these studies point to the fact that it is the social and psychological success or failure of a family that determines whether the children will be well adjusted, and not the presence of two parents (Burchinal, 1964a; Nye, 1957). One parent, therefore, who is consistently loving and firm, who is secure within herself or himself, and who is free of resentment and hostility toward family members, is more desirable than two parents who despise each other but stay together "for the children's sake."

In view of the crucial importance of a father figure in the development of both boys and girls, a woman who is the sole parent in a family can avert many problems for her children by providing them with father figures in the form of uncles, grandfathers, or friends. The same is true for the single father who may be worried about the absence of female role models. A close relationship with a male or female relative or family friend can give a boy or girl a role model and a chance to learn how to relate in a natural, trusting manner.

Adjustment period after remarriage. The experience of an unhappy marriage does not appear to deter people from remarriage. Remarriage after divorce has become increasingly common over the past two decades, with 75 percent of the women and 83 percent of the men remarrying again within three years of a divorce (*Newsweek*, May 15, 1978). This tendency among divorced men and women to remarry within a relatively short period of time may stem from feelings of incompetency in maintaining relationships and a resultant loss of self-esteem caused by failure of the first marriage. One study (Hetherington, Cox & Cox, 1977) showed that divorced individuals seek a long-lasting relationship. Numerous short-term relationships reportedly added to their feelings of depression. The subjects saw the formation of a relationship that involved concern for each other as contributing strongly to the rebuilding of their self-esteem and happiness. Interestingly, a large proportion of the remarriage population consists of divorced persons who have remarried other divorced persons. It may be that with a partner who has been divorced, the individual finds a greater understanding of the stresses that a divorce produces.

Adjustment after remarriage is almost always more difficult than adjustment within a first marriage, and the time needed varies greatly from couple to couple. Many factors are involved, including: how mature each partner is, how long they have known each other, whether or not they have lived together before marriage, and whether either or both has children. It may be a particularly trying period if children are part of the scene. The adjustment will include the responsibilities of the new spouse to the partner's children from the previous marriage as well as the children's stress of adapting to a new parent.

In one study of couples who had remarried after divorce (Messinger, 1976) the respondents were asked to rank in order of importance the conflicts occurring in the first marriage and in the present marriage. In their first marriage, couples ranked the partner's immaturity highest, sexual difficulties second, followed by personal lack of marriage readiness, in-law interferences, and factors such as differences in values and interests. Problems concerning child rearing, financial problems, and cultural differences ranked quite

402 Special Families

low. By contrast, in the remarriage, the biggest source of conflict centered around children. As Gagnon and Greenblatt (1978) point out:

Reconstituted families may seem very much like primary families, but in fact they differ from them in several ways. First, time is needed to assume new parental, child and sibling roles. Individuals may have played the roles of mother, father, or children, but they have not been stepmothers, stepfathers, stepchildren, or stepsiblings. Second, the full "family" constellation comes into existence all at once. There is no period for the two adults to develop a relationship without children and then to develop relationships with one child at a time. Third, it is unclear what "success" as a member of a reconstituted family means. Fourth, although it has undoubtedly diminished in recent years, there remains some stigma from the external world.

Unfortunately, statistics show that individuals are quicker to dissolve a second or third marriage. It may be that having gone through the trauma of divorce the first time makes it an easier and tried solution when the remarriage presents so many new and unexpected problems. Clearly, the remarriage family will continue as an evolving social form even though it has inherent conflicts. Individuals contemplating remarriage need to be adequately prepared and to develop realistic expectations in order to insure a more fulfilling marriage.

MIXED MARRIAGES

As a social concern, one-parent families probably receive more focus than do racially or religiously mixed marriages, but mixed marriages touch, directly or indirectly, almost every individual in America.

Interracial marriages. So far as interracial marriages are concerned, it is usually a marriage between a Caucasian and a Negro that causes outrage and condemnation. Marriages between Anglo-Americans and Latin-Americans, or between Caucasians and Orientals or Indians do not excite as much disapproval. The curious fact about the black-white marital taboo in our society is that black female-white male sexual unions have been given tacit approval since slavery was introduced into the United States, and the many mulattoes in our society attest to these unions (Smith, 1972). So-

"Ralph, you're black and I'm white, you're Jewish and I'm Catholic, you're a Democrat and I'm a Republican, you like sex and I don't, you go to bed early and I go to bed late, you don't want children and I do, you like entertaining guests and I don't, you're well educated and I'm not, and you like to keep the house twenty degrees colder than I do. Fine. None of that bothers me. But how can you expect our marriage to last if you can't learn to like pizza?''

CHRISTIANSON

ciety seems more outraged at legal sexual unions between the two races than at illicit sexual relations between them.

The most condoned black-white unions, of course, have been between the white male—the superordinate race and sex—and the black female—the subordinate race and sex. As long as the racial pairing followed that pattern, and as long as the resulting children went unacknowledged as children of a white man, society was relatively unmoved by black-white unions. But when black men and white women began to openly date and legally marry, that was a different story. To a racially and sexually prejudiced society, the pairing of black male—subordinate race but dominant sex—with white female—superordinate race but subordinate sex—seemed contrary to nature and God. It also threatened the supremacy of the white man's position. In the past, the white man could govern the social, political, educational, and financial structure of our society, having complete dominion over the earth, the animals on it, all people with dark skin, and all white women. The structure of society has now changed, and blacks, as well as liberated white women, have become conscious of their equality. To the white man, then, the prejudice against a black man marrying a white woman is not really to "protect the flower of white womanhood," but to protect his own image as supreme being. White bigots reason—reason is not the right word—white bigots *fear* that if a black man can take a white woman from a white man today, tomorrow he may take the white man's job and his membership in the country club, and the white man will be reduced to just another human being, instead of being allowed to believe himself a superior human being.

Those who strenuously object to interracial marriages usually do so on the grounds that the races should be kept "pure" by prohibition of sexual union between them. Anthropologists recognize from 2 to over 100 races (Saxton, 1968), but most agree that there is no such thing as a "pure" race (UNESCO, 1952), and skin pigmentation alone usually determines the race to which a person is assigned (Saxton, 1968). The white pigmentation of a person's skin, however, rarely classifies him as Caucasian if there is any black, red, yellow, or brown pigmentation in his ancestry. If a person's parents are both white, he is Caucasian; if both parents are black, he is Negroid; if one parent is white and one is black, he is still a Negro and his children will also be Negroes, even if he marries a white person. The classification of Negro remains for his grandchildren and great-grandchildren, even if all of his descendants marry white persons. The "purity" of the races, then, seems to be reserved for whites and not for darker races. While almost every other large society in the world legally and socially accepts interracial marriages, the United States, along with the Republic of South Africa and, to a lesser extent, Great Britain, continues to view interracial unions with bigotry and illogical fear, especially if one of the pair is black.

The discrimination an interracial couple receives varies according to their socioeconomic level, their place of residence, and the race of the nonwhite partner. If one partner is black, the couple will encounter more prejudice than if he or she is of another race, such as oriental. Even though the person comes from the same socioeconomic level, has the same amount of education, belongs to the same church, and uses the same kind of mouthwash as the anglo mate, if his skin is darker in color, rejection will be forthcoming from many people of both races.

In the face of the almost certain rejection that an interracial couple can expect, why do they marry? Most marry for the same reasons that white-white or black-black or brown-brown couples marry—because they love one another and find pleasure in each other's company. There may also be other factors involved in the decision to marry outside one's own race. A person may be attracted to a member of another race because of the exotic aura that surrounds someone who is different. The more different the other is, the more enticing the difference may be. The black athlete with the slim, blonde white woman make an especially attractive couple because of the contrast between them, and each may be partially attracted to the other because they are aware of that contrast.

Others may begin to date members of other races to demonstrate their lack of bigotry and their liberal philosophy. They may choose a person of another race as a marriage partner from the same urge to demonstrate the liberality of their racial views. In some cases, the marriage of a racially mixed pair indicates a rebellion against parental authority, and one or both may be secretly enjoying the discomfort their marriage is causing their parents. In other cases, a member of a race that is not accorded equal status in society may marry a member of a "superior" race in order to achieve social status.

According to a 1971 Louis Harris survey, the incidence of interracial dating is on the increase, and there is evidence that interracial marriage is also on the increase (Porterfield, 1973). The survey found that almost one American in five has dated someone of another race, with the incidence being highest on the West Coast where one in three has done so, and lowest in the South, where less than one in ten has dated across racial lines. Young people between the ages of 21 and 25 are more likely to have dated people of other races than are older people.

The term "interracial" holds different meanings for different people, and statistics reporting interracial dating and marriage must be viewed with some caution. For example, California was reported in 1959 to have had an intermarriage rate of 1.4 percent of all marriages (Barnett, 1963). However, these "interracial" marriages included fewer than one-tenth of 1 percent of white males marrying black females, and fewer than three-tenths of 1 percent of white females marrying black males. The "interracial" marriages were primarily between Caucasians and other nonblacks whose ethnic or national identification was other than Caucasian or American.

The number of black-white marriages in the United States is not known, but there were 51,400 black-white marriages reported by the 1960 U.S. Census, indicating a rate of 2500 such marriages a year, or 1 in every 800 American marriages. Of these, 1 in 50 was between a black groom and a white bride, and 1 in 1,000 was between a white groom and a black bride. That number has undoubtedly increased since the United States Supreme Court ruling in

1967 that declared laws forbidding interracial marriage unconstitutional. Some estimates have placed the number of black-white marriages in the United States at 1 million (Porterfield, 1973).

The determining factor in the success or failure of a black-white marriage seems to lie primarily in the white partner's willingness to give up all white status and to allow the children to be brought up as blacks. Surprisingly, children of black-white marriages seem to adjust to their racial mixture more easily than children of religiously mixed marriages adjust to their religious mixture. Mixed Negroid and Caucasian children probably feel less conflict between their two heritages because they are considered black and raised with other black children (Blood, 1969). Problems, if they occur, are more likely during the early teen years when the child begins to date. Prejudice may then be encountered from parents of black peers and from parents of white peers. The teenager may at this time undergo identity confusion and need a great deal of emotional support from his or her parents. It is at this time that the parents will probably experience the greatest feelings of guilt for having crossed socially sensitive racial lines when they married.

Like other mixed marriages, conflicts in a black-white marriage arise primarily because of different traditions, customs, and attitudes. If the backgrounds of the two are similar, there will be fewer adjustment problems. A black man from the South who enjoys soul

food and blues music will have more difficulty adjusting to a white wife from Boston who enjoys baked beans and brown bread and chamber music. And a rural white woman from Oklahoma will have difficulty adjusting to the lifestyle of a black sophisticate from New York. For this reason, it is especially important that couples from different racial and cultural backgrounds have a long engagement period during which they can discover their differences and begin their mutual adjustment. A large percentage of racially mixed couples decide during their engagement period that the differences are too great to be surmounted (Blood, 1969), and only 0.08 percent of all marriages in the United States involve individuals of different races (Jacobson, 1959). Since most black-white couples have given long thought to the advisability of marriage, their marriages have a good chance of survival (Golden, 1954). In fact, black-white marriages are more stable than black-black marriages, which are twice as likely to end in divorce as white-white marriages (Monahan, 1970).

Interfaith marriages. Religiously mixed couples, while not as uncommon as racially mixed couples, represent only 6.4 percent of all marriages in the United States. Catholics more often marry outside their faith (22 percent), while Protestants (9 percent) and Jews (7 percent) are less likely to do so (U.S. Bureau of the Census, 1958). If there are a great many Catholics in a given area, there are few Catholic-non-Catholic marriages, but if there are relatively few Catholics in an area, there will be more interfaith marriages. The same is true, of course, in the case of Jews and Protestants, which is simply to say that people marry the people they know. Those who are very young, elderly, or low in socioeconomic status are more likely to intermarry than are others (Burchinal & Chancellor, 1962). For all three religious groups, interfaith marriage rates have doubled in the last generation (Bumpass, 1970).

A religiously mixed couple actually may be more dissimilar in attitude and tradition than racially mixed couples are, especially if their religious differences are part of national or cultural differences. A German Catholic from Minnesota married to a German Lutheran from Minnesota may have many similarities in cultural background, but a German Lutheran from Minnesota married to a French Catholic from New Orleans may find their differences too great to overcome.

If a couple's commitment to their religions is strong, and if there is a great difference between the religions, they will experience a considerable amount of conflict as their two faiths collide. A Jew and a Christian, for example, will have basic differences in their religious beliefs, as well as differences in their traditional religious holidays. Observances of Easter and Passover, Christmas and Hanukkah, will have entirely different meanings for the two, and their differences may cause unhappiness for both. There may be similar conflicts, of course, if a Reformed Jew marries a Conservative Jew, or if a Mormon marries an Episcopalian. The differences are not merely in different beliefs, but in different cherished memories and traditions. A religious ceremony that seems sacred to one may appear ludicrous to the other, and the same difference of opinion and custom will extend to daily observances of religious rites in the home.

Until the very recent past, the Roman Catholic Church had strict rules governing the valid marriage of a Catholic to a non-Catholic. The non-Catholic partner was required to sign an antenuptial agreement in which he promised that his children would be reared as Catholics and that he would never dissolve the marriage. The antenuptial agreement was dispensed with in 1966, and the non-Catholic partner now need only make an oral promise to raise his children in the Catholic Church, but the Catholic partner is still required to sign a written agreement. Marriages still must be performed by a Catholic priest to be valid in the eyes of the Catholic Church, but a non-Catholic clergyman may now serve a subsidiary role to the priest, and the couple is now allowed to have an elaborate nuptial mass if they wish.

The Roman Catholic Church strongly discourages interfaith marriages by advising young people to avoid dating non-Catholics so there will be no temptation to marry them (Landis & Landis, 1973). The Roman Catholic position on mixed marriage was codified in the mid-sixteenth century by the Council of Trent, and was based on New Testament texts such as Second Corinthians 6:14, in which the Apostle Paul urged the members of his flock, "Do not be mismated with unbelievers," and on the pronouncement of the Council of Elvira at the beginning of the fourth century forbidding the marriage of Christian women and "infidels, Jews, heretics or priests of the pagan rites."

In A.D. 339, the Roman Emperor Constantine prohibited all Jewish and Christian marriages, and in A.D. 398, such marriages were declared adulterous. This law remained until the eighteenth century, when a degree of separation of church and state was achieved in a few European countries, and religious intermarriage became possible in some areas.

An interfaith marriage between a Catholic and a non-Catholic is considered by the Roman Catholic Church to be either valid or invalid. If **valid**, the marriage is sanctioned by the Church, and if invalid it is not. The fact that a marriage is *religiously* invalid, of course, does not mean that it is *legally* invalid. Estimates are that at least a third of all Catholics who married during the last two decades have married non-Catholics (Vincent, 1972), and, in view of the past trend, between 15 and 25 percent of these marriages were probably invalid (Bishop's Committee on Mixed Marriages, 1943; Schnepp, 1942). A Catholic marriage may be **invalid** because a person is nominally Catholic and therefore willing to dispense with the promises exacted by the Church. Or a non-Catholic partner may be unwilling to accept the conditions of the Church. In other cases, one of the married pair may be divorced and therefore ineligible to contract a valid Catholic marriage (Blood, 1969). Only 30 percent of all valid Catholic marriages between 1940 and 1950 were mixed (Schnepp, 1942; Thomas, 1951, 1956). Of Catholics who marry non-Catholics, in valid or invalid marriages, 30 percent are lost to the Catholic Church (Bishop's Committee on Mixed Marriages, 1943; Schnepp, 1942; Thomas, 1956).

The Protestant position regarding interfaith marriage is that a person's religious faith may be weakened by a marriage to a person of another faith, and that an interfaith marriage leads to marital discord and divorce. Although some Protestant denominations have passed resolutions in the last decade discouraging Protestant-Catholic marriages, there are rarely any codified restrictions against them (Vincent, 1972), and Protestant churches recognize the validity of marriages performed by a Catholic priest. The problem that most frequently arises in Catholic-Protestant marriages, and that poses the biggest threat to their success, is the difference in the official stance of the two religious groups on birth control. Of the three major religious groups in the United States—Catholic, Protestant, and Jewish—only the Roman Catholic Church forbids effective methods of birth control. A Protestant woman whose Catholic husband forbids the use of the pill, IUD, condom, foam, diaphragm, or any other "artificial" means of contraception will be likely to react with resentment and sexual coldness. A Catholic wife, on the other hand, whose rhythm method of contraception results in more children than her Protestant (and protesting) husband can afford will often be shunned sexually by her husband, and the marital rift may eventually become a chasm.

Unlike either the Jewish or Catholic faiths, Protestant groups have the problem of **interdenominational marriages** that may affect individual church membership. One study found that in 70 percent of interdenominational marriages, one spouse switched his church membership to that of the partner, and 12 percent of the interdenominational couples compromised and joined an entirely different church. Only 19 percent retained their original denominational memberships, in contrast to half of the interfaith couples who marry across Catholic, Protestant, or Jewish lines and continue to adhere to their original religion (Prince, 1962). One of every three or four interfaith marriages results in a change of church membership by one spouse (Bossard & Letts, 1956; Landis & Landis, 1973; Leiffer, 1949; Pike, 1954). It is possible that the increase in interdenominational marriages accounts for the reported increase in church membership in recent years. If a person remains on the membership rolls of his original church after he has become a member of a new church, the dual affiliation will be reflected in a seeming increase in church membership (Vincent, 1972).

Family and cultural solidarity among the Jews has resulted in strong objection to marriage with Gentiles because of the consequent weakening of the Jewish partner's commitment to Judaism. Jewish-Gentile marriages are said to be the cause of more depletion of the Jewish ranks than persecution has been (Barron, 1946; Resnik, 1933; Slotkin, 1942), and rabbinical sentiment against interfaith marriage was so strong a few decades ago that in 1947 a resolution completely forbidding Jew-Gentile marriages was defeated

"The Methodist Panthers and the Jewish Pythons are having a rumble. Which side do I belong on?"

Mixed Marriages **411**

by only a two-vote margin at the Central Conference of American Rabbis in Montreal (*Family Life*, 1947).

In the recent past, Orthodox Judaism found the marriage of a Jew to a Gentile so offensive that a child who married a Gentile was considered dead by the parents, and his or her name was never mentioned afterwards. The child was shunned by the family, and omitted from the parents' wills. Such extreme measures are seldom the case now, but there is still strong feeling among Orthodox Jews about marrying Gentiles, and no Orthodox rabbi would officiate at a mixed marriage (Landis & Landis, 1973). Jews who marry Gentiles are more often Reform Jews, rather than Conservative or Orthodox (Gordon, 1964), but there are many Reform and Conservative rabbis who refuse to officiate at a Jewish-Gentile marriage.

If the non-Jew converts to Judaism, the marriage is not considered a mixed marriage, but is rather called an **intermarriage** (Freehof, 1947), and is allowed by Orthodox, Reform, or Conservative rabbis. The feeling, however, is that a Jewish convert will not be a faithful Jew, and intermarriages are discouraged.

The Jewish attitude toward mixed marriage is based on Old Testament texts such as Deuteronomy 7:1–4, which commanded the Hebrews to utterly destroy the people whom they conquered, showing no mercy toward them and allowing no covenants or marriages with them, "for they would turn away your sons from following me, to serve other gods" (Deuteronomy 7:4).

The fear today is not that a mixed marriage will result in the Jew's "serving other gods" but that it will weaken the group solidarity of Judaism, traditionally a tight community united by persecution and discrimination. As discrimination lessens, mixed marriages between Jews and Gentiles become more frequent, and the solidarity of Judaism is therefore weakened, with the children of such marriages usually not identifying with the Jewish people (Fine & Himmelfarb, 1963). The trend, however, is toward more mixed marriages among Jews, as Jews become more integrated into the larger community.

Until very recently, Jewish men have had more opportunity and freedom to meet and mingle with Gentiles, and therefore they have entered into mixed marriages five times more often than Jewish women have (Barron, 1946; Landis & Landis, 1973; Resnik, 1933; Zimmerman & Cervantes, 1960). Today, Jewish women have greater freedom, and there are probably a greater number of Jewish women marrying Gentile men than was true in the past.

The trend toward more mixed marriages among American Jews has paralleled their integration into American society. In Greater Washington in the late 1950s, for example, the rate of mixed mar-

riages among Jews was 1.4 percent among first-generation Jews, 10.2 percent among second-generation Jews, and 17.9 percent among third-generation Jews (Fine & Himmelfarb, 1963). In 70 percent of these marriages, the children failed to consider themselves Jews. Undoubtedly, the percentages are higher today.

When a Jew and a Gentile marry, they are eventually more likely to divorce than are a Catholic and Protestant couple (Zimmerman & Cervantes, 1960). The reason for the higher divorce rate among Jews and Gentiles may not indicate more dissatisfaction in these marriages as much as it reflects the fact that a Catholic is less willing to terminate an unhappy marriage.

There are, however, strains on Jewish-Christian mixed marriages that may contribute to their higher divorce rate. Cultural differences may exist that create adjustment difficulties. A Jew and a Christian will have different food habits, they will celebrate different holidays, and they may have different days of rest. The family of the Jewish partner may have extreme family solidarity that is difficult for the Christian to penetrate, and the Jewish family may be less accepting than the Christian family is (Landis & Landis, 1973). There may be tension between the Jewish-Christian pair due to the Christian family's belief that they have a moral obligation to convert their Jewish son- or daughter-in-law to Christianity, and to their fear that the child's Christian faith is endangered by the mixed marriage. If the children are brought up in the Jewish faith, as they more frequently are if the Jewish partner is the father (Baber, 1953), the Christian grandparents may react with bitterness, anger,

Mixed Marriages **413**

and fear, making a rift between themselves and their child, and tension between the married couple.

Success or failure. Whether a marriage is mixed racially or religiously, there are certain expectations that are almost universal. In-law problems occur in almost every mixed marriage, for example, and conflict over the heritage that should be emphasized to the children or over their religious training. Whether or not the parents are religiously devout or strongly identified with their own cultural group, they may firmly resist having their child raised in the partner's faith or with the partner's cultural customs.

Both partners in a mixed marriage can also expect to encounter some discrimination and ostracism from their own and their partner's family and racial or religious group. Finding mutual friends may be a problem, depending on the extent of the differences between the pair, and a couple may have to have individual friends rather than mutual friends. In some cases, especially in racially mixed marriages, finding adequate and desirable housing will be a problem, and a racially mixed couple may have to live in a neighborhood that they would reject if given a choice.

While the picture appears dismal for mixed marriages, nevertheless, the majority of them succeed (Vernon, 1970). It should be noted, however, that racially mixed couples are more likely to divorce than are religiously mixed couples (Saxton, 1970a) because of the greater social and familial discrimination. The fact that there is discrimination against the children of racially mixed couples probably accounts for a significant amount of disrupting marital tension in a racially mixed marriage (Gordon, 1964). In religiously mixed marriages, there is a higher divorce rate if both partners hold to their separate faiths (Landis & Landis, 1973). Marriage counselors and sociology textbooks have concentrated on the fact that statistics comparing religiously mixed and nonmixed marriages have shown that couples in mixed marriages divorce with two or three times greater frequency than do couples in nonmixed marriages, representing a 200 to 300 percent difference in the divorce rate. With statistics like these, few counselors would advise a couple to enter a marriage if they were of different religious faiths. But, as Glen Vernon has pointed out (1970), the same set of figures, when they are reversed, show only about a 10 percent difference in the divorce rate of religiously mixed and nonmixed marriages. The accompanying table illustrates how the same statistics appear in a different light when viewed in a positive rather than in a negative manner.

414 Special Families

Religious affiliation of married couples	Percent ending in divorce or separation (Landis, 1949)	Percent enduring (Vernon, 1970)
Both Catholic	4.4	95.6
Both Jewish	5.2	94.8
Both Protestant	6.0	94.0
Mixed, Catholic-Protestant	14.1	89.9
Both none	17.9	82.1
(No Jewish-Protestant figures available		

The important point about both sets of figures is that the majority of these marriages endure, whether both are of the same religion, or both have no religion. To be sure, religious differences add to the adjustment problems of a married pair, but there need not be insurmountable problems associated with religious differences. When a couple, and their advisors, expect serious problems to arise because of religious differences, there is a strong possibility that the couple will fulfill their own prophecy and create problems where none needed to exist. Religious differences therefore become the scapegoat for problems that may be due to immaturity, inflexibility, and selfishness on the part of the married pair. In these instances, the marriage may have been a failure in any case, but having religious differences as a convenient whipping post allows the couple to part without trying to work out their differences.

For a racially or religiously mixed marriage to succeed, there are certain conditions that must be met within the marriage (Blood, 1969). First, the couple must be more compatible than the members of a nonmixed marriage need to be. The closer they are in their individual likes and dislikes, in their philosophies and values, and the closer they are in their ability to express themselves emotionally, the more compatible they are likely to be, and the more satisfaction they will find in their marriage. Couples in mixed marriages also must have superior coping ability with which to meet the common problems of marriage as well as the uncommon ones associated with a mixed marriage. If both partners are able to react to expressions of discrimination from others with a measure of humor and disregard, they will find much greater happiness than they will if they react with moodiness or anger. A black wife in a white neighborhood who can laugh off a new neighbor's assumption that she is her white husband's maid will have fewer unhappy moments than the woman who reacts with bitterness and indignation. And the white woman who receives hostile stares and vicious remarks as she leads her black children through a department store must keep her equanimity and patience toward the bigotry expressed, or else she will find only misery in her life and in her marriage. Obviously, such reactions require much more effort and more emotional maturity on the part of the mixed pair. More love is required, more sacrifice, and more concern for the spouse, as well as more commitment to the marriage.

Both partners must be able to discuss rationally the problems that crop up because of their racial or religious differences, and solve them as best they can, with their primary concern being the happiness of the other and the stability of the marriage, and not the winning of a racial or religious point. If a couple is lucky enough to receive the support of their families and their community, their problems will be lessened considerably. If hostility persists from family or community, a couple in a mixed marriage would be wise to move to a community that is more accepting of them and their differences. A racially or religiously mixed couple require the best of social circumstances if their marriage is to succeed, and they must be willing to separate themselves from family and familiar surroundings for the sake of their marriage.

What are the effects on children of having parents who differ in race or religion? How can a child, the embodiment of the physical union of two people, also be the embodiment of disparate religions or races? The union of black and white people does not result in a family of children who are either black or white, as it may in a litter of puppies with a white mother and a black father, but in children who are honey-colored, with genes whose genetic codes come from widely different heritages. And like the color, the child of a black-white marriage is not clearly one or the other in his orientation and identity, but a blending of the two—a part of each, but like neither.

Similarly, a child of a Jew and a Christian cannot be simply a Jew or a Christian, because the child is exposed to both heritages; whatever the religious training is, it will be colored and affected by this exposure. A child growing up in a home with a Jewish father and a Baptist mother may be reared as a Jew, with the full support and sanction of the mother, but the child will still be affected by the mother's unconscious expression of her Baptist background. The Jewish heritage may be emphasized and the Christian heritage ignored, but he or she is likely to be rocked to sleep to the tune of "Rock of Ages," and the religious orientation cannot be purely Jewish, as it would be if both parents were Jewish and their lullabies were "Shma Yisra'el" or "En Kaylohaynu."

Confusion of identity is probably the most common problem of children of mixed marriages, and it is perhaps for this reason that mixed marriages have fewer children than unmixed marriages do (Blood, 1969). Children of mixed marriages may react to their identity confusion by asocial behavior and by rejection of any religious or racial identity at all. It is better, in religiously mixed marriages, for all the children in the family to be raised in the same faith because if some of the children are raised according to one parent's heritage, and the other children are raised according to the other's, the child's personal insecurity and confusion will be increased (Gordon, 1964).

In some European countries in the nineteenth century, the problem of the child's religious future was settled by government decree. Prussia, for example, decreed in 1825 that the father was to choose the religion of all children, and Austria passed a similar law in 1868. Until 1940, male children in Poland were legally obliged to follow their father's religion, while female children were required to follow their mother's religion.

In the United States, the most common pattern is for the children to follow their mother's religion (Landis & Landis, 1973), although if the father is Jewish the children are more often brought up in the Jewish faith (Baber, 1953). The fact that Catholic and Protestant marriages more often allow the children to be raised in the mother's church probably reflects both apathy on the part of the father and the fact that women are usually responsible for their children's religious instruction.

However a family copes with the identity problems of their children that are due to the mixed marriage of the parents, and however the children adjust to their dual races or religions, the success or failure of such a family largely depends on the emotional strength of the married pair, and on their degree of self-actualization (Blood, 1969). Because self-actualized persons are less rigid in thinking, and better able to tolerate differences in others, they will be less fearful of customs and traditions unlike their own, and will instead appreciate them for their differentness. It is for this reason that a mixed marriage is an area in which only the very strong should tread, and the average person would be well advised to steer clear of a mixed marriage in favor of one that requires less sacrifice. Under the best of circumstances, marriage is a relationship that requires constant effort to make it satisfying to both parties. Under the adverse circumstances that usually surround a mixed marriage, even greater effort is required, and a mixed couple must embrace a philosophy that is accepting, patient, forgiving, and compassionate in order to assure that their marriage will be a success.

CONCLUSION

There are those who believe that all these examples of exceptional families—the unwed mother, the solitary parent, and the mixed marriage—spell an end to the orderly structure of the institution of the family in our society. They see the changes in the family structure as disruptive and destructive.

There is no doubt that the institution of the family is in a state of flux, and the increase in the number of exceptional families reflects that flux. But these are changes that represent evolvement, rather than disruption. And it will be the manner in which society copes with the evolving structure of the American family that determines whether the institution of the family is destroyed or strengthened by the changes it is undergoing.

It is perhaps time for the family to be viewed in terms of human *relationships*, rather than in terms of role classifications and assignments. Anything that interferes with the relationships within the family is disruptive to the institution of the family, and anything that promotes those relationships is strengthening to that institution.

When viewed in that light, it is not the changes in the family structure that are disruptive or destructive, but society's attitude toward the changes. Rather than viewing the unwed mother with destructive scorn and abuse, society instead could be favorably impressed with the love and dedication that made her keep her children and make sacrifices for them. Approval for the unwed mother would do much to create an atmosphere for her children that would enable them to develop self-confidence and feelings of personal worth—feelings that are strengthening to the family.

Similarly, by viewing divorce as evidence of human failure, rather than as a turning point in the lives of a family, society discourages growth and satisfaction in the lives of the divorced couple and their children, and therefore creates a disruptive and destructive atmosphere that leads to a breakdown in the close relationships within the family. By acknowledging divorce as an indication of changed goals and sharpened self-awareness, and by accepting the divorcée and her children not as combat casualties, but as human beings who chose to travel a particular road as best they could, the structure of the divorcée's family would be strengthened and much parent-child conflict and family disruption would be eliminated.

More than for the difficulties of any other exceptional family, society is responsible for the pain and struggle that characterize a mixed marriage. It is the *relationship* between the married pair that matters, not their color or nationality or religion. What does it matter what the colors of a family are, so long as there is love and devotion among them? And what does it serve society to try to disrupt their family and destroy their love by treating them with hostility and bigotry?

And who is to say that a person's faith in God is weakened because someone he or she loves worships the same God in a different way? Are the religious bodies more concerned with people's religious faith, or with their membership rolls? Again, it is not the exceptional family that threatens the institution of the family. Instead, it is society's reaction to the exceptional family that threatens change, growth, and viability, and it is the attitude of society that must change as the form of the family changes.

CHAPTER 14

THE TROUBLED MARRIAGE

Nothing is easier than fault finding; no talent, no self-denial, no brains, no character are required to set up in the grumbling business.
ROBERT WEST

"How'd we get into this trap?"

Sheila and Joe Wescott have been married for five years, and they have two children. When they married, Joe was 19 and Sheila was barely 18, and they would sit for hours planning their dream home and the trips they would take to Europe and the Orient. Their first child was born just 11 months after their marriage and was a colicky, sickly baby who needed continual care from Sheila and a great deal of medical attention. As the doctor bills mounted, Joe dropped his night classes at the university, and also dropped his dreams of completing college by taking two evening courses a semester. He took a second job in order to pay all the bills. He and Sheila quit making plans for trips abroad, and they were too tired to look at magazine pictures of beautiful homes. As the baby grew older, both Sheila and Joe became more responsible, mature people, and they carefully weighed the merits of spending money on a movie or of applying that money to debts they owed. Joe became especially sensitive about the fact that his income was not enough to cover all their expenses every month, and Sheila learned to avoid the subject of money in their conversations.

By their third anniversary, both Sheila and Joe were unhappy in their marriage, but each believed that the fault lay in the fact that they had so many financial worries. Sheila's mother agreed to take care of the baby while Sheila worked, so she took a secretarial job. Her added income helped, but there were so many new expenses connected with Sheila's job—bus fare, extra clothing, etc.—that there was only a small difference in their total income. In time, Sheila began to be aware that she was attractive to some of the men in her office, and she felt vaguely uncomfortable when flirtatious remarks were made to her. There were some single girls in the office, and Sheila found herself listening with wistful envy when they talked during coffee breaks about their dates. At home, Sheila felt that her baby was forgetting her, because he was asleep when she came home in the evening, and her mornings were so hectic with preparing breakfast and getting dressed for work that she had no time to play with him. In the evening, she and Joe watched television and went to bed, frequently with only a perfunctory goodnight kiss. Their sex life was dull and monotonous, with no spontaneity or fun involved, and Sheila frequently cried quietly after Joe was asleep.

Sheila pretended to be dismayed when she became pregnant again, but she was secretly pleased because she felt that another baby would draw her and Joe closer together. She also was relieved not to have to continue working, because she was finding it increasingly difficult to avoid the temptation of responding to the men in the office who found her sexually attractive. She sternly told herself that she was a married woman and a mother, and that dating and good times were behind her.

The Troubled Marriage **421**

The birth of the second baby failed to bring the feeling of closeness and sharing that Sheila had hoped for in their marriage. Instead, Joe felt firmly trapped in the life of a laborer without hope of ever getting a college education, and he felt guilty because he had secretly hoped that Sheila would continue working so that he could eventually go back to school. He had never mentioned it to her, because he felt it was a selfish wish. He was ashamed of his resentment toward the new baby and toward Sheila for killing his dream, but his resentment was there nonetheless.

Sheila and Joe began to prick each other with small jabs of sarcasm and criticism. On the surface, they were polite and considerate, but their hostilities simmered beneath the surface. Their sex life deteriorated further, and Joe began to treat Sheila with a kind of cold indifference during sexual intercourse. Sheila responded with a lack of responsiveness, and for a time suffered from painful vaginismus and a complete lack of vaginal lubrication. She was unable to sleep, and often got up in the night and cried alone in the living room. Joe established the habit of stopping at a tavern for several beers before coming home in the evening. Their older child added to the unhappy atmosphere in the home by whining and anxious clinging to Sheila, as he sensed his parents' irritation and unhappiness, and the baby continually fretted and cried.

One night while watching TV, Sheila and Joe saw a program about a family service agency in their city. The program featured a report on a young couple who had come to the agency for marriage counseling. As they watched the program, both Sheila and Joe realized that their own marriage was in deep trouble, and for the first time in years they had an honest discussion of their feelings of unhappiness and despair. Both agreed to go to the agency and try to revive their dying marriage.

From that point on, the story of Sheila and Joe's marriage may take many different turns, depending on their maturity and self-understanding, their commitment to the marriage, their ability and willingness to put forth effort for the marriage, and the skill and experience of the person who counsels them about their marriage. If their individual commitment is great, if they are both eager to make any necessary changes within themselves for the sake of their marriage, if they are both flexible and emotionally mature enough to accept counseling without becoming defensive and resentful, and if their counselor is attuned to their problems so that he or she can offer sound and insightful guidance, the chances are excellent that their marriage will stabilize and remain successful through the coming years.

On the other hand, if each is determined to make the other the "problem," or if one or both is unwilling or unable to make any significant changes in the self or to gain any insights into his or her own behavior, or if they are unlucky enough to find a marriage counselor who treats all marital problems in exactly the same manner, without regard to individual personalities and circumstances, the chances are excellent that the marriage will founder more and more and eventually fall apart.

There is also a third possibility: Both Sheila and Joe may be willing and able to make changes within themselves; they may be emotionally mature and insightful; and their marriage counselor may be flexible, experienced, and emotionally stable, with a warm rapport with both. And Sheila may decide, after intense, candid soul-searching, that she would rather be single and alone with her children than married and living with Joe. And Joe may decide that marriage before college was a mistake that he will always regret, and that he would rather try to find a way to finish college than to have the responsibility of marriage. If this is the case, marriage counseling has not failed, and neither have Sheila and Joe. Instead, counseling will have enabled them to see that they have been the victims of a cultural system that encourages people to keep themselves in perpetual hock to their dreams of possession. Does a man want to be considered successful and achieving? Then he should buy a new car (and make payments to the bank for it for the next

three years, when it is time to trade it in and buy another one). Does a couple want to be a part of the "in" suburban group? Then they should buy a house with simulated Georgian columns across the front and furnish it with Early American furniture and braided rugs, bought at their friendly furniture store at what may be an interest rate of 18 percent or more per annum, although through gimmicks and clever advertisement it may appear to be a much lower rate. Or should their house have arches instead of columns, they may furnish it with Mediterranean-style furniture bought at the same store at the same interest rate. Intellectual conversation is held vicariously via David Frost matching wits with Dick Cavett on the Early American or Mediterranean-style TV set (color, of course). In such a system, a vulnerable, naive, inexperienced young couple like Sheila and Joe are almost bound to have marital difficulties. Disturbed when their romantic dreams of a continual honeymoon are not realized, their frustrations increase when they feel their slice of the good life is not as great as that of others. They suffer further disillusionment when their children prove to be smelly, messy little beings who throw up on the not-yet-paid-for couch. Having realized the basis of their own discontent, they will still be saddled with the responsibility of their children, and the manner in which they meet their obligations to those children will have great bearing on the course their children's lives take.

Whatever the outcome, a large amount of the credit or blame must go to the marriage counselor. There are marriages that endure without satisfaction to either party, exacting a heavy toll in anxiety and confusion for the marital partners and their children, because a marriage counselor influences them to keep the marriage together at all costs. And there are marriages that split without the partners having the opportunity to examine the marriage or their own needs, because a marriage counselor has played God with their lives and told them that their marriage was hopeless.

CHOOSING A MARRIAGE COUNSELOR

People choosing a marriage counselor frequently do so without any knowledge of licensing laws in their state or of the criteria for a qualified marriage counselor. They assume that the title of "Marriage Counselor" implies specialized training and that anyone bearing that title has been scrutinized by some qualifying body and found competent. The sad fact is that there are many more incompetent people calling themselves marriage counselors than there are qualified marriage counselors. Only six states—California,

Georgia, Michigan, Nevada, New Jersey, and Utah—recognize marriage and family counseling as a legally independent profession, although 20 states are in the process of obtaining such independence (Williamson, 1979). In many states, almost anyone can present himself or herself as a marriage counselor, and ministers, educators, social workers, physicians, psychiatrists, and psychologists who have had no specialized training in marriage counseling may do considerable harm, however unwittingly, by counseling marriages in trouble and applying their own biases and personal beliefs to someone else's marriage. For example, in a study (Knapp, 1975) where 465 questionnaires were sent to a random sample of the clinical membership of the American Association of Marriage and Family Counselors, there was some indication of counselor bias toward client behavior and personality, particularly in the area of recreational swinging, in 43 percent of the respondents.

In addition to marriage counselors in private practice, there are counselors working for groups such as the Jewish Community Services, the Catholic Cana Conference of Charities, or Protestant counterparts. Various community services also provide marriage counseling, such as those sponsored by local United Fund agencies. In some cases these religious and public agencies provide adequate counseling, but in other cases there are too many clients for the available counselors to provide adequate counseling for all.

A marriage counselor may be a happily married middle-aged psychologist with an accepting, approving orientation toward life and marriage and people, or a dour, middle-aged man or woman whose own marriage is empty and who approaches a marital problem as if a marriage without problems is simply the lesser of two evils. Sometimes marriage counselors are very directive in their approach, to the point of becoming impatient and irritated if their clients fail to immediately follow their suggestions, and sometimes they are so timidly nondirective that the clients may feel that they are simply providing their counselor with an interesting hour in which the two make their own plans, for good or ill, without any guidance from the counselor. A marriage counselor may have a moralistic attitude toward sex, toward divorce, and toward life itself, which is conveyed to the married pair in a condemning, judging attitude. Or there may be a hedonistic, irresponsible, totally libertine attitude, which is conveyed to the pair, leading to even more confusion and uncertainty on their part.

Many times, married couples seeking a marriage counselor are so afraid that their neighbors or their families or their employers will find out that their marriage is less than perfect that they simply look in the yellow pages of the telephone book for the names of marriage counselors and hope for the best. Unfortunately, those who are the most unethical or the most untrained may have the most alluring advertisements in the telephone directory, and the naive married pair may therefore fall victim to quacks or incompetents. A better method of finding a competent marriage counselor would be to get referrals from several sources. The family doctor, lawyer, or minister, a school counselor, or a next-door neighbor may know several marriage counselors they can recommend, either because they have consulted them themselves or because they have heard of them. In most cases, it is wiser to avoid telling what the marital problem is when asking for the name of a qualified marriage counselor, because few family doctors, lawyers, ministers, school counselors, or next-door neighbors are qualified to be marriage counselors. While they may offer good advice and sympathetic understanding, and while clergymen and family doctors provide two-thirds of all marriage counseling (Saxton, 1968), they are rarely trained in providing the couple with a completely new approach to their problems and a fresh start with each other.

The cost of counseling. If several people are asked for the name of a good marriage counselor, and the same counselor's name is mentioned more than once, he or she is probably a good place to start. Often, the marriage counselors most often suggested are in private practice, with fees ranging from $30 to $70 an hour, and a married couple will hopelessly conclude that their marriage cannot be helped because they cannot afford the fees. It is remarkable that middle-class couples will think nothing of borrowing $3000 or $4000, or more, to finance a new car, but they react with horror to the idea of paying much less than that for counseling for themselves and their marriage. To be sure, there are couples whose incomes are not sufficient to pay any amount for private marriage counseling, but there are many other people who simply feel that payment for such an intangible service is wasted money. They resent being charged for something they cannot drive, eat, wear, or show off, even when they have reasonable assurance of the counselor's competence. It is these people who swell the caseloads of marriage counselors working in community agencies that exist for those who are unable to pay for private services.

Some insurance companies now pay a portion of the cost of private marriage counseling and, hopefully, others will include this service in their allowable expenses in the future. A call to a marriage counselor's office or to the insurance carrier will tell a couple if their insurance policy pays for this service. If it does not, they should question their own reasons for being reluctant to pay for marriage counseling. If they are sincere in their wish to clarify the issues driving them apart, they will look upon the cost of marriage counseling as they would look upon the cost of medical or dental care. The symptoms of an ailing marriage are not as dramatic or urgent as the symptoms of appendicitis or an abscessed tooth, but they are as real and deserve as much attention. Sadly, of course, there are many Americans who are unable to pay for medical or dental care or for private marital counseling. To be sure, there are agencies that provide such services, but their caseloads are understandably very large, and clients receiving counseling from such agencies are less likely to have the intensive care they would receive in a private setting. Hopefully, proposed government-sponsored insurance programs will provide for the services of marriage counselors as well as other mental health workers as a part of the fee-paid services. Certainly healthy marriages should be considered important to the emotional and physical well-being of the American people.

Training and qualifications. In a private setting, a marriage counselor probably will be either a psychiatrist or a clinical psychologist. If a psychiatrist, the counselor is a medical doctor (MD) who probably has had an internship and a residency in psychiatry. He or she may or may not have had intensive specialized training in marital counseling, but has probably had at least some limited training. In some states, any medical doctor can call himself or herself a psychiatrist or a marriage counselor without having had any training at all in either psychology or marriage counseling. Couples seeking marriage counseling should check a psychiatrist's background and training before entrusting themselves and their marriage to his or her care.

A clinical psychologist is a doctor of philosophy (PhD) who has had approximately five years of graduate school and internship that were devoted to the study of psychology and original psychological research. Like a psychiatrist, he or she has probably had some general training in marriage counseling, and may or may not have had intensive specialized training in marriage counseling. A psychologist may not prescribe drugs as a psychiatrist may. If there is a need for chemotherapy, the psychologist will refer the patient to a medical doctor for a prescription. In many cases, the psychologist will administer a battery of psychological tests to a couple in marital counseling so that their personality types and unconscious fears, desires, and motivations can be assessed much more quickly.

Some psychologists hold master's degrees (MA or MS) and have had a minimum of one year, and usually two or more years, of graduate school devoted to the study and practical application of psychological theory. Depending on the state in which they practice, master's-level psychologists may be in private practice or under the direct supervision of a clinical psychologist. Like PhD psychologists, subdoctoral psychologists may or may not have had intensive specialized training in marriage counseling.

Sometimes a social worker, with a master's degree in social work (MSW), will work in a private setting or with clinical psychologists or psychiatrists. Social workers with master's degrees have had approximately two years of graduate work that is heavily weighted with practical experience in dealing with familial problems. They may or may not have had specialized training in marriage counseling.

Some marriage counselors are ministers who may or may not have had special training in pastoral marital counseling. In some cases, a church will employ pastoral counselors to provide their members with counseling that includes marital counseling. Such pastoral counselors usually have counseling orientations that reflect the particular stances of their church on divorce, sex, contraception, abortion, and marriage.

Marriage counselors may also be educators, physicians in general practice, social service workers, and sociologists. These professionals, like the others, may or may not have had specialized training in marriage counseling.

Obviously, the title of "Marriage Counselor" does not imply that the holder is trained to counsel people whose marriages are in trouble. So, in the absence of a referral from a trusted friend or professional, how does one go about finding a counselor who is qualified? One excellent way is to write the American Association for Marriage and Family Therapy at 225 Yale Avenue, Claremont, California 91711 (714:621-4749) and ask for a list of qualified marriage counselors in one's immediate area. This organization of more than 5000 members sets rigid qualifications for membership. To become a member, a counselor must have a graduate degree in one of the behavioral sciences and must have had at least two years' experience in marriage counseling, with one of those years under supervision approved by the Association. Membership is at least a guarantee to the client that the counselor is qualified to practice marriage counseling, and when one considers that there are probably more than 40,000 marriage counselors in the United States (*Successful Marriage*, Feb. 1974), that guarantee is valuable.

Armed with the names of qualified marriage counselors, a couple should visit the first on their list and discuss frankly their financial situation and the amount of time they have to spend in counseling. They should ask the counselor what the fees are, how counseling sessions are conducted, and what the goals in marriage counseling are. A couple may have to visit two or three counselors before they find one who is acceptable to both, but the visits will be well worth the added expense if they result in finding a marriage counselor who seems sympathetic, accepting, flexible, and nonbiased. He or she should be oriented toward helping the couple as they struggle to solve their own problems. No counselor can solve the problems alone while the couple sit passively and wait for a miracle.

EFFECTIVENESS OF COUNSELING

Considering the high probability of finding a marriage counselor whose training is less than it should be, the percentage of couples who are helped by marriage counseling is high. According to one study, 66 percent of the people who had received marriage counseling felt that the experience had helped their marriage. This is in contrast to 88 percent of subjects who found counseling helpful for personal problems not related to marital problems (Gurin et al., 1960).

One of the reasons for the difference in effectiveness between personal and marital counseling lies in the fact that in personal counseling the client has only one person's feelings to consider, and in marital counseling, there are two sets of needs and desires that are in conflict, so the chances of complete success are less. Another complicating factor in marriage counseling is that couples frequently wait until every last shred of respect and love has been destroyed by their conflicts, and by the time they consult a marriage counselor they may be doing so only in order to say to the world, "We tried everything!" before they file for divorce. Couples who consult a marriage counselor when they still feel affection and concern for one another have a greater chance of success in marital counseling.

Unrealistic expectations. Sometimes, couples' dissatisfaction with their marital counseling experience is related to unrealistic expectations. Many people believe that marriage counselors can make their marriage happy. They cannot. They can point out to the partners the factors that create unhappiness in their marriage, and they can help them view their marriage from a different perspective, but they cannot wave a magic wand and bestow instant happiness on them or on their marriage.

People also frequently believe that marriage counseling can eliminate all problems in a marriage. It cannot. It can provide clarifi-

"What a cute counselor."

CHRISTIANSON

cation of the problems, alternative solutions if there are any, and suggestions as to how to live with the problem if their are no solutions.

Other people expect a marriage counselor to be an arbiter of their differences, so that each will know who is "right" and who is "wrong." But a good marriage counselor will avoid taking sides on the issues presented, and may even avoid the issues themselves, instead dealing with the emotions and feelings behind the issues. A husband may accuse his wife of extravagance, for example, asking with self-righteous indignation, "Can you believe she spent $5 for a bar of soap?" If the marriage counselor chastizes the wife for such extravagance, he may be sure of being paid promptly, but he has done nothing but become an ally of the husband. When the two divorce, the husband may find cold comfort in the knowledge that his marriage counselor thought his wife was extravagant, too. If the counselor deals with the feelings of being unloved that both the husband and the wife have, and with the fact that the wife tests her husband's love by buying expensive things, while the husband tests the wife's love by setting monetary limits on his acceptance, he may save a marriage and help two people understand themselves and each other.

In other cases, couples will expect a marriage counselor to do all the work for them, while they passively sit like lumps of clay. A marriage counselor who is easily frustrated may do an hour-long monologue every week in which he or she gives them suggestions and advice for putting some zip into their marriage. A wise and experienced therapist, on the other hand, may either out-frustrate the couple by being a bigger and more silent lump, so that they turn on the therapist in anger and disgust and finally take responsibility for their own problems, or the therapist may simply tell them that they are being lumps and that he or she cannot deal with their marital problems unless they are willing to work on them.

A counterpart of the passive lumps are the couple who come in, not for marital counseling, but for hypnosis to *make* them change for the better. These are people who, again, want the therapist to do all the work, while they remain passive and feel no pain. While they recognize the need for change, they are so fearful of the pain involved and so reluctant to take any emotional risks that they want someone to change them in spite of themselves. Needless to say, hypnosis is rarely of any value in marital counseling.

Ineffective counselors. These are some of the reasons that people may find marriage counseling less than effective, but it is unfair to place all the blame on the persons coming for marriage counseling and none on the therapist. As was said, the sad fact is that there are more ineffective marriage counselors than there are effective ones, and there are some who are even damaging. The majority are ineffective not because they are quacks or because they are unscrupulous, but because they are too concerned with their own image and with being liked by the couple they counsel. Or they may have unresolved marital conflicts or personal problems of their own that interfere with their objectivity and prevent them from approaching certain problems in a viable and efficient way. They may be too ready to agree, too quick to sympathize, too willing to offer support and commendation for the things that a couple are doing *right,* and too hesitant to be honest about the things they are doing *wrong.*

A woman who is a warm, loving, efficient mother, for example, may be treating her husband as one of the children rather than as her husband. The husband may be reacting to the lack of romance in his marriage by being stubborn about money, irritable in his relations with the children, and rude to his wife. A therapist who fears hurting the feelings of such a good woman may instead praise her homemaking talents in the vain hope that she will see the light herself. He may also praise the husband for being such a good provider, for being loyal to his wife, and for being a good community leader, while hoping that the husband will see the real problem for himself and confront his wife with it. A couple with such a therapist may find satisfaction in his praise and encouragement, but not in their marriage, and the counseling experience may not help them at all. A more confrontive therapist, on the other hand, may in one session point out to the wife that she is her husband's mate, not his mother, and that while she excels at being a mother, she fails at being a lover. He may also point out to the husband that his reactions are neither effective nor honest, and urge both of them to explore their personal relationship with candor and thoroughness. The wife's feelings may be hurt, and the husband may be angry, but the couple have been given the truth that their marriage needed. They may then choose to ignore it and continue in their old unhappy way, or they may choose to pursue it and see if there is a better way.

COUNSELING TECHNIQUES

Just as there are many types of marriage counselors, there are also many types of marriage counseling techniques. Some counselors see each marital partner separately, and some do **conjoint therapy**, in which the two are seen together. Other therapists see each partner separately as well as seeing the two together. There are some therapists who insist that individual counseling is the only way; others insist that only conjoint therapy is effective. Most experienced counselors tailor their technique to fit the situation and the persons. For some couples, individual counseling may be preferable, at least at the beginning of their counseling; for others, conjoint therapy may bring the best results.

In some cases, especially in a private clinic with several therapists, one therapist will see the wife and another therapist will see the husband. This has both advantages and disadvantages. The advantages are that the therapist who best suits the husband's personality can see the husband, while the therapist who best fits the wife's personality can see the wife. A man may resent seeing a woman therapist, while his wife may feel awkward talking to a male therapist. In other cases, the situation is reversed, and a man may prefer talking to a woman, while a wife may feel more at ease talking to a man. The disadvantages are that the two therapists may not be able to work closely enough together to have a good understanding of the dynamics within the marriage, and the underlying issues may be overlooked in favor of the presenting issues.

In most cases, it is probably best for the couple if they see the marriage counselor individually at least once every one or two weeks, so that they can discuss aspects of their relationship that they may feel would be destructive to their marriage if discussed in a conjoint session. If either spouse is having a sexual affair, for example, and fears that the knowledge would be damaging to the other spouse, he may prefer to talk to the therapist about it and get an opinion about the advisability of telling his spouse. Or, one or both partners may have emotional problems that need to be explored in an individual setting.

Seeing the couple as a couple, on the other hand, allows the therapist to observe their pattern of interaction and to break up old habits of interaction that are self-defeating. The value to the clients of conjoint therapy may depend solely on the insight and skill of the therapist. For two people to continue to have the same arguments in front of their therapist that they have at home does nothing but provide entertainment and wonder for the therapist. But if the therapist can interpret their argument in a new light, and show them that they are reacting to unfulfilled needs and desires, rather than to the actions of the other, their pattern of interaction can be redirected and their argument can instead become communication.

To the dismay and horror of many people in marriage counseling, communication does not necessarily lead to closeness, at least initially. We hear so frequently that if two people can only communicate, they will solve all their problems. Actually, two people who begin to communicate may discover that they dislike what the other is communicating, and they may decide that their differences are too great to allow any closeness *ever* to exist between them. Communication, in fact, may not depend on one's ability to *express* one's feelings and beliefs clearly, but on the ability to *hear* and understand the feelings and beliefs of the other. Most people do express their feelings, at least in an indirect way, and communicative skills frequently involve teaching a spouse to interpret the messages the mate sends out. It is when a marital pair learn to correctly decode each other's expressed messages that they may react with dismay and hurt, and say "We don't communicate!" They are communicating; they are simply communicating messages that neither wants to hear. Marriage counseling can help a couple learn to decode each other's messages, and to accept them as communication. Sometimes the communication experiences bring a couple closer together in their relationship, and other times honest communication drives them farther apart.

THE GOAL OF COUNSELING

The goal of marriage counseling is *not* to keep all marriages together. Instead, it is to help couples clarify their own needs and wishes and feelings and to identify in their spouses those traits that meet their needs and those that do not. Marriage counseling aims at helping each spouse arrive at a bargaining position in many of their transactions, so that one provides for a need in the other in return for having a need of his own met. It also helps each spouse learn to give to the mate without demands for exact exchange. If a couple insist on a purely *quid pro quo* (something for something) relationship, they are each denied the pleasure of giving to the other spontaneously. Without a quid pro quo basis to their relationship, however, they may each have so many unfulfilled needs and desires they cannot feel enough generosity and lovingness toward the other to give freely without expectation of return.

Only about 8 percent of the total married population consult marriage counselors (Gurin et al., 1960), but it is very probable that there would be many more satisfying marriages if people consulted competent marriage counselors when they are unable to work out marital problems satisfactorily.

SEPARATION AND DIVORCE

The process of disengagement is rarely a smooth transition. Many people are unprepared for the abrupt change in lifestyle that accompanies the transition from being married to being single. In addition, the situation is made more complex by the ambivalence that is usually characteristic of people who are breaking away from what was once a close, intimate attachment.

The period of separation is often punctuated with alternating feelings of high intensity: anger as well as nostalgia; euphoria as well as despair; bright hope for the future, as well as cynicism and bitterness about the past. Nearly always, feelings of rejection and guilt are heightened during separation and must be faced and eventually worked through. Not everyone is entirely confident of the decision to separate, and frequently they discover attributes of the spouse or aspects of the relationship that were taken for granted during the marriage and only come to their awareness when they are absent.

Redefinition of roles also must be accomplished with the new status of being divorced. This includes roles in regard to others outside the family and also in interactions among the family members as well (Gagnon & Greenblatt, 1978). This is particularly true with regard to the parental roles toward the children. If, after marriage counseling, a couple decide that their marriage is unworkable, their next decision is whether to remain together in name only, or to separate through a legal separation or divorce. If their choice is between a legal separation and a divorce, it is time to consult an attorney.

In selecting an attorney to handle the legality of ending a marriage, couples who have joint holdings totaling more than $10,000 should probably consult a specialist in domestic relations matters (Walzer, 1974). Names of such specialists can be obtained by calling the local bar association. If Joe and Sheila decide to divorce, their total assets consist of furniture and household furnishings, china and silver wedding gifts, $1000 cash value on a life insurance policy, $200 in a savings account, $300 in a checking account, and their four-year-old Ford. The total market value would be less than $10,000, and any attorney that they trusted could probably handle their divorce action to their mutual satisfaction.

It would be far better if Joe and Sheila consulted separate attorneys, even though there is relatively little in the way of cash, real estate, or other property to divide. Having separate attorneys can prevent one spouse—usually the husband—from agreeing to larger alimony or child-support payments than he can really afford. Or it can prevent the wife from agreeing to less than she and the children will actually need. For the majority of Americans, however, two attorneys are simply out of the question, and even the attorney fees charged by a single attorney create a hardship for many couples. It is unfortunate that the dissolution of a marriage is usually a costly process, even when there is very little property to divide. A license to marry costs less than the cost of a good steak dinner. The petition to end the marriage costs as much as a weekend in Acapulco, a skiing trip to Colorado, a Caribbean cruise, or a nose job, any one of which might be more beneficial to a divorcing person than the services of an attorney, especially in routine, noncontested divorces. Hopefully, future laws will provide for automatic divorces in cases in which the couple mutually decide to end the marriage and when no minor children are involved.

In most cases, an out-of-court settlement that is negotiated by the attorneys representing the husband and wife is more advantageous and less costly in money and emotions than a court settlement, and it usually takes six months to a year less time than a court settlement does (Warner, 1974).

In discussing their marriage with the attorneys, it is imperative that both husband and wife be absolutely candid with their respective attorneys about personal matters such as sexual affairs, drinking or drug problems, and inappropriate conduct in the presence of their children, as these matters can affect the court's decision about

"I suppose, Paul, we have to ask ourselves whether this marriage is <u>worth</u> destroying."

CHRISTIANSON

custody and visitation rights. The information a client gives his attorney is both **confidential**—it will not be divulged to anyone else—and **privileged**—a judge cannot force the lawyer or the client to reveal the contents of their conversations—unless the client waives his right of privilege (Walzer, 1974).

Grounds for divorce. There is a growing acceptance of no-fault divorces; that is, it is not necessary to prove that one spouse was "at fault" in order to obtain a divorce, and property division is simply based on the amount of assets involved. Although the assumptions behind the no-fault concept have been shown to be invalid in most cases, the traditional legal grounds for divorce reflect ideas such as that one person is to blame and that strict divorce laws preserve the family. These two reasons for divorce are often quite different from the psychological reality. The two most common legal reasons for divorce are cruelty and desertion, but a study of divorces showed that "real" reasons for divorce are more often financial nonsupport, alcoholism, infidelity, and incompatibility

Separation and Divorce **437**

(Fersch & Vering, 1976). If a divorce is in a no-fault state like Washington or California, it is not necessary to prove that one spouse was "at fault" in order to obtain a divorce, and property division is simply based on the amount of assets involved. In New York, fault grounds for divorce do not have to be proved against one of the spouses, but divorce is made more difficult in that two people must first enter into a separation agreement that can be finalized into a divorce agreement after one year. Even in a state such as Illinois where grounds for divorce must be alleged, the burden of proof is very weak, as in mental cruelty. No longer is the amount of alimony or division of property determined by which partner is found to be "at fault." In most states, judges prefer to divide property equally, unless one partner has intentionally depleted or diminished the assets (Walzer, 1974).

THE PROPERTY SETTLEMENT AGREEMENT

The primary function of a divorce attorney is to help the client arrive at a property settlement agreement with the spouse that is fair and equitable to both parties. A signed written contract between a husband and wife, a **property settlement agreement** divides both marital property and marital liabilities; it settles the amount and duration of alimony and child-support payments; and it determines which parent will have custody of the children and sets the visitation rights of the other parent (Warner, 1974).

In order to arrive at a fair settlement, the two attorneys should be provided with complete records detailing the marital assets and liabilities involved. Then, in a neutral atmosphere, each attorney can negotiate for his client and arrive at fair compromises for each spouse.

Marital assets. In many cases, both husband and wife approach a settlement agreement without any idea of their total assets and liabilities or without any idea of the distinction between marital assets and liabilities and personal assets and liabilities. **Marital assets** consist of that property that has been acquired during the marriage and is jointly owned by both husband and wife. It is this property that is divided between the spouses when they divorce. Separate, or **personal property**, is that property that is solely owned by one spouse and is not divided except under unusual circumstances. A gift of money to one of the spouses, or property owned prior to the marriage, for example, would be separate property. In some cases, there is outraged astonishment when one spouse learns that assets he had thought were marital are really separate, or when a spouse learns that property long considered separate is really marital. A couple may be given a house, for example, by the parents of the wife. If they divorce, the house is marital property despite the fact that the wife always may have considered it to be her own, and despite her parents' wish for the house to remain hers. On the other hand, if the house is a gift to their daughter alone, and not to the couple, then it is separate property, and is not ordinarily considered in a property settlement agreement.

Marital property may be **tangible**—like a bank account—or **intangible**—like a patent on some invention or a copyright on published literary material. These assets may have been either bought with earnings of the husband or wife, or acquired as gifts or through joint inheritance. A couple might own a home, they might have jointly owned real estate and contracts and options to buy other real estate, they may share mortgages, trust deeds, leases, insurance policies, stocks, bonds, and shares in mutual funds and other corporate securities that would all be subject to property division. In addition, they probably own such things as automobiles, boats, art objects, and household furnishings that must also be divided. If there are business interests or interests in patents, trademarks, or copyrights, these are also subject to division between the spouses, as are job-related stock options, deferred salary benefits, and interests in job-related pension and profit-sharing plans (Warner, 1974).

Ideally, a divorcing couple will provide their attorneys with factual, precise records of their assets and liabilities so that a fair division of property can be made. In actual practice, however, one or both partners may become greedy or panic-stricken at the thought of having to share the marital assets and liabilities and may withhold information from the other. In most cases, it is the wife who is ignorant about the extent of marital assets, and it is she who must discover the true property that should be divided (Warner, 1974).

An attorney who has to investigate the marital assets of a couple may begin with an inspection of community income tax returns, including all attached schedules, for the past several years. He or she may analyze joint or individual checking account receipts for the past several years to ascertain the names of mortgage and insurance companies, names of insurance agents, stockbrokers, and accountants, as well as the location of any safe-deposit boxes. Canceled checks of payments made to the local tax collector will reveal how much is paid in taxes every year and help to determine the location of real estate owned.

A wife has the right to request copies of real estate tax bills of any jointly held real property from local property tax authorities, and she also can obtain information as to the nature and extent of the husband's pension rights, profit-sharing rights, stock options, and deferred payment rights from her husband's employer. In addition, she should become knowledgeable about the nature, extent, and financial worth of marital property. The **nature** of a life insurance policy, for example, may be that it is a standard life insurance policy; its face value of $50,000 is its **extent**; while its financial worth may be a present dollar value of $3000 (Warner, 1974). In most states, the wife has the right to examine all community financial records, since the assets and the liabilities are partially hers. If a wife can provide her attorney with information such as this, he or she can then negotiate the best possible settlement for her. If the attorney has to discover these details alone, it will be time-consuming and costly. Complete cooperation with one's attorney is essential in most divorce cases.

The property settlement. In arriving at a **property settlement**—the portion of a property settlement agreement that is concerned solely with the division of marital assets and liabilities between the husband and wife—the present fair market value is the basis used, and not the value that a spouse attaches to an asset, or the amount that it costs new, or the amount it would bring at a crash sale. The **present fair market value** is the amount that a buyer would be willing to pay for it, if a reasonable amount of time were given to find a buyer. In the case of antiques, art objects, and household furnishings, reasonable compromises as to their actual value must be worked out by the attorneys, since these objects may be difficult to appraise to the satisfaction of both spouses. In the case of stock and mutual funds, the fair market value is the price that each could be sold for on the stock market. Savings and checking accounts, of course, are valued at whatever their current balances are (Warner, 1974).

In **community property** states, such as California, Texas, Washington, New Mexico, and Arizona, the law specifies that each party shall receive half of the net value of the assets—in other words, the value of the assets after the total amount of the liabilities is subtracted. In **common law** states like New York and Illinois, however, the courts are allowed to award the "innocent" spouse more than half of the net marital assets in order to punish the "guilty" party—the one guilty of misconduct such as adultery or infliction of mental cruelty (Warner, 1974). In some common law states, a wife might get no part of the marital assets at all, although she might still get alimony, at least for a limited period of time. In several of these states, a husband may sue his wife for divorce, charging her with adultery or mental cruelty, and the wife could be denied both property and alimony, since the judges in these states have discretionary power over awarding alimony and property division.

Whether a state is community property or common law in its laws makes a difference in the income taxes that may be assessed. In a community property state where property is divided equally, for example, an unequal division will result in taxation as if each spouse had sold half of the property to the other, with a possible capital-gains tax. In a common law state, a husband may be taxed on the gain on any property that has appreciated in value that is turned over to the wife. If a wife gets the house in a common law state, for example, and the house has gone up in value since it was purchased, the husband will have to pay income tax on the amount the house has increased in value unless he purchases another house within a year. In such a case, he might be better off to pay cash to his wife instead of giving her the house (Asimow, 1974).

When marital assets are equally divided, there are certain traditional rules. The wife usually gets the house, most of the silver, china, furniture, one of the automobiles, and the savings account. The husband, on the other hand, most likely ends up with a small part of the household furnishings, most of the investment portfolio, one of the automobiles, and *all* of the marital debts. The reason for the inequity in liabilities is that the husband is usually the one with a regular income (Warner, 1974).

Often, the wife wants the house because it represents security to her and to her children, and it will allow the children to remain in their known school and neighborhood. In many cases, however, the cost of the house is greater than a woman's income will allow, and she should look carefully at all the expenses involved before assuming the responsibility.

On a $30,000 house, for example, the mortgage payments will be approximately $250 a month. A wife may have total support payments totaling $500 a month. She will have to pay the $250 mortgage payments, plus homeowner's insurance policy payments of approximately $15 a month, roughly $25 a month in repairs, and real estate taxes of approximately $40 a month, with a total house expense of $330 per month, before paying the utility bills. She would have less than $170 a month to pay for utilities, groceries, clothing, and all the other family expenses—an obvious impossibility (Warner, 1974). She would probably be better off financially and emotionally to sell the house, divide the profit with her husband, and move to an apartment, unless she has a job that will net enough income to pay for the necessary expenses after the house expenses are paid.

In many cases, the property settlement agreement will specify that the husband is required to make the children beneficiaries of a significant amount of his life insurance so that they will not be penalized if he should die before they reach adulthood with their educations completed. If a husband and wife own a business together, and the business is transfered to the husband, the wife may get a promissory note from the husband to equalize the division. She would receive a monthly payment in addition to any support payments until the note was paid.

Marital liabilities. Couples who are divorcing must also divide the liabilities that were incurred during the course of their marriage *for the benefit of the married couple*. In some states, **marital liabilities** also include debts husband and wife had before they married, or debts one or the other incurred during the course of the marriage that were not for the benefit of the married couple (Warner, 1974). A husband who had charged the cost of a skiing trip to a resort in Colorado, therefore, might share the debt with his wife when they divorced, even though she did not accompany him on the trip.

A divorcing couple might have to share liabilities such as a mortgage on their home, due and payable real property taxes, premium payments on life or medical insurance policies, and department store and oil company credit accounts. Loans such as those for car purchases and furniture and appliance purchases are also joint liabilities, as are finance company loans, medical and dental bills, automobile and home insurance, and miscellaneous credit card accounts (Warner, 1974).

Support rights. In determining **support rights**, another major area of the settlement agreement, the earning capacity of the spouses, the length of the marriage, the health of each party, the financial needs of each, the educational achievements of each, their accustomed standard of living, the age of the children, the wife's ability to support herself, and the health of the children and any special requirements they may have are taken into consideration. Generally speaking, courts award between 30 and 40 percent of the husband's after-tax income as support to the wife and children (Warner, 1974).

Support for the wife and children may be paid as **alimony**—an amount of money paid on a weekly or monthly basis for the wife's support, as **spousal support**—the term used in no-fault states instead of alimony, or as **child support**—money paid to the wife by the husband on a weekly or monthly basis for the care of the children in custody of the wife. Alimony, spousal support, and child support also may be paid by the wife to the husband, of course, but in most cases the husband pays support to the wife because the wife usually has the children and the lesser income.

Alimony is tax deductible to the husband, but child-support payments are not. A wife pays income taxes on alimony, but not on child-support payments. A tax exemption of $1000 per child per year can be allowed the father if he pays child support of more than $600 per child per year, and if the wife agrees to his claim in writing. Otherwise, the parent who contributes the most to the child's support is allowed to claim the child as a tax exemption. A recent IRS ruling allows a stepparent's contributions to a child's support to be counted in determining which parent paid the most for support. The parent who claims the children as tax exemptions can also claim medical and childcare expenses as deductions. In some cases, it is more advantageous to both husband and wife if the bulk of support payments are in the form of alimony or spousal support, and in other cases it is more advantageous if the payments are primarily in the form of child support. The best plan depends on the tax bracket that both husband and wife are in. In either case, the children should receive the benefit of the savings in tax dollars. As in other tax questions, an attorney should handle the tax problems and the decision of whether support payments should be in the form of alimony or child support (Asimow, 1974).

Custody of children. The third area covered by a settlement agreement is the **custody** of the children. Decision as to the proper custodial parent is based on the parental fitness of the respective spouses, the needs of the children, their ages, and their personal desires. Before the age of 14, the usual tendency is to award custody to the mother, although this trend is changing to some extent. Unless there are mitigating reasons to limit visitation, the father is usually awarded liberal visitation rights and custody on certain holidays and possibly during the summer months. Custody and visitation should remain flexible since the needs and circumstances of children and parents change with time, and the custody and visitation provisions may need to be changed to fit the new circumstances (Warner, 1974).

OBTAINING THE DIVORCE

Once the details of a settlement agreement have been worked out, the procedure for obtaining a divorce is simple. A bill of complaint is filed and after a certain waiting period, the final decree is granted

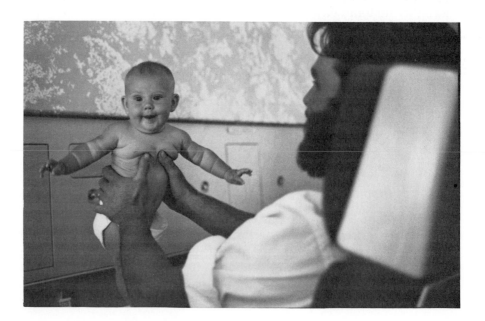

unless the action is contested. The waiting period varies from state to state, with 60 days being common. When a property settlement agreement has been worked out and signed by the married couple, the actual courtroom procedure may take only a few minutes for the granting of a divorce. In cases where there are small children, the judge may refuse to grant a divorce until the couple have consulted a marriage counselor.

In some states, there is a specified time set before a couple can marry other persons, but they may immediately remarry each other. In other states, either spouse can marry another person immediately after the divorce decree is granted.

DIVORCE LAWS

There are 8.1 million divorced men and women in the United States or 84 divorced persons for every 1000 persons in an intact marriage. The divorce rate is 5.1 per 1000 population and the marriage rate is 10.1 per 1000. Thus, the number of marriages is only twice the number of divorces. Forty-nine percent of the first marriages for women with an incomplete education and 29 percent for women with four years of college will end in divorce. In spite of these statistics, the divorce rate—the highest in the world—may be starting a reverse in the trend toward more divorce in the future as it increased only 2 percent in 1976 as compared with an annual average increase of 11.5 percent over the past several years.

Divorce laws have failed to keep pace with the changing marriage and divorce patterns. The laws vary greatly from state to state, and the statistics on divorce patterns frequently reflect the laws of particular states rather than the actual conduct of the married partners involved. In states with stringent divorce laws like New York, for example, the percentage of annulments is high, whereas in states like New Mexico where divorces are granted because of "incompatibility," annulment is extremely rare (Kephart, 1966).

There is a great need for uniformity in divorce laws and for an end to fault laws. Despite the fact that the decision to divorce is usually mutual, with only 10 percent of all divorces being contested (Kephart, 1966), a divorce is still a legal contest in many states, and one partner *must* bring charges against the other in order to dissolve the marriage. This law results in charges that have little to do with the actual reasons for divorce, and admission of guilt on the part of the charged party as a means to an end rather than as a truthful admission of any "guilt." Couples who mutually agree to end their marriage can be charged with "collusion" and legally punished, although enforcement of the law against collusion is rare (Rheinstein, 1953). Furthermore, if the "innocent" party indicates in court that he or she has forgiven the "guilty" party for the charged offense, the divorce will be denied. It also will be denied if the "innocent" party has consented to the behavior with which the "guilty" party is charged (Clark, 1957).

The voiced rationale behind such a ridiculous situation is that the institution of marriage is stabilized by the legal obstacles put in the way of divorce. But unvoiced is the desire on the part of many in our society to punish those who are deemed immoral for wishing to dissolve their marriages.

Currently, domestic relations law is moving toward a more equal relationship between men and women. Thus, the Equal Rights Amendment, although facing a difficult road to passage, has the potential of influencing the area of divorce reform quite directly with its philosophy of egalitarianism. Should the ERA be passed, state statutes covering several areas important to divorce reform would be directly affected. Under ERA, state statutes that permit alimony awards only to the wife will be unconstitutional. If decreed at all, alimony must be available to either sex. Also the presumption that a man, because of his sex, should bear the primary duty of child support would give way to the equal responsibility of both parents. Presumptions that the mother should be favored in custody suits would not be allowed. Grounds for divorce that use sex as the sole criterion would be unconstitutional. Thus, the wife would not have a legal duty to live at the husband's choice of domicile. Statutes that allow a woman a divorce for nonsupport must grant the man the same right or be declared illegal. Overall, the ERA would require legislators either to invalidate those laws that limit the rights of one sex or to extend those laws to both sexes (Myricks, 1977).

The need for divorce laws that reflect the needs and actual behavior of the society governed by the laws is also apparent in changing divorce laws around the world. In Great Britain, it is now possible for couples whose children are older than 16, and who have been separated for at least two years, to get divorced by mail. A form is filled out by one partner, agreed to by the other partner, and sent to the judge, who may, if he approves, send the divorce decree through the mail.

Swedish law now allows instant divorce for couples with no small children. No reasons need to be given for the divorce to be granted. Couples with small children will have to wait six months before a final decree is issued. The old law required a year's waiting period before a divorce was granted.

In Libya, a man may no longer divorce his wife by the traditional manner of saying three times in public, "Divorced." Instead, the court appoints mediators to try to arrange for a reconciliation between the married partners. If none is possible, the husband must pay some recompense to his wife when the divorce is granted.

In the Philippines, divorce is not allowed at all except in very unusual circumstances in which one partner usually has to be jailed for adultery or concubinage. Rather than divorcing, Filipinos in growing numbers are simply leaving their spouses, either with or without a legal separation, and moving in with another person. So widespread is the custom that the term "Number Two" is used to denote the illegal husband or wife. In the Philippines, divorce is out of the question because of the influence of the Roman Catholic Church, but broken marriages exist nevertheless, and are increasing in number.

Russia has one of the higher divorce rates among the world's major countries, but divorce frequently does not physically separate a couple because of the shortage of housing in Russia. Newlyweds are given priority for new apartments, and unless one of the divorced parties is guilty of "systematically violating the rules of community life" (whatever that means), a divorced couple are not granted separate apartments.

CONCLUSION

As this chapter has indicated, the institution of marriage is so vital to the orderly existence of society that laws have been enacted to control the right of married persons to end their marriages. But marriages do end, and the laws are often penalizing or ineffective. Child-support laws are frequently ignored, so that the mother frequently has the major or total burden of supporting a couple's children. Alimony may be unfairly awarded to women who are capable of supporting themselves, with a resulting unfair burden placed on the divorced husband. And older women who are not able to support themselves frequently receive too little in property settlement to survive on and have to turn to state welfare for assistance. A final case history will illustrate an unfortunate situation that is dismally common.

"You don't need a career"

Sonja and Fred marry while still in college, he a pre-med student and she a sociology major. After graduation, Sonja goes to work in a lawyer's office to support Fred while he is in medical school. After Fred receives his medical degree and completes his internship and residency, Sonja quits her job and has a baby, finally forgoing for good her original dream of doing graduate work in sociology. After a few years, Fred tells her that he is in love with his office nurse, and they divorce. Fred is ordered to pay $200 a month in child support, and Sonja goes back to work as a legal secretary. She yearns to go back to school and get her graduate degree, but she must support her child. Her attorney (and her ex-husband) patronizingly tell her, "Baby, you're young and pretty. You don't *need* a career, you'll find another husband!" At first she feels she'd rather die first, but in a few years' time, when the drudgery of trying to make ends meet on a too-meager salary begins to be too much for her, she convinces herself that she is in love with a widowed salesman with two children. She does not like his children and realizes that he is primarily interested in finding a mother for them, but he represents financial security to her.

The outcome of the marriage is depressingly predictable. More equitable child-support laws would help prevent such situations, as would an end to the false notion that a husband's career is more important than a wife's.

Furthermore, it would seem that reform laws should place heavier emphasis on enforcing child-support laws and remove the present procedure whereby the woman has to file contempt-of-court charges against her children's father before the court makes any attempt to enforce child-support laws. The government has no trouble collecting income tax payments, and surely child-support payments could be as systematically collected if states utilized the computerized techniques that are available to them. An illuminating sidelight to the question of child-support payments is that men who are most vocal in their insistence that a woman's place is in the home during their marriages are usually the very men who angrily insist that their wives should support their children virtually alone after their divorces. A woman who was labeled a good mother when she was home with her children before her divorce is, after her divorce, labeled a lazy freeloader if she does not leave her children in order to work to support them.

In the case of older couples, it would seem fair to assess alimony payments when the wife is unable to support herself and has no independent income. But for younger women, alimony appears to be simply a punitive measure directed toward the man, especially when no young children are involved.

And in every case, the need to make false accusations against one of the spouses should be abandoned. Especially when there are no children, divorces should be granted on demand, with an equal division of marital property.

Until reforms such as these exist, couples who want to end their marriages should consult attorneys who can advise them about the divorce laws in their own state. They should plan their futures realistically, with full attention paid to future income and expenses. In some cases, they may decide that divorce would be too destructive to their security and work out a compromise whereby their legal union is preserved if their psychological one is not. In other cases, they will hopefully be able to end their marriages with dignity and mutual respect.

THE FUTURE
OF MARRIAGE

As the foregoing chapters have attempted to make clear, the institution of monogamous marriage, with the family unit a nuclear one, is frequently inadequate for the needs of modern men and women. The inadequacy stems from several sources: the lack of marriage education and parent education in our schools and universities; a lack of sex education in the home, school, and church; usually inadequate feelings of self-worth and self-confidence on the part of marrying couples; a new emphasis on personal fulfillment and individual freedom for all, but especially for women; and a general romanticization of sex, marriage, parenthood, and man--woman relationships that leads to disillusionment and despair for many people who face reality too late.

The increasing necessity for restructuring the character of marriage has come about as a consequence of major cultural and societal changes that have occurred in this century. Schulz and Rodgers (1975, pp. 231–232) list six of these changes that are considered to be significantly influential:

1. "The declining influence of religion . . ." Marriage is now considered more a "personal" contract than a sacred one.
2. "The widespread use of products such as the birth control pill and the automobile. . . ." These have resulted in much greater freedom, independence and mobility of men and women.
3. "The increasing antipersonalization of our society. . . ." Professionalism, with the attendant aggressiveness, manipulation, and productivity associated with it, leads to difficulties with intimacy.
4. "The creation of an enormous job market, including some 31.7 million jobs for women. . . ." Marriage now has less utilitarian advantage to women; they are less economically dependent.
5. "The increasing demand for advanced training. . . ." This results in postponement of marriage and, thus, to changes in attitude toward cultural restrictions, such as premarital sex.
6. "The 'population explosion'. . . ." There are more young people than ever before, and their number increases their influence on matters of social norms, fashion, etc.

With these changes, the demands on marriage have increased, and they are qualitatively different from past requirements. But just as the bearer of bad tidings is often blamed for the news he reports, one who introduces questions or voices concern over the signs of deterioration in the institution of marriage in our society is quickly declared to be against the American way of life and to be actively working for the quick demise of marriage and the family as cultural institutions. This, of course, is utter nonsense. Instead of passively watching the institution of marriage be eroded by decay, we can be making moves to adapt it to new demands, so that it will be rewarding and fill the needs of people who choose it. To turn our heads away from the problem does not make the problem go away. And to face the fact that marriage styles will almost inevitably change in the future is not to say that marriage itself is dead or dying. On the contrary, the changes that will occur in marriage in the future may well make it much more effective than it would be if it did not change.

In a recent survey of young college students (Whitehurst, 1973), 96 percent reported feeling that they were capable of having a satisfactory marriage, and 60 percent believed that they could love, sexually and psychically, more than one person at a time. Over half of those sampled planned to have marital and sexual lifestyles different from those of their parents, but only about 12 percent felt that monogamy was dying as a way of life. Not surprisingly, women were much more concerned with matters such as equality, openness of marriage, better family planning, more careful mate selection, and inadequate communication than were men. These were middle-class students, mostly in their first college year, and their views may become less at variance with traditional views as they grow older, but it is still evident that the *trend* in attitudes toward marriage styles is away from the closed, conventional, monogamous marriage and toward more open marital styles. Only time will tell if the open marital style, with or without sexual freedom for both wife and husband, will be more or less satisfactory than the marital styles that we now have. It might be speculated that it will be less boring and also less comfortable.

Future changes in marital forms will parallel the changes in our society in general. As women realize their determination to have an equal share of life, traditional sex roles are bound to be altered, with men and women moving back and forth across the formerly rigid line that divided "men's work" from "women's work." Furthermore, daycare centers will likely replace, to a large extent, the family home as the primary source of socialization for the young. Occupational roles are also becoming less rigid, and the future may see both men and women having two or more careers in one lifetime, as one occupation becomes obsolete or unfulfilling. This, too, will affect the institution of marriage. With increased occupational equality for women, there will be increased occupational flexibility for men. Men will therefore be able to change jobs more easily and move to more challenging or interesting occupations at will, since they will not have to support a family by themselves. And the

CHRISTIANSON

"Just think — no two are alike."

women who have an equal responsibility for the family will also have an equal voice in its management and direction. Such changes are inevitable, and probably will save the institution of marriage by establishing marriage as a partnership between two people who *prefer* to spend their lives together.

In the future rarely will a woman say, "I got married because I was pregnant," or "I was not a virgin, and I thought no other man would want me," or "I wanted to get away from my family." Neither will a man say, "I didn't really want to marry her, but one thing led to another, and once I'd asked her, I couldn't humiliate her by jilting her," or "She tricked me by telling me she was pregnant, and by the time I knew better, it was too late."

Future women are not likely to marry for security and escape, and future men are not likely to marry for domestic comfort and for sex. Instead, both men and women are likely to marry for the emotional satisfaction found in their relationships, and they are likely to base their interaction on mutually satisfying emotional re-

The Future of Marriage **453**

wards. Some people will go from one relationship to another, without ever having an involvement of any depth with anyone, but others will work to make their relationships deep and permanent.

As has been true for many centuries, the transfer of family property and inheritance rights in general will probably necessitate some legal recognition of female-male relationships that produce or adopt children, and some provisions will undoubtedly have to be made for surviving widowers and widows. But marriage in the future will quite likely become more a private than a public institution, with a greater emphasis on morality than on legality.

To ask if the anticipated future changes in marriage forms are good or bad is analogous to asking if the changes from infancy to adulthood are good or bad. All change and progress involves giving up some things that were valuable and satisfying. When an infant becomes a toddler, she no longer receives beaming smiles from all her family whenever she coos or gurgles. Instead, she may receive frowns and harsh words when she toddles into forbidden areas. The same child loses some of the approval accorded to children by her parents when she moves into adolescence and begins the process of cutting the parental umbilical cord by being rebellious and sometimes obnoxious. Leaving adolescence to enter the world of adults means leaving behind a relatively responsibility-free life for one that imposes responsibility from all sides. In every case, however, the desire for autonomy and individuality prompts the child to move from one stage of development to the next, regretfully leaving behind some of the benefits of the previous stage and philosophically taking on some of the disadvantages of next stage.

So it is with our evolving marriage styles. To say that all change in marriage is for the better is untruthful. There is much in our present marriage form that is comfortable and fulfilling, and some of that comfort and security will be discarded in the next stage of marriage. But we will probably leave it behind nonetheless in order to attain the desired personal freedom that is now so vital to the needs of modern human beings. Undoubtedly, the future marriage forms will contain some new advantages as well as some new disadvantages, and men and women will have to cope with the disadvantages while basking in the advantages. The point is that the changes taking place in marriage forms do not simply reflect a restless impulsiveness on the part of married people, but instead reflect genuine needs for growth that are as inevitable as the needs of a child to move from one stage of growth to another.

It should be remembered, however, that there are some basic needs of human beings that will never change, and these needs must be considered in the new marriage forms. The needs for love, for affection, for recognition, for respect, and for sexual satisfaction remain vitally important to all marital relationships, and any surviving marital form must provide for the fulfillment of these needs. If these human needs are met, and if new generations continue to be cared for and prepared for responsible adulthood, the particular form that marriage takes is immaterial. We must never lose sight of the fact that *people and their needs are the only important consideration*, and not the preservation or initiation of any particular style of life or of marriage.

TWO WEDDING CEREMONIES

Following are two wedding ceremonies that reflect the change of our times. The first is a traditional Protestant ceremony that is still commonly used in marriages today, although the trend is now away from its "locked-in" vows and away from its comments and overtones that place the wife in a somewhat subservient position to the husband.

The second, more liberal, ceremony reflects an attitude of equality of the sexes and the independence of the husband and the wife as individuals while, at the same time, allowing for the unity of two people in the joint venture of marriage. This ceremony, or variations of it, is not at this time widely used in marriages, but the movement in the direction of its increasing use is rapid and significant.

TRADITIONAL CEREMONY

It is a happy and holy hour when a man and a woman come to this sacred altar to consecrate their love and commitment to one another. Our Lord said, "Where two or three are gathered together in my name, there am I in the midst of them." We are instructed by the Apostle Paul, "Whatever you do, in word or deed, do all in the name of the Lord Jesus, giving thanks to God." Let us pray asking for God's blessing in this sacred hour. (*Prayer*)

Bob Williams and Dana Stevens, you have come to this altar to pledge your love for one another and to be joined in Christian marriage.

Bob, will you have this woman to be your wife, and will you pledge yourself to her in all love and honor, to live with her forsaking all others, in the holy bond of marriage? (*Answer*)

Dana, will you have this man to be your husband, and will you pledge yourself to him in all love and honor, to live with him forsaking all others, in the holy bond of marriage? (*Answer*)

Who gives this woman to be married? (*Answer*)

Marriage was established in the dawn of human history by the creative act of God. In his wisdom and providence, God purposed that a man and a woman should share their life together in the covenant relationship of marriage. As in all of God's divine plans for our life, marriage calls for our deepest commitment to the will of God. In discipleship to Christ, we find the truth of God's word which, when practiced in life, lifts us beyond mere human achievement.

God created woman "out of man" and gave her to him as a "helpmate or soul-mate." Adam recognized woman as "bone of my bone and flesh of my flesh." So marriage creates the oneness that God purposed: The two become one flesh. It is as though one heart beats in two bodies and one mind controls two lives. We are not surprised then that the Bible says, "The man who finds a wife finds a good thing. She is a blessing to him from the Lord." The manner of creation suggests God's will for the marriage relationship. Woman was not taken from man's foot to be dominated by him. Neither was she taken from man's head, to rule him. Instead, she was taken from his side to be equal with him, and from near his heart to be loved and protected by him. Jesus honored a marriage celebration as the occasion for his first miracle. He spoke many times of the sacredness and responsibility of marriage. Our Lord used the marriage relationship to describe His relationship to the Church: It is the bride of Christ.

The Apostle Paul gives divine instruction expressing God's will for Christian marriage: "Submit yourselves one to another, because of your reverence for Christ. Wives, submit yourselves to your husbands as to the Lord . . . in the same way that Christ has authority over the church . . . so wives must submit themselves completely to their husbands. . . . Husbands, love your wives in the same way that Christ loved the church and gave his life for it. . . . A man who loves his wive loves himself. . . ."

I charge you to hold in memory and to practice in life the teachings of God's word about marriage. Believing it to be your desire to be joined together in Christian marriage, I ask you to join right hands and make your vows of commitment.

Bob, in taking the woman whom you hold by the right hand to be your wife, I require you to promise and covenant—before God and these witnesses—to be Dana's faithful and loving husband: to love and cherish her, according to the Laws of God, until death alone shall part you. Do you so promise? (*Answer*)

Dana, in taking the man whom you hold by the right hand to be your husband, I require you to promise and covenant—before God and these witnesses—to be Bob's faithful and loving wife: to love and cherish him, according to the Laws of God, until death alone shall part you. Do you so promise? (*Answer*)

Our Lord said, "A new commandment I give unto you that you love one another. . . . Love is patient and kind. Love is not jealous nor boastful. Love is not arrogant nor rude. Love does not insist on its own way. It is not irritable nor resentful. It does not rejoice at wrong but rejoices in the right. Love bears all things, endures all things. So Faith, Hope, Love abide, these three; but the greatest of these is Love."

The ring is a symbol of marriage recognized by all. You have chosen to seal the vows just made by the giving and receiving of rings. These rings given and proudly worn are a constant reminder and public testimony of your love for each other and your commitment to marriage.

Notice the ring is a circle, symbol of the unending and eternal covenant made this hour. God's will for Christian marriage is one man/one woman forever. Notice also the ring is made of finest metal and precious stone, suggesting that your love is to be pure and faithful. As the ring passes through my hand it gives expression to the fact that God's blessing and will are sealed into your marriage covenant. He will always be a part of your life, and will richly bless you so long as you allow Him to do so. Jesus taught us to pray, "Thy will be done, on earth as it is in heaven."

Bob, do you give this ring as a pledge of your love for Dana and promise to be true to its meaning? (*Answer*)

Dana, do you accept this ring as a token of Bob's love for you and will you wear it as a witness of your love and faithfulness to him? (*Answer*)

Dana, do you give this ring as a pledge of your love for Bob and promise to be true to its meaning? (*Answer*)

Bob, do you accept this ring as a token of Dana's love for you and will you wear it as a witness of your love and faithfulness to her? (*Answer*)

Having publicly pledged your love for one another, having promised your faithfulness to Christian marriage, and having sealed your covenant by the giving and receiving of your rings, by the authority committed unto me as a minister of the gospel and by the Laws of the State of Texas, I declare that Bob and Dana Williams are husband and wife. "What therefore God hath joined together, let not man put asunder."

From a ceremony performed by
James K. Varner, Pastor,
Woodhaven Baptist Church,
Houston, Texas

458   Two Wedding Ceremonies

CONTEMPORARY CEREMONY

Love is a thing to walk with hand in hand,
Through the everydayness of this workaday world. . . .

What greater thing is there for two human souls than to feel that
they are joined together to strengthen each other in all labor,
to minister to each other in all sorrow, to share with each other
in all gladness, to be with each other in the silent unspeakable
memories?

. . . let there be spaces in your togetherness,
And let the winds of the heavens dance between you.
Love one another, but make not a bond of love:
Let it rather be a moving sea between the shores of your souls.
Fill each other's cup but drink not from one cup.
Give one another of your bread but eat not from the same loaf.
Sing and dance together and be joyous, but let each one of you be
alone,
Even as the strings of a lute are alone though they quiver with
the same music.
Give your hearts, but not into each other's keeping.
For only the hand of Life can contain your hearts.
And stand together yet not too near together.
For the pillars of the temple stand apart,
And the oak tree and the cypress grow not in each other's shadow.

We are gathered together to unite this man and this woman in
marriage, which is an institution founded in nature, ordained by
the state, sanctioned by the church, and made honorable by the
faithful keeping of good men and women in all ages. It is, therefore,
not to be entered into unadvisedly, or lightly, but reverently, dis-
creetly, soberly, and in the presence of God. This celebration is the
outward token of a sacred and inward union of hearts, which the
church may bless and the state make legal, but which neither state
nor church can create or annul, a union created by loving purpose
and kept by abiding will. Into this estate these two persons come to
be united.

(*To the man*) Ed, do you unite yourself with Kit, to establish a
home with her? Do you commit yourself to the union made today,
promising to give your time, your thought, and your effort to make
it a union rewarding to your wife and to yourself? (*Answer*)

(*To the woman*) Kit, do you unite yourself with Ed, to establish
a home with him? Do you commit yourself to the union made today,

promising to give your time, your thought, and your effort to make it a union rewarding to your husband and to yourself? (*Answer*)

(*To the man*) Do you pledge to Kit that you will be as loving, as patient, as respectful, and as honest as you are able to be, and that you will support her in her times of weakness, encourage her in her times of doubt, console her in her times of grief, and rejoice with her in her times of triumph? (*Answer*)

(*To the woman*) Do you pledge to Ed that you will be as loving, as patient, as respectful, and as honest as you are able to be, and that you will support him in his times of weakness, encourage him in his times of doubt, console him in his times of grief, and rejoice with him in his times of triumph? (*Answer*)

(*The man and woman join right hands.*)

As an outward sign of the inner love between you, you have chosen to exchange rings so that others may know of your commitment to one another.

(*To the woman*) Do you, Kit, give this ring to Ed as a symbol of your love for him? (*Answer*)

(*To the man*) Do you, Ed, accept Kit's ring as a symbol of her love for you, and will you wear it as a symbol of your love for her? (*Answer*)

(*To the man*) Do you, Ed, give this ring to Kit as a symbol of your love for her? (*Answer*)

(*To the woman*) Do you, Kit, accept Ed's ring as a symbol of his love for you, and will you wear it as a symbol of your love for him? (*Answer*)

This woman and this man have pledged their commitment to one another and to their union together, and have exchanged rings as outward symbols of their love. I now pronounce them husband and wife. Let us all share with them the joy of this occasion.

> *Modified form of*
> *marriage ceremony*
> *used by*
> *Judge Miron Love,*
> *Houston, Texas*

REFERENCES

Abernathy, V. D. American marriage in a cross-cultural perspective. In H. Grunebaum & J. Christ (Eds.), *Contemporary marriage: Structure, dynamics, and therapy.* Boston: Little, Brown, 1976.

Adler, A. *Understanding human nature.* Philadelphia: Chilton, 1927.

Albee, E. *Who's afraid of Virginia Woolf?* New York: Atheneum, 1962.

Albrecht, R. A study of dates that failed. In R. E. Albrecht & E. W. Bock (Eds.), *Encounter: Love, marriage, and family.* Boston: Holbrook, 1972.

Albrecht, R. E., & Bock, E. W. (Eds.). *Encounter: Love, marriage, and family.* Boston: Holbrook, 1972.

Allport, G. W. *Personality: A psychological interpretation.* New York: Holt, 1937.

Allport, G. W. *Pattern and growth in personality.* New York: Holt, 1961.

Amelar, R. D. *Infertility in men.* Philadelphia: Davis, 1966.

Arnold, M. Pension plans provide hope for many but pay-offs for the few. *Houston Post,* Sept. 16, 1973.

Arnott, C. C. Husbands' attitudes and wives' commitment to employment. *Journal of Marriage and the Family,* 1972, 34, 673–684.

Aronson, E. Who likes whom and why. *Psychology Today,* 1970, 4(3), 48–50.

Asimow, M. Tax planning and divorce: Let Uncle Sam ease the financial pain. *Marriage and Divorce,* 1974, March/April, 64, 65.

Athanasiou, R., Shaver, P., & Travis, C. Sex. *Psychology Today,* 1970, 4(2), 39–52.

Baber, R. *Marriage and the family.* New York: McGraw-Hill, 1953.

Bach, G., & Wyden, P. *The intimate enemy.* New York: Morrow, 1969.

Bardwick, J. M. Her body, the battleground. *Psychology Today,* 1972, Feb., 50–82.

Barnett, L. D. Research on international and interracial marriages. *Marriage and Family Living,* 1963, 25, 105–107.

Barron, M. The incidence of Jewish intermarriage in Europe and America. *American Sociological Review,* 1946, 11, 6–13.

Bartell, G. Group sex among Mid-Americans. In J. S. DeLora & J. R. DeLora (Eds.), *Intimate life styles: Marriage and its alternatives.* Pacific Palisades, Calif.: Goodyear, 1972.

Bates, A. Parental roles in courtship. *Social Forces,* 1942, 20, 483.

Bauman, K. E., & Wilson, R. R. Premarital sexual attitudes of unmarried university students: 1968 vs. 1972. *Archives of Sexual Behavior,* 1976, 5, 29–37.

Beigel, H. G. Love: Courtly, romantic, and modern. *American Sociological Review,* 1951, 16, 326–334.

Bell, R. R. Female sexual satisfaction as related to levels of education. *Sexual Behavior,* 1971, Nov., 6–14. (a)

Bell, R. R. *Marriage and family interaction.* Homewood, Ill.: Dorsey, 1971. (b)

Bell, R. R., & Balter, S. Premarital sexual experiences of married women. *Medical Aspects of Human Sexuality*, 1973, Nov., 111–123.

Bell, R. R., & Bell, P. L. Sexual satisfaction among married women. *Medical Aspects of Human Sexuality*, 1972, Dec., 136–144.

Bell, R. R., & Blumberg, L. Courtship intimacy and religious background. *Marriage and Family Living*, 1959, Nov., 356–360.

Bell, R. R., & Chaskes, J. B. Premarital sexual experience among coeds, 1958 and 1968. *Journal of Marriage and the Family*, 1970, 32, 81–84.

Berardo, F. Widowhood status in the United States: Perspective on a neglected aspect of the family life-cycle. In M. E. Lasswell & T. E. Lasswell (Eds.), *Love, marriage, family: A developmental approach*. Glenview, Ill.: Scott, Foresman, 1973.

Berger, B., Hackett, B., Cavan, S., Zickler, G., Millar, M., Noble, M., Theiman, S., Farrell, R., & Rosenbleeth, B. Child-rearing practices of communal family. In A. S. Skolnick & J. H. Skolnick (Eds.), *Family in transition*. Boston: Little, Brown, 1971.

Bergler, E. *Unhappy marriage and divorce*. New York: International Universities Press, 1946.

Bernard, J. The adjustments of married mates. In H. T. Christensen (Ed.), *Handbook of marriage and the family*. Chicago: Rand McNally, 1964.

Berne, E. *Games people play*. New York: Grove Press, 1964.

Bieber, T. The lesbian patient. *Medical Aspects of Human Sexuality*, 1969, Jan., 6–12.

Biller, H. B. Father absence and the personality development of the male child. *Developmental Psychology*, 1970, 2(2), 181–201.

Bishop's Committee on Mixed Marriages. *A factual study of mixed marriages*. Washington, D.C.: National Catholic Welfare Conference, 1943.

Blood, R. *Marriage*. New York: Free Press, 1969.

Blood, R., & Wolfe, D. *Husbands and wives*. Glencoe, Ill.: Free Press, 1960.

Bossard, J., & Letts, H. Mixed marriages involving Lutherans. *Marriage and Family Living*, 1956, 18, 308–311.

Boulding, K. Conflict management as a learning process. In A. De Reuck & J. Knight (Eds.), *Conflict in society*. Boston: Little, Brown, 1966.

Broderick, C., & Fowler, S. New patterns of relationships between the sexes among preadolescents. *Marriage and Family Living*, 1961, Feb., 28.

Broverman, I. K., Broverman, D. M., Clarkson, F. E., Rosencrantz, P., & Vogel, S. R. Sex-role stereotypes and clinical judgments of mental health. *Journal of Consulting Psychology*, 1970, 34, 1–7.

Brownfield, D. Communication—key to dynamics of family interaction. *Marriage and Family Living*, 1953, 15, 316–319.

Bumpass, L. The trend of interfaith marriage in the United States. *Social Biology*, 1970, 17(3), 253–259.

Bumpass, L. L., & Sweet, J. A. Differentials in marital instability: 1970. *American Sociological Review*, 1972, 37, 754–766.

Bunzel, R. Economic organizations of primitive peoples. In F. Boas (Ed.), *General Anthropology*. New York: Heath, 1938.

Burchinal, L. Characteristics of adolescents from unbroken, broken, and reconstituted families. *Journal of Marriage and the Family*, 1964, 26, 44–51. (a)

Burchinal, L. The premarital dyad and love involvement. In H. T. Christensen (Ed.), *Handbook of marriage and the family*. Chicago: Rand McNally, 1964. (b)

Burchinal, L. G. Personality characteristics of children. In F. I. Nye & L. W. Hoffman (Eds.), *The employed mother in America*. Chicago: Rand McNally, 1963.

Burchinal, L. G., & Chancellor, L. E. Proportions of Catholics, urbanism, and mixed-Catholic marriage rates among Iowa counties. *Social Problems*, 1962, 9(4), 359–365.

Burgess, E. W., & Cottrell, L. S. J. *Predicting success or failure in marriage*. New York: Prentice-Hall, 1939.

Burgess, E. W., Locke, H., & Thomas, M. *The family*. New York: American Book, 1963.

Burgess, E. W., & Wallin, P. *Engagement and marriage*. Philadelphia: Lippincott, 1953.

Byrne, D. Opinion: What makes people sexually appealing? *Sexual Behavior*, 1971, June, 75–77.

Cadwallader, M. Marriage as a wretched institution. *Atlantic Monthly*, 1966, 218(5), 62–66.

Campbell, A. A., & Cooking, J. D. The incidence of illegitimacy in the United States. *Welfare in Review*, 1967, May, 1–6.

Cavan, R. S. *The American family*. New York: Thomas Crowell, 1953.

Charny, C. W. The husband's sexual performance and the infertile couple. *Journal of the American Medical Association*, 1963, 185(2), 43.

Charny, I. Opinion: How does marital quarreling affect sexual relations? *Sexual Behavior*, 1971, Nov., 52–55.

Charny, I. *Marital love and hate*. New York: Macmillan, 1972.

Christensen, H. T. (Ed.). *Handbook of marriage and the family*. Chicago: Rand McNally, 1964.

Christensen, H. T. Children in the family: Relationship of number and spacing to marital success. *Journal of Marriage and the Family*, 1968, 30, 283–289.

Christensen, H. T., & Gregg, C. F. Changing sex norms in America and Scandinavia. *Journal of Marriage and the Family*, 1970, 32, 616–627.

Clark, H. I. *Social legislation*. New York: Appleton-Century-Crofts, 1957.

Clark, L. Sterility in the female. *Sexology*, 1959, Sept., 308–314.

Clark, L. Painful intercourse. *Sexology*, 1965, Oct., 194–196.

Coleman, J. C. *Abnormal psychology and modern life* (4th ed.). Chicago: Scott, Foresman, 1972.

Commission on population growth and the American future. New York: New American Library, 1972.

Constantine, L. L., & Constantine, J. M. The group marriage. In M. E. Lasswell & T. E. Lasswell (Eds.), *Love, marriage, family: A developmental approach*. Glenview, Ill.: Scott, Foresman, 1973.

Coombs, R. Reinforcement of values in the parental home as a factor in mate selection. *Marriage and Family Living*, 1962, 24, 155.

Crosby, J. F. *Illusion and disillusion: The self in love and marriage*. Belmont, Calif.: Wadsworth, 1973.

Cuber, J. How new ideas about sex are changing our lives. In J. S. DeLora & J. R. DeLora (Eds.), *Intimate life styles: Marriage and its alternatives*. Pacific Palisades, Calif.: Goodyear, 1972.

Cuber, J. F., & Harroff, P. *Significant Americans: A study of sexual behavior among the affluent*. New York: Appleton-Century-Crofts, 1965.

Cutler, B. R., & Dyer, W. G. Initial adjustment processes in young married couples. In J. Hadden & M. Borgotta (Eds.), *Marriage and family*. Itasca, Ill.: F. E. Peacock, 1969.

Cutright, P. Income and family events: Marital stability. *Journal of Marriage and the Family*, 1971, 33(2), 291–306.

Davis, K. The sociology of parent-youth conflict. *American Sociological Review*, 1940, 5, 524.

Davis, K. E. Sex on campus: Is there a revolution? *Medical Aspects of Human Sexuality*, 1971, Jan., 128–142.

DeLora, J. R. Social systems of dating on a college campus. *Marriage and Family Living*, 1963, 25(1), 81–84.

DeLora, J. S., & DeLora, J. R. (Eds.). *Intimate life styles: Marriage and its alternatives*. Pacific Palisades, Calif.: Goodyear, 1972.

Demos, J. Myths and realities in the history of American family-life. In H. Grunebaum & J. Christ (Eds.), *Contemporary marriage: Structure, dynamics, and therapy*. Boston: Little Brown, 1976.

Denfeld, D., & Gordon, M. The swingers. In G. F. Streib (Ed.), *Changing family: Adaptation and diversity*. Reading, Mass.: Addison-Wesley, 1973.

Dengrove, E. Myth of the captive penis. *Sexology*, 1965, Feb., 447–449.

DeRougemont, D. The crisis of the modern couples. In R. N. Ashen (Ed.), *The family: Its function and destiny*. New York: Harper, 1959.

Deutscher, I. The quality of post-parental life: Definitions of the situation. *Journal of Marriage and the Family*, 1964, Feb., 52.

Dizard, J. *Social change in the family*. Chicago: Community and Family Study Center, University of Chicago, 1968.

Donahue, W., Orbach, H., & Pollak, O. Retirement: The emerging social pattern. In C. Tibbits (Ed.), *Handbook of social gerontology*. Chicago: University of Chicago Press, 1960.

Douvan, E. Employment and the adolescent. In F. I. Nye & L. W. Hoffman (Eds.), *The employed mother in America*. Chicago: Rand McNally, 1963.

Duvall, E. *In-laws: Pro and con*. New York: Association Press, 1954.

Duvall, E., & Hill, R. How can you cope with conflict constructively? In R. E. Albrecht & E. W. Bock (Eds.), *Encounter: Love, marriage, and family*. Boston: Holbrook, 1972.

Dyer, E. Parenthood as crisis: A re-study. *Marriage and Family Living*, 1963, 25(2), 196–201.

Ehrenwald, J. Opinion: How does marital quarreling affect sexual relations? *Sexual Behavior*, 1971, Nov., 52–55.

Eichenlaub, J. E. *The marriage art*. New York: Dell, 1961.

Ellis, A. A study of human love relations. *Journal of Genetic Psychology*, 1949, 75, 61–71.

Ellis, A. *Sex without guilt*. New York: Lyle Stuart, 1958.

Ellis, A. *The art and science of love*. New York: Lyle Stuart, 1960.

Ellis, A. Frigidity. In A. Ellis & A. Abarbanel (Eds.), *The encyclopedia of sexual behavior*, 1. New York: Hawthorn, 1961. Also Aronson, 1973.

Ellis, A. *Sex and the single man*. New York: Lyle Stuart, 1963.

Ellis, A. Group marriage: A possible alternative? In G. F. Streib (Ed.), *Changing family adaptation and diversity*. Reading, Mass.: Addison-Wesley, 1973.

England, R. W., Jr. Images of love and courtship in family magazine fiction. *Marriage and Family Living*, 1960, 22, 162–165.

English, O. S. Sexual adjustment in marriage. In M. Fishbein & R. Kennedy (Eds.), *Modern marriage and family living*. New York: Oxford University Press, 1957.

Epstein, N. B., & Santa-Barbara, J. Conflict behavior in clinical couples: Interpersonal perceptions and stable outcomes. *Family Process*, 1975, 14, 51–65.

Erickson, E. *Identity: Youth and crisis*. New York: Norton, 1968.

Estellachild, V. Hippie communes. In J. S. DeLora & J. R. DeLora (Eds.), *Intimate life styles: Marriage and its alternatives*. Pacific Palisades, Calif.: Goodyear, 1972.

Family Life, 1947, 7(9), 8.

Feld, S. Feelings of adjustment. In F. I. Nye & L. W. Hoffman (Eds.), *The employed mother in America*. Chicago: Rand McNally, 1963.

Fine, M., & Himmelfarb, M. (Eds.). *American Jewish Yearbook*. Jewish Publication Society, 1963.

Fisher, C., Gross, J., & Zuch, J. Cycle of penile erection synchronous with dreaming (REM) sleep. *Archives of General Psychiatry*, 1965, 12, 29–45.

Flapan, M. A paradigm for the analysis of child-bearing motivations of married women prior to birth of the first child. *American Journal of Orthopsychiatry*, 1969, 39(3), 410.

Folsom, J. F. *The family*. New York: John Wiley & Sons, 1934.

Frankl, V. E. *Man's search for meaning*. Boston: Beacon Press, 1963.

Frede, M. C. *Sexual attitudes and behavior of college students at a public university in the Southwest*. Unpublished doctoral dissertation, University of Houston, 1970.

Freehof, S. Report on mixed marriage and intermarriage. *Yearbook*, vol. 57. Philadelphia: Central Conference of American Rabbis, 1947.

Fritsch, C. *The layman's Bible commentary*, vol. 2. Richmond, Va.: John Knox Press, 1960.

Fromm, E. *Man for himself*. New York: Holt, 1947.

Fromm, E. *The art of loving*. New York: Harper, 1956.

Gadpaille, W. J. Opinion: What makes people sexually appealing? *Sexual Behavior*, 1971, June, 75–77.

Gagnon, J. H., & Greenblatt, C. S. *Life designs: Individuals, marriages, and families*. Glenview, Ill.: Scott, Foresman, 1978.

Gallup, G. The woman's mind: America's young mothers. *Ladies Home Journal*, 1962, March, 96.

Gaylin, J. The single father is doing well. *Psychology Today*, 1977, 10(11), 36–37.

Gebhard, P. H. Factors in marital orgasm. *Journal of Sociological Issues*, 1966, 22(2), 88–95.

Gelles, R. J. Violence and pregnancy: A note on the extent of the problem and needed services. *Family Coordinator*, 1975, 24, 81–86.

Gibney, F. The strange ways of Staphorst. *Life*, 1948, Sept. 27, 2–8.

Giele, J. Z. Changing sex roles and the future of marriage. In H. Grunebaum & J. Christ (Eds.), *Contemporary marriage: Structure, dynamics, and therapy*. Boston: Little, Brown, 1976.

Gilder, C. The suicide of the sexes. *Harper's Magazine*, 1973, July, 42–54.

Ginzberg, S. L. *Life styles of educated women*. New York: Columbia University Press, 1966.

Gold, M. *A social psychology of delinquent boys*. Ann Arbor: Institute for Social Research, University of Michigan, 1961.

Golden, J. Patterns of Negro-white intermarriage. *American Sociological Review*, 1954, 19(2), 144–147.

Goode, W. J. The theoretical importance of love. *American Sociological Review*, 1959, 24, 38–47.

Gordon, A. *Intermarriage*. Boston: Beacon Press, 1964.

Greenblat, B. R. *A doctor's marital guide for patients*. Chicago: Budlong Press, 1962.

Greenstein, J. Father characteristics and sex typing. *Journal of Personality and Social Psychology*, 1966, 3, 271–277.

Grunebaum, H., & Christ, J. (Eds.). *Contemporary marriage: Structure, dynamics, and therapy*. Boston: Little, Brown, 1976.

Gurin, G., Veroff, J., & Feld, S. *Americans view their mental health*. New York: Basic Books, 1960.

Hand, H. B. Working mothers and maladjusted children. *Journal of Educational Sociology*, 1957, 30(5), 245–246.

Harari, H., & McDavid, J. W. Teachers' expectations and name stereotypes. *Journal of Educational Psychology*, 1973, 65, 222–225.

Harlow, H. F. The nature of love. *American Psychology*, 1958, 13, 673–685.

Harlow, H. F. Love in infant monkeys. In S. Coopersmith (Ed.), *Frontiers of psychological research*. San Francisco: Freeman, 1966.

Harlow, H. F., Harlow, M. K., Dodsworth, R. O., & Arling, G. L. Maternal behavior of rhesus monkeys deprived of mothering and peer associations in infancy. *Proceedings of the American Philosophical Society*, 1966, 110(1), 58–66.

Harper, R. A. Overcoming impotence. *Sexology*, 1965, May, 680–682.

Harris, T., *I'm OK, you're OK*. New York: Harper & Row, 1967.

Haughey, J. C. The commune—child of the 1970's. In J. S. DeLora & J. R. DeLora (Eds.), *Intimate life styles: Marriage and its alternatives*. Pacific Palisades, Calif.: Goodyear, 1972.

Havighurst, R. J. *Human development and education*. London: Longmans, 1953.

Henry, J. *Pathways to madness*. New York: Random House, 1971.

Herman, R. D. The going steady complex: A re-examination. *Marriage and Family Living*, 1955, 17, 38.

Hess, D. What pension reform bill means to average worker. *Houston Post*, Oct. 7, 1973.

Hetherington, E. Effects of paternal absence on sex-type behaviors in Negro and white preadolescent males. In R. Parke (Ed.), *Readings in social development*. New York: Holt, 1969.

Hetherington, E. M. Girls without fathers. *Psychology Today*, 1973, Feb., 47–52.

Hetherington, E. M., Cox, M., & Cox, R. Divorced fathers. *Psychology Today*, 1977, 10, 42–46.

Hill, R. Campus values in mate selection. *Journal of Home Economics*, 1945, 37.

Hobart, C. Some effects of romanticism during courtship on marriage role opinions. *Sociology and Social Research*, 1958, 42, 336–343.

Hobbs, D. F. Parenthood as crisis: A third study. *Journal of Marriage and the Family*. 1965, Aug., 367–372.

Hoffman, L. W. Effects on children: Summary and discussion. In F. I. Nye

& L. W. Hoffman (Eds.), *The employed mother in America*. Chicago: Rand McNally, 1963.

Hollender, M. H. Women's wish to be held: Sexual and nonsexual aspects. *Medical Aspects of Human Sexuality*, 1971, Oct., 12–26.

Hollingshead, A. B. Cultural factors in the selection of marriage mates. *American Sociological Review*, 1960, 15, 627.

Horney, K. *The neurotic personality of our time*. New York: Norton, 1937.

Horowitz, I. Consensus, conflict, and cooperation. In N. J. Demerath III, & R. A. Peterson (Eds.), *System, change, and conflict*. New York: Free Press, 1967.

Horton, D. The dialogue of courtship in popular songs. *American Journal of Sociology*, 1957, 62, 569–578.

Hudson, J., & Henze, L. F. Campus values in mate selection: A replication. In R. E. Albrecht & E. W. Bock (Eds.), *Encounter: Love, marriage, and family*. Boston: Holbrook, 1972.

Hunt, M. *The natural history of love*. New York: Knopf, 1959.

Hunt, M. *Her infinite variety*. New York: Harper & Row, 1962.

Hunt, M. Sexual behavior in the 1970's. *Playboy*, 1973, 20(10), 84–88, 194–207. (a)

Hunt, M. Sexual behavior in the 1970's. Part II: Premarital sex. *Playboy*, 1973, 20(11), 74–75. (b)

In the news. *Medical Aspects of Human Sexuality*, 1970, July, 130.

Is the American family in danger? *U.S. News and World Report*, 1973, April 16, 71–74.

Jackson, D. D. Family interaction, family homeostasis and some implications for conjoint family psychotherapy. In J. H. Masserman (Ed.), *Individual and family dynamics*. New York: Grune & Stratton, 1959.

Jacobson, P. *American marriage and divorce*. New York: Holt, 1959.

Janson, H. W. *History of art*. Englewood Cliffs, N.J.: Prentice-Hall, 1967.

Kaats, G. R., & Davis, K. E. The dynamics of sexual behavior of college students. *Journal of Marriage and the Family*, 1970, 32, 390–399.

Kaplan, H. S. *The new sex therapy: Active treatment of sexual dysfunctions*. New York: Quadrangle, 1974.

Karpel, M. Individuation: From fusion to dialogue. *Family Process*, 1976, 15, 65–82.

Kaufman, S. Menopause and sex. *Sexual Behavior*, 1971, May, 58–64.

Kelly, G. L. Impotence. In A. Ellis & A. Abarbanel (Eds.), *The encyclopedia of sexual behavior*, 1. New York: Hawthorn, 1961. Also Aronson, 1973.

Keniston, K. Youth: A "new" stage of life. *American Scholar*, 1970, Autumn, 631–653.

Kephart, W. M. Drinking and marital disruption. *Quarterly Journal of Studies on Alcoholism*, 1954, March, 63–73.

Kephart, W. M. *The family, society, and the individual*. Boston: Houghton Mifflin, 1966.

Kephart, W. M. Oneida: An early American commune. In A. S. Skolnick & J. H. Skolnick (Eds.), *Family in transiton*. Boston: Little, Brown, 1971.

Kierkegaard, S. *The sickness unto death*. Princeton, N.J.: Princeton University Press, 1941. (a)

Kierkegaard, S. *Concluding unscientific postscript*. Princeton, N.J.: Princeton University Press, 1941. (b)

King, E. Personality characteristics—ideal and perceived in relation to mate selection. Doctoral dissertation, Library of the University of Southern California, Los Angeles, 1961. In J. A. Peterson, *Education for marriage*. New York: Scribner, 1964.

Kinsey, A. C., Pomeroy, W. B., & Martin, C. E. *Sexual behavior in the human male*. Philadelphia: Saunders, 1948.

Kinsey, A. C., Pomeroy, W. B., Martin, C. E., & Gebhard, P. H. *Sexual behavior in the human female*. Philadelphia: Saunders, 1953.

Kirkpatrick, C. Community of interests and the measurement of marriage adjustment. *The Family*, 1937, 18, 133–137.

Kirkpatrick, C. *The family*. New York: Ronald, 1955.

Kleegman, S. J. Frigidity. *Quarterly Review of Surgery, Obstetrics and Gynecology*, 1959, 16, 243–248.

Kleegman, S. J., Amelar, R. D., Sherman, J. K., Hirschhorn, K., & Pilpel, H. Roundtable: Artificial donor insemination. *Medical Aspects of Human Sexuality*, 1970, May, 84–111.

Knapp, J. J. Some non-monogamous marriage styles and related attitudes and practices of marriage counselors. *Family Coordinator*, 1975, 24, 505–514.

Kohlberg, L. Stages of moral development as a basis for moral education. In C. Beck & E. Sullivan (Eds.), *Moral education*. Toronto: University of Toronto Press, 1971.

Komarovsky, M. *Blue-collar marriage*. New York: Random House, 1962.

Komarovsky, M. Cultural contradictions and sex roles: The masculine case. *American Journal of Sociology*, 1973, 77, 873–884.

Krantzler, M. *Creative divorce*. New York: M. Evans, 1974.

Krich, A. Marriage and the mystique of romance. *Redbook*, 1970, Nov.

Landis, J. Length of time required to achieve adjustment in marriage. *American Sociological Review*, 1946, 11, 668ff.

Landis, J. Marriages of mixed and non-mixed religious faith. *American Sociological Review*, 1949, 14, 401–407.

Landis, J., & Landis, M. *Building a successful marriage*. Englewood Cliffs, N.J.: Prentice-Hall, 1973.

Landis, P. H. *Making the most of marriage* (3d ed.). New York: Appleton, 1965.

Langdon-Davies, J. *A short history of women*. New York: Literary Guild of America, 1927.

Lantz, H. R., & Snyder, E. C. *Marriage: An examination of the man-woman relationship*. New York: John Wiley & Sons, 1969.

Lasswell, M. E., & Lasswell, T. E. (Eds.), *Love, marriage, family: A developmental approach*. Glenview, Ill.: Scott, Foresman, 1973.

Lederer, W. J., & Jackson, D. D. *The mirages of marriage*. New York: Norton, 1968.

Lehfeldt, H. Artificial insemination. In A. Ellis & A. Abarbanel (Eds.), *The encyclopedia of sexual behavior*, 1. New York: Hawthorn, 1961.

Leiffer, M. Mixed marriages and church loyalties. *Christian Century*, 1949, 66, 78–80.

Leighton, D., & Kluckhohn, C. *Children of the people*. Cambridge, Mass.: Harvard University Press, 1947.

LeMasters, E. E. Parenthood as crisis. *Marriage and Family Living*, 1957, Nov., 352–355.

LeMasters, E. E. Parents without partners. In M. E. Lasswell & T. E. Lasswell (Eds.), *Love, marriage, family: A developmental approach*. Glenview, Ill.: Scott, Foresman, 1973.

468

Lerner, B., Raskin, R., & Davis, E. On the need to be pregnant. *International Journal of Psycho-Analysis*, 1967, 48, 295.

Leslie, G. *The family in social context.* New York: Oxford University Press, 1967.

Liddick, B. Practicing marriage without a license. In G. Roleder (Ed.), *Marriage means encounter.* Dubuque, Iowa: Wm. C. Brown, 1973.

Lief, H. Sex in older people. *Sexual Behavior*, 1971, Oct., 72–74.

Linton, R. *The study of man.* New York: Appleton-Century, 1936.

Lloyd, C. W. *Human reproduction and sexual behavior.* Philadelphia: Lea & Febiger, 1964.

Locke, H. *Predicting adjustment in marriage.* New York: Holt, 1951.

Lopata, H. The secondary features of a primary relationship. *Human Organization*, 1965, Summer, 116–123.

Lowrie, S. H. Dating theories and student response. *American Sociological Review*, 1951, 16, 334–340.

Lowrie, S. H. Early marriage: Premarital pregnancy and associated factors. *Journal of Marriage and the Family*, 1965, Feb., 52.

Lowrie, S. H. Early and late dating: Some conditions associated with them. In B. Farber (Ed.), *Kinship and family organization.* New York: John Wiley & Sons, 1966.

Lynn, D. B. Divergent feedback and sex-role identification in boys and men. *Merrill-Palmer Quarterly*, 1964, 10(1), 17–23.

Mace, D. R. Contemporary issues in marriage. In R. E. Albrecht & E. W. Bock (Eds.), *Encounter: Love, marriage, and family.* Boston: Holbrook, 1972.

Mace, D. R., & Mace, V. *Marriage East and West.* Garden City, N.Y.: Doubleday, 1960.

MacLean, R. Trial marriage among the Peruvian aborigines. *Mexican Sociology*, 1941, 1, 25–33 (in Spanish).

Malinowski, B. *The sexual life of savages in Northwest Melanesia.* New York: Liveright, 1929.

Marcus, P. In-law relationship adjustment of couples married between two and eleven years. *Journal of Home Economics*, 1951, 43, 35–37.

Maslow, A. H. A theory of sexual behavior in infra-human primates. *Journal of Genetic Psychology*, 1936, 48, 310–338. (a)

Maslow, A. H. The determination of hierarchy in pairs and in a group. *Journal of Genetic Psychology*, 1936, 49, 161–190. (b)

Maslow, A. H. The dominance drive as a determiner of the social and sexual behavior of infra-human primates, I. Observations at Vilas Park Zoo. *Journal of Genetic Psychology*, 1936, 48, 261–277. (c)

Maslow, A. H. The role of dominance in the social and sexual behavior of infra-human primates, III. A theory of sexual behavior of infra-human primates. *Journal of Genetic Psychology*, 1936, 48, 310–338. (d)

Maslow, A. H. A theory of human motivation. *Psychological Review*, 1943, 50, 370–396.

Maslow, A. H. *Toward a psychology of being.* Princeton, N.J.: Van Nostrand, 1962.

Maslow, A. H. Self-esteem (dominance-feeling) and sexuality in women. In M. F. DeMartino (Ed.), *Sexual behavior and personality characteristics.* New York: Grove Press, 1966.

Massey, C., & Warner, R. *Sex, living together, and the law.* Occidental, Calif.: Nolo Press, 1975.

Masters, W. H., & Johnson, V. E. Vaginal pH: The influence of the male ejaculate. *Report of the thirty-fifth Ross Conference: Endocrine dysfunction and infertility.* Columbus, Ohio: Ross Laboratories, 1960.

Masters, W. H., & Johnson, V. E. Intravaginal environment: I. A lethal factor. *Fertility and Sterility,* 1961, 12, 560–580.

Masters, W. H., & Johnson, V. E. *Human sexual response.* Boston: Little, Brown, 1966.

Masters, W. H., & Johnson, V. E. Major questions in human sexual response. Lecture presented to the Harris County Medical Society, Houston, March 1967.

Masters, W. H., & Johnson, V. E. *Human sexual inadequacy.* Boston: Little, Brown, 1970.

Masters, W. H., & Johnson, V. E. Sexual values and sexual function. A paper delivered at the 40th anniversary meeting of the Marriage Council of Philadelphia, Dec. 1971.

May, R. *Love and will.* New York: Norton, 1969.

McCary, J. L. *Sexual myths and fallacies.* New York: Van Nostrand, 1971.

McCary, J. L. Sexual advantages in middle-aged men. *Medical Aspects of Human Sexuality,* 1973, Dec., 139–160.

McCary, J. L. *McCary's human sexuality* (3d ed.). New York: Van Nostrand, 1978.

McDavid, J. W., & Harari, H. Stereotyping of names and popularity in grade school children. *Child Development,* 1966, 37, 453–459.

McGinnis, R. Campus values in mate selection: A repeat study. *Social Forces,* 1959, May, 36.

Mead, M. *Growing up in New Guinea.* New York: New American Library, 1930.

Mead, M. New design for family living. *Redbook,* 1970, Oct.

Mead, M., & Kaplan, F. B. (Eds.). *American women: The report of the President's Commission.* New York: Scribner, 1965.

Meerlo, J. A. M. *Conversation and communication.* New York: International Universities Press, 1952.

Menninger, K. *Love against hate.* New York: Harcourt, Brace, 1942.

Messinger, L. Remarriage between divorced people with children from previous marriages: A proposal for preparation for remarriage. *Journal of Marriage and Family Counseling,* 1976, 2, 193–200.

Monahan, T. P. Are interracial marriages really less stable? *Social Forces,* 1970, 48, 461–473.

Montague, M. F. A. *The meaning of love.* New York: Julian Press, 1953.

Morgan, E. *The descent of woman.* New York: Stein and Day, 1972.

Mozes, E. B. Premature ejaculation. *Sexology,* 1963, Nov., 274–276.

Murdock, G. P. *Social structure,* New York: Macmillan, 1949.

Murstein, B. Opinion: What makes people sexually appealing? *Sexual Behavior,* 1971, June, 75–77.

Murstein, B. I. *Love, sex and marriage through the ages.* New York: Springer, 1976.

Myricks, N. The equal rights amendment: Its potential impact on family life. *Family Coordinator,* 1977, 26, 321–324.

Newsweek, 1978, 41(20), May 15.

Newton, N. Trebly sensuous woman. *Psychology Today,* 1971, July, 68–99.

Nye, F. I. Child adjustment in broken and in unhappy unbroken homes. *Marriage and Family Living,* 1957, 19, 356–361.

470 References

Nye, F. I. *Family relationships and delinquent behavior*. New York: John Wiley & Sons, 1958.

Nye, F. I. The adjustment of adolescent children. In F. I. Nye & L. W. Hoffman (Eds.), *The employed mother in America*. Chicago: Rand McNally, 1963.

Nye, F. I., Carlson J., & Garrett, G. Family size, interaction, affect, and stress. In J. S. DeLora & J. R. DeLora (Eds.), *Intimate life styles: Marriage and its alternatives*. Pacific Palisades, Calif.: Goodyear, 1972.

Nye, F. I., & Hoffman, L. W. (Eds.) *The employed mother in America*. Chicago: Rand McNally, 1963.

Nye, F. I., Perry, J. B., Jr., & Ogles, R. H. Anxiety and anti-social behavior in pre-school children. In F. I. Nye & L. W. Hoffman (Eds.), *The employed mother in America*. Chicago: Rand McNally, 1963.

Ogburn, W. F., & Nimkoff, M. F. *Technology and the changing family*. Boston: Houghton Mifflin, 1955.

Ogren, D. J. Sexual guilt, behavior, attitudes, and information. (Doctoral dissertation, University of Houston, 1974). *Dissertation Abstracts International*, 1975, 35–10B, 5126. (University Microfilms No. 75–08246)

O'Neill, W., & O'Neill, G. *Open marriage*. New York: Avon, 1972.

O'Neill, W. L. *Divorce in the progressive era*. New Haven, Conn.: Yale University Press, 1967.

Overholser, C., Jr. Marriage 1973 style. *Family Circle*, 1973, 82, 32ff.

Packard, V. *The sexual wilderness*. New York: McKay, 1968.

Parson, S. T. *Essays in sociological theory*. Glencoe, Ill.: Free Press, 1949.

Perry, J. P., Jr., & Pfuhl, E., Jr. Adjustment of children in solo and remarriage homes. *Marriage and Family Living*, 1963, 15, 516–540.

Perutz, K. *Marriage is hell*. New York: Morrow, 1972.

Peterson, E. T. The impact of maternal employment on the mother-daughter relationship. *Marriage and Family Living*, 1961, 23(4), 355–361.

Peterson, J. A. *Education for marriage*. New York: Scribner, 1964.

Piaget, J. *The moral judgment of the child*. New York: Harcourt, Brace & World, 1932.

Pike, J. *If you marry outside your faith*. New York: Harper, 1954.

Pineo, P. C. Disenchantment in the later years of marriage. *Marriage and Family Living*, 1961, 23(1), 3–11.

Plath, D. W., & Sugihara, Y. A Japanese commune. In A. S. Skolnick & J. H. Skolnick (Eds.), *Family in transition*. Boston: Little, Brown, 1971.

Pocket Data Book, USA, 1976. U.S. Dept. of Commerce, Bureau of the Census.

Poloma, M. M., & Garland, T. N. The married professional woman: A study in the tolerance of domestication. *Journal of Marriage and the Family*, 1971, 33, 531–540.

Poponoe, P. *Modern marriage*. New York: Macmillan, 1940.

Porterfield, E. Mixed marriage. *Psychology Today*, 1973, Jan., 72–78.

Price, R. Trial marriage in the Andes. *Ethnology*, 1965, 4, 310–322.

Prince, A. A study of 194 cross-religion marriages. *Family Life Coordinator*, 1962, 11(1), 3–7.

Raboch, J. Penis size: An important new study. *Sexology*, 1970, June, 16–18.

Rainwater, L. Some aspects of lower class sexual behavior. *Journal of Sociological Issues*, 1966, 22(2), 96–108.

Ramey, J. W. Intimate groups and networks: Frequent consequence of sexually open marriage. *Family Coordinator*, 1975, 24, 515–530.

Rapoport, R., & Rapoport, R. N. Dual-career families re-examined: New integrations of work and family (2nd ed.). London: M. Robertson Biblio Distr., 1976.

Reed, R. B. Social and psychological factors affecting fertility: The interrelationship of marital adjustment, fertility control, and the size of family. *Milbank Memorial Fund Quarterly*, 1947, 25, 383–425.

Reichard, G. Social life. In F. Boas (Ed.), *General Anthropology*. New York: Heath, 1938.

Reik, T. *A psychologist looks at love*. New York: Grove Press, 1944.

Reik, T. *Of love and lust*. New York: Strauss & Cudahy, 1957.

Reiss, I. L. How and why America's sex standards are changing. *Transaction*, 1960, March, 26–32. (a)

Reiss, I. L. *Premarital sexual standards in America*. Glencoe, Ill.: Free Press, 1960. (b)

Reiss, I. L. Premarital sex permissiveness among Negroes and whites. *American Sociological Review*, 1964, 29, 688–698.

Reiss, I. L. Social class and campus dating. *Social Problems*, 1965, 13(2), 165.

Reiss, I. L. The influence of contraceptive knowledge on premarital sexuality. *Medical Aspects of Human Sexuality*, 1970, Feb., 71–86.

Reiss, I. L. Premarital sex codes: The old and the new. In D. L. Grummon & A. M. Barclay (Eds.), *Sexuality: A search for perspective*. New York: Van Nostrand Reinhold, 1971.

Renne, K. Correlates of dissatisfaction in marriage. *Journal of Marriage and the Family*, 1970, Feb., 65.

Resnik, R. Some sociological aspects of intermarriage of Jew and non-Jew. *Social Forces*, 1933, 12, 94–102.

Rheinstein, M. Trends in marriage and divorce laws of western countries. In Duke University School of Law, *Law and contemporary problems*. Durham, N. C.: Duke Univ., 1953.

Richardson, H. B. Love and the psycho-dynamics of adaptation. *Psychoanalytic Review*, 1956, 43, 337–347.

Ripley, J. Money matters. *Houston Post*, Sept. 16, 1973.

Rodman, H. *Marriage, family, and society*. New York: Random House, 1965.

Rogers, C. R. *On becoming a person: A therapist's view of psychotherapy*. Boston: Houghton Mifflin, 1961.

Rogers, C. R. *Becoming partners: Marriage and its alternatives*. New York: Delacorte Press, 1972.

Roleder, G. (Ed.). *Marriage means encounter*. Dubuque, Iowa: Wm. C. Brown, 1973.

Rollin, B. Motherhood: Who needs it? In A. S. Skolnick & J. H. Skolnick (Eds.), *Family in transition*. Boston: Little, Brown, 1971.

Rollins, B. C., & Feldman, H. Marital satisfaction over the family life cycle. *Journal of Marriage and the Family*, 1970, 32, 20–28.

Rosen, H. S. A survey of the sexual attitudes and behavior of mate-swappers in Houston, Texas. Unpublished master's thesis, University of Houston, 1971.

Rossi, A. S. The mystique of parenthood. In A. S. Skolnick & J. H. Skolnick (Eds.), *Family in transition*. Boston: Little, Brown, 1971.

Rubin, I. *Sexual life after 60*. New York: Basic Books, 1965.

Rubin, I. Sex after forty—and after 70. In R. Brecher & E. Brecher (Eds.),

An analysis of human sexual response. New York: New American Library, 1966.

Russell, B. *Marriage and morals.* New York: Liveright, 1929.

Ryder, N. B., & Westoff, C. F. Fertility planning status: United States, 1965. *Demography,* 1969, 6, 435–444.

Salk, L. *What every child would like his parents to know.* New York: McKay, 1972.

Santrock, J. Paternal absence, sex typing, and identification. *Developmental Psychology,* 1970, 2(2), 264–272.

Satir, V. Marriage as a statutory five year renewable contract. Paper presented at APA 75th Annual Convention, Washington, D.C., Sept. 1, 1967.

Saxton, L. *The individual, marriage, and the family.* Belmont, Calif.: Wadsworth, 1968.

Saxton, L. Interracial marriage. In L. Saxton (Ed.), *A marriage reader.* Belmont, Calif.: Wadsworth, 1970.

Saxton, L. *The individual, marriage, and the family* (3rd ed.). Belmont, Calif.: Wadsworth, 1977.

Scanzoni, J. A social system analysis of dissolved and existing marriages. *Journal of Marriage and the Family,* 1968, 30, 452–461.

Schnepp, G. *Leakage from a Catholic parish.* Washington, D.C.: Catholic University of America Press, 1942.

Schulterbrandt, J., & Nichols, E. Ethical and ideological problems for communal living: A caveat. In M. E. Lasswell & T. E. Lasswell (Eds.), *Love, marriage, family: A developmental approach.* Glenview, Ill.: Scott, Foresman, 1973.

Schulz, D. A., & Rodgers, S. F. *Marriage, the family, and personal fulfillment.* Englewood Cliffs, N.J.: Prentice-Hall, 1975.

Scriven, M. Putting sex back into sex education. *Phi Delta,* 1968, 49, 9.

Second income: It dwindles quickly. *Houston Post,* Dec. 15, 1972.

Sex around the world. *Sexology,* 1974, Aug., 38.

Shatil, J. Development trends in the kibbutz. *New Outlook,* 1971, May, 33.

Shaw, G. B. *Pygmalion.* Baltimore: Penguin Books, 1967.

Shaw, W. *Operative gynaecology.* Baltimore: Williams & Wilkins, 1954.

Sherfey, M. J. The evolution and nature of female sexuality in relation to psychoanalytic theory. *Journal of the American Psychoanalytic Association,* 1966, 14, 28–128.

Shettles, L. B. Predetermining children's sex. *Medical Aspects of Human Sexuality,* 1972, June, 172.

Shlein, J. Mother-in-law: A problem of kinship terminology. In H. Rodman (Ed.), *Marriage, family, and society.* New York: Random House, 1965.

Shostrom, E. L. The measurement of growth in psychotherapy. *Psychotherapy: Theory, Research, and Practice,* 1972, 9(3), 194–198.

Shostrom, E. L., & Kavanaugh, J. *Between man and woman.* Los Angeles: Nash Publishing, 1971.

Siegel, A. E., Stolz, L. M., Hitchcock, E. A., & Adamson, J. Dependence and independence in the children of working mothers. *Child Development,* 1959, 30, 533–546.

Siegel, J. S. Demographic aspects of aging and the older population in the United States. *Current Population Reports,* Special Studies, Series P-23, No. 59, January 1978, U.S. Dept. of Commerce, Bureau of the Census.

Silverman, A., & Silverman, A. *The case against having children.* New York: McKay, 1971.

Silverman, P. R. (Ed.), et al. *Helping each other in widowhood.* New York: Health Sciences Publishing, 1974.

Sirjamaki, J. *The American family in the twentieth century.* Cambridge, Mass.: Harvard University Press, 1955.

Skolnick, A. S., & Skolnick, J. H. (Eds.). *Family in transition.* Boston: Little, Brown, 1971.

Slotkin, J. S. Jewish-Gentile intermarriage in Chicago. *American Sociological Review,* 1942, 7, 34–39.

Smith, C. E. Negro-white intermarriage: Forbidden sexual union. In R. E. Albrecht & E. W. Bock (Eds.), *Encounter: Love, marriage, and family.* Boston: Holbrook, 1972.

Smith, G. P. For unto us a child is—legally. *American Bar Association Journal,* 1970, 56, 143–145.

Snyder, E. E., & Spreitzer, E. Attitudes of the aged toward non-traditional sexual behavior. *Archives of Sexual Behavior,* 1976, 5, 249–254.

Spiro, M. The Israeli kibbutz. In A. S. Skolnick and J. H. Skolnick (Eds.), *Family in transition.* Boston: Little, Brown, 1971.

Sprey, J. The family as a system in conflict. In J. S. DeLora & J. R. DeLora (Eds.), *Intimate life styles: Marriage and its alternatives.* Pacific Palisades, Calif.: Goodyear, 1972.

Statistical Abstract of the United States, 1977, Dept. of Commerce, Bureau of the Census, 98th ed.

Steele, B., & Pollock, C. The battered child's parents. In A. S. Skolnick & J. H. Skolnick (Eds.), *Family in transition.* Boston: Little, Brown, 1971.

Steinzor, B. *When parents divorce.* New York: Pantheon, 1969.

Stephens, W. *The family in cross-cultural perspective.* New York: Holt, 1963.

Stephens, W. Predictors of marital adjustment. In L. Saxton (Ed.), *A marriage reader.* Belmont, Calif.: Wadsworth, 1970.

Stewart, B. The relationship of marijuana usage and sexual activity in university students. Unpublished master's thesis, University of Houston, May 1972.

Stoller, F. The intimate network of families as a new structure. In G. Roleder (Ed.), *Marriage means encounter.* Dubuque, Iowa: Wm. C. Brown, 1973.

Stroup, A. L. *Marriage and family: A developmental approach.* New York: Appleton-Century-Crofts, 1966.

Stryker, S. The adjustment of married offspring to their parents. *American Sociological Review,* 1955, April, 149–154.

Stuckert, R. R. Role perception and marital satisfaction—a configurational approach. *Marriage and Family Living,* 1963, Nov., 415–419.

Successful Marriage (pamphlet), 1974, Feb.

Sussman, M. B. Family continuity, selective factors which affect relationships between families at generational levels. *Marriage and Family Living,* 1954, 16, 112–120.

Sussman, M. B. *Sourcebook in marriage* and the family (2d ed.). Boston: Houghton Mifflin, 1963.

Teen-age sex: Letting the pendulum swing. *Time,* 1972, Aug. 21, 34–38.

The teenagers. *Newsweek,* 1966, March 21, 60.

Terman, L. *Psychological factors in marital happiness.* New York: McGraw-Hill, 1938.

Thomas, J. L. The factor of religion in selection of marriage mates. *American Sociological Review,* 1951, 16, 487–491.

Thomas, J. L. *The American Catholic family.* Englewood Cliffs, N.J.: Prentice-Hall, 1956.

Thosteson, G. Health. *Houston Post,* Nov. 30, 1973.

Uddenberg, N. Mother-father and daughter-male relationships: A comparison. *Archives of Sexual Behavior,* 1976, 5, 69–79.

Udry, J. R. *The social context of marriage* (3d ed.). Philadelphia: Lippincott, 1974.

Uhr, L. M. Personality changes in marriage. Unpublished doctoral dissertation, University of Michigan, 1957.

UNESCO. *Statement of the nature of race and race differences.* 1952.

United States Bureau of the Census. *Current population reports,* 1958, Series P-20 (79).

United States Bureau of the Census. *Population Characteristics,* Series P-20, No. 316, 1977.

United States Bureau of the Census. *Population Characteristics,* Series P-20, No. 324, 1978.

Vassilikos, V. *The plant; the well; the angel: A trilogy,* translated from the Greek by E. & M. Keeley. New York: Knopf, 1964 (1st American ed.).

Vernon, G. Interfaith marriages. In L. Saxton (Ed.), *A marriage reader.* Belmont, Calif.: Wadsworth, 1970.

Vincent, C. E. Interfaith marriages: Problem or symptom? In R. E. Albrecht & E. W. Bock (Eds.), *Encounter: Love, marriage, and family.* Boston: Holbrook, 1972.

von Wiese, L. *Systematic sociology,* adapted and amplified by H. Becker. New York: John Wiley & Sons, 1932.

Wallace, K. M. An experiment in scientific matchmaking. In R. E. Albrecht & E. W. Bock (Eds.), *Encounter: Love, marriage, and family.* Boston: Holbrook, 1972.

Waller, W. The rating-dating complex. *American Journal of Sociology,* 1937, 2, 727–734.

Waller, W., & Hill, R. *The family.* New York: Dryden Press, 1951.

Walster, E., & Berscheid, E. Adrenaline makes the heart grow fonder. *Psychology Today,* 1971, June, 46–50, 62.

Walster, E., Piliavin, J., & Walster, G. The hard-to-get woman. *Psychology Today,* 1973, Sept., 80–83.

Walzer, S. When should you see a lawyer? *Marriage and Divorce,* 1974, March/April, 36–42.

Warner, J. A house divided: Arriving at a property settlement. *Marriage and Divorce,* 1974, March/April, 86–91.

Way, P. Address to United Church of Christ, All Lutheran Youth Gathering: Discovery '73, Houston, Texas, Aug. 6, 7, 1973.

Wells, J. G. A critical look at personal marriage contracts. *Family Coordinator,* 1976, 25, 33–37.

Westermarck, E. *The history of human marriage.* New York: Allerton, 1922.

Westman, J. C., & Cline, D. W. Divorce is a family affair. In M. E. Lasswell & T. E. Lasswell (Eds.), *Love, marriage, family: A developmental approach.* Glenview, Ill.: Scott, Foresman, 1973.

Westoff, L. A., & Westoff, C. F. *From now to zero: Fertility, contraception and abortion in America.* Boston: Little, Brown, 1971.

White, R. W. *Lives in progress.* New York: Holt, 1966.

Whitehurst, R. N. Youth views marriage: Some comparisons of two generation attitudes of university students. In R. Libby & R. Whitehurst (Eds.), *Renovating marriage*. Danville, Calif.: Consensus Publishers, 1973.

Williams, F. Children of divorce: Detectives, diplomats, or despots? *Marriage and Divorce*, 1974, March/April, 24–28.

Williamson, D. S. Personal communication to G. F. Sternes, May 1, 1979.

Williamson, P. The erotic zones. *Sexology*, 1961, June, 740–743.

Williamson, R. C. *Marriage and family relations*. New York: John Wiley & Sons, 1966.

Wilson, G., & Ryland, G. *Social group work practice*. Boston: Houghton Mifflin, 1949.

Winch, R. F. *The modern family*. New York: Holt, 1952.

Winch, R. F. *The modern family* (rev. ed.). New York: Holt, 1963.

Winett, R., Fuchs, W., & Moffatt, S. A comparative study of daycare and non-daycare children and their families. Unpublished manuscript, University of Kentucky, 1974.

Zimmerman, C. C., & Cervantes, L. F. *Successful American families*. New York: Pageant Press, 1960.

PHOTO CREDITS

477

Chapter 7

Chapter 8

Chapter 9

Chapter 10

Chapter 11

Chapter 12

Chapter 13

Chapter 14

SUBJECT INDEX

479

and togetherness, 2, 133–135
(example), 335
utilitarian, 291
(*See also* Conflict, marital; Success, marital)
Adjustment after remarriage, 402–403
Adolescence, 113
attitudinal formation in, 44–45, 166–169, 400–401
and "falling in love," 166
independence needs of, 153, 178
and infatuation, 150–151
security needs of, 11, 176
sexual activity in, 166–169, 205–207, 400
(*See also* Dating; Homosexuality; Intercourse, sexual, premarital; Masturbation; Orgasm, nocturnal; Petting)
Adoption, 356, 358, 359
Adrenal glands, 220
Adultery, 51–54, 76
(*See also* Intercourse, sexual, extramarital; Swinging)
Aging process and sexuality:
in men, 207, 208, 217, 245, 251, 255, 273–274
in women, 207, 208, 245, 246, 251, 258, 270–273
(*See also* Menopause)
Alcohol, effect of, on sexual functioning, 254–256, 267–268
Alcoholism, as cause of divorce, 278
Alimony (*see* Divorce)
Amnion, 359–360
Amniotic fluid, 360
Amyl nitrite, 269
Anal intercourse, 250
Anaphrodisiacs, 267–269
Androgen, 215, 220, 271
Androgyny, 42
Animal behavior patterns, 43, 49–50, 163, 219, 350
Anniversary grief reaction, 387
Annulment, 201, 445
Antogamy, 89
Aphrodisiacs, 267–269
Artificial insemination, 357–358
Assisted insemination, 358
Attitudes, sexual:
in ancient Greece, 155
of ancient Hebrews, 51, 155

double standard in, 50–51, 194, 229–231
toward extramarital intercourse, 2, 48–57, 103, 106–109, 121, 383
toward homosexuality, 149, 155
toward marital intercourse, 85–87
(group marriage), 245, 246, 376, 410
in modern communes, 98
toward premarital intercourse, 93, 169, 213, 229–233, 383
toward sexuality in childhood and adolescence, 168–169, 263
of women, culturally imposed, 226, 257, 347–348

"Bachelors' houses," 109
"Bag of waters" (amniotic sac), 360, 361
Bartholin's glands, 223
Behavior, sexual, forms of, 205–214
(*See also* Bisexual activity: Homosexuality; Intercourse, sexual; Masturbation; Orgasm, nocturnal; Petting)
"Being in love," 24–25
Bestiality, 205
Betrothal, 178–180
(*See also* Engagement)
Bigamy, 201
Bigotry, 382, 405, 416
Birth:
average size at, 361
multiple, 220, 363
premature, 361
(*See also* Childbirth)
Birth control, 233–241, 253, 354, 383, 410
(*See also* Abortion; Abstinence, sexual; Coitus interruptus; Condom; Contraception, chemical methods of; Diaphragm; Douching; Oral contraceptives)
Birth-control pills (*see* Oral contraceptives)
Birth date, calculating, 361
Birth positions, 361
Birth rate in U.S., 351
Bisexual activity, 60, 87, 106–108
Bisexuality, 210
Bladder:
female, 220 (illus.), 258
male, 216 (illus.), 217
Blind dates, 108–181
B-love, definition of, 24
B-needs, definition of, 24

Breastfeeding, 362
Breasts:
    changes in, during puberty, 223
    as erogenous zone, 262–265
    in lactation, 362
    in sexual response, 227, 362–363
Bride-price, 73, 79, 179, 198–200
Budget, family, 300–304
"Bundling," 160

Caesarean section, 241, 361
Cantharides, 267–268
Cardio-respiratory love, 154, 167
Celibacy, 101, 155
Cervix, 220 (illus.), 221, 236, 362
Chancre, 241–242
Chancroid, 242
Cheaper by the Dozen (Gilbreth), 346
Child abuse, 368–370
Childbirth:
    attitude toward: in communes, 99–100
        of women, 347–348
    leaves of absence for, from job, 298, 366
    "natural," 362
    process of, 361–362
    (*See also* Birth)
Childrearing:
    in alternative forms of marriage, 85–86, 91–95, 99–100
    and child abuse, 368–370
    as function of wife, 37–39, 45, 253, 294, 296–298
    and perpetuation of romantic love concept, 166–169
    and personality orientation of parents, 31–34
    and societal attitudes toward sexual expression in children, 168–169, 263
    (*See also* Children; Family; Parenthood)
Children:
    cost of having, 347
    effect of divorce on, 388–394
    effect of interfaith marriage on, 416–417
    effect of interracial marriage on, 407, 416–417
    effect of single-parent family on, 399–402
    legal rights of, 93–94, 113, 200–203

and pre-marriage contract, 112
    religious upbringing of, 416–417
    socialization of, 11–15, 42–45, 163–165, 399–402
        in kibbutzim, 94, 365
    of working mothers, 364–366
    (*See also* Adjustment, marital, and children; Childrearing; Family)
Child-support payments, 112, 386, 393, 394, 435, 438, 442–444, 447–449
Chromosomes, 216, 359, 360 (illus.)
Circumcision, 218–219, 256
Climacteric:
    in men, 273
    in women, 225, 226, 270–273
Clitoris, 215, 220 (illus.)
    changes in, during puberty, 224
    description of, 222–223
    in sexual intercourse, 222–223, 227, 266, 273
    (*See also* Cunnilingus)
Cluster marriages, 83
Coital positions, 265–267
    facilitating conception, 358
Coitus (*see* Intercourse, sexual)
Coitus interruptus (withdrawal), 217, 237
Coitus reservatus, 91
College, effects on dating, 172
Collusion, in divorce cases, 445
Colostrum, 362
Common-law marriage, 201–202
Communes:
    examples of: kibbutzim, 88, 92–95
        modern communes, 74, 88, 95–103, 130–132 (example)
        Oneida Community, 88–92
"Companionate Marriage," 110
Conception, 359
    favorable coital positions for, 358
    and predetermining sex of child, 358–359
    (*See also* Ovulation)
Conceptus, 220, 359–361
Condom, 237, 258, 357
Conflict, marital:
    causes of: conflicting needs, 335
        different frames of reference, 332–335
        hate and disappointment, 329–332
        internal conflict, 335–336
        togetherness, 335

Extramarital sexual activity, 51–54, 75–76
(*See also* Adultery; Intercourse,
sexual, extramarital; Swinging)

Failure, marital, 344
annulment in, 200–201, 445
divorce in (*see* Divorce)
incidence of, 445
legal separation in, 435, 445, 448
"Falling in love," 2, 160–169, 188–190
Fallopian tubes, 220, 220 (illus.), 253–254, 356
Family:
American, 77
in ancient cultures, 68, 71–74
communal, 82, 88–103
definition of, 93
effect of working mothers on, 364–366
exceptional, societal attitude toward,
380–384, 418–419
extended, 74–76, 82, 95
in household grouping, 74–75
and incest taboos, 66–69, 95, 191–192
as institution, change in, 418–419
necessity for, 4
nuclear, 51, 66, 67, 69, 74–77, 82, 94,
109
or orientation, definition of, 69
prehistoric forms of, 65
in primitive societies, 68–74
of procreation, definition of, 69
reconstituted, 403
single-parent: effect on children of,
388–391, 399–402
problems of, 385–387
societal attitude toward, 383–384
size of: desired, 351
effect on marriage of, 352–354
(*See also* Adjustment, marital, and in-laws; Childrearing; Children;
Motherhood; Parenthood)
Fantasy:
as defense mechanism in marital
adjustment, 278
of revenge, in marital conflict, 332
sexual, 108, 207
Feedback, in conflict-solving, 279–280
Fellatio, 249, 263
definition of, 249
incidence of, 209
in swinging, 106
(*See also* Oral-genital contact)
Female superiority, concept of, 42

"Feminine" stereotypes, 40–45, 350
learning of, 42–45
Fertility:
drugs to aid, 220
reduced, in men, 356
Fertilization, 359, 360 (illus.)
without ejaculation, 217
site of, 220
(*See also* Conception; Ovum;
Pregnancy; Sperm)
Fetus, 360–361
(*See also* Development, prenatal)
Fight-training, marital, 338–341
Foam, contraceptive, 234, 236 (illus.), 237
Follicles, ovarian, 219, 225
Follicle-stimulating hormone (FSH), 215
Foreskin (*see* Prepuce)
Forgiveness, connotations of, 2–3
Fraternal twins, 363–364
"Free love," 89, 101
Friends, Intimate (IF), 108–109
Frigidity (*see* Orgasmic dysfunction, female)
Fusion, in relationships, 15, 292–293

Game-playing, marital, 336–338, 343
Games People Play (Berne), 336, 343
Gender, error in identification of, 215
General paresis, 242
Genitalia:
female, 219–223
(*See also* Menstruation)
male, 215–219
pubescent changes in, 223–225
(*See also* Sexual response cycle)
Glands (*see* Adrenal glands; Bartholin's
glands; Cowper's glands; Pituitary gland;
Prostate gland, Sebaceous glands)
Glans:
clitoral, 222–223
penile, 216 (illus.), 218–219, 222
Going steady, 176–178
Gonorrhea, 241
Granuloma inguinale, 242
Greed, as motive in relationships, 188
Group marriage, 84–88, 103, 114
advantages of: economic and social,
85–86
experiential, 87–88
in the Oneida Community, 88–92
sexual sharing in, 86–87
Group sex:
in group marriage, 87
in swinging, 105–107

incidence of, in U.S., 406–408
laws concerning, 191, 407
and marital adjustment, 407–408, 414–417
motivations in entering, 405–406
societal attitudes toward, 382, 383, 403–405, 418–419
success of, 407–408, 414–417
Interstitial cell-stimulating hormone (ICSH), 215
Intimate Enemy, The (Bach), 338
Intimate Friends (IF), 108–109
Intrauterine contraceptive device (IUD), 234, 236–237, 253

Jealousy:
assumed role of, in origin of incest taboos, 68
in origin of sexual exclusiveness, 49–51
basis of, 15–18, 57–62, 101
coping with, 59–62, 322
in nontraditional marriages, 55, 86, 87, 98–101, 107–108, 140–142
in polygynous marriages, 74
in traditional marriages, 2
Judaism:
attitude of: toward adultery, 51–52
toward homosexuality, 155
toward interfaith marriage, 191, 384, 410–414, 417
toward woman's role in marriage, 376
(*See also* Religious belief)
Juvenile delinquency, 165, 366, 399–401

Kibbutzim, 74, 88, 92–95, 365
"King Kong Complex," 370–372
Kinship:
and households, 74–75
and incest taboos, 66–69, 191
in kibbutzim, 95
and polygamy, 71–74

Labia majora, 222
changes in, during puberty, 224
description of, 222
in oral-genital contact, 249
in sexual response, 227
Labia minora, 222
changes in, during puberty, 224
description of, 222

in oral-genital contact, 249
in sexual response, 227
Labor (*see* Childbirth)
Lactation, 362
Laparoscopy, 253
L-dopa, 269
Legal separation, 435, 445, 448
Leisure time, as marital problem, 309–312
Lesbianism, origin of term, 155
(*See also* Homosexuality)
Levirate, 71–72
Likeableness, aspects of, 183–186
Lion in Winter, The (film), 321
Living together, 109, 112–113
Love:
altruistic, 148
aspects of (infatuation, mature love, romantic love), 150–163
cardio-respiratory, 154, 167
"courtly," 156–158
definitions of, 27, 146–148
dependent, 27–29
and developmental needs, 27–29
development of capacity for, in childhood, theories of, 163–165
"at first sight," 149, 151
"free," 89, 101
and hate, 323, 329–332
and infatuation, 150–151, 167
mature, 162–163
preconditions for "falling in love," 188–190
romantic, 75, 79, 151–162, 166–169, 281
historical development of, 75–76, 155–162
perpetuation of, as concept, 166–168
and sex, societal separation of, in childhood and adolescence, 168–169
Lymphogranuloma venereum, 242

Macho myth, 370
Maculopapular sex flush, 227
Madonna concept, 375
Maidenhead, 221
Male superiority, concept of, 40–42, 370
Manipulation:
jealousy as tool of, 59–62
patterns of, in marriage, 29–31
Marijuana, and sexual functioning, 268–269

Marital adjustment (*see* Adjustment, marital)
Marital conflict (*see* Conflict, marital)
Marital failure (*see* Failure, marital)
Marital success (*see* Success, marital)
Marquesan tribe (of Polynesia), 58, 71
Marriage:
    adjustment in (*see* Adjustment, marital)
    age requirements for, 192, 200–203
    average age at, 351
    cluster, 83, 103
    common-law, 201–202
    "Companionate," 110
    "complex," in Oneida Community, 89
    conflict in (*see* Conflict, marital)
    cooperation in, 341–342
    creative, 120–123, 138, 142–144
        examples of, 138–142
    dyadic, definition of, 84
    emotional rewards of, 3–5
    exploitation in, 341–342
    failure in (*see* Failure, marital)
    forms of: attitudes of college students toward, 452
        future changes in, 451–455
    group, 82–88, 103, 109, 114
    individual, 110
    as institution: function of, 4, 37
        history of, 65–79
    interdenominational, 410
    interfaith (*see* Interfaith marriage)
    interracial (*see* Interracial marriage)
    in kibbutzim, 94–95
    legal aspects of, 191–192, 200–203
    as means of transferring property, 69, 73–79
    mixed (*see* Interfaith marriage; Interracial marriage)
    and number of children wanted, 351
    parental, 110
    patterns of manipulation in:
        Bitch-Nice Guy, 30
        Daddy-Doll, 29–30
        Dove, 30–31
        Hawks, 30
        Master-Servant, 30
        Mother-Son, 29
    personality orientations toward:
        exploitative, 32
        hoarding, 32–33
        marketing, 33–34
        receptive, 31
    pseudocreative, examples of, 124–138
    and romantic love, 151–155, 158–281
    and self-actualization, 1–5, 18–20, 31, 38, 142–144, 299
    sex roles in, 38–39, 45–48, 196, 283, 293–296
        (*See also* Adjustment, marital, and role fulfillment)
    sexual adjustment in (*see* Adjustment, marital, and sexual adjustment)
    sexual exclusiveness in, 48–51, 54–57
    sexual freedom in, 52–57, 67, 86–88, 103–109, 121
    sexual variety in, 54, 86–87, 103, 107, 109, 259–261
        examples of, 124–125, 140–142
    status in, equated with earning 287–288
    success in (*see* Success, marital)
    swinging in (*see* Swinging)
    symmetry of work roles in, 48
    three-step, 111
    traditional form of, 1–3, 48, 51, 65, 79
        alternatives to, 82–109
        need for change in, 1–5, 37, 114–115, 451
    trial, 103, 109–112
    two-step, 110
    and woman's status, 37–42, 373
Marriage counseling, 423–434
    cost of, 426–427
    effectiveness of, 429
    goal of, 434
    techniques in, 432–434
    training and qualifications for, 427–429
    unrealistic expectations of, 430–431
Marriage customs, 79, 197–203
"Masculine" stereotypes, 38–45, 231, 370
    learning of, 42–45
Masturbation, 168, 205–208, 223
Maternal death, 234
"Maternal instinct," 38, 348–350, 366–368
    (*See also* Motherhood; Parenthood)
Mate selection:
    through computer dating services, 182
    and dating, 171–173, 176–178, 182, 194
    endogamous factors in, 191–192
    exogamous factors in, 191

Ovaries:
    changes in, during puberty, 224
    description and function of, 219–220
    in menopause, 271
    removal of, 220, 254, 272
    (*See also* Estrogen; Progesterone
    (progestin))
Ovulation, 219–220, 225–226, 271
    after childbirth, 363
    and conception, 225–226, 234, 237, 359
    initial, 224
    multiple, during menstrual cycle, 220,
    238
    prevention of, 234
Ovum (egg), 219–220, 224, 271
    disorders involving, 356
    fertilization of, 359, 360 (illus.)
    in menstrual cycle, 225–226
    in multiple births, 363–364
Ownership, in marriage, concept of, 52

Pair-bonding, 49
Parent-child relationship, in
nontraditional marriages, 85–86, 92–94,
99–100
    (*See also* Childrearing; Children;
    Family)
Parenthood:
    attitudes toward, traditional, 346–348,
    377
    and childbearing years, average age of
    women at end of, 38
    and marital adjustment, 352–355
    and marital success, 354–355
    and "maternal instinct," 348–350,
    366–368
    and motivations for having children,
    346–348, 370–377
    present trends in, 351–352
    as a religious obligation, 376
    societal promotion of, 346–348, 377
    task of, change in, 62–63
    training for, lack of, 366–368
    and unwanted children, 355
    (*See also* Childrearing; Children;
    Family; Motherhood)
Paresis, general, 242
Parturition, 361
PCPA, 269
Penicillin, in treatment of venereal
disease, 242
Penis, 215, 216 (illus.), 217–219, 222
    changes in, during puberty, 225

in coition, 218, 226–229, 250
description of, 217–219
in sexual excitement, 217, 218, 226
size of, 217–219
and venereal-disease infection, 241,
242
(*See also* Circumcision; Erection,
penile; Fellatio)
Penis captivus, 219
Pension plans, 317–318
Perfectionism, Noyes's doctrine of, 88–89
Petting, 205
    definition of, 208
    incidence of, 208–210
    marital, 246
    premarital, 176, 208–210, 229
Pill (*see* Oral contraceptives)
Pituitary gland, 215, 225, 362
Placenta, 360, 362
Plateau phase in sexual response cycle, 227
Polyandry, 57–58, 71–72
Polygamy, 57–58, 71–74, 84
Polygyny, 71, 73–74
Polyps, 258
Population control, 253
    (*See also* Birth Control)
Positions:
    birth, 361
    coital, 265–267, 358
Postpartum depression, 347
Potassium nitrate, 269
Power, relationship roles and, 286
Precoital fluid, 217, 237
Predetermining child's sex, 358–359
Pregnancy:
    crisis during, 352
    fear of, 39, 233, 249, 252
    and men's need to prove masculinity,
    370–371
    possibility of, and menopause, 226
    premarital, 173, 192, 196, 233
    prevention of (*see* Birth control)
    sexual activity in last weeks of, 250
    and women's need for identity or
    attention, 373
    (*See also* Conception; Development,
    prenatal; Motherhood)
Premarital sexual intercourse (*see*
Intercourse, sexual, premarital)
Pre-marriage contract, 111–112
Premature birth, 361
Premature ejaculation (*see* Ejaculatory
dysfunction)

in modern communes, 95
and negative emotions, 23–24
and parenthood, 377–378
and personality orientation, 34
and sexual expression, 243
steps in, through psychotherapy, 20–21
Self-disclosure, in conflict resolution, 280
Self-esteem, 24–28
inability of marriage to provide, 27–28
and negative feedback in marriage, 334
and wanting children, 370–377
and women's sexual activity, 231
Self-fulfillment (*see* Self-actualization)
Self-identity, sense of:
blocked by conformity, 8–10
and caring, 13–15
growth of, 10–15
lack of, 8
and one's name, 364
and personal relationships, 11–18
and values, 11–14
Semen, 216–217, 356
Seminal vesicles, 216–217
Seminiferous tubules, 215
Sensate focus, 263–265
Separation, 392–393
emotional reaction to, 435
Separation, legal, 435, 445, 448
Sex:
and aging (*see* Aging process and sexuality)
predetermining child's, 358–359
Sex appeal (*see* Sexual attraction)
Sex differences:
in economic achievement and marital status, 298
in length of life, 42, 51
in marital adjustment, 280–283
in motivations for wanting children, 370–377
nonbiological, explanations for, 40–42
and personality traits, 39–40
in premature birth, 42
in sex drive, 245, 251, 312
in sex-role learning, 42–45
in status, 39–42, 45–48
Sex drive:
and aphrodisiacs, 267–269
differences in: between individuals, 206
between the sexes, 245, 251, 312

hormonal influences on, 219, 272
inequality in, within a marriage, 132 (example), 248, 251, 257
and pregnancy, fear of, 253
Sex education (*see* Education, sex)
Sex flush, maculopapular, 227
Sex roles:
in colonial America, 77
learning of, 42–45, 172–173, 399–402
in marriage (*see* Adjustment, marital, and role fulfillment; Marriage, sex roles in)
Sexual adjustment, in marriage (*see* Adjustment, marital, and sexual adjustment)
Sexual arousal, techniques of, 218, 261–265
(*See also* Erogenous zones)
Sexual attitudes (*see* Attitudes, sexual)
Sexual attraction, 186–188
and "falling in love," 2, 152, 166–169, 188–190
Sexual behavior (*see* Behavior, sexual)
Sexual dysfunction, 254–259
(*See also* Erectile dysfunction)
Sexual excitation, causing ovulation, 220, 238
Sexual exclusiveness, 48–51, 54–57
(*See also* Marriage, sexual exclusiveness in)
Sexual fantasies, 207
Sexual fidelity, 48–51, 54–57
(*See also* Marriage, sexual exclusiveness in)
Sexual freedom, 52–57, 67, 86–88, 103–109, 121
(*See also* Marriage, sexual freedom in)
Sexual ignorance, 246–249
Sexual intercourse (*see* Intercourse, sexual)
and older people (*see* Aging process and sexuality)
oral-genital (*see* Oral-genital contact)
Sexual permissiveness, 52–57, 67, 86–88, 103–109, 121
(*See also* Marriage, sexual freedom in)
Sexual physiology, 214–223
Sexual response cycle: phases of:
excitement, 222, 226–227
orgasmic, 228–229

492   Subject Index

AUTHOR INDEX

494

Author Index **497**

498 Author Index